T0295955

Entrepreneurship Development in the Balkans

LAB FOR ENTREPRENEURSHIP AND DEVELOPMENT

Series Editors: Bruno S. Sergi and Cole C. Scanlon

Lab for Entrepreneurship and Development is Emerald's innovative book series on the study of entrepreneurship and development, striving to set the agenda for advancing research on entrepreneurship in the context of finance, economic development, innovation, and the society at large.

The *Lab for Entrepreneurship and Development*, a now-independent research lab that first started at the Institute of Quantitative Social Sciences at Harvard University, with the overarching and ambitious aim of using the book series as to synthesize interdisciplinary research by academics and students to advance our understanding of modern entrepreneurship and development across cultural and disciplinary boundaries.

Previous volumes:

Entrepreneurship and Development in the 21st Century – Edited by Bruno S. Sergi and Cole C. Scalon

Entrepreneurship for Social Change – Edited by Bruno S. Sergi, Cole C. Scalon and Luke R. I. Heine

Entrepreneurship Development in the Balkans: Perspective from Diverse Contexts

EDITED BY

VELAND RAMADANI
South-East European University, North Macedonia

SASHO KJOSEV
Ss. Cyril and Methodius University, North Macedonia

AND

BRUNO S. SERGI
Harvard University, USA

United Kingdom – North America – Japan – India – Malaysia – China

Emerald Publishing Limited
Emerald Publishing, Floor 5, Northspring, 21-23 Wellington Street, Leeds LS1 4DL.

First edition 2023

British Library Cataloguing in Publication Data
A catalogue record for this book is available from the British Library

ISBN: 978-1-83753-455-5 (Print)
ISBN: 978-1-83753-454-8 (Online)
ISBN: 978-1-83753-456-2 (Epub)

To professor Domigo Ribeiro-Soriano, for his outstanding support in making my research gain meaning and purpose and reaching a global audience.
Veland Ramadani

To my parents, Divna and Aleksandar, for their invaluable sacrifices; and to my son Vojdan and my wife Nina, for their continuous support.
Sasho Kjosev

To my brother Enzo and my sisters Nunziatella and Fiorenza.
Bruno S. Sergi

Contents

About the Editors

Veland Ramadani is a Professor of Entrepreneurship and Family Business at the Faculty of Business and Economics, South-East European University, Tetovo, North Macedonia. His research interests include entrepreneurship, small business management, and family businesses. He authored or co-authored around 180 research articles and book chapters, 12 textbooks, and 25 edited books. He has published in *Journal of Business Research*; *Technological Forecasting and Social Change*; *Review of Managerial Science*; *Business Ethics, the Environment and Responsibility; International Journal of Entrepreneurial Behaviour and Research; International Entrepreneurship and Management Journal*, among others. In 2021, in a study conducted by Stanford University (USA), he was ranked among the Top 2% of the most influential scientists in the world.

Sasho Kjosev is a Professor at the Faculty of Economics at the University, Ss. Cyril and Methodius, in Skopje and the President of the Association for Regional Development "Balkan Economic Forum." He holds a PhD in Development Economics and a Graduate Diploma Program in Development Planning Techniques from the International Institute of Social Studies of Erasmus University Rotterdam, the Netherlands. His professional interests include macroeconomic (development) planning, development planning techniques, national accounting, sustainable development, regional and local economic development, economics of innovation, labor economics, and agricultural policy.

Bruno S. Sergi is an Instructor on the Economics of Emerging Markets at Harvard University and an Associate of the Harvard's Davis Center for Russian and Eurasian Studies and the Harvard Ukrainian Research Institute. He co-directs the *Lab for Entrepreneurship and Development* (LEAD). He also teaches Political Economy and International Finance at the University of Messina. He is the Series Editor of *Cambridge Elements in the Economics of Emerging Markets* (Cambridge University Press), as well as the Editor for *Entrepreneurship and Global Economic Growth* and a co-Series Editor of *Lab for Entrepreneurship and Development* (Emerald Publishing). He has published in *Business Strategy and the Environment, Corporate Social Responsibility and Environmental Management, Economic Modelling, Energy, Energy Research & Social Science, Finance Research Letters, International Journal of Production Research, Journal of Economics & Business, Journal of Intellectual Capital, Management Decision, Resources Policy*, among others. He has published numerous books as well.

About the Contributors

Hyrije Abazi-Alili is an Associate Professor at South-East European University, Republic of North Macedonia. She holds a PhD in Economics from Staffordshire University, UK. She teaches undergraduate, postgraduate, and doctoral courses in Economics and Econometrics. She was Affiliate Fellow at CERGE-EI, Prague for the period 2014–2020. Her research interests include economics of innovation, ICT, entrepreneurship, labor market, gender, social issues, etc., with advanced application of econometrical models. She authored dozen research articles in highly ranked journals, several international conferences, and book chapters (international publisher). She was also engaged as a Senior Expert in several international projects: EU Projects, IPA, UNDP, RRPP, etc.

Selajdin Abduli is an Associate Professor at the Faculty of Business and Economics at South-East European University, Republic of North Macedonia, where he teaches both undergraduate and postgraduate courses in the field of Economics and Management. He served as a Pro-dean for post-graduate studies from 2012 to 2015. His research interests include human resources management, labor market, family business, and entrepreneurship. He authored and co-authored many research articles in different peer and refereed journals.

Abdul Wahab Aidoo is an Assistant Professor of Management at the Faculty of Business Administration at the International University of Sarajevo (IUS), Bosnia & Herzegovina (B&H). He obtained his undergraduate degree in Economics from the Kwame Nkrumah University of Science and Technology in Ghana. He also completed his MBA from Istanbul Commerce University in Istanbul-Turkey followed by his PhD in Innovation Management from IUS in B&H. He has years of experience in the corporate industry before ending up in Academia. He has co-authored articles in internationally recognized journals such as *Periodicals of Engineering and Natural Sciences*, *Economic Review: Journal of Economics and Business*, and *Heritage and Sustainable Development*. His research interest is in the fields of innovation management, marketing, entrepreneurship, and consumer behavior.

Fernando Angulo-Ruiz is an Associate Professor in the Department of International Business, Marketing, Strategy & Law, at MacEwan University (Canada). He studies entrepreneurs and hybrid organizations, marketing capabilities, and marketing of higher education institutions. His research has been published in high-impact international academic journals. He is involved in various international research projects that have received financial support from several organizations, including the Social Sciences and Humanities Research Council of Canada. He is an Editorial Review Board Member of the *Journal of Business Research* and reviews for many other highly regarded international journals.

Boštjan Antončič is a Professor of Entrepreneurship at the School of Economics and Business, University of Ljubljana. His areas of expertise include corporate entrepreneurship, entrepreneurial networks, entrepreneurial personality, and international entrepreneurship. He has written several books – more than 10 in the area of entrepreneurship alone, as well as several business research articles. His papers have been published in academic journals such as the *Journal of Business Venturing*, *Entrepreneurship and Regional Development*, *Industrial Management & Data Systems*, *Technovation*, *Frontiers in Psychology*, *Transformations in Business and Economics*, *Journal of Business Economics and Management*, and *Journal of Small Business Management*.

Jasna Auer Antončič is an Associate Professor of Entrepreneurship at the Faculty of Management, University of Primorska, where she teaches and conducts business research work. Her main research interests include employee satisfaction, the psychology of entrepreneurship, intrapreneurship, and business growth. She has written three books in the area of entrepreneurship, as well as several business research articles. Her articles have been published in scientific and academic journals such as *Industrial Management & Data Systems*, *Frontiers in Psychology*, *Journal of Small Business and Enterprise Development*, *Journal of Developmental Entrepreneurship*, and *Journal of Enterprising Culture, Behavioral Sciences, and Management*.

Mehmet Bağış received his PhD from Sakarya University Business Institute in 2018. Since 2022, he has been an Associate Professor at Sakarya University of Applied Sciences, Faculty of Applied Sciences, Department of International Trade and Finance. His professional interests include strategic management, entrepreneurship, resource-based view, dynamic capabilities, behavioral strategy, and competitive strategy.

Nadica Jovanovska Boshkovska is an Assistant Professor at the School of Business Economics and Management, University American College Skopje. She has accumulated professional experience of 16 years as a Lecturer in the field of Marketing. She holds MSc in International Economics from Tor Vergata University, Italy, and a Professional Development Fellowship at Cornell University, USA. Her doctoral degree is focused on territorial marketing, earned at the St. Cyril and Methodius University, Skopje. She has attended numerous national and international conferences, earned certificates, and published many articles in domestic and international journals and conference proceedings. She also works as Chief Project Officer for Europa RE, a Swiss reinsurance company.

Stefan Chichevaliev has a PhD in Business Administration and is a postdoctoral researcher at Vrije Universiteit Brussel, and Executive Director at the Social Entrepreneurship Observatory, with more than a decade of experience in the private, public, and civil sectors. He has a solid track record of published research, analyses, and publications in social and sustainable entrepreneurship. He is a consultant for many international organizations in creating and implementing innovative and sustainable solutions with significant impact on people's well-being. He is committed to building bridges between science and practice. He is a developer of partnerships and an advocate for social entrepreneurship and attainment of sustainable development goals.

Dragana Ćirović is a Teaching Assistant and a PhD candidate at the Faculty of Economics, University of Montenegro. She was hired as a Teaching Assistant at the University of Montenegro in 2017. In February–September 2019, she was engaged as a Marketing Assistant at Klikovac DOO Company. Currently, she is working at the Faculty of Economics, University of Montenegro as a Teaching Assistant for several subjects in the field of marketing, management, and entrepreneurship. She is fluent in English and has a basic level of knowledge of Russian, Italian, and Spanish language. During her academic career, she has participated in several international and bilateral projects and numerous conferences. She has published a monograph and several scientific papers and some of them are indexed in high-rated databases, such as SSCI and Scopus.

Mladen Čudanov is a Full professor at the University of Belgrade, Faculty of Organizational Sciences, Serbia, where he acquired an MSc and PhD degrees. He was teaching abroad in ZHCPT (PR China), JCIT (PR China), Roma TRE University (Italy), and University of Zilina (Slovakia). Has 20+ years of consultant experience in systems with 20,000+ employees, large, medium, and small companies, on projects of job systematization, organizational structure, process, and strategy design and analysis. His main research interests are organizational design, entrepreneurship, restructuring of business systems, organizational change management, and ICT application. He has published more than 140 research papers, has 1,000+ citations, ~1/4 of it from the WoS. He also serves as the editor and reviewer in several journals.

Stojan Debarliev is a Professor at the Department of Management at the Faculty of Economics – Skopje, Ss. Cyril and Methodius University in Skopje. He received his master's degree and doctorate in the field of business management, more specifically in strategic and business planning. He has been employed at the Faculty of Economics – Skopje since 2005. Previously, he gained work experience in the business sector working in marketing and sales at Macedonian On-line and Pekabesko. His educational and research interest is in the fields of management, business planning, strategies, business models, social entrepreneurship, and sustainable development. He is the author of university textbooks, as well as research papers in scientific journals and proceedings of international conferences. He has delivered lectures at summer schools, workshops, and seminars. He actively teaches first-, second-, and third-cycle studies. He is currently appointed head of the Yunus Center for Social Businesses at the Faculty of Economics-Skopje.

Jordi Diaz is the Dean and Faculty of EADA Business School and Director of the Executive Academy of the European Foundation for Management Development (EFMD Global). He holds an Executive Doctorate of Business Administration (EDBA) program from Ecole des Ponts Business School ParisTech (France), a Master's in Human Resources Management from EADA Business School (Spain), and professional certificates from Harvard Business School. He serves on Advisory Boards at several business schools, including Burgundy School of Business, and is an Associate Editor of the *International Journal of Technology-Enhanced Learning*. His community service memberships include Business Fights Poverty and Excellence in Sustainability Club in Spain.

Mark Esposito is a Professor of Business and Economics and Director of the Futures Impact Lab at the Hult International Business School. He holds a doctoral degree in Business Administration from École des Ponts ParisTech and is a Resident Fellow and Professor of Economic Policy at Mohammed Bin Rashid School of Government in Dubai. He is on the Faculty at Harvard University's Division of Continuing Education and Institutes Council and Co-Leader, of the Microeconomics of Competitiveness Program at the Institute of Strategy and Competitiveness at Harvard Business School. He is a Global Expert on the World Economic Forum, and currently, serves as Subject Matter Expert for the Prime Minister's Office in the UAE.

Daphne Halkias is a Professor and distinguished research Fellow at École des Ponts Business School Paris Tech, a Fellow at the Institute of Coaching, McLean Hospital at Harvard Medical School, a Research Affiliate at the Institute for Social Sciences, Cornell University, and a Research Associate at the Center for Comparative Immigration Studies, University of California, San Diego. She is CEO of Executive Coaching Consultants and Editor of the *International Journal of Teaching and Case Study*, the *International Journal of Technology-Enhanced Learning*, and the *International Journal of Social Entrepreneurship and Innovation*. She is a Member of the Academy of Management, Business Fights Poverty, American Psychological Association, and has authored/edited 14 academic books and over 100 peer-reviewed papers.

Tatiana Harkiolakis is an academic researcher and Director of Communications at Executive Coaching Consultants. She holds a Master of Science in Media and Communications from The London School of Economics and Political Science and is a PhD candidate in Media, Culture and Creative Industries at the City, University of London. She has presented her research at international media, business conferences and journals. Her research interests include journalism and social media, digital entrepreneurship, the future of work, online activism, gender equality in Greece, and alternative media. She is a Member of the International Communications Association, the Online News Association, and Business Fights Poverty.

Sadudin Ibraimi is a Professor of Management and Applied Statistics at the Faculty of Business and Economics, South-East European University, North Macedonia. His research interests include decision-making, operation management, statistics, and entrepreneurship. He authored or co-authored around 20 research articles. He has published in *International Entrepreneurship and Management Journal*, *Journal of Balkan and Near Eastern Studies*, among others. From 2019, he served as a Member of the Higher Education Accreditation Board. He conducted several trainings and projects in the Business and Innovation Center.

Nicholas Mmaduabuchi Ikpogu is a Maritime Administration and Transportation Management Professional and is an Adjunct Professor at Capstone Edge College in Calgary, Alberta, Canada. He holds a PhD in Management and is a Surveyor and Auditor with the American Bureau of Shipping. His professional experience cuts across the Merchant Navy as a Deck Officer (navigation), Marine Science Technician with the United States Coast Guard Reserve, Department of Defense employee with the US Navy Military Sealift Command, and Flag State Inspector with the Liberia International Ship Corporate Register. He has worked in offshore and marine operations, ship operations, and inspections to enforce International Maritime Organization and United States Coast Guard regulations, port and waterways management, and commercial vessel international safety management and International Ship and Port Facility Security audits.

Aleksandra Janeska Iliev is an Assistant Professor at the Department of Management at the Ss. Cyril and Methodius University in Skopje Faculty of Economics-Skopje which is the largest state university in Macedonia. There she teaches different subjects related to entrepreneurship, small business, and organizational behavior, at the bachelor, master level, and PhD levels, which also includes mentoring candidates at various milestones of their studies. Her main research interest revolves around entrepreneurship and organizational behavior, further specializing in sustainability, social business, entrepreneurial education, and generational differences. Her participation in various national and international projects has enabled her to grow her applicative experience concerning topics she is engaged in. As a scholar, she is trying to detangle what and how education in a formal and non-formal context can stimulate flourishing grounds for entrepreneurship. She has frequently participated in conferences and events within the entrepreneurial ecosystems regionally and locally. She has published and presented in various publications journals, conference proceedings, book chapters, and co-authored books.

Ondrej Jaško is a Full Professor at the University of Belgrade, Faculty of Organizational Sciences, where he teaches at all three levels of academic studies in the fields of organizational design, management consulting, entrepreneurship, and public sector management. He has been the Head of the Department of Business System Organization for many years. He performed the function of Vice-Dean on several occasions and was a Member of various management bodies at the Faculty of Organizational Sciences and at the University in Belgrade. He is a co-author of more than 150 scientific papers and 17 textbooks and monographs. He was a reviewer of numerous books and articles in international scientific journals. He led more than 50 consulting and development projects that were implemented for the needs of the economy and the public sector.

Tomislav Jukić is an Associate Professor at the University Josip Juraj Strossmayer in Osijek, Croatia. He is a successful owner of a private business, as one of the most reputable businesses in Southeastern Europe. He has published numerous reputable academic journal articles and book chapters on organizational behavior – personality traits and health care management topics.

Marko Kolaković, PhD, is a Tenured Professor, Head of the Department of Entrepreneurship at the Faculty of Economics and Business, University of Zagreb and President of Student Business Incubator, University of Zagreb and International Institute of Entrepreneurship. He is a leader of the postgraduate study "Strategic Entrepreneurship," a Guest Lecturer at several other postgraduate studies at the Faculties of Economics in Croatia and Bosnia and Herzegovina and a Visiting Researcher at the University of Johannesburg. He is a member of the Board of Directors of the World Scientific Association "Business & Economics Society International," Worcester, MA, USA. He has published four books namely *International Business in the Conditions of Globalization, Entrepreneurship in the Knowledge Economy, Virtual Economy, and Entrepreneurship in the 21st Century* and a huge number of scientific and professional papers. He has presented his papers at about 40 international and domestic scientific conferences and proceedings.

Besnik A. Krasniqi is a fulbright postdoctoral scholar, who holds MA and PhD in Economics from Staffordshire University (UK). He teaches Small Business and Entrepreneurship, Innovation Management, and Research Methods at the University of Prishtina in graduate and postgraduate studies. His professional career spans teaching and research in entrepreneurship at Maastricht School of Management (the Netherlands), Indiana University (USA) and University of Michigan (USA), Staffordshire University (UK), State University of Tetovo (Macedonia), and Riinvest Institute for Development Research (Kosovo). He has authored several books, numerous research reports, and consultancy assignments. His research work in the area of entrepreneurship, firm growth, institutions, SME finance, informal economy, and transition and emerging economies appeared in international journals such as *Entrepreneurship Theory and Practice*, *Small Business Economics*, *International Entrepreneurship and Management Journal*, and *Economic Systems*. He is a Member of the Academy of Sciences and Arts, Republic of Kosovo.

Jovan Krivokapić is an Assistant Professor at the Faculty of Organizational Sciences in Belgrade, at the Department of Business Systems Organization. His areas of interest are Business Consulting, Organizational Design, and Event Management, and he holds the international certificate "Certified KPI Professional." He was the Head or Member of project teams in more than 30 commercial and research projects in the field of organizational design. As an author or co-author, he published 4 books and more than 50 papers at scientific conferences and in foreign and domestic journals.

Liridon Kryeziu obtained a PhD in Business Administration at Sakarya University, Turkey. He currently teaches at University for Business and Technology-UBT/ESLG College and holds a position as a Senior Researcher at Riinvest Institute. His research interests are family firms, institutions, firm internationalization, social networks, SMEs, behavioral strategy, and strategic management.

Selma Kurtishi-Kastrati is an Associate Professor at the American University of Middle East Kuwait – currently serving as the Head of the HRM Department at the College of Business Administration. She holds a PhD in Foreign Direct Investments from South-East European University, MA in International Business from Webster University, and BA (Hons) in Business and International Management from Oxford Brookes University. She has 20 years of experience in academia, teaching different courses such as international business, business organization and management, introduction to leadership, and career planning. Her research interests include FDI, business ethics, corporate social responsibility, female entrepreneurship, and small business management.

Mehmet Nurullah Kurutkan graduated from Sakarya University, Labour Economics, and Industrial Relations, Sakarya, Turkey in 2000. He started his career in the hospital sector as an X-ray Technician, and later, worked as a Quality Management Director, and then he became a Faculty Member in a Business School at Duzce University. He is currently a Full-time Academic Member of Duzce University, Faculty of Healthcare Management (2011–present). His professional interests mainly include bibliometric analysis, entrepreneurship, professionalism, and lean healthcare. He authored 40 articles, 9 books, and 5 book chapters in Turkish and English.

Tatiana S. Manolova is a Professor of Management at Bentley University, USA. Her research interests include entrepreneurial strategy, international entrepreneurship, and management in emerging economies. She is the author of over 70 scholarly articles and book chapters, has co-authored two books, and has co-edited two compendia of research on women entrepreneurs published by Edward Elgar Publishing. She is a Senior Editor for the *International Journal of Emerging Markets*, and a Consulting Editor for the *International Small Business Journal* and the *International Journal of Management Reviews*.

Boban Melović is a Professor at the University of Montenegro, Head of the Department of Management and Marketing, and Member of the Scientific Board of the University of Montenegro. He teaches groups of subjects in the field of Marketing and Management. In three mandates, he performed the function of Vice-Dean (twice as Vice-Dean for Academic Affairs and once as Vice-Dean for International Cooperation). He is the author or co-author of five books, several chapters in international monographs, and a large number of scientific papers in the field of marketing, management, entrepreneurship, brand, and tourism. He owns WorldSkills Europe Expert Certificate in Entrepreneurship. He is a two-time winner of the Award of the University of Montenegro for the achieved results and special contributions in the development of scientific research work and international positioning of the university.

Ivona Mileva is an Assistant Professor at the School of Business Economics and Management, University American College Skopje. She graduated on the topic of luxury management and her doctoral dissertation is focused on the organizational behavior field, specifically on the topic of organizational culture. She has been part of the Leadership Summit Ambassador Program, organized by People to People at Harvard University, and lately, she has been awarded with a certificate in Entrepreneurship from Harvard Business School. Her academic research is focused on the area of organizational behavior, entrepreneurship, and management fields. She has attended a wide range of conferences and co-authored academic articles both, domestically and internationally.

Isa Mustafa received his MA from the University of Belgrade in Organizational Sciences and his PhD from the University of Prishtina in Economics. He was Full Professor at the University of Prishtina in courses of Microeconomics, Managerial Economics, and Financial Management, both in graduate and postgraduate studies. His main research interest includes private sector development, informal economy, fiscal policies, and financial system. He published numerous research articles, books, reports, and studies. He is full member of Kosovo Academy of Sciences and Arts.

Andrei Stefan Nestian is the Head of the Management, Marketing, and Business Administration Department and Professor Habil at the Alexandru Ioan Cuza University in Iasi, Romania, at the Faculty of Economics and Business Administration. He lectures in management, human resource management, competency and talent management, quality management, and organizational performance. He completed the International Management Teachers Academy program organized by CEEMAN and is a Member of the Academy of Management (USA). He has 17 years of experience as a consultant and trainer, and extensive project management experience. He is co-owner of a business consultancy company since 2007, managing projects of organizational development based on attracting European non-reimbursable funding.

Ramo Palalić is an Assistant Professor of Entrepreneurship and Family Business Management at the College of Economics and Political Science (EQUIS accredited), Sultan Qaboos University, Oman. His research is in the area of entrepreneurship, leadership, and management. He has authored and co-authored many articles in globally recognized journals like *Management Decision*, *International Journal of Entrepreneurial Behavior & Research*, *International Entrepreneurship and Management Journal*, and alike. Additionally, he has co-authored/co-edited several books and many book chapters in the field of business and entrepreneurship published with internationally prominent publishers (Springer, Routledge, and World Scientific). Moreover, he is serving as the Associate Editor of the *Journal of Enterprising Communities*, Co-EiC of Gestion 2000, Associate Editor of *Heritage and Sustainable Development*, as well as a Board Member in several well-established international journals. His research field of interest is entrepreneurship, SMEs, and family businesses.

Albena Pergelova is an Associate Professor at the School of Business, MacEwan University (Canada), where she currently holds the Board of Governors Research Chair position. Her research interests include entrepreneurship, digital technologies, and consumer well-being. Her research has appeared in a wide range of international journals across disciplines, such as the *Journal of Business Ethics, Entrepreneurship & Regional Development*, *Journal of Business Research*, *International Small Business Journal*, *Journal of Small Business Management*, *Journal of Advertising*, *Journal of Consumer Affairs*, *International Journal of Advertising*, and among others. Her research has been recognized with many "best paper" awards from international conferences.

Nadezda Pop-Kostova is a PhD candidate and a Lecturer at the School of Business Economics and Management at the University American College Skopje. She holds BBA and MBA – Management degrees in Business Economics and Management. She has professional work experience in the business consulting industry as a Management Consultant. During the past 10 years, she has been part of a number of Entrepreneurial workshops and received several important acknowledgments for her contribution. Her academic research interests span in the fields of entrepreneurship, entrepreneurial intentions, strategic and international management, and businesses.

Mohammad Rezaur Razzak is an Assistant Professor of Strategic Management, Entrepreneurship, and Family Business at the College of Economics & Political Science (EQUIS accredited), at Sultan Qaboos University in Oman. He obtained his bachelor's degree in Mechanical Engineering from the University of Texas at Austin followed by MBA from Southern Methodist University. He completed his PhD with distinction from the University of Malaya specializing in strategy and family business. He has over 35 years of experience that includes industrial and corporate positions followed by a full-time engagement in academia. At present, his research interests are in the areas of family business, digital entrepreneurship, emerging business models in the industry 4.0 era, and sustainable manufacturing and supply chain practices through digitalization.

Gadaf Rexhepi is a Professor of Strategy and Innovation at South-East European University, Republic of North Macedonia (RNM). He has published around 60 research articles in different peer and refereed journals among which are *Business Strategy and the Environment, Sustainable Development, Corporate Social Responsible and Environment Management, Review of Managerial Science*, and *Industrial Marketing Management*. Most of his work in the past seven years has been in the field of CSR and sustainability. Starting in 2020, he is a Member of the Council of the National Bank of RNM for a seven-year term. He received the Award for Excellence 2016 – Outstanding Paper by Emerald Group Publishing (*Journal of Enterprising Communities: People and Places in the Global Economy*).

Goran Riđić is an Associate Professor of International Business and Management and the University of Applied Management Studies (HDWM) in Mannheim, Germany. He also teaches a Strategic Management course at the prestigious Frankfurt Finance School. He has earned his Bachelor of Arts degree majoring in Economics and minoring in German at Trinity College, Hartford, Connecticut, USA, his Master of Business Administration (MBA) from the University of Connecticut Graduate School of Business Administration in Storrs and Stamford, Connecticut, and his doctorate degree from Northeastern University in Boston, Massachusetts, USA. He has published numerous publications in the areas of management, organizational behavior, and personality traits including the prestigious, Science Citation Index (SCImago) Q1-ranked *Journal of Personality* titled "Country-Level Correlates of Dark Triad in 49 Countries." At the present time, he has 431 Google Scholar citations and business experience in top world corporations such as United Technologies – Pratt & Whitney, General Electric, ING, and Hartford Insurance Inc.

Ognjen Riđić is an Associate Professor of Management at the College of Economics and Political Science, International University of Sarajevo, and Bosnia and Herzegovina. His research focuses on management, organizational behavior, personal financial management, health care management, leadership, and entrepreneurship. He has authored and co-authored numerous articles in internationally recognized journals, such as *Psychological Assessment* (the *Official Journal of the American Psychological Association (APA)*), *Assessment-SAGE Journals, Current Psychology, International Journal of Human Resources Development, Croatian Operational Research Review, Periodicals of Engineering and Natural Sciences*, and *Dynamic Relationships Management Journal and Economic Review*. Additionally, he has co-authored one book and several book chapters in the field of business and entrepreneurship published with internationally prominent publishers (Springer Nature, World Scientific, etc.). Moreover, he is serving as the Reviewer of *Emerald Journal of Enterprising Communities, Heritage and Sustainable Development, Economic Review*, and *EdTech Journal*, in addition to being an Editorial Board Member of *Inquiry: Sarajevo Journal of Social Sciences*.

Justina Shiroka-Pula received his MA from the Faculty of Economics, University of Zagreb and PhD in Economics from the University of Prishtina. She was Full

Professor at the University of Prishtina and taught courses of Operation Management, Operation Research, Small Business Management, and Managerial Decision-making in both undergraduate and postgraduate studies. Her research interests include SME management, informal economy, operations research, and decision-making. She published numerous research articles, books, reports, and studies. She is full member and Vice President of Kosovo Academy of Sciences and Arts.

Marsela Thanasi-Boçe is an Associate Professor of Marketing at the American University of the Middle East, College of Business. She teaches different marketing courses at the undergraduate and graduate levels, such as principles of marketing management, international marketing management, retail and merchandising, new product development, and new ventures and product design. She has published several research articles in leading marketing journals. Her research interest is focused on customer relationship management, brand management, consumer behavior, retail, social media marketing, entrepreneurship education, and corporate social responsibility.

Ivan Todorović works at the University of Belgrade, Faculty of Organizational Sciences. His field of expertise includes organizational design, restructuring, management consulting, business model development, and entrepreneurship. He has participated in more than 30 consulting projects in the largest companies in Serbia and in numerous research projects financed by the Republic of Serbia or international institutions like EBRD, UNIDO, and USAID. He is a co-author of more than 70 articles in international monographs, journals, and conference proceedings, and he is hired as a reviewer in several international scientific journals and conferences. He was a Visiting Lecturer at the University of Maribor, Faculty of Organizational Sciences, in Slovenia. As a mentor, he has supported several start-up companies and coached student teams for international case study competitions.

Ivan Turčić is a Postdoctoral Researcher and Senior Assistant at the Department of Entrepreneurship, Faculty of Economics and Business (FEB), University of Zagreb and Vice President of International Institute of Entrepreneurship. He obtained his PhD degree in 2022 with summa cum laude at FEB. Since 2016, he has been employed at FEB, as an Assistant and Senior Assistant/Postdoctoral Researcher. He is the (co)author of over 10 papers published in scientific journals and conference proceedings, is a member of the Organizing Committee of *Business and Entrepreneurial Economics Conference* and is Co-editor of *BEE Conference Proceedings*. He took several training courses and workshops in quantitative methods and teaching competencies. His main areas of research interest include social entrepreneurship, digital entrepreneurship, entrepreneurial intentions, entrepreneurship education, SME finance, generation Z and entrepreneurship, and innovative business models.

Mladen Turuk, PhD, is an Assistant Professor at the Department of Entrepreneurship, Faculty of Economics and Business (FEB), University of Zagreb. He received additional education at the University of Ljubljana and the University of Hong Kong, studying qualitative and quantitative methods of scientific research. Since 2011, he has been employed at the FEB, as a Research Fellow, Postdoctoral Fellow, and Assistant Professor. As a Guest Lecturer, he has been engaged at Macquarie University in Sydney, Shanghai University of International Business and Economics, University of Ljubljana, and Montpellier Business School and he is a Visiting Researcher at the University of Johannesburg. He is the Secretary of the specialist postgraduate study "Strategic Entrepreneurship." He has published over 20 scientific and professional papers. He is the Editor-in-Chief of the *International Journal of Contemporary Business and Entrepreneurship* and the President of the Entrepreneurship Club.

Ana Iolanda Voda is a Lecturer at the Department of Management, Marketing, and Business Administration, Faculty of Economics and Business Administration, Alexandru Ioan Cuza University of Iași, Romania. Her research interests include entrepreneurship, social inclusion, and smart cities. She attended over 50 conferences worldwide (e.g., Portugal, Spain, and the Czech Republic), published over 30 papers indexed in the WOS, and over 10 books/book chapters. She has been a Principal Investigator/Member of the project team of 16 national and international projects/grants (e.g., "Research & Innovation for Cities & Citizens – RI4C2" project, EC2U Alliance, Horizon 2020 "Science with & for Society" SwafS call for European Universities (2021–2024); Principal Investigator, ERASMUS+ Program Jean Monnet Activities 2019 Call, European Smart Cities for Sustainable Development (SmartEU) (620415-EPP-1-2020-1-RO-EPPJMO-MODULE (2020–2023). She is also a Romanian representative in 2 COST Projects (e.g., CA 18115 (TRIBES) – 2019–2023; and CA 20115 (ENIS-2021–2025).

Desislava I. Yordanova is a Professor at the Department of Business Administration of Sofia University "St. Kliment Ohridski." Her research interests include entrepreneurship, small business management, and family business management and succession. She has published articles in various international journals including *International Small Business Journal*; *Journal of Small Business Management*; *Journal of International Management*; *Sustainability*; *International Journal of Entrepreneurial Behaviour & Research*; *Journal of Developmental Entrepreneurship*; *Service Business*; *World Review of Entrepreneurship, Management, and Sustainable Development*; and *International Journal of Business and Globalisation*.

Rasim Zuferi is engaged as a Lecturer at the Faculty of Business and Economics at South-East European University, Republic of North Macedonia. He has taught Accounting and Marketing courses in undergraduate and postgraduate courses. He has been teaching for more than 20 years at the undergraduate and graduate levels at South-East European University in Tetovo, Macedonia, and in other institutions. His research interests include promotion, consumer behavior, marketing research, and entrepreneurial marketing. He has published several research articles in different peer and refereed journals.

Foreword

My mother grew up in Egypt, where – at the time – it was the dream of many girls to marry King Farouk, a highly respected leader whose origins were Balkan. Eventually, she married my father, and she got to meet Farouk, who happened to be a friend of his. Not surprisingly, I grew up constantly reminded that the Balkan people are among the kindest in the world, the most trustworthy, and the warmest friends one could imagine.

Hence, I have insufficient words to describe my delight in writing the *Foreword* of this important book about wonderful people from an area that has throughout history been of great importance. It is assembled by dedicated editors bringing together a variety of authors who specialize in different topics, and the volume is worth much more than the sum of its parts.

The Balkans was the area where the Austro-Hungarian Empire met the mighty Ottoman Empire. This in itself is exciting for me, being the nephew of my mother's brother – whose documents stated the Ottoman Empire as his country of birth. More importantly, the meeting of empires enriched this area with the cross-fertilization of ideas and a unique blend of worldly architectures.

I first visited the Balkans during the 1970s. The Soviet Union had considerable influence over the Warsaw Pact countries at the time. Meanwhile, in what was then Yugoslavia, Tito had much power. Entrepreneurship was obviously not the flavor of the day. Of course, Greece and Turkey had many small firms, but entrepreneurship development was not yet a priority.

In 1982, in Bulgaria, I learned that merely speaking about entrepreneurship could lead to trouble. Later that decade I spent much time in the Yugoslav republics.

As the Berlin Wall fell, the world changed, and I was invited to teach in 1995 at the Academy of Economic Sciences in Romania. The following year I spent much time in Albania, writing an article that appeared in the *Journal of Small Business Management.* My love for the Balkans and its people increased and I authored a book as well as several articles about the transition in the region. Now I am happy to see this present volume and I commend the editors for their genius in putting it together.

Léo-Paul Dana

Professor, Dalhousie University, Canada & ICD Business School, France

Visiting Professor, Lappeenranta University of Technology, Finland

Honorary Professor, Amity University Uttar Pradesh, India

Chapter 1

Entrepreneurship Development in the Balkans: Past, Present, and Future

Veland Ramadani, Sasho Kjosev and Bruno S. Sergi

1. Introduction

The book *Entrepreneurship Development in the Balkans: Perspective from Diverse Contexts* is the first of a series of books in the area of entrepreneurship and development that are planned to be produced under the MoU signed between the Balkan Economic Forum[1] (regional LEAD office for the Balkans) and the Lab for Entrepreneurship and Development (LEAD).[2]

The association for regional development Balkan Economic Forum is an NGO based in Skopje (North Macedonia), independent of any national government, political party, or other vested interest. It operates with an inclusive approach that respects universal human rights and recognizes the potential of every individual to actively contribute to the achievement of tangible economic development for the region's social welfare. Balkan Economic Forum's focus is on developing and implementing innovative strategies and creative solutions to the current economic challenges facing the Balkan countries to stimulate economic growth, which, in turn, strengthens regional cooperation, peace, and security.

The new book treats different topics in the field of entrepreneurship and small businesses, such as innovation, risk management, women entrepreneurship, social entrepreneurship, migrant entrepreneurship, corporate entrepreneurship, institutional support of entrepreneurial initiatives, sustainability, green entrepreneurship, and so on, from the perspective of different Balkans' countries: Albania,

---

[1]Balkan Economic Forum: https://www.balkaneconomicforum.org/.

[2]LEAD is a research lab based in Cambridge, USA, that spun out of Harvard's IQSS in 2018: https://www.leadresearchteam.com/ and https://www.iq.harvard.edu/?utm_source=aws&utm_medium=iq&utm_campaign=redirect_analysis.

Entrepreneurship Development in the Balkans: Perspective from Diverse Contexts, 1–14

Published under exclusive licence by Emerald Publishing Limited
doi:10.1108/978-1-83753-454-820231001

Bosnia and Herzegovina, Bulgaria, Croatia, Greece, Kosovo, Montenegro, North Macedonia, Romania, Serbia, Slovenia, and Türkiye.

2. The Balkans: History, Present, and Future

Within the geographical borders of the Adriatic, Ionian, Mediterranean, Aegean, and Black Seas, which outline the Balkan Peninsula, the origin of human society dates back to the Paleolithic period. Following the development of grain farming and livestock raising practices in the area which spread from the Middle East during the Neolithic period around 7000 BC, human settlements expanded with the aid of human migration, multi-ethnic cultures took root, regional trade developed, the population grew amidst waves of conflict, and human ingenuity led the region in becoming the site of Europe's first advanced civilization located in Greece beginning in 3200 BC at the beginning of the Bronze Age in Europe (Boyadzhiev, 2020; Gimbutas, 1972).

At the turn of the century, the Balkan region was more sparsely populated and underdeveloped than Western Europe, with few natural resources and low economic prize. The main value of Balkan was its geographical position and geopolitical interest (Llewellyn & Thompson, 2017). Considering that the Balkan's position represented a crossroad between three great empires, Ottoman, Austro-Hungarian, and Russian, with access to several waterways, which were important for many peoples and places of the world, made this region to be of vital and strategic importance. This made the Balkans for centuries, but why not even today, to be considered a gate between the East and the West, where many cultures intermingled, trade developed, and many ethnic groups and peoples mixed and merged with each other (Alpha History, 2023).

Modernly, within those geographical borders, lies a region commonly known as the Balkans, which is a term coined in the early twentieth century that is used to describe the culturally diverse, resource-rich area shared by countries in southeastern Europe, including Albania, Bosnia and Herzegovina, Bulgaria, Croatia, Greece, Kosovo, North Macedonia, Montenegro, Romania, Slovenia, Serbia, and Türkiye (Fig. 1).

Not long ago, many Balkan countries operated under an economic system based on state control and central government planning that restricted private enterprise and became uncompetitive in global trade markets. Since then, these countries have undertaken the challenging yet eminently worthwhile transition to free market economies characterized by the deregulation of prices and markets and the liberalization of capital, labor, and product markets; however, in the absence of strong and effective support mechanisms, this transition does not automatically lead to economic development and improved social welfare. During this transitional period, these economies have experienced severe contractions due in part to the collapse of many uncompetitive, state-owned enterprises and the spread of the global economic crisis, which, along with other factors, have resulted in massive unemployment, increased poverty, social instability, and widespread corruption. During the latter stages of the global economic crisis, Balkan regional income levels have dropped below their 1989 values (Monastiriotis & Petrakos, 2010).

Fig. 1. Geographic Map of the Balkan Peninsula. *Source*: Based on Google Maps.

Looking on the bright side of things, many of these countries possess memberships in various international organizations that were established to facilitate economic development and security, such as the World Bank, World Trade Organization, International Monetary Fund, Organization for Economic Cooperation and Development, Organization for Security and Cooperation in Europe, North Atlantic Treaty Organization, and Council of Europe. Another significant socio-economic alliance is shared by Bulgaria, Croatia, Greece, and Romania as European Union (EU) Member States, while Albania, Bosnia and Herzegovina, North Macedonia, Montenegro, Serbia, and Türkiye are EU candidate countries. Kosovo is considered to be a potential candidate for EU membership.

In this regard, Constantine Alexander, the President Emeritus of the Balkan Economic Forum, noted:

> These alliances, along with diverse cultures and natural resources, represent economic assets, the responsible management of which can contribute to the long-term economic performance of the individual nations; however, Balkan development potential, economic growth, and inter-state cooperation have been hindered by the consequences of multi-faceted regional conflicts. Reliance upon external economic development aid is neither a viable nor a sustainable long-term solution to the region's current challenges, including the need for socio-economic stability, security, and inter-state cooperation. (Alexander, n.d., p. 2)

Balkan countries can collaborate toward an even brighter future as long as they remain mindful of history, showing us there will be no future if they remain divided. Regional exchange can be a source of growth and development and of enhancing good governance. An old African proverb says, "if you want to go fast, go alone … but if you want to go far, go together." The Balkans represent one of the most diverse parts of Europe, culturally and naturally. As such, it presents valuable gifts to the oldest continent, Europe.

Further, the Balkan countries' strengths

> lie in their diversity and determination to be part of the European family of democratic nations. Balkan countries' dream envisions a Balkan Peninsula with good governance, responsible economic growth, sustainable employment, environmentally sustainable development, regional cooperation, and widening educational opportunities. To achieve these goals, the pathway to the future is sustainable development for the Balkan region. It offers a framework to generate economic growth, achieve social justice, exercise environmental stewardship, and strengthen accountability. (Alexander, 2022)

Considering that Balkan belongs to Europe, the EU should support this part to achieve (a) long-term economic recovery (private sector and human capital); (b) green (environment and climate/clean energy) & digital transition (digital future); (c) faster regional integration; and (d) convergence with the EU (European Union, 2021).

3. Entrepreneurship in the Balkans: in a Nutshell

Entrepreneurship in the Balkans, in the past, precisely before the 1990s of the twentieth century, did not present a topic of interest to researchers and policymakers; probably, this was because these countries were governed according to the socialist system, where the free initiative was not seen as a development option and everything was done to suppress it, at any cost (Ramadani, Dana, Gërguri, & Tašaminova, 2013). Many countries did not do enough even after the 1990s. Svetozar Janevski, a successful entrepreneur from North Macedonia, will say

> we should consider ourselves lucky to have put behind the times filled with political crisis, wars, economic turbulence, high inflation, no proper conditions for free trade and a constant lack of access to finance to invest in development projects. However, these periods have created clusters of people with shady values and unclear merits. (Janevski, 2018, p. 3)

Based on the literature, the pioneer of studies on entrepreneurship in the Balkan countries is the well-known scholar Léo-Paul Dana, with his works about Albania (Dana, 1996), Macedonia (Dana, 1998), Bosnia and Herzegovina (Dana, 1999a), Greece (Dana, 1999b), Bulgaria (Dana, 2000), and Croatia (Dana, 2005a). The books of Dana (2005b) and Ramadani and Schneider (2013) can be considered as more thoughtful and comprehensive publications, where in detail was described the development of entrepreneurship in each Balkan country, addressing all the vicissitudes and challenges faced by entrepreneurs as well as the efforts and opportunities that were offered to evoke the entrepreneurial spirit, innovation, and risk-taking in these endeavors. Then, many other publications continued to appear in the form of scientific articles, books, and presentations at scientific conferences, with created a good base in the literature, sufficient to open new paths for studying entrepreneurship activities in this region, such as women entrepreneurship (Palalic et al., 2020; Ramadani et al., 2013), ethnic entrepreneurship (Ramadani, Rexhepi, Gërguri-Rashiti, Ibraimi, & Dana, 2014), corporate entrepreneurship (Antoncic & Hisrich, 2004), social entrepreneurship (Halberstadt et al., 2021; Palalic, 2014; Phillips, De Amicis, & Lipparini, 2016; Varga, 2017), sustainable and green entrepreneurship (Abazi-Alili, Ramadani, & Hughes, 2023; Ivanova & Mustafa, 2021), digital and technology entrepreneurship (Gërguri-Rashiti, Ramadani, Abazi-Alili, Dana, & Ratten, 2017; Krasniqi & Peci, 2017), and so on.

Global Entrepreneurship Monitor (GEM) is among the most used and reliable databases to present the state and development of respective countries. GEM was established in 1999 by Babson College (USA) and London Business School (UK) to study the economic impact of entrepreneurship and the factors influencing the development of entrepreneurial activities at the national level. With its coverage of more than 120 countries worldwide, GEM represents the most coordinated approach to researching the entrepreneurial activity of a population or a relevant country (Bosma et al., 2021). GEM's almost worldwide presence and rigorous scientific methodology have made it the world's most influential and authoritative source of empirical data and expertise on the potential and development of entrepreneurship among different countries. Every year, GEM provides a vast collection of data on social attitudes, individuals' participation levels in different stages of the entrepreneurial process, and characteristics of entrepreneurs and their businesses. This information enables comparisons within and between individual economies, geographic regions, and levels of economic development (Hisrich & Ramadani, 2017). Among the most used GEM indicators is the *TEA index* (total early-stage entrepreneurial activity) which shows the percentage of the population between 18 and 64 years old (this age is used for all GEM indicators) who are either nascent entrepreneurs or new business owners-managers (Bygrave & Zacharakis, 2008). Data about entrepreneurial activity in some Balkan countries are presented in Table 1.

The other indicators' descriptions and meaning in Table 1 are as follows (Hill, Ionescu-Somers, & Coduras, 2022):

- *Established business ownership*: Percentage of the population who currently own their business for more than 42 months.
- *Female/male TEA ratio*: Percentage of females who are either nascent entrepreneurs or new business owners-managers, divided by the male counterparts percentage.

Table 1. Entrepreneurship Indicators in the Balkan Countries.

No.	Country	Year	Total Early-stage Entrepreneurial Activity (TEA)	Established Business Ownership	Female/ Male TEA	Motivational Index	Entrepreneurial Intentions	Entrepreneurship as a Good Career Choice	Fear of Failure Rate	Innovation
1	Bosnia and Herzegovina	2010	7.74	6.64	0.37	0.64	16.76	75.99	27.45	N/A
2	Bulgaria	2018	6.00	8.35	0.87	0.96	3.91	62.57	30.98	14.89
3	Croatia	2021	12.35	4.03	0.59	1.37*	21.68	62.44	45.58	24.59*
4	Greece	2021	5.53	14.68	0.71	3.05*	9.58	64.79	51.46	28.44*
5	Kosovo	2014	4.03	2.06	0.69	1.32	6.31	68.28	26.73	28.55
6	Montenegro	2010	14.94	7.81	0.54	1.03	31.86	80.99	30.42	N/A
7	North Macedonia	2010	7.88	7.58	0.34	0.4	26.69	71.27	30.91	N/A
8	Romania	2021	9.68	4.10	0.98	1.59*	9.72	67.78	48.25	N/A
9	Serbia	2009	4.90	10.12	0.40	N/A	22.2	68.89	27.96	N/A
10	Slovenia	2021	6.66	8.49	0.85	1.96*	15.38	68.21	42.97	25.54*
11	Slovenia	2009	5.36	11.01	0.32	N/A	9.70	55.75	29.68	N/A
12	Türkiye	2021	15.69	6.64	0.49	1.73*	31.30	66.8	39.84	30.8*

Source: Based on GEM data published on https://www.gemconsortium.org/data.

Notes: Albania is not included in GEM; Data with * are for 2018.

- *Motivational index*: Percentage of TEA-involved people that are motivated by an opportunity, divided by the percentage of those that are motivated by a necessity.
- *Entrepreneurial intention*: Percentage of people who are latent entrepreneurs and plan to start their own business within three years.
- *Entrepreneurship as a good career choice*: Percentage of people who consider starting their own business as a desirable career choice.
- *Innovation*: Percentage of those involved in TEA who indicate that their product/service is new to at least some customers and that few/no businesses offer the same product.
- *Fear of failure*: Percentage of people who indicate that fear of failure would prevent them from entering entrepreneurship.

If we compare the TEA index of the Balkans countries, there can be seen that Türkiye leads the list, where 15.69% of Turkish people between 18 and 64 years old are either nascent entrepreneurs or new business owners-managers, followed by Montenegro with 14.94 and Croatia with 12.35 TEA index, respectively. Greece has the most significant percentage of the population who have owned their business for more than 42 months, respectively 14.68, followed by Slovenia and Serbia. Türkiye, Kosovo, and Greece have the highest innovation rate, while people from Montenegro, Bosnia and Herzegovina, and North Macedonia see entrepreneurship as a good career choice. People from Greece, Romania, and Croatia have the highest percentage in terms of showing fear of failure from entering entrepreneurship in comparison with other Balkans people, while only 26.73% of Kosovars say that the fear of failure will prevent them from opening their own businesses. People from Greece, Slovenia, and Romania are more motivated by an opportunity in the market rather than by necessity. Montenegro, Türkiye, and North Macedonia have the highest rate of entrepreneurial intentions, respectively, the percentage of people who are latent entrepreneurs and plan to start their own business within three years. Since that Albania is not part of GEM, other studies show that the people of Albania have an entrepreneurial spirit, but the government and other actors, despite some positive efforts and initiatives, should do more to support the entrepreneurial initiatives and create a better ecosystem, where entrepreneurs show a little trust in the government capacities, low budget is dedicated for entrepreneurship and innovation, little cooperation among triple helix actors, lack of information about supporting programs and organizations, entrepreneurship as a concept is not part of the most universities programs yet, etc. (Kapo, 2022; Ramadani, Bexheti, Rexhepi, Ratten, & Ibraimi, 2017). Engjëll Rraklli, an IT serial entrepreneur, regarding the entrepreneurial ecosystem in Albania, will say

> I've had entrepreneurial tendencies since high school, from forming a rock band and then starting to build games with the intentions of monetizing them, providing programming courses and so on. When it comes to the start-up ecosystem, I personally believe that start-ups are a way of innovating but also of improving

> economies, especially in the Balkans. So as an entrepreneur in the start-up scene right from its inception in Albania, it's a responsibility for me to give back and to try to help grow the ecosystem as much as I can. (Stojkovski, 2022, p.1)

Entrepreneurs in the Balkans face several challenges. Culkin and Simmons (2018) found that the Balkans' entrepreneurs mostly face the following challenges: the confusion of real entrepreneurs with the so-called "predatory entrepreneur" creates bad image about their companies and business activities; continued difficulties in creating a stable customer base and establishing connections with larger markets; insufficient internal investments and the distance from the main supply chains to the big markets deprive the Balkan entrepreneurs from the key sources of new businesses contracts, innovation, and access to affordable funds to finance their further development; underdeveloped venture capital and business angels market, which creates additional difficulties in the process of business ideas concretizations and turn them into profitable businesses; the mistaken perception that entrepreneurship is exclusively related to hi-tech, somehow contributes to many individuals shying away from the idea of opening their own businesses; insufficient possession and development of entrepreneurial skills; and insufficient technical knowledge about regulatory issues.

4. Structure of the Book

This book consists of 15 chapters, including this introductory chapter. Every chapter discusses a particular entrepreneurship topic in a respective Balkan country, while chapters two and three covers all Western Balkan countries.

Chapter 2 – "Family Ties Shaping the Entrepreneurial Intentions" is written by Ivona Mileva, Nadezda Pop-Kostova, and Nadica Jovanovska Boshkovska. The authors provide readers with a thorough grasp of family enterprises' entrepreneurial aspirations. It will also assess how previous experience in family businesses affects one's ambition to start their own firm. For this matter, the authors have used data acquired from the GUESSS (Global University Entrepreneurial Spirit Students' Survey), the survey carried out among college students in different Balkan countries: North Macedonia, Albania, Greece, Croatia, and Bulgaria.

Chapter 3 – "How Is Social Entrepreneurship Pursuing the Path of Development? Regional Perspectives in the Western Balkans" written by Stefan Chichevaliev, Stojan Debarliev, and Aleksandra Janeska Iliev portray the development of social entrepreneurship in the Western Balkans and present a regional overview. Social entrepreneurship has become a globally known contributor to alleviating societal, economic, social, and environmental concerns. Its influence on increasing people's quality of life has put the concept on a pedestal, and the Balkans are no different. To provide a regional development overview, the authors have used the institutional perspective.

Hyrije Abazi-Alili, Gadaf Rexhepi, Selajdin Abduli, Sadudin Ibraimi, and Rasim Zuferi in Chapter 4, "Green Entrepreneurship and Firm Performance: The Case of Albania," by using enterprise data for the Republic of Albania (ALB), examine the effects of green entrepreneurship on firm performance. They found that when the determinants of firm performance were investigated, green entrepreneurship, certification, innovation activities, foreign ownership, and monitoring energy appears to have a positive impact on firm performance, while the effect of direct export is negative.

Ramo Palalić, Ognjen Riđić, Tomislav Jukić, Abdul Wahab Aidoo, Goran Riđić, and Mohammad Rezaur Razzak in Chapter 5, "Entrepreneurship Ecosystem in Bosnia and Herzegovina: Perspectives and Challenges," describe 10 elements of the entrepreneurial ecosystem and their implications on entrepreneurial ecosystem outlook of Bosnia and Herzegovina. As the authors noted, Bosnia Herzegovina similarly to other countries of former Yugoslavia is still regarded to be a transitional economy, both from the social, political, and economic perspectives. In this regard, it is important to note that political agendas and economic strategies are still not satisfactory for the development of entrepreneurial activities.

Chapter 6 – "Entrepreneurial Implementation Intentions among Bulgarian STEM Students: Facilitators and Constraints," coauthored by Desislava I. Yordanova, Albena Pergelova, Fernando Angulo-Ruiz, and Tatiana S. Manolova, based on a sample of 299 STEM students, who reported technology-based entrepreneurial intentions, discuss the importance of entrepreneurial implementation intentions for closing the intention-behavior gap. A binary logistic regression is applied to examine four specific mechanisms that facilitate or impede the students' actual implementation intentions.

Marko Kolaković, Mladen Turuk, and Ivan Turčić in Chapter 7, "Social Entrepreneurship: Perspective of Croatia," analyze the development of social entrepreneurship in Croatia over the last 10 years; the current state and perspective of the development of social entrepreneurship; and the strategic documents related to social entrepreneurship with an emphasis on the Strategy for the Development of Social Entrepreneurship 2015–2020, which was an essential document for the promotion and financing of social entrepreneurship. They concluded that social entrepreneurship in this country is still in its initial development phase, and a colossal opportunity has been missed. The authors recommended that the government and other stakeholders must make additional efforts to develop social entrepreneurship in Croatia.

Chapter 8 – "Digital Entrepreneurship and Disruptive Innovation in the Greek Maritime Industry: The Case of Harbor Lab," coauthored by Daphne Halkias, Mark Esposito, Tatiana Harkiolakis, Jordi Diaz, and Nicholas Mmaduabuchi Ikpogu, aims to answer the questions of who the Greek digital entrepreneur in the maritime sector is and how their entrepreneurial actions contribute to a growing knowledge base of digital entrepreneurship for future theoretical research and professional practice. This chapter contributed a fresh perspective of scholarly knowledge on digital entrepreneurship for future theoretical research and professional practice.

Chapter 9 – "Informal Entrepreneurship in Kosovo: An institutionalist Approach," contributed by Isa Mustafa, Justina Pula-Shiroka, Besnik A. Krasniqi, Veland Ramadani, and Liridon Kryeziu, examines the informal sector entrepreneurship in Kosovo using institutional theory lenses. Using a survey with 500 owners/managers of private companies, the study finds that the service industry has the highest participation in the informal economy compared to other sectors. On average small firms, compared to larger ones, report a higher percentage of unreported incomes. Findings also suggest that when informal entrepreneurs perceive penalties for tax avoidance from tax authorities as high, they tend to have higher compliance with reporting their income. In addition, it was found that the higher the vertical (trust in formal institutions) and horizontal distrust (trust in business partners), the higher the involvement in the informal economy.

Chapter 10 – "Multi-Context Analysis of the Environment for the Development of Entrepreneurship in Montenegro," written by Boban Melović and Dragana Ćirović, provides an overview of entrepreneurship in Montenegro, through various aspects of the analysis. In the beginning, the authors discuss the role and importance of the development of entrepreneurship in Montenegro, followed by an analysis of the institutional and strategic framework for supporting the development of entrepreneurship. The authors concluded that entrepreneurship is a concept that is increasingly used in Montenegrin economic theory, but also that it is increasingly present in everyday life, which is confirmed by numerous examples from practice.

Chapter 11 – "Sustainable Entrepreneurship in North Macedonia: Challenges and Perspectives," coauthored by Marsela Thanasi-Boçe, Selma Kurtishi-Kastrati, Veland Ramadani, and Rasim Zuferi, provides a detailed description of sustainable entrepreneurship drivers and outcomes with a focus on the challenges and perspectives of sustainable entrepreneurship in North Macedonia. The authors provide also some lessons from challenges and best practices of sustainable ventures in North Macedonia together with suggestions for these practices to be adopted in other countries associated with the actions required for implementation.

Ana Iolanda Voda and Andrei Stefan Nestian in Chapter 12, "Gender Differences in Early-stage Entrepreneurship: The Case of Romanian Entrepreneurs," explore gender inequalities in the entrepreneurial landscape in Romania, based on GEM data, highlighting similarities and differences between women and men entrepreneurs. They found that identifying opportunities proved to be positive and significant for both genders, while fear of failure had the opposite effect. Further, they concluded that the external knowledge that an entrepreneur's environment gives rise to can prove to be supportive in the discovery of opportunities and their exploitation.

Chapter 13 – "Development of Entrepreneurship in Serbia: Main External Factors and Influences" is written by Ondrej Jaško, Mladen Čudanov, Jovan Krivokapić, and Ivan Todorović. They have systematized observations regarding changes in entrepreneurship in Serbia during the previous decade, having in mind some key factors such as High-Impact Low-Probability (HILP) events, dynamic development in the sphere of information technologies (IT), and foreign direct investments (FDI). The authors created a set of reports that indicate the strength and direction of the influence of the mentioned factors and their consequences in the sphere of entrepreneurship at the level of Serbia and selected cities, based on the fact that the entrepreneurial ecosystem in those cities faced greater than average challenges.

Chapter 14 – "Intrapreneurship, Ecopreneurship and Digitalization in Slovenia," written by Jasna Auer Antončič and Boštjan Antončič, covers intrapreneurship, ecopreneurship, and digitalization, and presents qualitative research findings on eco-innovations and digitalization in Slovenia. Eco-innovations and digitalization are important aspects of intrapreneurship and the performance of existing companies. Practices of the participating company in circular economy and eco-innovations and digitalization are presented and discussed.

Mehmet Bağış, Mehmet Nurullah Kurutkan, and Liridon Kryeziu in the last chapter, "Entrepreneurship Studies in Türkiye: Where Are We? Where Should We Go? Analysis of International Publications," examined the contribution of publications in the context of Türkiye to the international entrepreneurship literature between 2005 and 2022. They analyzed 471 articles published in international journals in the Web of Science (WoS) Core Collection database using Biblioshiny+Bibliometrix, SciMAT, and VOSViewer. The authors have used performance, theme and evolution, co-authorship, and document analysis in their examination.

5. Conclusion and Future Research Avenues

During the past few decades, the Balkans Peninsula has undergone significant changes in entrepreneurship development. In the communist era, private entrepreneurs were not allowed in most Balkan countries, as the state handled all aspects of the economy. Following the fall of communism, the transition to a market economy began, although the process was complex and slow. Many countries needed more infrastructure, institutions, and legal frameworks for entrepreneurial activities.

Even with challenges, some entrepreneurs established and expanded successful businesses. Today, the entrepreneurial ecosystem in the Balkans is changing quickly, thanks to increased support from governments, investors, and international organizations. Many Balkan countries have introduced policies and initiatives to encourage entrepreneurship, such as tax incentives, business incubators, and funding programs.

Younger generations are also driving entrepreneurial activity and embracing innovation and technology. The future of entrepreneurship in the Balkans looks promising, as the area offers the potential to become a thriving hub for innovation and an entrepreneurial environment. Policymakers must prioritize challenges such as access to finance, talent retention, and reducing red tape. The EU membership could provide access to a more business-friendly environment and a market with over 500 million consumers, significantly increasing their potential customer base and financial resources. The other side is that EU membership would come with stringent regulations and standards, which can be difficult and expensive for smaller businesses. Also, competition in the European market can be tough, so it will be a hard requirement for Balkan entrepreneurs to compete with EU businesses. The larger EU market can provide resources and opportunities for entrepreneurs looking to set about and develop their businesses in the Balkans. Entrepreneurship in the Balkans must keep growing with a focus on innovation, technology, and collaboration with a new geography of regional value chains and benefit from being strategically located at the crossroads of Europe and Asia.

Governments, investors, and accelerators have recognized the potential of the region's entrepreneurs. They must help foster a culture of innovation and collaboration, which is essential for developing regional value chains and intertwined business activities.

In conclusion, the sections in *Entrepreneurship Development in the Balkans: Past, Present, and Future* discuss entrepreneurship topics closed tied to developing regional value chains and EU membership. The region maintains the potential for agriculture, manufacturing, and technology. The IT and agriculture sectors can represent thriving regional value chains. Both examples can increase their market reach and export their products to potential markets. By collaborating with businesses in neighboring countries, Balkan entrepreneurs can tap into the resources and expertise and compete on a regional and international scale. The growth of entrepreneurship and regional value chains in the Balkans represent an effective development for the region. The Balkans have come a long way in entrepreneurship development and considerable potential for steady growth exists.

References

Abazi-Alili, H., Ramadani, V., & Hughes, M. (2023). Green entrepreneurship and productivity: Firm-level evidence from the BEEPS Survey in the Republic of North Macedonia. In *Proceedings dedicated to Academician Alajdin Abazi on the occasion of the 80th anniversary of his birth*, Skopje: Macedonian Academy of Science and Arts.

Alexander, C. (2022). Speech of Constantine Alexander at the 2022 Balkan Economic Forum (BEF). Retrieved from https://www.facebook.com/MediumskaInformativnaAgencija/videos/861146784892278/. Accessed on January 17, 2023.

Alexander, C. (n.d.). *Balkan economic forum (BEF) ethos and mission*. Athens: Balkan Economic Forum.

Alpha History. (2023). The Balkans. Retrieved from https://alphahistory.com/worldwar1/balkans/. Accessed on January 17, 2023.

Antoncic, B., & Hisrich, R. D. (2004). Corporate entrepreneurship contingencies and organizational wealth creation. *Journal of Management Development*, *23*(6), 518–550.

Bosma, N., Hill, S., Ionescu-Somers, A., Kelley, D., Guerrero, M., & Schott, T. (2021). *Global entrepreneurship monitor 2020/2021 global report*. Babson Park and London: Babson College and London Business School.

Boyadzhiev, K. (2020). The transition to the late neolithic in the upper Thracian Plain. *Quaternary International*, *560–561*(9), 45–56.

Bygrave, W., & Zacharakis, A. (2008). Entrepreneurship, 1st Edition, New York: Wiley.

Culkin, N., & Simmons, R. (2018). *Study of the challenges that hinder MSME development in the Western Balkans*. London: British Council.

Dana, L. P. (1996). Albania in the twilight zone: The *përsëritje* model and its impact on small business. *Journal of Small Business Management*, *34*(1), 64–70.

Dana, L.-P. (1998). Waiting for direction in the former Yugoslav Republic of Macedonia (FYROM). *Journal of Small Business Management*, *36*(2), 62–67.

Dana, L. P. (1999a). Business and entrepreneurship in Bosnia–Herzegovina. *Journal of Business and Entrepreneurship*, *11*(2), 105–118.

Dana, L. P. (1999b). Preserving culture through small business: Government support for artisans and craftsmen in Greece. *Journal of Small Business Management*, *37*(1), 90–95.

Dana, L. P. (2000). Bulgaria at the crossroads of entrepreneurship. *Journal of Euromarketing*, *8*(4), 27–50.

Dana, L. P. (2005a). Recent research about entrepreneurship and small business in Croatia. *International Journal of Entrepreneurship & Small Business*, *2*(3), 209–210.

Dana, L. P. (2005b). *When economies change hands: a survey of entrepreneurship in the emerging markets of Europe from the Balkans to the Baltic States*. Oxford: Routledge.

European Union. (2021). Economic and investment plan for the Western Balkans 2021–2027. Retrieved from https://www.wbif.eu/. Accessed on January 17, 2023.

Gërguri-Rashiti, G., Ramadani, V., Abazi-Alili, H., Dana, L. P., & Ratten, V. (2017). ICT, innovation and firm performance: The transition economies context. *Thunderbird International Business Review*, *59*(1), 93–102.

Gimbutas, M. (1972). The neolithic cultures of the Balkan Peninsula. In H. Birnbaum & S. Vryonis (Eds.), *Aspects of the Balkans: Continuity and change: Contributions to the international Balkan conference held at UCLA* (pp. 9–49). Boston: De Gruyter Mouton.

Halberstadt, J., Niemand, T., Kraus, S., Rexhepi, G., Jones, P., & Kailer, N. (2021). Social entrepreneurship orientation: Drivers of success for start-ups and established industrial firms. *Industrial Marketing Management*, *94*(1), 137–149.

Hill, S., Ionescu-Somers, A., & Coduras, A. (2022). *Global entrepreneurship monitor 2021/2022 global report: Opportunity amid disruption*. London: GEM.

Hisrich, R., & Ramadani, V. (2017). *Effective entrepreneurial management*. Cham: Springer.

Ivanova, A., & Mustafa, S. (2021). *Green entrepreneurship roadmap of Western Balkans*. Prishtina: Balkan Green Foundation.

Janevski, S. (2018). *Challenges for entrepreneurship in Western Balkans*. Zagreb: Svjetski Kongres Poduzetnika.

Kapo, K. (2022). *Challenges of strengthening the Albanian start-up ecosystem*. Ljubljana: University of Ljubljana.

Krasniqi, B., & Peci, F. (2017). The determinants of technological innovation: The role of anti-competitive behaviour and access to finance. *International Journal of Economic Perspectives*, *11*(2), 309–316.

Llewellyn, J. & Thompson, S. (2017). The Balkans. Retrieved from https://alphahistory.com/worldwar1/balkans/. Accessed on May 13, 2023.

Monastiriotis, V., & Petrakos, G. (2010). Twenty years of economic transition in the Balkans: transition failures and development challenges. *Southeastern Europe*, *34*(2), 154–174.

Palalic, R. (2014). A study on business ethics and corporate social responsibility (CSR): Evidence from Bosnia and Herzegovina. *Southeast Europe Journal of Soft Computing*, *3*(1), 26–31.

Palalic, R., Dana, L. P., & Knezović, E. (2020). *Women's entrepreneurship in the former Yugoslavia*. Cham: Springer.

Phillips, J., De Amicis, L., & Lipparini, F. (2016). *Social entrepreneurship in the Western Balkans: State of play*. London: PlusValue.

Ramadani, V., Bexheti, A., Rexhepi, G., Ratten, V., & Ibraimi, S. (2017). Succession issues in Albanian family businesses: Exploratory research. *Journal of Balkan and Near Eastern Studies*, *19*(3), 294–312.

Ramadani, V., Dana, L. P., Gërguri, S., & Tašaminova, T. (2013). Women entrepreneurs in the Republic of Macedonia: Waiting for directions. *International Journal of Entrepreneurship and Small Business*, *19*(1), 95–121.

Ramadani, V., Rexhepi, G., Gërguri-Rashiti, S., Ibraimi, S., & Dana, L. P. (2014). Ethnic entrepreneurship in Macedonia: The case of Albanian entrepreneurs. *International Journal of Entrepreneurship and Small Business*, *23*(3), 313–335.

Ramadani, V., & Schneider, R. (2013). *Entrepreneurship in the Balkans: Diversity, support and prospects*. Heidelberg: Springer.

Stojkovski, B. (2022). From rock bands to software and gaming: This serial entrepreneur pushes Albania's ecosystem forward. Retrieved from https://therecursive.com/albanian-entrepreneur-stubbornness-precondition-success/. Accessed on January 15, 2023.

Varga, E. (2017). *Social enterprise ecosystems in Croatia and the Western Balkans: A mapping study of Albania, Bosnia & Herzegovina, Croatia, Kosovo, FYR Macedonia, Montenegro and Serbia*. London: European Bank for Reconstruction and Development.

Chapter 2

Family Ties Shaping the Entrepreneurial Intentions

Ivona Mileva, Nadezda Pop-Kostova and Nadica Jovanovska Boshkovska

Abstract

The study of entrepreneurship has advanced quickly in recent decades; however, despite its extraordinary importance, the information on the influence of family on entrepreneurial intentions remains fragmented and hard to compare. Therefore, the main objective of this chapter is to give readers a thorough grasp of family enterprises' entrepreneurial aspirations. It will also assess how previous experience in family businesses affects one's ambition to start their own firm. For this matter, the authors will use data acquired from the GUESSS (Global University Entrepreneurial Spirit Students' Survey), the survey carried out among college students in different Balkan countries: North Macedonia, Albania, Greece, Croatia, and Bulgaria. The reader will be introduced to the up-to-date scientific research in the area of entrepreneurial intentions, through receiving an increased understanding of whether the role of parents has influence over the entrepreneurial intentions of their offspring.

Keywords: Entrepreneurship; entrepreneurial intentions; family background; family influence; Balkan countries; family enterprises

1. Introduction

In this fast-paced environment, entrepreneurship is "enjoying" its momentum as it continues to grow. Entrepreneurship, according to Harvard School Professor Stevenson (1983), is "the pursuit of opportunity without regard to existing

Entrepreneurship Development in the Balkans: Perspective from Diverse Contexts, 15–32

Published under exclusive licence by Emerald Publishing Limited
doi:10.1108/978-1-83753-454-820231002

controlled resources." It is a process of discovery and action that is a crucial component in generating jobs and raising the productivity of a nation's economy (Junaid, Durrani, Mehboob-ur-Rashid, & Shaheen, 2015; Stevenson, 1983). Consequently, entrepreneurship is strongly related to the future of economic growth (Shneor, Jenssen, & Vissak, 2016).

Why do some people start their own businesses while others don't? Despite the prevalence of entrepreneurship and its goals, few studies have sought to examine entrepreneurship inside family enterprises. The literature on entrepreneurship, however, claims that there are a variety of variables that affect this decision.

The assumption that intentions are the best predictor of particular behavior arises from the explanation offered by many authors that becoming an entrepreneur emerges from planned activity (Mboko, 2011). Entrepreneurial intents are therefore regarded as being drivers of one's conduct toward it for the decision to start new businesses as a planned action (Kautonen, van Gelderen, & Tornikoski, 2013; Krueger, Reilly, & Carsrud, 2000; Liñán & Chen, 2009; Linan, Rodríguez-Cohard, & Guzman, 2011). People who have great aspirations for starting a business are more likely to do so than those who have low goals (Thompson, 2009). A few key variables, including the person's attitude toward behavior, the subjective norm, and perceived behavioral control, provide a detailed explanation of the intent (Ajzen, 1991). The family business environment, though, is one of these factors that stands out the most (Ajzen, 2001; Liñán & Chen, 2009; Solesvik, Westhead, Kolvereid, & Matlay, 2012).

2. Literature Review

2.1. Entrepreneurial Intentions

Intentions guide actions, but not all of them are carried out; some are completely abandoned, while others are modified to account for the evolving situation (Ajzen, 1991). Entrepreneurial intention is influenced by psychological traits such as the urge for achievement, self-confidence, and personal attitudes (Ferreira, Raposo, Gouveia Rodrigues, Dinis, & do Paço, 2012). The findings of the research conducted by Ferreira et al. (2012) could be related to the event that triggers the decision to become an entrepreneur and the stage of making that decision, where psychological factors have the greatest influence, according to the models of the entrepreneurial process developed by Bygrave and Zacharakis (2011) and Barringer and Ireland (2010).

The research study by Liñán and Chen (2009), which used the Ajzen's model of entrepreneurial intention, demonstrates that subjective norm has a significant impact on entrepreneurial intention and that this influence is consistent across national boundaries. When attitude and subjective norm are more favorable and perceived behavioral control is higher, an individual's intention is stronger (Ajzen, 1991). Thus, having an entrepreneurial intention is a requirement for both becoming an entrepreneur and engaging in particular activities following the start-up phase (Liñán & Chen, 2009). It was determined that as powerful as the intention is, the stronger the performance would be. Intentions might be characterized as a motivating force that influences toward executing some activity (Ajzen, 1991).

According to Crant (1996), a person's entrepreneurial goals are highly correlated with their proactive personality. Personal traits of an individual, such as age, gender, education, and role model, are referred to as proactive personality. They all have an impact on people's entrepreneurial intentions and decisions to start their own businesses. Rebrenik and Shirec (2011) claimed that entrepreneurial intentions are requirements for entrepreneurial activity and of pivotal importance for understanding the entrepreneurial process, in contrast to Krueger and Brazeal (1994), who contend that entrepreneurial potential is a prerequisite for entrepreneurship. The first element that emerges and results in entrepreneurial intention is entrepreneurial potential, and both of these factors create the possibility for entrepreneurship development. On the other hand, Singh and Singh (2015) came to the conclusion that the choice to launch a new business is linked to a prior plan and is therefore preceded by an intention to do so.

Bilgiseven and Kasımoğlu (2019) state that there are several aspects, including psychological (personal), environmental, cognitive, and demographic factors, that contribute to entrepreneurial intentions. In addition, Murphy, Liao, and Welsch (2006) have demonstrated in the literature that an entrepreneurial stream is a two-way approach, namely, person and environment.

Additionally, it was shown by Zhao, Seibert, and Hills (2005) that psychological traits as well as acquired skills and talents have an impact on entrepreneurial inclinations, yet other authors made the case that environmental effects and environmental support have an effect on entrepreneurial inclinations when it comes to the contextual elements.

2.2. Theory of Entrepreneurial Intentions – Theory of Planned Behavior

As an intention-centered theory, Ajzen's Theory of Planned Behavior (Fig. 1) is well-founded in theory and effectively predicts a wide range of planned behaviors (Krueger & Carsrud, 1993). It is an expansion of the theory of reasoned action (Ajzen, 1991; Fishbein & Ajzen, 2005), and it uses attitudes, perceived behavioral control, and arbitrary standards to explain intentions (Van Gelderen et al., 2008). The individual's purpose to carry out specific conduct is a key component of the idea of planned behavior, just like it was in the original theory of reasoned action (Ajzen, 1991). Both the theory of reasoned action and the theory of planned behavior are thought to be purposefully processing theories that suggest that people's attitudes are formed after a thorough examination of the information that is readily available (Conner & Sparks, 2005). To predict behavior from behavioral intents, which are functions of the independent theory of planned behavior components, such as attitude toward behavior, subjective norm, and perceived behavioral control, is the main goal of the theory of planned behavior (Barua, 2013).

The theory holds that intentions play a crucial role since they have a direct impact on how people behave. On the other hand, intentions are a result of personal motivational variables that affect behavior. Because people frequently engage in the activities they want to undertake, there is a relationship between intention and behavior (Conner & Sparks, 2005).

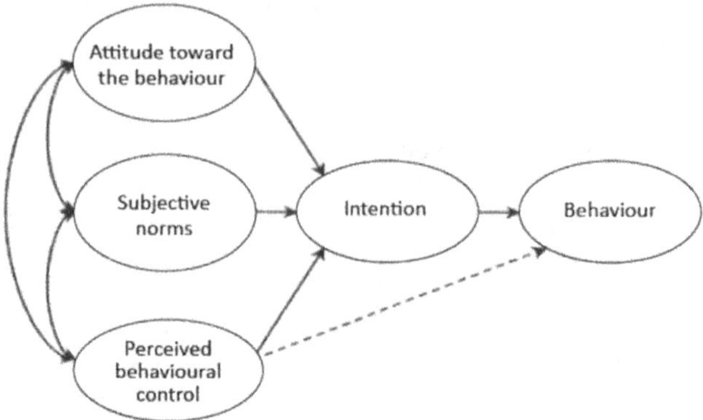

Fig. 1. Theory of Planned Behavior. *Source*: Adapted from Ajzen (1991).

Along with motivating variables, behavior is also influenced by non-motivational elements, commonly referred to as a person's actual power over behavior, like time, money, skills, and cooperation with others. The theory of planned behavior places the greatest emphasis on perceived behavioral control, which is also known as an individual's confidence in their ability to carry out the behavior. Perceived behavioral control is influenced by control beliefs, such as those regarding the existence of elements that might make it easier to carry out an action, and the perceived influence of those factors (Ajzen, 1991). As an external factor that influences behavior both directly and indirectly through intentions, perceived behavioral control is included (Madden, Ellen, & Ajzen, 1992).

According to Ajzen (1991) and Conner and Sparks (2005), personal and contextual barriers affect how well an intention is carried out, therefore "the addition of perceived behavioral control should become increasingly effective as volitional control over behavior decreases." Moreover, two additional factors are included in the theory as well as how behavior will be intended and carried out. The first one, attitude toward behavior, is defined as a positive or negative assessment of the accomplishment of the primary behavior. Attitude-based beliefs, or more specifically, beliefs about the likely consequences of the behavior and evaluations of these consequences, influence one's attitude toward that behavior (Ajzen, 1991). The second is a subjective norm or social factor that affects the accomplishment of the main behavior. Subjective norms are influenced by normative ideas, normative expectations of others, and the desire to live up to those standards (Ajzen, 1991).

According to the theory of planned behavior, which is a popular model in applied social psychology, perceptions of behavioral control and intentions have a direct impact on the behavioral success (Barua, 2013). The intentions are stronger for carrying out the attainment of the primary behavior, the more favorable the attitude toward behavior, the more beneficial impact of social norms, and the larger the perceived behavioral control. Ajzen and Madden's study on students' attendance in class served as the first test based on the theory of planned behavior. After adjusting for attitudes and subjective norms, the results of their experiments revealed that perceived behavioral control was a major predictor of intents, supporting the theory of planned behavior (Madden et al., 1992).

2.3. Entrepreneurial Parents and Offspring's Entrepreneurial Intentions

For centuries, people have been curious about how parents pass on their entrepreneurial spirit to their offspring. It is thought that generational transmission of entrepreneurial career ambitions and practices occurs (Laspita, Breugst, Heblich, & Patzelt, 2012). Some authors claimed that genetic inheritance explains how entrepreneurial activity is passed from parents to children (Hofman, Uitterlinden, & Rooij, 2010).

Without a doubt, family, as a social structure, exerts a significant influence on the choices made by those who belong to that social unit. Yet, according to Turkur and Selcuk's (2009), the influence of parental occupation on an individual's choice of career may be understood from a social perspective. As a result, an individual's decision to launch a business frequently results from continual interactions and consultations with his or her social milieu. Parents are thought of as role models for their children, from whom they learn information, values, and business abilities (Jahmurataj et al., 2023; Wyrwich, 2015). However, it's possible that parents will encourage their children's entrepreneurial goals by providing them with human, social, and financial capital (Dunn & Holtz-Eakin, 2000). Family members' decisions are significantly influenced by the family as a social structure.

A person who comes from an entrepreneurial family is more likely to choose an entrepreneurial career than someone from a non-entrepreneurial household. According to Krueger and Carsrud's (1993) study, the family plays a variety of roles in the decision-making processes that lead to the development of new businesses. These responsibilities can be represented by various informational resources, financial aid, human resources, technological advancements, role models, raw materials, and supplies. Due to this, the family plays a crucial and significant part in strategy, especially during the early phases of the establishment of new businesses (Klyver, 2007). However, many academics have suggested that the importance of prior family experience in business goes beyond the involvement of family members in the decision-making process when starting a new enterprise or when family-owned businesses handle succession (Katz, 1992; Shapero & Sokol, 1982). Evaluation of recent research has also revealed that the study of the role of the family in new business creation and decision-making has gained greater attention on a broader scope, including issues relating to family business exposure, family prior business experience, family ownership, business transition, and family occupation (Turkur & Selcuk, 2009). Yet, because earlier family experience plays a crucial role as an intergenerational influence on entrepreneurial attempts, experts are asking for more empirical information in this particular field.

The family as a social system plays an essential role in creating entrepreneurship awareness, by exercising great impact on the desirability and feasibility for further entrepreneurial intention and for the creation of an entrepreneurial new business (Shapero & Sokol, 1982). Childhood socialization impacts an individual's thoughts, processes, and feelings toward entrepreneurial activity (Dyer & Handler, 1994) as family members' engagement in entrepreneurial tasks creates an opportunity for the individual to develop similar or same perceptions (Chua, Chrisman, & Steier, 2003). It is well known that people from entrepreneurial families are expected to be aware of these effects (Carr & Sequeira, 2007). A particular environment in which professional ambitions are formed is growing up in a family where the parents are the managers and owners of a family business. This idea was supported by Andersson and Hammarstedt (2010, 2011) who demonstrate that due to the socialization factor and the entrepreneurial spirit felt by the offspring, having an entrepreneurial parent increases a child's likelihood of becoming an entrepreneur by 30% to 200%.

Children who grow up working in the family business are frequently exposed to the chances and obstacles associated with an entrepreneurial career. It has been suggested that youngsters from business families should be more inspired to launch their own business than children without this background if parents act as good role models. This may be connected to improved awareness of the difficulties associated with an entrepreneurial career, learning effects, or family support for the resources required to launch a business (Dimitrova, Vadnjal, & Petrovska, 2014). However, those who have had prior family business experience may take those perspectives into account, which could have a favorable or negative impact on their attitudes and intents toward self-employment and entrepreneurial activity (Carr & Sequeira, 2007). This underlines the fact that family businesses play a significant role in influencing people's attitudes toward entrepreneurship.

Another crucial idea is that role models were created because researchers believed that, to some extent, entrepreneurial aspirations could be transmitted due to a genetic tendency for entrepreneurship (Nicolaou & Shane, 2010). Role modeling describes learning through imitation as being more like a direct experience. When someone is being modeled after, they unintentionally and casually observe the behavior and eventually adopt it (Tkachev & Kolvereid, 1999). According to Crant (1996), being raised in an entrepreneurial household has a major impact on an individual's plans to launch their own business. According to other studies, entrepreneurs' children see starting a new business as a logical career choice because they are already familiar with the aspects that go into the process (Woo, Cooper, & Dunkelberg,1988).

According to Birley and Westhead (1994), having role models is another crucial aspect of wanting to launch a business, and having self-employed parents typically makes them particularly useful as mentors for young people launching their own firms (Matthews & Moser, 1996). Entrepreneurial parents set an example and develop management skills for aspiring individual entrepreneurs in family settings (Papadaki & Chami, 2002). Additionally, according to prior studies (Fairlie & Robb, 2007), established entrepreneurs often have a self-employed mother or father in their family history. They were also likely to have children who grew up with entrepreneurial parents. According to Mueller (2006), parental role modeling is the most important element influencing children's entrepreneurial intentions. According to Drennan, Kennedy, and Renfrow (2005), people who have a favorable impression of their family's business history see establishing a business as both desired and doable. This suggests that a family business can help foster the emergence of entrepreneurship among family members. Chaudhary (2017) comes to the conclusion in a recent study that having a self-employed family background will have a favorable link with entrepreneurial intent.

It is emphasized in both empirical and theoretical studies how much families affect their children's desires for a job. For instance, Roe's (1957) theory emphasizes the significance of early parent–child interaction with regard to career development, whereas Holland (1985, p. 93) emphasizes the surroundings that parents create for their children, or, to put it another way, "types produce types." Super (1990) identified the family as the primary source of influence on self-reflection and vocational maturity in another theoretical framework.

Eccles (1993) emphasizes parents as role models, supporters, and suppliers of knowledge, opportunities, and numerous resources for their children and supports the idea that parents have a significant influence on their children's professional decisions.

From a different angle, Kuckertz and Wagner (2010) indicate that entrepreneurial parents have no career-related influence on their children. This alludes to the absence of a link between previous experience in family businesses and business aspirations. Even the authors Zellweger, Sieger, and Halter (2011) showed that there is a bad correlation between entrepreneurial parents and their children's intentions to pursue entrepreneurship. It mostly depends on parental failure in self-employment as to whether entrepreneurial parents have an impact on their children's intentions (Mungai & Velamuri, 2011). The likelihood of children becoming entrepreneurs is lower for those whose parents experienced failure than for those whose parents experienced success.

Yet, most of the literature review suggests that the entrepreneurial intention among children who belong to entrepreneurial families is higher in comparison to children who do not have any entrepreneurial family background, despite some authors' findings that there is no relationship or even a negative relationship between entrepreneurial intentions and family businesses. In other words, kids who have business-minded parents are more likely to launch their own companies. The authors will therefore try to strengthen these conclusions by thoroughly examining the connection between entrepreneurial aspirations and family enterprises.

3. Methodology

For the purpose of this research, data from the newest Global University Entrepreneurial Spirit Survey (GUESSS) is used. GUESSS is an international research initiative exists since 2003, which the main purpose is conducting national and international reports and publications collected from surveys about entrepreneurship among students worldwide with the aim to support further development of entrepreneurial thought and suggest practical improvement in the educational segment. The survey itself asks a variety of questions on respondents' plans for their careers, their intentions for starting their own businesses and taking over family businesses, as well as their plans for succession. As it is one of the largest student entrepreneurship surveys in the world, Albania, Bulgaria, Croatia, Greece, and North Macedonia took involvement and participation in the research. The number of participants for further research is composed as follows: Albania with 434 participants, Bulgaria with 717, Croatia with 1,660, Greece with 1,594, and North Macedonia with 175 completed online surveys. The target population is university students, and the sample size is a combination of graduate, undergraduate, and PhD students, from public and private educational institutions, with a total of 4,580 university students. Questions relative to the family business environment were taken into account and were further analyzed and presented.

4. Results and Discussion

For the purpose of this chapter, the results of university students' responses from five countries were further presented and discussed. Regarding the number of participants, the results are as follows: 36.2% students from Croatia, 34.8% from Greece, 15.7% from Bulgaria, 9.5% from Albania, and 3.8% from North Macedonia. The total number of university students is 4,580 (Table 1).

The family business environment in GUESSS Survey is analyzed through the following questions:

(a) Are your parents self-employed?
(b) Are your parent's majority owners of a business?

Table 1. Number of Participants.

Participants by Country				
Country	**Frequency**	**Percent**	**Valid Percent**	**Cumulative Percent**
Albania	434	9.5	9.5	9.5
Bulgaria	717	15.7	15.7	25.1
Croatia	1,660	36.2	36.2	61.4
Greece	1,594	34.8	34.8	96.2
North Macedonia	175	3.8	3.8	100.0
Total	4,580	100.0	100.0	

Source: Authors' compilation.

(c) If you would pursue a career as an entrepreneur, how would people in your environment react (1=very negatively, 7=very positively)?

- Your close family.
- Your friends.
- Your fellow students.

Regarding the purpose of this chapter, the question under C is excluded because it is more related to the general environment of the participants. The first two questions are directly related to the family business experience of university students.

Results from the first question (a) show that the range of students with non-family business experience is 52–66%, while the range of students with such experience is 34–48%. Based on the portion of respondents, the majority of students, or almost 48% with family business experience are from Albania and North Macedonia. The majority of students with non-family business experience or 66.6% are from Croatia (Table 2).

The majority of university students have family business experience as a result of a self-employed father or both parents. This conclusion is in relation to the results of the question: "Are your parents' majority owners of a business?" where the majority of students stated that the major owner is their father. On the opposite, a minority of them have experience as a result of being a self-employed mother (Table 3).

Further on, students with family business experience were asked to answer the question "Do you regard this business as a family business?" It can be concluded that the majority of them see the business of their parents as a family business in the future. The results of these questions are a good indicator for the future development of entrepreneurial intentions among students with a family business background (Table 4).

Table 2. Are Your Parents Self-employed?

		Country					Total (%)
		Albania (%)	**Bulgaria (%)**	**Croatia (%)**	**Greece (%)**	**North Macedonia (%)**	
Are your parents self-employed?	No	52.8	60.1	66.6	55.8	52.6	60.0
	Yes, father	20.0	16.6	16.2	23.4	19.4	19.3
	Yes, mother	5.5	7.1	5.4	6.3	3.4	5.9
	Yes, both	21.7	16.2	11.9	14.6	24.6	14.9
Total		100.0	100.0	100.0	100.0	100.0	100.0

Source: Authors' compilation.

Table 3. Are Your Parents' Majority Owners of a Business?

		Country					
		Albania (%)	Bulgaria (%)	Croatia (%)	Greece (%)	North Macedonia (%)	Total (%)
Are your parents' majority owners of a business?	No	59.7	66.8	72.3	69.3	62.9	68.8
	Yes, father	18.7	15.1	16.0	17.5	17.7	16.7
	Yes, mother	4.1	5.9	4.2	5.3	3.4	4.8
	Yes, both	17.5	12.3	7.6	7.8	16.0	9.7
Total		100.0	100.0	100.0	100.0	100.0	100.0

Source: Authors' compilation.

The next set of questions is giving insight into students' intentions for the possibility of taking over the business of their parents (Table 5). We add these questions for identifying the potential influence of family businesses on entrepreneurial intentions among students. Questions are measured on a seven-point Likert scale whose level of agreement ranged from 1=not at all to 7=very much.

According to the results, the majority of Greek students (44.8%) state that they are not ready to do anything to take over their parents' business, while Croatian students (37.2%), followed by Albanian students (26.8%) state that they agree with the statement of taking over their parents' business. Most of the students in Greece do not consider their professional goal as becoming a successor in their

Table 4. Do You Regard this Business as a "Family Business"?

		Country					
		Albania (%)	Bulgaria (%)	Croatia (%)	Greece (%)	North Macedonia (%)	Total
Do you regard this business as a "family business"?	No response	7.6	3.4	7.8	5.8	9.1	6.4
	No	24.1	42.8	32.8	41.4	16.7	36.1
	Yes	68.2	53.8	59.4	52.8	74.2	57.5
Total		100.0	100.0	100.0	100.0	100.0	100.0

Source: Authors' compilation.

Table 5. Your Parents' Business.

Your parents' business	Six items with a seven-point Likert scale (from 1=strongly disagree to 7=strongly agree) Please indicate your level of agreement with the following statements: 1. ... I am ready to do anything to take over my parents' business. 2. ... My professional goal is to become a successor in my parents' business. 3. ... I will make every effort to become a successor in my parents' business. 4. ... I am determined to become a successor in my parents' business in the future. 5. ... I have very seriously thought of taking over my parents' business. 6. ... I have a strong intention to become a successor in my parents' business one day.

Source: Authors' compilation.

parents' business (52%), which is the opposite situation among the majority of Macedonian (6.9%), Albanian (26.7%), and Croatian (39.7%) students.

When it comes to making efforts to become a family business successor, the majority of the students from Albania (24.8%), Bulgaria (20.5%), and North Macedonia (7.8%) are ready to undertake the challenges and put every effort to step in the business, yet the majority of students from Greece (47.7%) do not agree that they will work hard and put efforts to become successors. In addition, the majority of the students from Croatia (39.4%), North Macedonia (6.8%), and Bulgaria (20.5%) believe they are determined to become a successor in their parent's business, which is the opposite of the beliefs of most Greek students (45.9%); they believe they are not determined to become a successor in their parents' business in the future.

The results show that the majority of the students from Croatia (40%), Albania (22.9%), and Bulgaria (18.5%) believe that they are very serious about the idea of taking over their parents' business, in comparison with the majority of Greek students (45.8%), who perceive themselves as not that serious. Most of the participants in all of the countries which are subject to this research (Albania (22.9%), Croatia (38.2%), Bulgaria (20.9%), and North Macedonia (7.6%)), except Greece have a strong intention to become a successor in the businesses owned by their parents. As per the results, more than 40% of the students from Greece do not have intentions to succeed in the family business, while the highest intention is seen among the Croatian students. The majority of the students from Albania, North Macedonia, and Bulgaria consider entrepreneurial succession as an option and they perceive themselves as ready to undertake the business. These results are presented in Figs. 2–7.

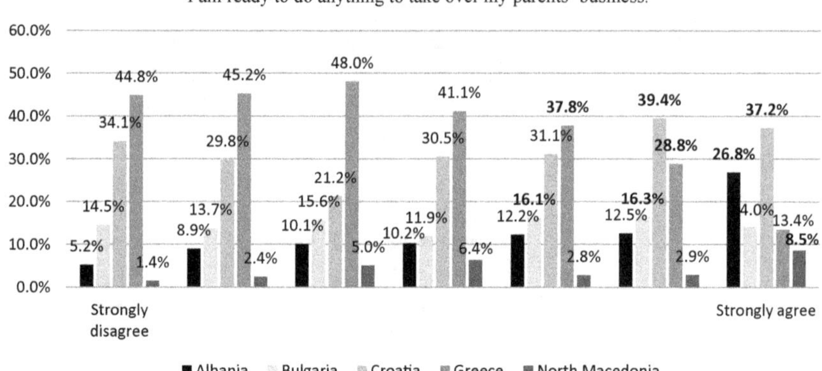

Fig. 2. I Am Ready To Do Anything To Take Over My Parents' Business. *Source*: Authors' compilation.

Fig. 3. My Professional Goal Is to Become a Successor in My Parents' Business. *Source*: Authors' compilation.

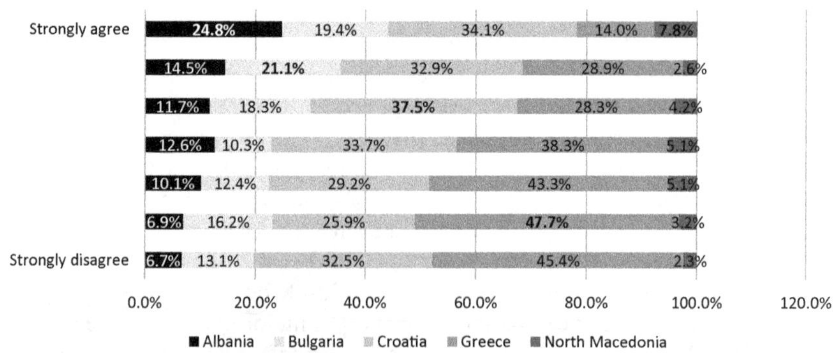

Fig. 4. I Will Make Every Effort to Become a Successor in My Parents' Business. *Source*: Authors' compilation.

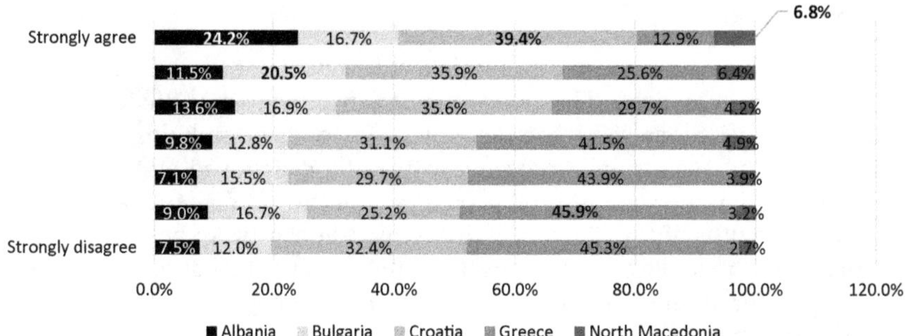

Fig. 5. I Am Determined to Become a Successor in My Parents' Business in the Future. *Source*: Authors' compilation.

Fig. 6. I Have Very Seriously Thought of Taking Over My Parents' Business. *Source*: Authors' compilation.

Fig. 7. I Have a Strong Intention to Become a Successor in My Parents' Business One Day. *Source*: Authors' compilation.

5. Conclusion

The goal of this study is to provide insight into students' entrepreneurial goals and succession intentions. This study aims to investigate how students in the various Balkan nations view themselves in terms of their ambitions for entrepreneurship and succession. According to the aforementioned research, it can be concluded that the parents' professional careers and entrepreneurial goals are related. The results of this study may therefore be applicable to both theory and practice in understanding the elements that influence a person's decision to pursue an entrepreneurial career or choose to take over the family firm. The study adds to previous research by providing a deeper knowledge of students in the Balkan region's objectives about succession and entrepreneurship. This would add to our understanding of the ideas of entrepreneurial goals and succession intentions in family enterprises because it had not been done before in the Balkan setting and with a family focus. Furthermore, we think that our research will offer potential advantages of this knowledge for managers and owners of family businesses. The first step in producing more qualified individuals in the field of entrepreneurial business is having an awareness of how students view entrepreneurship and their possible professional careers.

In view of the study's conclusions about the goals for succession, the study suggests that parents provide their children the opportunity to work for the family business. This will provide the children an inside look at the business, improve their intent for succession, increase their likelihood of believing they can run the family business successfully, and increase their sense of loyalty to it. As a result, the children will be able to look up to their parents as role models and develop important managerial abilities while working. Because of this, family businesses should be supported in educating the next generation by fostering a strong bond between the parents, who serve as the owners, and the children, who serve as the successors (Dickinson, 2000). They should also be clarified the frequent dual roles of the family members and the dual characteristics of the family businesses (Tagiuri & Davis, 2016).

6. Research Limitations

The limitations of this study are not exempt. The first limitation is the risk of social desirability bias. Although the undertaken research was completely anonymous, there is still a risk that respondents may not have been completely honest and provided an honest answer. The second risk is the student's education, that is, GUESSS research was done mostly by business school students. The third risk is the limited sample size or non-representative sample size since it is not known whether the respondents in the survey are representative of the total population of a specific country. All these restrictions, however, may be fully extended in a subsequent study. Future research can make use of bigger samples, perhaps even representative samples, to expand our understanding of the country's student population's entrepreneurial and succession ambitions, as well as the relationship between these intentions with prior family business experience.

References

Ajzen, I. (1991). The theory of planned behavior. *Organizational Behavior and Human Decision Processes*, *50*(1), 179–211.

Ajzen, I. (2001). Attitudes. *Annual Review of Psychology 52*, 27–58.

Andersson, L., & Hammarstedt, M. (2010). Intergenerational transmissions in immigrant self-employment: Evidence from three generations. *Small Business Economics*, *34*(3), 261–276.

Andersson, L., & Hammarstedt, M. (2011). Transmission of self-employment across immigrant generations: The importance of ethnic background and gender. *Review of Economics of the Household*, *34*(3), 261–276.

Barringer, B. R., & Ireland, R. D. (2010). *Entrepreneurship*. Hoboken, NJ: Wiley.

Barua, P. (2013). The moderating role of perceived behavioral control: The literature criticism and methodological considerations. *International Journal of Business and Social Science*, *4*(10), 57–59.

Bilgiseven, E. B., & Kasımoğlu, M. (2019). Analysis of factors leading to entrepreneurial intention. *Procedia Computer Science*, *158*, 885–890.

Birley, S., & Westhead, P. (1994). A taxonomy of business start-up reasons and their impact on firm growth and size. *Journal of Business Venturing*, *9*(11), 7–31.

Bygrave, W., & Zacharakis, A. (2011). *Entrepreneurship*. Hoboken, NJ: Wiley.

Carr, J. C., & Sequeira, J. M. (2007). Prior family business exposure as intergenerational influence and entrepreneurial intent: A theory of planned behavior approach. *Journal of Business Research*, *60*(10), 1090–1098.

Chaudhary, R. (2017). Demographic factors, personality and entrepreneurial inclination: A study among Indian university students. *Education + Training*, *59*(2), 171–187.

Chua, J. H., Chrisman, J. J., & Steier, L. P. (2003). Extending the theoretical horizons of family business research. *Entrepreneurship Theory and Practice*, *27*(4), 331–338.

Conner, M., & Sparks, P. (2005). Theory of planned behaviour and health behaviour. *Predicting Health Behaviour*, *2*(1), 170–222.

Crant, J. M. (1996). The proactive personality scale as a predictor of entrepreneurial intentions. *Journal of Small Business Management*, *34*(3), 42–49.

Dickinson, T. M. (2000). *Critical success factors for succession planning in family businesses*. Unpublished Master thesis, Faculty of Business Administration, University of the Witwatersrand, Johannesburg.

Dimitrova, M., Vadnjal, J., & Petrovska, I. (2014). Should I become an entrepreneur or an employee: Dilemmas of students from Macedonia and Slovenia? In *International May conference on strategic management –IMKSM2014*. Retrieved from https://www.academia.edu/28394418/Should_I_Become_an_Entrepreneur_or_an_Employee_Dilemmas_of_Students_in_Macedonia_and_Slovenia

Drennan, J., Kennedy, J., & Renfrow, P. (2005). Impact of childhood experiences on the development of entrepreneurial intentions. *International Journal of Entrepreneurship and Innovation*, *6*(4), 231–238.

Dunn, T., & Holtz-Eakin, D. (2000). Financial capital, human capital, and the transition to self-employment: Evidence from intergenerational links. *Journal of Labor Economics*, *18*(2), 287–305.

Dyer, W. G., Jr., & Handler, W. (1994). Entrepreneurship and family business: Exploring the connections. *Entrepreneurship Theory & Practice*, *19*(1), 71–83.

Eccles, J. S. (1993). School and family effects on the ontogeny of children's interests, self-perceptions, and activity choice. In R. Dienstbier & J. E. Jacobs (Eds.), *Developmental perspectives on motivation* (pp. 145–208). Lincoln, NE: University of Nebraska Press.

Fairlie, R., & Robb, A. (2007). Why are black-owned businesses less successful than white-owned businesses? The role of families, inheritances, and business human capital. *Journal of Labor Economics*, *25*(2), 289–323.

Ferreira, J. J., Raposo, M. L., Gouveia Rodrigues, R., Dinis, A., & do Paço, A. (2012). A model of entrepreneurial intention: An application of the psychological and behavioral approaches. *Journal of Small Business and Enterprise Development*, *19*(3), 424–440.

Fishbein, M., & Ajzen, I. (2005). The influence of attitudes on behavior. *The Handbook of Attitudes*, *1*(1), 173–222.

Hofman, A., Uitterlinden, A. G., & Rooij, F. J. A. (2010). Genome-wide association studies in economics and entrepreneurship research: Promises and limitations. *Small Business Economics*, *35*, 1–18. doi:10.1007/s11187-010-9286-3

Holland, J. L. (1985). *Making vocational choices: A theory of vocational personalities and work environments* (2nd ed.). Englewood Cliffs, NJ: Prentice-Hall.

Jahmurataj, V., Ramadani, V., Bexheti, A., Rexhepi, G., Abazi-Alili, H., & Krasniqi, B. (2023). Unveiling the determining factors of family business longevity: Evidence from Kosovo. *Journal of Business Research*, *159*(4), 113–745.

Junaid, M., Durrani, M., Mehboob-ur-Rashid, & Shaheen, N. (2015). Entrepreneurship as a socially constructed phenomenon: Importance of alternate paradigms research. *Journal of Managerial Sciences*, *9*(1), 35–48.

Katz, J. (1992). A psychological cognitive model of employment status choice. *Entrepreneurship Theory and Practice*, *17*(1), 29–37.

Kautonen, T, van Gelderen, M., & Tornikoski, E. T. (2013). Predicting entrepreneurial behavior: A test of the theory of planned behavior. *Applied Economics*, *45*(6), 697–707.

Klyver, K. (2007). Shifting family involvement during the entrepreneurial process. *International Journal of Entrepreneurial Behavior and Research*, *13*(5), 258–277.

Krueger, N. F., Jr, & Brazeal, D. V. (1994). Entrepreneurial potential and potential entrepreneurs. *Entrepreneurship Theory and Practice*, *18*(3), 91–104.

Krueger, N. F., & Carsrud, A. L. (1993). Entrepreneurial intentions: Applying the theory of planned behaviour. *Entrepreneurship and Regional Development*, *5*(4), 315–330.

Krueger, N. F., Reilly, M. D., & Carsrud, A. (2000). Competing models of entrepreneurial intentions. *Journal of Business Venturing*, *15*, 411–432.

Kuckertz, A., & Wagner, M. (2010). The influence of sustainability orientation on entrepreneurial intentions – Investigating the role of business experience. *Journal of Business Venturing*, *25*(5), 524–539.

Laspita, S., Breugst, N., Heblich, S., & Patzelt, H. (2012). Intergenerational transmission of entrepreneurial intentions. *Journal of Business Venturing*, *27*(4), 414–435.

Liñán, F., & Chen, Y. (2009). Development and cross-cultural application of a specific instrument to measure entrepreneurial intentions. *Entrepreneurship Theory and Practice*, *33*(3), 593–617.

Linan, F., Rodríguez-Cohard, J. C., & Guzman, J. (2011). Temporal stability of entrepreneurial intentions: A longitudinal study. In O. J. Borch, A. Fayolle, P. Kyro, & E. Ljunggren (Eds.), *Entrepreneurship research in Europe: Evolving concepts and processes* (pp. 34–65). Cheltenham: Edward Elgar.

Madden, T. J., Ellen, P. S., & Ajzen, I. (1992). A comparison of the theory of planned behavior and the theory of reasoned action. *Personality and Social Psychology Bulletin*, *18*(1), 3–9.

Matthews, C., & Moser, S. (1996). A longitudinal investigation of the impact of family background and gender on interest in small firm ownership. *Journal of Small Business Management*, *34*(1), 1–15.

Mboko, S. (2011). Towards and explanation of the growth in young entrepreneurship activities: A cross country survey of work values of college students. *Journal of Marketing Development and Competitiveness*, *5*(1), 108–118.

Mueller, P. (2006). Exploring the knowledge filter: How entrepreneurship and university–industry relationships drive economic growth. *Research Policy*, *35*(10), 1499–1508.

Mungai, E., & Velamuri, S. R. (2011). Parental entrepreneurial role model influence on male offspring: Is it always positive and when does it occur? *Entrepreneurship Theory and Practice*, *35*(2), 337–357.

Murphy, P. J., Liao, J., & Welsch, H. P. (2006). A conceptual history of entrepreneurial thought. *Journal of Management History*, *12*(1), 12–35.

Nicolaou, N., & Shane, S. (2010). Entrepreneurship and occupational choice: Genetic and environmental influences. *Journal of Economic Behavior & Organization*, *76*(1), 3–14.

Papadaki, E., & Chami, B. (2002). Growth determinants of micro-businesses in Canada. Retrieved from https://www.researchgate.net/publication/242465130_Growth_Determinants_of_Micro-Businesses_in_Canada. Accessed on February 15, 2023.

Rebrenik, M., & Shirec, K. (2011). Building entrepreneurship careers via entrepreneurship education: The case of Slovenia. In *Fostering education in entrepreneurship* (pp.15–41). Hoboken, NJ: Wiley.

Roe, A. (1957). Early determinants of vocational choice. *Journal of Counseling Psychology*, *4*(2), 212–217.

Shapero, A., & Sokol, L. (1982). The social dimensions of entrepreneurship. In C. Kent, D. Sexton, & K. Vesper (Eds.), *The encyclopedia of entrepreneurship* (pp. 72–90). Englewood Cliffs, NJ: Prentice-Hall.

Shneor, R., Jenssen, J. I., & Vissak, T. (2016). Introduction to the special issue: Current challenges and future prospects of entrepreneurship in Nordic and Baltic Europe. *Baltic Journal of Management*, *11*(2), 134–141.

Singh, T., & Singh, S. (2015). Entrepreneurial intentions among university students in Manipur. *International Journal of Management and Social Science Research Review*, *1*(7), 55–64.

Solesvik, M., Westhead, P., Kolvereid, L., & Matlay, H. (2012). Student intentions to become self-employed: The Ukrainian context. *Journal of Small Business and Enterprise Development*, *19*(3), 441–460.

Stevenson, H. H. (1983). *A perspective on entrepreneurship*. Harvard Business School Working Paper 384–131.

Super, D. E. (1990). A life-span, life-space approach to career development. In D. Brown & L. Brooks (Eds.), *Career choice and development: Applying contemporary theories to practice* (pp. 197–261). San Francisco, CA: Jossey-Bass.

Tagiuri, R., & Davis, J. (2016). Bivalent attributes of family firms. *Family Business Review*, *9*(2), 199–208.

Thompson, E. R. (2009). Individual entrepreneurial intent: Construct clarification and development of an internationally reliable metric. *Entrepreneurship Theory and Practice*, *33*(4), 669–694.

Tkachev, A., & Kolvereid, L. (1999). Self-employment intentions among Russian students. *Entrepreneurship & Regional Development*, *11*, 269–280. https://doi.org/10.1080/089856299283209

Turkur, D., & Selcuk, S. (2009). Which factors affect entrepreneurial intention of university students? *Journal of European Industrial Training*, *33*(2), 142–159.

Van Gelderen, M., Brand, M., van Praag, M., Bodewes, W., Poutsma, E., & Van Gils, A. (2008). Explaining entrepreneurial intentions by means of the theory of planned behaviour. *Career Development International*, *13*(6), 538–559.

Woo, C. Y., Cooper, A. C., & Dunkelberg, W. C. (1988). Entrepreneurial typologies: Definitions and implications. In B. A. Kirchoff, W. A. Long, W. McMullan,

K. H. Vesper, & W. E. Wetzel, Jr. (Eds.), *Frontiers of entrepreneurship research* (pp. 165–176). Wellesley, Mass: Babson College.

Wyrwich, M. (2015). Entrepreneurship and the intergenerational transmission of values. *Small Business Economics*, *45*(1), 191–213.

Zellweger, T., Sieger, P., & Halter, F. (2011). Should I stay or should I go? Career choice intentions of students with family business background. *Journal of Business Venturing*, *26*(5), 521–536.

Zhao, H., Seibert, S., & Hills, G. (2005). The mediating role of self-efficacy in the development of entrepreneurial intentions. *Journal of Applied Psychology*, *90*(6), 1265–1272.

Chapter 3

How is Social Entrepreneurship Pursuing the Path of Development? Regional Perspectives in the Western Balkans

Stefan Chichevaliev, Stojan Debarliev and Aleksandra Janeska Iliev

Abstract

In this book chapter, we analyse social entrepreneurship (SE) development in the Western Balkans and present a regional overview. SE has become a globally known contributor to alleviating societal, economic, social, and environmental concerns. Its influence on increasing people's quality of life has put the concept on a pedestal, and the Balkans are no different. The new advances have increased the efforts from the third sector in advocating for increased visibility, recognition, and support for social enterprises (SEs) as contributors to the development of resilient communities and facilitating the countries' recovery from economic, social, and environmental crises. To provide a regional development overview, we use the institutional perspective. We base the analysis on data by applying qualitative methods, including document analysis, conference speeches, round tables, consultations, and other impactful events conducted over the last decade. The evidence suggests that the Western Balkan countries are similar in their development and lack a clear vision, a strategic pathway, and sustainable solutions to accelerate the sector's growth. The awareness of the SEs' contributions is still low, hindering their impact and potential scalability. Raising awareness campaigns is much needed to increase SEs' visibility, recognition, revenues, and financial sustainability. Intersectoral collaboration is not at a suitable level, and the coordination and partnerships between the SE actors are lacking. The region needs to make a significant and

Entrepreneurship Development in the Balkans: Perspective from Diverse Contexts, 33–68

Published under exclusive licence by Emerald Publishing Limited
doi:10.1108/978-1-83753-454-820231003

consistent effort to facilitate the sector's development and support SEs to provide the expected societal impact.

Keywords: Social entrepreneurship; sector development; institutional perspective; social enterprises contribution; SE ecosystem; Western Balkan

1. Introduction

SE aims to improve society while pursuing social, cultural, environmental, and economic goals. It creates sustained social and economic value through creative solutions and public–private–non-profit alliances (Harris, Renko, & Caldwell, 2013). SE can boost regional economies by creating new products, services, and businesses (Friedman & Desivilya, 2010).

In the last decade, we witnessed SE development in the Western Balkans. The European Union (EU), the United Nations (UN), and other non-governmental organisations (NGOs) have driven regional sector growth. These actors provide grants and capacity-building to social entrepreneurs, create an enabling environment for entrepreneurship, and promote SE (European Commission, 2022). Moreover, the Western Balkan's national governments support social enterprise development alongside international development actors. These include new policies and legislation, tax incentives, special access to public procurement, and supporting local SE networks. However, Western Balkan SE is behind other European regions (European Commission, 2020). Despite that, social entrepreneurs and public awareness of SE are rising. The European Commission has funded regional SE programs. Thus, Western Balkan SE is developing slowly.

This book chapter provides a regional perspective by utilising institutional theory and analysing the political, legal, institutional, and social dimensions. We offer novel information about SE development in the region and each country individually. Thus, the contribution of this chapter is threefold: (a) we provide a much-needed review of the contemporary literature and organisational reports published on the topic; (b) we provide a comparative analysis and explicate the SE development level in the region; and (c) we provide a future research agenda to further the sector's exploration and facilitate its development.

2. Social Entrepreneurship Research Development

SE, as a concept, has been developing for the last three decades. The increased attention from all sectors has put SE on a pedestal, contributing to its rise in research and development. Governments have also started sponsoring SE activities and creating new organisational frameworks to facilitate the development of new SE ventures. In the past 10 years, there have been an increasing number of SE centres established at universities around the globe, as well as new academic publications on SE, social enterprise, and social innovation. Additionally, there are now much more conferences and special issues of scientific publications devoted to the subject (Choi & Majumdar, 2014). Scholars and practitioners have seen this momentum as an opportunity to increase the body of knowledge, theory, and practice, investigating various topics surrounding the field. SE as a concept (Dacin, Dacin, & Matear, 2010; Kuratko, 2018), SE culture (Choi, 2010), process (Mair & Marti, 2006), activities (Austin, Stevenson, & Wei-Skillern, 2006; Zahra, Gedajlovic, Neubaum, & Shulman, 2009), hybridity (Chichevaliev, 2019; Pache & Santos, 2013), social value creation (Nicholls, 2008; Peredo & McLean, 2006), ecosystems and context (Chichevaliev, 2020; Muñoz & Kibler, 2016; Wry & Zhao, 2018) are some of the topics that have been studied.

Given that we are exploring SE development in the Western Balkans and applying the regional perspective, we focussed on the context and ecosystem development. The context, in particular, has been noted as having the potential to either accelerate or impede the sector's development (Weerawardena & Mort, 2006; Zahra & Wright, 2011). To investigate the countries' context, we identified several factors in the literature which are crucial for SE development, including legal and governmental (Fici, 2015; Sullivan, 2007), political, economic, and cultural (Griffiths, Gundry, & Kickul, 2013), religious (Choi, 2010), financial (Hoogendoorn, 2011), institutional (Stephan, Uhlaner, & Stride, 2014), and others. We focus on four main dimensions (political, legal, institutional, and social) that provide the overview and the foundation of the SE ecosystem and country context.

The political dimension portrays the environment's appeal, controls entrepreneurial activity, and establishes rules (Griffiths et al., 2013). It is essential that the government play a part in the formation of social entrepreneurial activity recognition. Issues that the government has delegated to the third sector are addressed by SE. Whether or not, the sector will develop depends on the disparity in power between these two actors. As a result, the political environment is crucial. The sector and the policy system could benefit from presenting pertinent policies and actions at all levels (national, regional, and local) to encourage social entrepreneurs and good practices in the regulations. SE integrates economic and social policies, is crucial to the welfare system, and is well-suited to encourage social incentives and the growth of social capital (United Nations Development Program, 2012).

Through the case of definition and regulation, we examine the legal aspect. The case of the definition has always been a challenge and varies from context to context. The SE difficulties affecting its promotion and expansion have been exacerbated by various definitions, forms, and models (Austin et al., 2006; Boschee, 1998; Dees, 1998; Dees & Anderson, 2003). Since so many distinct discourses are relevant to various facets of SE, it has become nearly impossible to define the notion (Dey & Steyaert, 2010; Nicholls, 2010). Also, no universal legal structure applies to SE, but numerous distinct legal frameworks exist globally, particularly in Europe. Some current legal entities that engage in SE are cooperatives, nonprofits, commercial businesses, social purpose firms, and social cooperatives. As a result, the discrepancies have proven to be a significant obstacle. They are making it impossible to compare the scale and scope of SE and firms on a national and international level (Haugh, 2005).

The institutions also have a pivotal role to play in the sector's development (Mair & Marti, 2009). Numerous researchers have stressed the significance of institutions in SE literature (Dacin et al., 2010; Estrin, Mickiewicz, & Stephan,

2013; Mair & Marti, 2009; Zahra et al., 2009). Two key ideas are covered: institutional support and institutional voids (Dacin et al., 2010; Stephan, Uhlaner, & Stride, 2014). Institutional gaps present chances for entrepreneurship and, in reality, SE. One of the institutional gaps that SE has filled is the institutions' failure to support the community (Mair & Schoen, 2007). According to Stephan et al. (2014), in a national setting, influences offered as needs or resource instruments motivate an individual to engage in SE. SE intentions are among the factors that make institutional support crucial for the growth and promotion of SE. Sud, VanSandt, and Baugous (2009) add that one strategy for fostering SE is the establishment of organisational legitimacy, which ought to give social firms a distinct organisational category. SEs may be better understood and given more options for funding if they are categorised.

We incorporated the financial aspect in the institutional dimension. It contains the availability and accessibility of funding for SEs. SEs must generate financial resources to carry out their social purpose and make a social effect (Dacin et al., 2010). However, enterprises often turn to government support or project grants. Most rely on various funding sources, including user fees, membership fees, subscription fees, government grants (subsidies), and other sources (Hoogendoorn, 2011). According to the literature, SEs find it challenging to obtain the same capital available to commercial enterprises (European Commission, 2011; Rangan, Leonard, & McDonald, 2008). This situation strengthens the concept of hybridity. Most SEs combine their social goal with a typical legal form of business, a commercial enterprise, to be eligible for more conventional income bases.

Lastly, in the social dimension, we touch upon education (Ferri & Urbano, 2011; Harris et al., 2013; Sahasranamam & Nandakumar, 2020), visibility (Saebi, Foss, & Linder, 2019), and recognition (Bacq & Janssen, 2011) of social entrepreneurs and enterprises as prerequisites for SE development. Harris et al. (2013) highlight that due to a lack of formal business education, some people may need to help turning an idea or expertise into a business or spotting a potential entrepreneurial opportunity. The educational system develops and controls skills and influences SE intentions (Sahasranamam & Nandakumar, 2020). These dimensions suggest that societal/institutional settings influence a potential social entrepreneur's awareness and recognition of SE's needs and potential (Saebi et al., 2019). That is why recognition of SE and entrepreneurs is essential to boost the intentions of new and upcoming social entrepreneurs and pave the way to the sector's development (European Commission, 2018, 2019, 2020).

3. Method

We used qualitative methodology for this book chapter. Specifically, we used document analysis to investigate national policies (strategies and action plans, laws, institutional documents, and funding calls), international reports, empirical articles and publications, conference speeches, round tables, consultations, and other impactful events conducted over the last decade.

Document analysis is the systematic assessment and evaluation of documents, including printed and electronic (computer-based and Internet-transmitted) content. Document analysis requires data to be reviewed and interpreted to extract meaning, gain insight, and create empirical knowledge, just like other analytical approaches used in qualitative research (Corbin & Strauss, 2008; Rapley, 2007). Document analysis is a research technique that is particularly useful for qualitative case studies, in this case, country profiles of the Western Balkans.

We started our analysis by investigating national macro policies that mention SE, social enterprise, social economy, sustainable economy, sustainable entrepreneurship, sustainable enterprise, green economy, green entrepreneurship, and green enterprise. Then, we analysed the micro-policies specifically related to the concepts. This activity concluded the investigation of the first dimension – policy. We applied the same approach to the legal dimension. In the case of the third dimension – institutional support, we focussed on the infrastructure and the institutional support related to raising awareness, available funding sources and access thereof, capacity building, and involvement in the sector's development. For the last dimension, social, we analysed SE education, visibility, and recognition.

In this chapter, the method's limitations consist of the availability and retrievability of data. We have mitigated both limitations by identifying the documents already used in contemporary international reports, including national policies published by the government – public records, and reports produced by local organisations and international consultants. We also looked for more current public documents. However, we do not consider what is foreseen given that it is not yet confirmed, and no particular steps were undertaken when writing this book chapter.

4. Social Entrepreneurship in the Western Balkans: Regional Perspective

4.1. Albania

4.1.1. Political Dimension. SEs in the Republic of Albania appeared within the civil sector around the start of the new millennium through projects supported by foreign donors. Later in 2011, the Agency for Social Business Promotion was established to support sustainable economic and social development by promoting sustainable, balanced, and cohesive social business at the national level. The civil sector is a leading factor in the development of the sector. In the following years, social and youth entrepreneurship was recognised in several policy documents such as Employment and Skills Strategy, the Business and Investment Development Strategy, National Strategy for Development and Integration, National Youth Action Plan 2015–2020, and others (Andjelic & Petricevic, 2020).

Without a national strategy for SEs, the National Strategy for Employment and Skills 2014–2020 supported government objectives in SE. It promotes quality jobs and is focussed on four strategic priorities: (1) foster decent job opportunities through effective labour market policies; (2) offer quality vocational education and training to youth and adults; (3) promote social inclusion and territorial cohesion; and (4) strengthen the governance of labour market and qualification systems (Ministry of Social Welfare and Youth, 2014).

4.1.2. Legal Dimension. In 2016, Parliament passed the Law on SEs in Albania, recognising non-profit organisations as a legal form of social enterprise (Government of Albania, 2016). The law explicitly defines the areas of activity of SEs: social services, employment of vulnerable categories of citizens, youth employment, health, education, environment, promotion of tourism, culture and heritage, sports activities, and promotion of the development of local communities. The legal framework defines criteria for identifying SEs: (1) there shall be at least three employees, of whom at least one from the vulnerable categories of citizens; (2) 20% to 30% of revenue during the second and third year of operation shall be generated from economic activity; (3) the generated profit, directly or indirectly, shall not be distributed and shall be used to increase the operations of SEs; and (4) the enterprise shall make participatory decisions and involve employees in strategic decision-making (Ilijevski & Iloska, 2019).

4.1.3. Institutional Dimension. Besides the incomplete legal framework, the SE sector in the country is faced with a need for more understanding of the importance of social enterprise among the key institutional stakeholders. The register for SEs is not functional yet, with a lack of data about the number of SEs and other relevant statistics. Based on the EU operational definition, Albanian SEs exist in several legal forms: associations, centres, and foundations (i.e., those carrying out the economic activity); agricultural cooperatives; and limited liability companies. Only six non-profits are recognize under the Law. Still, some SEs registered as conventional businesses within the National Business Center with growing activities. According to some information, 679 non-profit organisations (associations, foundations, and centres) undertake economic activity, of which 319 have a licence to offer social and educational services. Besides that, there are 58 agricultural cooperatives with a total of 1,000 employees. The primary industries in which established SEs operate are hotel/food service activity, manufacturing, social services, healthcare, and educational services. Regarding potential SEs, there is a concentration mainly on industries such as agriculture, farming, and educational services (Haska & Hoxha, 2020).

4.1.3.1. Financial Dimension. There are a few sources and types of financial instruments for social and young entrepreneurs: government funding which is still undeveloped, and foreign aid for development projects which is usually very structured and implemented through grants and private funds. Also, there are particular financial agriculture and tourism schemes for cooperatives. The Ministry of Culture and Ministry of Finances and Economy of Albania provide financial support to non-profits via public institution grant schemes. The Agency for Support of Civil Society supports non-profit organisations through grants that draw on the Albanian budget. Some financial support to new and existing entrepreneurs is also provided by the Ministry of Health and Social Protection, Ministry of Agriculture, Ministry of State for Entrepreneurship, and some municipalities (Andjelic & Petricevic, 2020). The banks in Albania serve only if they possess collateral, and some smaller banks, such as First Investment Bank and International Commercial Bank, exclusively lend to small and medium enterprises (SMEs). A few business angel networks connect investors to SMEs for investment and knowledge sharing (Culkin & Simmons, 2018).

4.1.3.2. Non-financial Support and Access to Resources. Besides the financial support from various sources, SEs in Albania are faced with a necessity for knowledge and skills development to improve their market research skill, seize new opportunities in the market, financial management, marketing, networking, design sustainable solutions to their social problems, and business plan development. Although several projects have been realised in cooperation with EU funds and organisations over the last several years, SEs require access to capacity-building programmes. Albania does not have a national network promoting its SEs' developmental demands and challenges, which inhibits their growth and is considered one of the main issues for further development.

4.1.4. Social Dimension. There is a lack of awareness among the general public due to the lack of understanding and narrow focus on SE. The concept is predominantly used by non-profit organisations, social enterprise practitioners, and some institutional actors. Academic institutions have yet to begin researching the topic, although universities and other formal and non-formal educational institutions provide, to some extent, social enterprise education. Some examples of awareness-raising activities are UNDP – Self-Employment Programme for youth; Beyond Barriers Association Albania – Western Balkan Civil Society Organisations for Youth Employment Support; YEA (Young Entrepreneur Albania) – Young Entrepreneurship Albania Summit & Award 2016; SDC – Return Roses for a Sustainable Environment and Tourism; Centre for Competitiveness Promotion (CCP) – 'Erasmus for Young Entrepreneurs Project in Albania'; and National Resource Centre for Civil Society – The Academy for NGOs, Hapide Combinator and Ide të Gjelbërta (Andjelic & Petricevic, 2020).

4.2. Bosnia and Herzegovina

Federation of Bosnia and Herzegovina (BiH), Republika Srpska, Brcko District, and 10 cantons make up BiH's complex administrative structure. About 10 cantons comprise the Federation of BiH, and each has its administration and ministries. Political instability, which emerges from polarisation along ethnic lines, negatively impacts the business context. It discourages investment, makes it challenging to make long-term plans, and most crucially, causes a rise in the exodus of young people from the country (Sumak, 2022). However, SE in BiH becomes extremely important when considering regional efforts and opportunities for cooperation, but even more so when considering how to reduce poverty and social exclusion (Social Inclusion Foundation in Bosnia and Herzegovina, 2012).

4.2.1. Political Dimension. Political instability has slowed SE in the country. SE-related policies are rare. Indirect disability employment policies have been the most relevant to the sector. These policies from ex-Yugoslavia do not promote SE. The Swiss Embassy's Youth Employment Project launched SE in BiH, which sparked the sector's development (Vilić, 2022). In recent times, the Social Inclusion Strategy is the most crucial document that includes SE to mitigate poverty, social exclusion, and integration of marginalised groups in the labour market. One of the fundamental forces behind the strategy's strategic objectives is SE, considered a mix of social protection and employment (Government of BiH, 2020).

The government often struggles to distinguish between NGOs and SEs; thus, they now apply the 'non-governmental sector and SE sector' title in their incentive measures. Insufficient knowledge of SE, the lack of an adequate institutional and legal framework to regulate and encourage it, sporadic programmes and initiatives for employment through SE, lack of initial capital, lack of necessary knowledge and skills, and others are the main challenges for SE development (Initiative for Better and Humane Inclusion, 2016). Overall, the lack of policies and instruments to support SEs and their operations constrains their growth and impact.

4.2.2. Legal Dimension. SEs are not legally defined. They are registered as associations, limited liability companies, or crafts. Associations and foundations can conduct economic activities connected to their founding agreements and legislation. Profits can only be used to enhance the organisation's goals. Donations and grants are tax-exempt, while other operations are treated as for-profit enterprises (Sumak, 2022).

The complex country structure also impacts the regulation and the different authorities under which the SEs operate. For example, Republika Srpska adopted a Law on Social Entrepreneurship in December 2021, which provides a broad definition focussed on opportunities for solving societal issues, mitigating social exclusion, and strengthening social solidarity and cohesion (Government of BiH, 2022; International Labour Organisation, 2022). Despite this development, several laws in the country encompass the indirect legal framework for social enterprise development and provide space for them to get involved. These laws are related to associations and foundations, cooperatives, SMEs, environment, refugees, lotteries, public–private partnerships, crafts and entrepreneurial activities, social protection, micro-credit organisations, freedom of religion, and churches' legal status and religious communities in BiH, and other (International Labour Organisation, 2016). To conclude, SE in the country is still not regulated at the federal level, which creates confusion and adds to the one that already exists with the country's complex political and legal structure.

4.2.3. Institutional Dimension. The young ecosystem needs policies, regulations, and institutional support for social entrepreneurs. Startups are getting institutional assistance, but SEs are not. In established social companies, international, private, and entrepreneurial ecosystem organisations are replacing state institutional assistance (startup incubators, accelerators, etc.). The lack of a legal category for social companies remains the biggest obstacle to development in this sector (Sumak, 2022). While employment bureaus provide training to help people learn specific skills that should increase their competitiveness in the job market, they are not enough. The Social Inclusion Strategy foresees training for women empowerment, teachers, upskilling, and reskilling with active measures for employment, but it is not explicitly related to SE. To guarantee that this concept and model are better known, SE must also be promoted in the public eye (and through the media). These efforts should also include the creation of infrastructure, intersectoral cooperation, and social entrepreneur networking (Government of BiH, 2020). Associations, charities, international organisations, and businesses provide other private funding. The Mozaik Foundation's Social Business

Incubator trains social entrepreneurs and community leaders. The Regional Incubator for Social Entrepreneurs, CEED, GLOBUS, and others offer programs and training (Andjelic & Petricevic, 2020; Rosandic & Kusinikova, 2018b).

4.2.3.1. *Financial Support.* There are no extensive financial instruments or incentives in BiH that are intended to promote the growth of the social economy. Most public funding for SEs comes from support aimed at particular legal entities or policy-specific help, like the Fund for professional rehabilitation and employment of persons with disabilities. The international support comes from several EU programs focussed on civil society organisations such as IPA, EIDHR, and Erasmus. Other available funding sources are micro-crediting, loans, philanthropic efforts from the private sector, development aid agencies, and embassies (Rosandic & Kusinikova, 2018).

4.2.3.2. *Non-financial Support and Access to Resources.* Non-financial support is available from the SE and business sector actors. This is one of the positive developments for SE growth. Through 12 business incubators, SEs can receive financial and consultancy support. Some organisations are facilitating the movement (informal networks 'Together we can do more', 'Coalition of Marginalised Groups in BiH', and Social Entrepreneurship Network for Youth Employment). Still, the biggest obstacle is that these networks were established on a project basis. Regional networking is also an opportunity. Some organisations are networked on a regional level through partnerships and joint projects for SE development in the Western Balkans.

4.2.4. Social Dimension. SE education still needs to be included in the curricula at different levels (Andjelic & Petricevic, 2020; Rosandic & Kusinikova, 2018). Schools and faculties should provide education in this area to enable young participation in social activities, prepare them as individuals to engage in socio-economic activities, and advance this process (Djermanović, 2019). Moreover, the visibility and recognition of SE at different societal levels are hindered due to a lack of legal framework (Halibashic, Osmankovic, & Talic, 2015) and bureaucratic processes that make it challenging to communicate with public institutions, which can result in organisations delivering services to society not receiving the proper acknowledgement (Djermanović, 2019).

4.3. Kosovo[1]

The development of social companies is in its early years in Kosovo, so there are misconceptions about how they operate. Historically built on the tradition of cooperatives, SEs have focussed on offering services to the community (Kartallozi & Xhemajli, 2017). The new Law for SE has been a major milestone for further social business development, although it is farfetched assuming the appropriate adoption of this law immediately.

[1]All references to Kosovo, whether the territory, institutions, or population, in this chapter, shall be understood in full compliance with United Nations Security Council Resolution 1244 and without prejudice to the status of Kosovo.

4.3.1. Political Dimension. Attained to the aim of joining the EU, Kosovo has tailored its strategy, legislation, and policy reforms accordingly. However, practitioners identify a social enterprise as a company or organisation that engages in economic activity but has a social focus (Philips, De Amicis, & Lipparini, 2016). SE has been mentioned in strategic documents such as the 'Employment and Social Policies' Strategy, the Government's Strategy for Cooperation with Civil Society 2013–2017, the Strategy for Decentralisation of Social Services 2013–2017, the 2012–2016 SME Development Strategy, also the Strategy for Supporting Innovation and Entrepreneurship (2019–2023), and Kosovo's National Development Strategy 2016–2021 (Andjelic & Petricevic, 2020; Rosandic & Kusinikova, 2018). Social enterprise development is currently regarded as a prospect for mitigating unemployment by opening job possibilities for vulnerable groups (Government of Kosovo, 2017), hence the MLSW's apparent preference for transforming NGOs into SEs.

4.3.2. Legal Dimension. Many draft laws were suggested, the first prepared in 2012, then again in 2016 by Kosovo's Ministry of Labour and Social Welfare, and approved in 2017, but then rejected by the National assembly (Government of Kosovo, 2017). Many stakeholders expressed concerns about the proposed legislation, especially SEs finding the current understanding of SE extremely narrow, thus limiting the purpose of business in helping address Kosovo's social and environmental challenges (Kartallozi & Xhemajli, 2017). Practitioners have described SE as a business that engages in economic activities with a primarily social purpose, declaring those as associations, foundations, and work integration organisations for vulnerable groups based on not-for-profit principles (Loku, Gogiqi, & Qehaja, 2018). The new phase is outlined with Kosovo Government adopting Law No. 06/L-022, as SEs are defined as

> a legal person irrespective of the manner of its establishment, which contains social objectives in its charter, conducts economic activities, carries out production of goods and services in the general interest of society and integrates people from vulnerable working groups.

4.3.3. Institutional Dimension. Kosovo views SEs as crucial players in the welfare system (Srbijanko, Korunovska, & Bashevska, 2016), and setting the grounds for social enterprising is challenging. Support initiatives come from the MLSW and other governmental actors (Table 1). Evident is a lack of institutional support, accentuating the need for bilateral and regional programs.

4.3.3.1. Financial Support. Grant funding is in extremely high demand from SEs (Philips et al., 2016). Most depend on grants and private donations, so they are treated more from a charitable than a business perspective (Kartallozi & Xhemajli, 2017). Occasionally SEs are also financed by their for-profit business ventures.

According to Kosovo's Law on Social Enterprises, some of the fiscal incentives that SE enjoys are exemption from tax on profit and Value Added Tax for imported goods and/or services (Government of Kosovo, 2017).

The civil sector implicates dominance, as organisations depend on grants and donations (Kartallozi & Xhemajli, 2017). Some of these organisations struggle with sustainability because they are often small-scale efforts supported by one-time project grants (Varga, 2017). Most active SEs have been founded and operate with grant funding, implying a project-driven approach for most. Meaning organisations are young and financially and technically unqualified for planning sustainability (Rosandic & Kusinikova, 2018).

There is no specific financial support, SEs depending on their eligibility, can apply for funding from the segment of civil society related to SMEs. This is troubled due to the majority of public funding for the civil society sector being distributed through unofficial, frequently opaque processes, raising severe concerns about their equity (Rosandic & Kusinikova, 2018). Traditionally, international donors recognise the positive socioeconomic benefits that a vibrant SE sector can deliver. Therefore, they fund both the infrastructure and development of SE through the funding of government programs.

The EU office in Kosovo is funding different programs supporting SE or SMEs, executed by different organisations (International Organisation of Migration (IOM), The project Support to Micro Small and Medium Enterprises in Kosovo (MSME Grants)). UNDP has had a longstanding role in the conceptualisation of the Law on Social Enterprises. USAID provided for the KSEF to apply Advocacy for Regulation on the Registration procedures of SEs. USAID has also initiated an 'Up to Youth' project, supporting SE coming from the youth. One organisation which very focussed and specialised in SE is Yunus Social Business Balkans. Kosovo has been using the following sources for funding: the Instrument for Pre-accession Assistance, European Instrument for Democracy and Human Rights, World Bank, USAID, UNDP, IOM, UNV, GIZ, The Danish Refugee Council, and others.

4.3.3.2. Non-financial Support and Access to Resources. Through the Corporate Social Responsibility (CSR) network, the private sector supports implementing best CSR practices in accordance with the Global Compact Principle (Babovic et al., 2015). Forum for Civil Initiatives (FIQ) and Helvetas Enhancing Youth Employment project is CSO support organisations. LENS and Create Foundation enable the transfer of knowledge and best practices through regional and global networks (Andjelic & Petricevic, 2020; LENS, 2016).

Incubators offering various support are The Social Business Incubator Foundation Mitrovica (established by DRC), Facility in Gracanica, The Innovation Centre Kosovo (ICK) (established by the Norwegian Ministry of Foreign Affairs), Advice for Small Business facility (supported by EBRD) Business Start-Up Centre (BSCK), founded by SPARK, UNICEF Innovations Lab Kosovo, and Forum for Civic Initiatives.

4.3.4. Social Dimension. A few articles and reports provide a basic overview of the social enterprise ecosystem, mostly with similar narratives (Dervishi, 2019; Philips et al., 2016). Measuring and reporting social impact instruments for reporting and evaluating social measures are still not in place. The impact is documented on the level of case studies and best practices (Rosandic & Kusinikova, 2018). Public awareness of SE and its successes are deficient. This affects SE's ability to be recognised as a viable form of organisation (Andjelic & Petricevic, 2020). There is a certain negligence in the educational system in approaching the issues of SE (Andjelic & Petricevic, 2020; Philips et al., 2016).

4.4. Montenegro

SE as a notion, as well as its potential, is yet not fully recognised. The general public does not view SEs as progressive institutional tools that can modernise and further democratise the welfare system. Therefore, advocacy and public awareness efforts are crucial for fostering a favourable ecosystem for social entrepreneurs (European Commission, 2018).

4.4.1. Political Dimension. SE is a novelty to Montenegro. The National Strategy for Employment and Human Resources (2012–2015) of the Montenegrin government recognised SE's potential a decade ago and mentioned SE as a way to tackle unemployment and help the most vulnerable (Government of Montenegro, 2012). The sector's development has proceeded with the TACSO-supported working group to design a SE statute. The government's program called for a preliminary draft of the law and the strategy on SE, with an action plan to be adopted in the second quarter of 2013. After the government's conclusion, the 2013 Work Program was changed, and the Law on SE and sectoral policy documents were halted (Government of Montenegro, 2013). Policy development has stalled due to leadership changes and shifting agendas. There are no specific SE policies. The Strategy for Improving the Enabling Environment for the Activities of Non-Governmental Organisations 2018–2020 aimed to boost non-profits' socioeconomic impact. However, it defined SE narrowly. The most significant and tangible move was adopting the Strategy for Micro and SMEs in Montenegro 2018–2020, which promotes youth entrepreneurship, women entrepreneurship, and SE (Andjelic & Petricevic, 2020).

4.4.2. Legal Dimension. The sector in Montenegro is not regulated. SEs follow the regulation depending on their legal form. SEs can operate under various legal structures, including associations, foundations, cooperatives, limited liability companies, and sheltered companies. Primarily, they are regulated by the Law on NGOs, but also by the Law on cooperatives, the Law on professional rehabilitation and employment of persons with disabilities, the Law on trade companies, and other regulations about their legal recognition. The sector's development is questionable without a comprehensive legal framework defining the many categories of social economy organisations. Such a situation contributes to the case of definition. Currently, no national definition exists, and the social economy actors largely agree with the EU definition (Andjelic & Petricevic, 2020). The failed attempt to regulate the sector in 2013 was the last effort to provide a legal framework for SE. The lack of legislation defining the categories of SE organisations, foundations, registration, operation, and funding processes reflects the underdevelopment of SE and SE in Montenegro (Regional Cooperation Council, 2015). However, Montenegrin law is neither exceptionally limiting nor particularly favourable to the growth of SE groups. Civil society pushes for social enterprise legislation, but so far, without any noticeable effect.

4.4.3. Institutional Dimension. This element relates to the range of support programs. This includes accounting, legal, IT, design, sector-specific support, and non-financial entrepreneurship-driven development services, including business management training, capacity building, mentoring, and coaching. Social companies need upskilling and structures, especially in their early stages (International Labour Organisation, 2021). The sector's development in Montenegro is hindered by data scarcity. First, the topic has little literature. Second, no policies or initiatives promote SE and offer statistics. Montenegro's SE sector is not officially sized or characterised. Since SE has no data collection framework, this analysis must leverage various sources (Andjelic & Petricevic, 2020).

The government supports SMEs, NGOs, and other legal entities, not SEs. Social companies need support to succeed, according to the literature. Training, advising, and mentorship to improve managerial, financial, and marketing skills should be the primary forms of support. Thus, sector actors advocate for a resource centre for social entrepreneurs and enterprises. Lack of resources and competence prevents social firms from entering the market. Social entrepreneurs lack national and regional networking and are inexperienced with European networks (European Commission, 2018; Jankovic, 2022). Most social sector institutions are inefficient, ineffective, and inadequate. A social enterprise's legal form is crucial for administrative, financial, and reporting purposes. These inquiries define stakeholder expectations, including management's (Jankovic, 2017). The Center for Economic Prosperity and Society and EFSE DF/Finance in Motion's Social Impact Award and social entrepreneur incubation program are important business support programmes (Andjelic & Petricevic, 2020).

4.4.3.1. Financial Support. Most social companies need donations and government money to buy materials and pay employees. Some use EU IPA financing for employee training and equipment purchases, while most use the Employment Agency's public works branch for public contracting (European Commission, 2018). The Ministries of Agriculture and Rural Development, Culture, Economy, and Science offer grant programs. The Development Fund, Employment Agency, and Montenegrin Business Angel Network give additional funding (Andjelic & Petricevic, 2020). Investments, crowdsourcing, and loans are rare, and loans are cautious with high-interest rates. Short-term projects and funding shortages hurt social entrepreneurs' operations (European Commission, 2018; Regional Cooperation Council, 2015). State funding is a major issue. Transparency and tracking project performance and impact are lacking in the allocation process (Vukovic & Bulatovic, 2016). Funding prioritises a few fields, leaving other organisations behind. These acts are also statutory violations that caused the Administrative Court of Montenegro to reverse the grant distribution and intensify SE development and enterprise assistance constraints (Parliament of Montenegro, 2013). Political instability and shifting objectives are preventing financial mechanism growth.

4.4.3.2. Non-financial Support and Access to Resources. It should come as no surprise that there is a paucity of the basic skills required to create SEs, given the relatively small sector. Business and financial management skills are feeble among SEs and will, in the future, impede sector development.

Although some organisations offer capacity-building activities for new and upcoming social entrepreneurs (Juventas, Fund for Active Citizenship, Centre for development of NGOs, and others), there is scarce non-financial support for SEs. The reports suggest the need for professional and in-kind support to SEs (Jankovic, 2017; Vukovic & Bulatovic, 2016). One of the suggested intervention areas is providing full access to SEs to all government, non-profit, or CSR-run training and mentoring programs for small- and medium-sized businesses to increase their capacities and contribute to society (Rosandic & Kusinikova, 2018).

4.4.4. Social Dimension. SE, in general, is not typically included in the traditional educational system. There is no systematic education about SE, which many see as a critical obstacle to the sector's development. Entrepreneurship has been added to the vocational education and training system, but not SE. It is one of the main reasons why SEs are still constrained by low visibility and recognition. The lack of specific policies and regulations adds to the constraints on the visibility and recognition of the field and its actors' operations (Rosandic & Kusinikova, 2018).

4.5. North Macedonia

4.5.1. Political Dimension. The Republic of North Macedonia has a constitutional and legal basis for developing the concept of social enterprise. The concept at the governmental level was introduced through strategies for cooperation with civil society (2012–2017) (European Commission, 2018). A broader discourse about SE started several years ago when the Ministry of Labour and Social Policy, supported by the IPA project 'Support to Social Enterprises', started developing a policy and legal framework. In response to these processes, the Work Programme of the Government for 2021 included the design and adoption of the National Strategy and an Action Plan for the Development of Social Enterprises, a Law on Social Entrepreneurship, and the establishment of the Centre for Social Enterprises.

The Strategy for Development of Social Enterprises provides a platform for implementing a package of measures, with a focus on five priorities: establishment of a legal framework that provides equal legal status and benefits for all types of social enterprise; creating a culture for SE and public recognition of SEs; organising mutual support, learning, and capacity building for SEs and key actors in the eco-system; entering and developing markets for SEs; and gaining access to external finance (Ministry of Labour and Social Policy, 2021).

4.5.2. Legal Dimension. The legislation in North Macedonia does not recognise and regulate SEs, as there is no Law on SEs. However, in February 2021, the Working Group was established to create policies and legislation for SE. In the absence of a Law for SEs, a sound basis and step forward is the definition of social enterprise within the Strategy for Development of Social Enterprises, where a social enterprise is defined as

> operator in a social economy whose primary goal is to have a societal impact by providing a wide range of social, economic, health, educational, cultural, environmental, and other products and services; and promote societal well-being by providing goods and services in the market in an innovative and entrepreneurial way, using its profit primarily to achieve social or environmental goals; and is managed in a transparent and accountable way, by including workers, consumers and stakeholders affected by its activities in decision-making. (Ministry of Labour and Social Policy, 2021)

Some of the existing legal acts allow the establishment and operation of entities that can be recognised as SEs or identify themselves as SEs, such as civil society organisations and foundations, cooperatives, sheltered companies, crafts organisations, trade companies, and others. SEs are established as legal bodies under the current laws (Law on Associations and Foundations, Law on Cooperatives, Law on Employment of Persons with Disabilities, and Law of Trade Companies) (Ilijevski & Iloska, 2019).

4.5.3. Institutional Dimension. Several institutions (the Ministry of Economy, the Agency for promotion and support of entrepreneurship, and the Fund for Innovation and Technology Development) were engaged in promoting and supporting SE initiatives. Also, several measures for supporting SEs have been undertaken over the last couple of years, including the National Deinstitutionalisation Strategy, the National Small and Medium Enterprise Strategy, the Strategy for Development of Women Entrepreneurship, the Mid-term Strategy on Corporate Social Responsibility, the Revised Employment and Social Reform Programme, etc.

The first public register of SEs in the country was recently created. The data from the register is publicly available and open for citizens and all interested parties, with the aim of visibility of existing SEs, further analysis of their capacities and needs, and encouragement of cooperation. In total, the register contains 57 SEs that offer diversified products and services, of which the most popular are the production of organic food and organic products, education for children and youth, inclusive and sustainable tourism, crafts, social services for vulnerable categories of citizens, and waste management. These enterprises employ 271 people or an average of fewer than five people per social enterprise. Half of the SEs that have provided data in the last three years have incomes up to 5,000 euros, while only ten have incomes higher than 15,000 euros (National Youth Council of Macedonia, 2022).

4.5.3.1. Financial Support. SEs have a hybrid financing model. Besides the revenues from their economic activities, they also have activities that are project-oriented and implemented through grant support from foreign donors and philanthropists, such as the USAID Aid Program, GIZ, UNDP, the Swiss Agency for Development and Cooperation, and the EU's IPA programs (Ilijevski & Iloska, 2019).

SEs are not eligible for funding through national programs for financing new companies unless registered as trade companies. A positive change in this direction is the call announced by the Fund for Innovation and Technological Development to encourage SE. Although loans are a regular source of financing for SMEs, banks rarely approve loans to these organisations. There are no offers designed to satisfy the specific financing needs of SEs to scale and develop their business activities (Ministry of Labour and Social Policy, 2021).

4.5.3.2. Non-financial Support and Access to Resources. Several government institutions, civil society organisations, advisory centres, accelerators, and hubs have recently started offering capacity-building support to SEs. Their advisory activities, training, or mentoring activities cover topics important for the development of SE and starting or running a SE, such as developing ideas, planning and managing business activities, financial management, social enterprise management, raising funds, preparing product and service offerings, building partnerships and networks, creating sales channels, and other (Ministry of Labour and Social Policy, 2021).

4.5.4. Social Dimension. SE has emerged as a new area that has attracted the attention of civil society in the last decade. However, the concept is insufficiently known to ordinary citizens, decision-makers, or the business community. The National Center has started a broader public campaign for SEs. In cooperation with its regional centres, the Centre has organised many fairs where the SEs have exhibited and presented their organic foods and products, handicrafts, and social service. Also, civil society organisations have organised several national and regional SE conferences in the last several years, contributing to increasing awareness about SE.

Within secondary and higher education, the part of the curricula contains a presentation of SE, integrated within subjects such as Business and Entrepreneurship. In addition, in the sphere of non-formal education, civil society organisations have implemented numerous non-formal education programs on this topic in the last decade. Such initiatives were also supported by government institutions such as the Ministry of Economy, the Agency for Support of Entrepreneurship, Fund for Innovation and Technology Development.

4.6. Serbia

SEs in Serbia were established through private initiatives to provide sustainable solutions for community development through social innovation in the environment and circular economy, social inclusion, and other sustainable development areas (Golubovic & Muhi, 2019). At the beginning of 2022, there has been structural progress in light of the recently adopted Law of Social Entrepreneurs.

4.6.1. Political Dimension. The start of EU integration (2013/14) has made Serbia eligible to participate in EU funding schemes (Rosandic & Kusinikova, 2017). The body responsible for SE is dominantly the Ministry of Labour, Employment, Veterans Affairs, and Social Protection, supported by various state institutions (Cvejic, 2018). The new Law on Social Entrepreneurship (article 19/20) enforces a Social Entrepreneurship Development Program and a Social Entrepreneurship Council as the main governing body. Traditionally based on the employment of people with disabilities, SEs are still a new phenomenon in the Serbian context but have developed due to social policy reform (Žarković Rakić et al., 2017). Social entrepreneurship is institutionally addressed through the Strategy for Cooperation of the Government with the Civil Society Sector (2012–2017) and the strategy for the Support of SMEs and Entrepreneurship (2015–2020), especially Pillar 6, referring to aspects of SE. In addition, The National Youth Strategy (2015–2025) and the Annual National Employment Action Plan engage in fundamental (self)employment measures, providing instruments for supporting SEs.

4.6.2. Legal Dimension. SE is governed by many legal frameworks (Golubovic & Muhi, 2019). The set of regulations supported the sector for quite a long time. Finally, in February 2022, the Law on SE was adopted after a decade of drafting, implying institutional recognition for SEs. The legal forms presented in the sector are associations/foundations of citizens, social cooperatives, enterprises for professional rehabilitation, and spin-off enterprises (limited liability or joint-stock companies).

4.6.3. Institutional Dimension. The social economy is inadequately recognised as a concept among public authorities in Serbia, attained employment opportunities for persons with disabilities (Rosandic & Kusinikova, 2017). SE has been more viable since 2008 after the global economic crisis. The complexity of the so-called institutionalisation includes policy incentives, training, or financing of SEs, which has been engaging diverse stakeholders.

The first survey of SEs was conducted by the Statistical Office in 2012, revealing 1,196 SEs operating. The performed mapping of SE in 2018 was based on the dataset of 2012, with methodological changes, so only 500 SEs were identified (Golubovic & Muhi, 2019). The alteration was made to exclude agricultural cooperatives since they were considered less organised and had conflicting goals. SEs have various legal forms in Serbia, so it is difficult to gather data, as the new Law on SE promises a separate registry. Due to undeveloped monitoring tools, without any standardization, still no presence of reliable data about the impact of SEs in Serbia (Rosandic & Kusinikova, 2017).

4.6.3.1. Financial Support. The work integration of SEs for people with disabilities (WISE) enables them to get subsidies from the state and have priority when competing for public tenders. According to the newly introduced Law on Social Entrepreneurship (article 17), social entrepreneurship entity may obtain benefits and exemptions following the regulations governing taxes, contributions for compulsory social insurance, fees for the use of public goods and other types of financial obligations.

Finance has frequently been disputed (Rosandic & Kusinikova, 2017). SEs relying on foreign financial aid provided is at a level of 87.5% (Stankovic & Stancic, 2017).

The most common funding tool for SEs is granted (Stankovic & Stancic, 2017). Grant programmes are financed by public bodies and private foundations, among which are USAID, Erste Bank, UniCredit Bank and Foundation, Rockefeller Brothers Fund, Norwegian Ministry of Foreign Affairs, British Council, and Delta Foundation. Traditional financing is scarce. However, loans for SEs have been piloted by UniCredit Foundation, UniCredit Bank, and Erste Bank on a small scale (loans up to 10,000 EUR, no collateral for loans up to 15,000 EUR, subsidised interest rates 5–7%, 5-year repayment period) (Andjelic & Petricevic, 2020).

The European Commission has been engaged in several funding activities. The most well-established tool is the Instrument of Pre-Accession (IPA) (2007–2013) which conforms to a series of programs (European Instrument for Democracy & Human Rights, ERASMUS, EaSI, COSME, WB EDIF, EaSI 2014–2020, and COSME funds). Organisations that have strongly supported SE development are also Smart Kolektiv, Yunus Social Business Balkans, and European Fund for South East Europe. International organisations have been engaged in the sector needs, among which: are USAID, the United Nations Development Program, the International Office of Migration, the International Labour Organisation, the British Council, The Henrich Boll Foundation, The German International Cooperation, UN, EBRD, and European Investment Bank.

4.6.3.2. Non-financial Support and Access to Resources. The 2016 'Year of Entrepreneurship' and 2017 'Decade of Entrepreneurship' were government initiatives offering non-financial support and resource access. Additionally, the organisation actively building capacities in the sector is the EU commission, the British Council, UN Global Compact Network Serbia, Delta Foundation, Trag Foundation, Group 484, Ana Foundation, and Vlade Divac Foundation. Smart Kolektiv via Smart Academy provides training, the City Centre for Social Entrepreneurship of Belgrade provides educational and training programs, and the Business Forum and Academy of Business Skills support young entrepreneurs through mentorship. The following organisations promote SE–Social Impact Award Serbia, Junior Achievement Serbia, In Centar, StartIn, StartUp Program, Association of Business Women in Serbia, Serbian Chamber of Commerce, and ID. Co-working spaces and hubs such as Impact Hub Belgrade, Rural Hub Vrmdza, and Centre for socially responsible business are also available.

4.6.4. Social Dimension. The education system offers partial options, so only entrepreneurship has been introduced into the secondary school curricula, also at some scale in the vocational education and training system (Rosandic & Kusinikova, 2017).

We provide the SE Development in Western Balkans: State-of-the-Art (Table 1) and the Comparative Analysis of SE Development in Western Balkan (Table 2) below for further reference.

Table 1. SE Development in Western Balkans: State-of-the-Art.

Country	Dimension	Situation	Gaps
Albania	Political	• SEs appeared within the civil sector around 2,000 through projects supported by foreign donors. • In 2011, the Agency for Social Business was established. • The National Strategy for Employment and Skills supports government objectives in the area of SEs	• The national strategy for SEs does not exist in the country. • SEs suffer from unfair competition associated with administrative burdens and bureaucracy

Table 1. (*Continued*)

Country	Dimension	Situation	Gaps
Albania	Legal	• In 2016, Parliament passed the Law on SEs. • The law explicitly defines the areas of activity of SEs • Based on the EU definition, SEs exist in several legal forms: associations, agricultural cooperatives, and limited liability companies	• The Law recognises only non-profit organisations as a legal form of social enterprise • The state disregards the importance of the economic aspect of SEs that can strengthen their sustainability
	Institutional	• Financial instruments for social entrepreneurs: government funding, foreign grants for development projects special financial agriculture, and tourism schemes for cooperatives • Several projects have been realised within the cooperation with EU funds for the capacity building of SEs	• The banks serve only if SEs possess collateral. There are a few business angel networks, and SEs are not included in these funding schemes • SEs are facing the necessity for knowledge and skills development • There is no national network promoting the development of SEs
	Social	• The concept of SEs is predominantly used by NPOs, SEs practitioners, and institutional actors • Foreign organisations are mostly included in supporting awareness-raising activities (UNDP, Beyond Barriers Association, YEA, SDC)	• There is a lack of awareness among the general public due to a narrow focus on SEs • Some SEs have attempted to cooperate with each other, but it has not yet been operationalized in concrete actions
Bosnia	Political	• Formal and non-formal educational institutions provide to some extent social enterprise education	• Academic institutions are not sufficiently included in researching SE topics

(*Continued*)

Table 1. (*Continued*)

Country	Dimension	Situation	Gaps
	Legal	• There is no SE regulation in the Federation of BiH • In 2022, Republika Srpska passed a Law on SE • Several laws in the nation include the de facto legal foundation for the growth of SEs	• Non-existent legal recognition of SEs • Various laws regulate various organisational legal forms of SEs • Legal confusion over the obligations and course of SEs
	Institutional	• Assistance from international organisations, private charities, the corporate sector, and the traditional entrepreneurial ecosystem is replacing state institutional support • There are no significant financial tools or incentives designed to encourage the development of the SEs • 'Together We Can Do More', the 'Coalition of Marginalized Groups in BiH', and the 'SE Network for Youth Employment' are informal national networks of SEs	• Lack of institutional support due to the low public, political and legal recognition • Lack of funding mechanisms due to lack of resources and legal identity • Lack of statistical data due to the nascency of the field
	Social	• The curricula at different levels still do not incorporate SE education	• Lack of SE education at all levels
Bosnia	Social	• Complicated bureaucratic result in organisations providing services to society not receiving the proper acknowledgment, which hinders the visibility and recognition of SE at different societal levels	• Lack of visibility and recognition of SE at different societal levels

Table 1. (*Continued*)

Country	Dimension	Situation	Gaps
Kosovo*	Political	• Efforts to align domestic policy with EU framework • SE represented partially in strategic documents such as: Strategy for Supporting Innovation and Entrepreneurship and National Development Strategy • Preference for transforming NGOs into SEs	• Limited profit generation • Focus on NGOs and bureaucracy • Government commitment
	Legal	• Government adopted Law on SEs in 2018 • SE are subject to the restriction on the distribution of profits, the distribution of goods and services defined by law, ensuring equal participation, employ people from disadvantaged groups, and remain compliant with legal requirements for financial reporting	• To narrow the focus of the Law for SEs, mainly on the engagement of vulnerable working groups • The development process is not viewed as inclusive enough by CSOs
	Institutional	• Dominantly governed by the Ministry of Labour and Social Welfare • Small-scale efforts donor funding, dependent on grants, project-based mentality • SEs may obtain benefits and exemptions in accordance with the regulations governing taxes and other financial obligations	• Undeveloped institutional infrastructure and support, both financial and in-kind, are deficient • Support infrastructure is centralised, local governments do not use SE as an inclusive problem-solving service • Most incentives are ad hoc, not specifically focussed on SEs, and not providing consolidated support

(*Continued*)

Table 1. (*Continued*)

Country	Dimension	Situation	Gaps
	Social	• Educational system is not substantially engaging in issues related to SEs • Public awareness/ understanding of SEs is negligible • A few publications locally and internationally on the SE topic	• Long-term educational opportunities are needed in order to drive the long-term development of SEs • Social impact is mostly documented on the level of case studies and best practice
Montenegro	Political	• SE is still a relatively new idea in social and economic activity. • Government leadership changes have caused stagnation and a change in priorities regarding SE • There are no sector-specific policies to encourage SE	• Lack of specific, micro-policies to facilitate the sector's development • Lack of inclusion of SEs in other policy documents and areas
Montenegro	Legal	• Several laws include the de facto legal foundation for the growth of SEs • The last effort to regulate the field was conducted in 2013	• Non-existent legal recognition of SEs • Various laws regulate various organisational legal forms of SEs • Legal confusion over the obligations and course of SEs
	Institutional	• Assistance from international organisations, private charities, the corporate sector, or the entrepreneurial ecosystem is replacing the state institutional support • There are no significant financial or incentives designed to encourage the development of the SEs • There are no SE networks promoting the growth of SE	• Lack of institutional support due to the low public, political and legal recognition • Lack of funding mechanisms due to lack of resources and legal identity • Lack of statistical data due to the nascency of the field • Lack of business development skills of social entrepreneurs needed for entering the market

Table 1. (*Continued*)

Country	Dimension	Situation	Gaps
	Social	• The curricula at different levels still do not incorporate SE education • Complicated bureaucratic procedures can result in organisations providing services to society not receiving the proper acknowledgment and recognition of SEs at different societal levels	• Lack of SE education at all levels • Lack of visibility and recognition of SE at different societal levels
North Macedonia	Political	• The concept of SEs was introduced through government strategies for cooperation with civil society • A wider discourse has continued with the IPA project 'Support to SEs' for developing a national strategy and legal framework for SEs • The National Strategy and Action Plan for support to SEs was adopted in 2022	• The concept of SE is insufficiently integrated into government policies that envisage the transition to an inclusive and sustainable economy • The partnership and networking are not appropriately developed at the regional and municipal levels
	Legal	• In 2021 a Working Group was established for creating legislation for SEs • Some of the existing legal acts allow the establishment of self-recognised SEs, such as civil society organisations, cooperatives, sheltered workspaces, crafts organisations, and trade companies	• Besides initiated activities, the country very long time does not have a law for SEs • The existent legal framework does not regulate SEs with their specifics, needs, and opportunities for concrete state support

(*Continued*)

Table 1. (*Continued*)

Country	Dimension	Situation	Gaps
	Institutional	• The SEs have a hybrid financing model, mostly funding through grants from foreign donors • The number, level of development, labour, and market share of SEs in the economy are at an insufficient level	• Most of the SEs do not pay attention to the improvement of products and building a recognisable name • The financial literacy of SEs is at a low level, demonstrating ignorance of economic activities
North Macedonia		• Several government institutions, civil society organisations, accelerators, and hubs have realised several activities for capacity-building support to SEs	• The SEs are not eligible for funding through national programs unless they are registered as trade companies
	Social	• Broader public campaign has been started led by the National Center for SEs, organising regional fairs for SEs • Civil society organisations have organised several conferences, contributing to increasing awareness • Secondary schools and universities have included the concept of SE partially in their curricula	• The concept of SE is insufficiently known to ordinary citizens, decision-makers, or the business community • Networking activities of SEs are missing in order to gather more relevant people around a unified idea
Serbia	Political	• Strategic documents in relationship to SE: the Strategy for Cooperation of the Government with the Civil Society Sector, Strategy for Support of SMEs and Entrepreneurship, and National Youth Strategy • Municipalities are developing the role of supporting SEs	• Weakly recognised concept among public authorities • SE topics are on the margins of the political agenda

Table 1. (*Continued*)

Country	Dimension	Situation	Gaps
Serbia	Legal	• In 2022 a Law on SE was adopted • Other legislation related to SEs: Law on Professional Rehabilitation and Employment of Persons with Disabilities, Law on Social Protection, and Law on Volunteers	• Rulebooks and additional legislative directives are still missing • Development of the SE Council legal framework is limiting for the SE sector
	Institutional	• Separate registry of SEs still under construction • In the pilot stage of innovative financing models, banks are trying out hybrid finance options • The private sector is actively engaged in CSR activities including technical support and providing access to commercial markets	• Public institutions lack knowledge and internal capacities • Financing infrastructure is not sufficiently developed • Ministry of Economy does not take an active role in tackling SE through their programs
	Social	• Informal education promotes SE • Formal education is only via entrepreneurship courses integrated into secondary schools and partially the VET sector • There are two networks (The Coalition for the Development of SE and the Social Economy Network of Serbia)	• No standardisations, no reliable data about the impact of SEs in Serbia

Table 2. Comparative Analysis of SE Development in Western Balkan.

Dimensions	Indicators	ALB	BiH	KOS	MNE	RNM	SRB	Lessons Learned and Future Perspectives
Political	Recognition at the central and local government level	√√	√	√	√	√√	√√	• SEs should be a cross-cutting issue for the ministries responsible for health, social welfare, finance, entrepreneurship, agriculture, etc. • The government should be more included in supporting SEs at the local level for balanced regional development. • BiH and MNE have low SE concept use and acceptance due to political instability and turbulences. • Kosovo has been focussing dominantly on the employment of vulnerable groups, whereas Serbia has been developing a wider concept taking into consideration wider societal problems.
	National strategy	X	X	X	X	√	X	• Most of countries do not have national strategies for SEs. North Macedonia e an exception, although this document is at the very beginning of its implementation. • A national strategy for SEs should be developed for developing and harmonizing different initiatives for supporting SEs.
Legal	SE law	√	X	√	X	X	√√	• Albania and Kosovo have had a law since 2016 and 2018 but now progress in bylaws. Serbia has had a law since 2022 and still awaiting bylaws. Republika Srpska has adopted a SE law but the Federation of BiH has not.

Table 2. (*Continued*)

Dimensions	Indicators	ALB	BiH	KOS	MNE	RNM	SRB	Lessons Learned and Future Perspectives
								• Countries with a law for SEs should be more engaged in encouraging more SEs to apply for the SE legal status, by reducing the restrictions within their legal framework criteria. • In countries with a Law for SEs, it should include a wider range of legal forms and products/services to tackle broader societal challenges through social innovation.
Institutional	Government and other forms of support	√√	√	√	√	√√	√√	• The state incentives for national donors, funding schemes, or tax deductions should be envisaged. • Most support measures for SEs in BiH and MNE are coming from employment measures for SMES and the employment of people with disabilities. • SRB has initiated some incentives but still lacks an overall support and coherent approach and special dedication to SEs is inconsistent.
	Social enterprise research and Statistics	√	X	X	X	√	√	• There is no available data on social enterprise research and statistics. There are only estimations that cannot be considered as a definite source of data. • Additional research efforts in the filed of SEs are needed for tailoring specific activities for supporting SEs.

(*Continued*)

Table 2. (*Continued*)

Dimensions	Indicators	ALB	BiH	KOS	MNE	RNM	SRB	Lessons Learned and Future Perspectives
	Measuring and reporting social impact	√	√	√	√	√	√	• The national unified methodology for measuring and reporting the impact of SEs should be developed for a broader understanding of the SEs activities and for creating better policies.
	Financial support	√	√	√	√	√	√	• SEs in the region are dependent on project grants, donations, and subsidies. • The international support comes from several EU programs focussed on civil society organisations such as IPA, EIDHR, Erasmus, and others. • There are no fiscal benefits for SEs. • Developing specific grants, investing schemes and credit lines is crucial for SEs growth.
	Capacity building for SEs	√√	√	√	√	√√	√√	• SEs require access to capacity-building programmes that help improve their entrepreneurship, management, marketing, and fundraising skills. • In BiH and Serbia, there are business incubators and other business support organisations that offer financial and technical support to SEs.
	Networks and mechanisms of mutual cooperation	√	X	X	X	√	√√	• BiH and SRB have several networks of SEs, active both on a central and local level.

Table 2. (*Continued*)

Dimensions	Indicators	ALB	BiH	KOS	MNE	RNM	SRB	Lessons Learned and Future Perspectives
								• Introducing SEs to national and international networks for greater response to the challenges in this sector is needed in all countries. • More cross-sectoral activities among SEs, donors, and public institutions are necessary to expand the opportunities for SEs
Social	SE education	√√	√	√	√	√√	√	• BiH, Montenegro, and Kosovo have not included SE education in the educational system. • SRB and North Macedonia have some initiatives attempting to integrate SE topics into education. • Skills that encourage social entrepreneurial behaviour need to be developed and promoted within the formal and non-formal education systems.
	Visibility and recognition of SE at different societal levels	√√	√	√	√	√√	√	• The visibility and recognition of SE at different societal levels in BiH, Montenegro, and Kosovo are very low given the issues with regulation, low raising awareness activities, and lack of government priority. • Increasing awareness among ordinary citizens, decision-makers, and the business community in Serbia in North Macedonia, by organising public events, conferences, and SEs fairs is crucial for the development of the sector.

Notes: SE – Social entrepreneurship; SEs – Social enterprises; Scale: High √√√ – Medium √√ – Low √; and Scale: Yes √ – No X.

5. Discussion

The engaging topic of SE is emerging in the Western Balkans. Even with a slow pace, the tendencies have been similar within the countries we have considered in our analysis. Our main findings have been grounded on scattered information and sublimated reporting found in relevant publications on the sector's development (Andjelic & Petricevic, 2020; Cvejic, 2018; NESsT, 2017; Philips et al., 2016; Rosandic & Kusinikova, 2018, 2017; Varga, 2017). The trending discussions are that it should be a cross-cutting issue for the ministries responsible for labour and social welfare, health, finance, entrepreneurship, agriculture, rural development, and others. It has been emphasised within all European Commission reporting documents that the government should be more included in supporting and advocating SEs at a local level for balanced regional development. Contextual considerations imply that BiH and MNE have low engagement in the SE concept due to political instability and turbulence. Whereas Kosovo has been focussing dominantly on the employment of vulnerable groups, Serbia has been developing a slightly broader concept considering wider societal problems.

Most Western Balkan countries have not prepared a national strategic frame related to SE. In this area, North Macedonia has been standing out, although this activity is in a very early stage. Hence, national strategies for SE should be established to develop and harmonise different initiatives for supporting SEs. From a legislative perspective, Albania in 2016, Kosovo in 2018, and Serbia in 2022 have introduced a law, but still, no progress in terms of bylaws and rulebooks is implicated. Interestingly, Republika Srpska has adopted a SE law, but the Federation of BiH has not. However, countries that have adopted Laws on SEs are missing application and operationalisation of SE legal status, especially the capacity of restrictive narrative within their legal framework should be considered. Countries with no Law on SEs, such as BiH, Montenegro, and North Macedonia, have been regulating SE depending on their legal registration/status. Their activities are based on the existing legal acts, enabling the establishment of self-recognised SEs, such as CSO, cooperatives, sheltered companies, crafts organisations, and trade companies.

State incentives considering national donors, funding schemes, or tax deductions should be envisaged. Most support measures for SEs in BiH, MNE, and Kosovo come from employment measures for SMEs and the employment of people with disabilities. SRB has initiated some incentives but still lacks overall support, and special dedication to SEs is inconsistent. SEs in the region are dominantly dependent upon project grants, donations, and subsidies (Andjelic & Petricevic, 2020; Rosandic & Kusinikova, 2017; Varga, 2017). The international support comes from several EU programs focussed on CSO, such as IPA, EIDHR, Erasmus, and others. Only Serbia has some private funding options, implicating a larger scale of opportunities. Developing specific grants, investing schemes, and credit lines for the SEs is vital. However, even more so, additional capacity building related to developing various management, marketing, and fundraising skills is a necessity.

Information related to SEs is scarce, so a unified methodology for measuring and reporting the impact of SEs is urgently needed for a broader understanding of the SEs' activities. Despite some low-key attempts from Serbia and North Macedonia, other countries have not included SE education in the educational system. Thus, skills that encourage social entrepreneurial behaviour must be developed and promoted within educational systems. This ultimately results in the overall argument that awareness of SE is low. Fair to say that some countries are further than others. The visibility and recognition of SE at different societal levels in BiH, Montenegro, and Kosovo are very low, given the lack of prioritising at many levels. It is evident that Serbia and North Macedonia have been more engaging and naturally have a slightly larger scale of engagement reflected at various societal levels.

6. Conclusion

SE in the region is continuously expanding. There have been projects, programs, and organisations in the area that are devoted to SE development, and people are becoming more aware of how SE may spur economic and social progress. In the last several years, most countries have adopted either regulation or policy for the sector's development and support for SEs. However, their operationalisation is still lacking. Low institutional support and available funding instruments and access constrain SEs operations, growth, and social impact. Countries need to develop the national capacity for SE. Education, training, and tailored support for social entrepreneurs, policymakers, and other stakeholders in the sector, including resources, technical assistance, and mentorship, are needed. One of the region's main challenges is measuring and evaluating social impact and the sector's development. Countries need to create systems to measure and evaluate the impact incorporating monitoring, assessing, and evaluating effectiveness. Lastly, fostering public–private–non-profit partnerships is a prerequisite for SE growth and will provide much-needed visibility and recognition of SEs activities and their impact.

References

Andjelic, J., & Petricevic, T. (2020). *Regional study and guidelines on social entrepreneurship in the Western Balkans: Albania, Bosnia and Herzegovina, Kosovo, Montenegro, North Macedonia, Serbia*. Tirana: RYCO.

Austin, J., Stevenson, H., & Wei-Skillern, J. (2006). Social and commercial entrepreneurship: Same, different, or both? *Entrepreneurship: Theory and Practice*, *30*(1), 1–22. https://doi.org/10.1111/j.1540-6520.2006.00107.x

Babovic, M. et al. (2015). Strategic Study on Social Economy Development in the Context of the South East Europe 2020 Strategy, Belgrade: European Movement in Serbia.

Bacq, S., & Janssen, F. (2011). The multiple faces of social entrepreneurship: A review of definitional issues based on geographical and thematic criteria. *Entrepreneurship and Regional Development*, *23*(5–6), 373–403. https://doi.org/10.1080/08985626.2011.577242

Boschee, J. (1998). *Merging mission and money: A board member's guide to social entrepreneurship*. Washington, DC: National Center for Nonprofit Boards.

Cvejic, S. (2018). *Social enterprises and their ecosystems in Europe: Country fiche Serbia*. Luxembourg: European Commission.

Chichevaliev, S. (2019). Conducive factors for development and promotion of social entrepreneurship in North Macedonia. *Journal of European and Balkan Perspectives*, *2*(1), 62–74.

Chichevaliev, S. (2020). *Key factors of conducive environment for development of social entrepreneurship in the Republic of North Macedonia*. Ph.D. thesis, University American College Skopje, Skopje.

Choi, H. (2010). Religious institutions and ethnic entrepreneurship: The Korean ethnic church as a small business incubator. *Economic Development Quarterly*, *24*(4), 372–383.

Choi, N., & Majumdar, S. (2014). Social entrepreneurship as an essentially contested concept: Opening a new avenue for systematic future research. *Journal of Business Ventures*, *29*, 363–376.

Corbin, J., & Strauss, A. (2008). *Basics of qualitative research: Techniques and procedures for developing grounded theory* (3rd ed.). Thousand Oaks, CA: Sage.

Culkin, N., & Simmons, R. (2018). *Study of the Challenges That Hinder MSME Development in the Republic of Albania*. Report for the British Council and Swedish Institute.

Dacin, P. A., Dacin, M.T., & Matear, M. (2010). Social entrepreneurship: Why we don't need a new theory and how we move forward from here. *Academy of Management Perspectives*, *24*(3), 37–57.

Dees, J. G. (1998). Enterprising nonprofits. *Harvard Business Review*, *76*(1), 55–67.

Dees, J. G., & Anderson, B. B. (2003). For-profit social ventures. *International Journal of Entrepreneurship Education*, *2*, 1–26.

Dervishi, M. (2019). *Being a social enterprise: Value-added or fuel to the misconceptions? The case of social enterprises in Kosovo*. Thesis, Rochester Institute of Technology, Rochester, NY.

Dey, P., & Steyaert, C. (2010). The politics of narrating social entrepreneurship. *Journal of Enterprising Communities*, *4*(1), 85–108. https://doi.org/10.1108/17506201011029528

Djermanović, S. (2019). *Study of national framework for social entrepreneurship in Bosnia and Herzegovina*. Network for Rural Development in Bosnia and Herzegovina.

Estrin, S., Mickiewicz, T., & Stephan, U. (2013). Entrepreneurship, social capital, and institutions: Social and commercial entrepreneurship across nations. *Entrepreneurship Theory and Practice*, *37*(3), 479–504.

European Commission. (2011). Social business initiative: European Commission, instrument for pre-accession assistance (IPA II) 2014–2020, Kosovo, support for better social services for the most vulnerable groups. Retrieved from https://neighbourhood-enlargement.ec.europa.eu/enlargement-policy/overview-instrument-pre-accession-assistance/kosovo-financial-assistance-under-ipa_en. Accessed on May 16, 2023.

European Commission. (2015). *A map of social enterprises and their eco-systems in Europe*. Synthesis Report Retrieved from https://ec.europa.eu/social/BlobServlet?docId=12987&langId=en. Accessed on May 16, 2023.

European Commission. (2018). *Social enterprises and their ecosystems in Europe: Country fiche: Former Yugoslav Republic of Macedonia*. Luxembourg: Publications Office of the European Union. Retrieved from http://ec.europa.eu/social/main.jsp?advSearchKey=socenterfiches&mode=advancedSubmit&catId=22. Accessed on February 2, 2023.

European Commission. (2019). *Social enterprises and their ecosystems in Europe. Country fiche*. Luxembourg: Publications Office of the European Union. Retrieved from https://europa.eu/!Qq64ny.

European Commission. (2020). *Social enterprises and their ecosystems in Europe. Comparative synthesis report*. Luxembourg: Publications Office of the European Union. Retrieved from https://europa.eu/!Qq64ny. Accessed on February 8, 2023.

Ferri, E., & Urbano, D. (2011). *Social entrepreneurship and environmental factors: A cross country comparison* (pp. 1–39). Universitat Autonoma de Barcelona. Barcelona, Spain.

Fici, A. (2015). *Recognition and legal forms of social enterprise in Europe: A critical analysis from a comparative law perspective*. Euricse Working Paper 82|15.

Friedman, V. J., & Desivilya, H. (2010). Integrating social entrepreneurship and conflict engagement for regional development in divided societies. *Entrepreneurship and Regional Development*, *22*(6), 495–514. https://doi.org/10.1080/08985626.2010.488400

Golubovic, D., & Muhi, B. (2019). Social entrepreneurship in Serbia: The state of play. *Revija za socijalnu politiku*, *26*(3), 359–378.

Government of BiH. (2022). Law on Social Entrepreneurship of Republic of Srpska. Retrieved from https://www.ilo.org/dyn/natlex/docs/ELECTRONIC/112343/140377/F73368202/BIH-112343.pdf. Accessed on January 20, 2023.

Government of Kosovo. (2017). Draft law on social enterprises. Retrieved from https://kryeministri.rks-gov.net/wp-content/uploads/2022/07/PROJEKTLIGJI_PER_NDERMARRJET_SOCIALE-1.pdf. Accessed on January 18, 2023.

Government of Montenegro. (2013). Government Work Program for 2013. Retrieved from https://www.gov.me/dokumenta/ac8d6c79-65cd-4e51-afc8-06a4d695f887. Accessed on January 18, 2023.

Government of Montenegro. (2012). National strategy for employment and human resources (2012–2015). Retrieved from https://www.etf.europa.eu/sites/default/files/m/0C9A33007F4C3B97C12580A7004BC611_212194_ETF_COUNTRY_NOTE_Montenegro.pdf. Accessed on January 18, 2023.

Government of Republic of Kosovo. (2011). SME development strategy for Kosova 2012–2016: With vision 2020.

Griffiths, D. M., Gundry, K. L., & Kickul, R. J. (2013). The socio-political, economic, and cultural determinants of social entrepreneurship activity: An empirical examination. *Journal of Small Business and Enterprise Development*, *20*(2), 341–357.

Halibashic, M., Osmankovic, J., & Talic, A. (2015). *Modeli socijalnog preduzetništva u Bosni i Hercegovini.* Youth Employment Project. Bosnia and Hercegovina: Ekonomski Institut Sarajevo.

Harris, S. P., Renko, M., & Caldwell, K. (2013). Accessing social entrepreneurship: Perspectives of people with disabilities and key stakeholders. *Journal of Vocational Rehabilitation*, *38*(1), 35–48. https://doi.org/10.3233/JVR-120619

Haska, E., & Hoxha, J. (2020). *Characteristics and challenges social enterprises Albania baseline study*. Tirana: Partners Albania for Change and Development.

Haugh, H. (2005). A research agenda for social entrepreneurship. *Social Enterprise Journal*, *1*(1), 1–12.

Hoogendoorn, B. (2011). *Social entrepreneurship in the modern economy warm glow, cold feet*. ERIM Ph.D. Series in Research in Management. Erasmus Research Institute of Management – ERIM. Erasmus Universiteit Rotterdam.

Ilijevski, K., & Iloska, A. (2019). *Social enterprises through the prism of cross-border cooperation between the Republic of North Macedonia and the Republic of Albania.* Skopje: Association for Research, Communication and Development Public.

Initiative for Better and Humane Inclusion. (2016). *Efekti politike podrške zapošljavanju OSI u FBiH i razvoj novih oblika podrške kroz socijalno poduzetništvo*. Initiative for Better and Humane Inclusion. Sarajevo, BiH.

International Labour Organisation. (2021). Inclusive entrepreneurship analysis in Montenegro. Geneva, Switzerland. Retrieved from https://www.ilo.org/empent/areas/entrepreneurship-and-enterprise-development/WCMS_803921/lang-en/index.htm. Accessed on May 16, 2023.

Jankovic, A. (2017). *Društveno Preduzetništvo u Funkciji Razvoja Crne Gore. Centar za ekonomski prosperitet i slobodu – CEPS*. Pogorica, Crna Gora.

Jankovic, A. (2022). *Country profile: Montenegro, Western Balkans conference for social entrepreneurship*. Social Entrepreneurship Observatory. Retrieved from https://seconference.online/wp-content/uploads/2022/05/01__FINAL_SE-Country-Profile_MNE.pdf. Accessed on January 26, 2023.

Kartallozi, I., & Xhemajli, V. (2017). *Rise of future leaders: Social enterprise in Kosovo*. SDC EYE Project is implemented by Helvetas Swiss Intercooperation and MDA. Pristina, Kosovo.

Kuratko, D. (2018). *Entrepreneurship: Theory, process, practice*. Boston: Cengage.

LENS. (2016). The cost of free money, YOU SEE! Platform for social innovations in youth employment. Retrieved from https://www.ngolens.org/wp-content/uploads/2017/03/The-cost-of-free-Money_web.pdf. Accessed on January 29, 2023.

Loku, A., Gogiqi, F., & Qehaja, V. (2018). Social enterprises like the right step for economic development for Kosovo. *European Journal of Marketing and Economics*, *1*(1), 18–23.

Mair, J., & Marti, I. (2006). Social entrepreneurship research: A source of explanation, prediction, and delight. *Journal of World Business*, *41*(1), 36–44.

Mair, J., & Marti, I. (2009). Entrepreneurship in and around institutional voids: A case study from Bangladesh. *Journal of Business Venturing*, *24*(5), 419–435.

Mair, J., & Schoen, O. (2007). Successful social entrepreneurial business models in the context of developing economies: An explorative study. *International Journal of Emerging Markets*, *2*(1), 54–68.

Ministry of Labour and Social Welfare. (2012). *National strategy for employment and development of human resources 2012–2015*. Podgorica. Montenegro.

Ministry of Labour and Social Welfare. (2013). *Strategy for development of the system of social and child protection 2013–2017*. Podgorica. Montenegro.

Ministry of Labour and Social Welfare. (2014). Strategjia Sektoriale 2014–2020. Pristina, Kosova.

Ministry of Labour and Social Policy. (2021). National strategy for the development of social enterprises in the Republic of North Macedonia (2021–2027). Skopje, North Macedonia.

Ministry of Social Welfare and Youth. (2014). National Strategy for Employment and Skills 2014-2020. Retrieved from https://financa.gov.al/wp-content/uploads/2018/09/NESS-ENG-8-1-15_final-version.pdf. Accessed on January 18, 2023.

Muñoz, P., & Kibler, E. (2016). Institutional complexity and social entrepreneurship: A fuzzy-set approach. *Journal of Business Research*, *69*(4), 1314–1318.

National Youth Council of Macedonia. (2022). *Baseline study for social enterprises in North Macedonia*. Organization for Social Innovation "ARNO". Skopje, North Macedonia.

NESsT. (2017). *Social enterprise ecosystems in Croatia and the Western Balkans: A mapping study of Albania. Bosnia & Herzegovina, Croatia, Kosovo, FYR Macedonia, Montenegro, and Serbia*. NESsT Global. USA.

Nicholls, A. (2008). Introduction. In A. Nicholls (Ed.), *Social entrepreneurship: New models of sustainable social change* (pp. 1–35). Oxford: Oxford University Press.

Nicholls, A. (2010). Institutionalizing social entrepreneurship in regulatory space: Reporting and disclosure by community interest companies. *Accounting, Organizations and Society*, *35*(4), 394–415. https://doi.org/10.1016/j.aos.2009.08.001

Parliament of Montenegro. (2013). *Committee for economics, finance and budget, consultative hearing on: Application of the law on non-governmental organisations in the field of financing*. Podgorica. Retrieved from https://www.skupstina.me/en/home. Accessed on November 21, 2013.

Pache, A. C., & Santos, F. (2013). Inside the hybrid organization: Selective coupling as a response to competing institutional logics. *Academy of Management Journal*, *56*(4), 972–1001. https://doi.org/10.1016/j.disc.2006.05.040

Peredo, A. M., & McLean, M. (2006). Social entrepreneurship: A critical review of the concept. *Journal of World Business*, *41*(1), 56–65.

Philips, J., De Amicis, L., & Lipparini, F. (2016). *Social entrepreneurship in the Western Balkans: State of play*. Plus Value Report. Retrieved from https://www.pvtest.org/wp-content/uploads/2017/02/se-in-w-balkans_state-of-play.pdf. Accessed on May 16, 2023.

Rangan, K., Leonard, H. B., & McDonald, S. (2008). *The future of social enterprise* (pp. 1–9). Working Paper, Harvard Business School.

Rapley, T. (2007). *Doing conversation, discourse and document analysis*. London: Sage.

Regional Cooperation Council. (2015). Strategic study on social economy development in the context of the South East Europe 2020 strategy. Retrieved from http://cepsmn.org/files/STRATEGIC_STUDY_ON_SOCIAL_ECONOMY_DEVELOPMENT.pdf. Accessed on January 18, 2023.

Rosandic, A., & Kusinikova, N. (2017). *Social economy in eastern neighbourhood and in the Western Balkans: Country report – Serbia*. European Union. Retrieved from https://ec.europa.eu/docsroom/documents/29642/attachments/11/translations/en/renditions/native. Accessed on May 16, 2023.

Rosandic, A., & Kusinikova, N. (2018a). *Social economy in eastern neighbourhood and in the Western Balkans: Country report – Kosovo*. European Union. Retrieved from https://ec.europa.eu/docsroom/documents/29642/attachments/7/translations/en/renditions/native. Accessed on May 16, 2023.

Rosandic, A., & Kusinikova, N. (2018b). *Social economy in eastern neighbourhood and in the Western Balkans: Country report – Bosnia & Herzegovina*. European Union. Retrieved from https://ec.europa.eu/docsroom/documents/29642/attachments/5/translations/en/renditions/native. Accessed on May 16, 2023.

Rosandic, A., & Kusinikova, N. (2018c). *Social economy in eastern neighbourhood and in the Western Balkans: Country report – Montenegro*. European Union. Retrieved from https://ec.europa.eu/docsroom/documents/29642/attachments/10/translations/en/renditions/native. Accessed on May 16, 2023.

Saebi, T., Foss, N. J., & Linder, S. (2019). Social entrepreneurship research: Past achievements and future promises. *Journal of Management*, *45*(1), 70–95. https://doi.org/10.1177/0149206318793196

Sahasranamam, S., & Nandakumar, M. K. (2020). Individual capital and social entrepreneurship: Role of formal institutions. *Journal of Business Research*, *107*(9), 104–117. https://doi.org/10.1016/j.jbusres.2018.09.005

Social Inclusion Foundation in Bosnia and Herzegovina. (2012). Assessment report on social entrepreneurship in Bosnia and Herzegovina. Retrieved from https://tacso.eu/publication/assessment-report-on-social-entreprenurship-in-bosnia-and-herzegovina/. Accessed on May 16, 2023.

Srbijanko, K. J., Korunovska, N., & Bashevska, M. (2016). *Social enterprises and work integration of vulnerable groups in Macedonia, Albania, and Kosovo: Reactor–Research in Action*. Skopje, North Macedonia.

Stankovic, N., & Stancic, I. (2017). *Social investment market in Serbia*. Smart Kolektiv. Retrieved from http://smartkolektiv.org/wp-content/uploads/2021/05/Social-Investment-Market-in-Serbia_Smart-Kolektiv.pdf. Accessed on February 6, 2023.

Stephan, U., Uhlaner, L. M., & Stride, C. (2014). Institutions and social entrepreneurship: The role of institutional voids, institutional support, and institutional configurations. *Journal of International Business Studies*, *46*(3), 308–331 https://doi.org/10.1057/jibs.2014.38.

Sullivan, D. M. (2007). Stimulating social entrepreneurship: Can support from cities make a difference? *Academy of Management Perspectives*, *21*, 77–78. https://doi.org/10.5465/amp.2007.24286169

Sud, M., VanSandt, C. V., & Baugous, A. M. (2009). Social entrepreneurship: The role of institutions. *Journal of Business Ethics*, *85*(1), 201–216. https://doi.org/10.1007/s10551-008-9939-1

Sumak, S. (2022). Country profile: Bosnia and Herzegovina – Western Balkans conference for social entrepreneurship. *Social Entrepreneurship Observatory*. Retrieved from https://seconference.online/wp-content/uploads/2022/05/01_FINAL_SE-Country-Profile_BiH.pdf. Accessed on January 26, 2023.

United Nations Development Program. (2012). Legal framework for social economy and social enterprises: A comparative report. Retrieved from https://ecnl.org/sites/default/files/2020-09/442_ECNL%20UNDP%20Social%20Econovmy%20Report.pdf. Accessed 16 May, 2023.

Varga, E. (2017). Social enterprise ecosystems in Croatia and the Western Balkans: A mapping study of Albania, Bosnia & Herzegovina, Croatia, Kosovo, FYR Macedonia, Montenegro and Serbia. Retrieved from https://connecting-youth.org/publications/publikim19.pdf. Accessed on January 9, 2023.

Vilić, D. (2022). Social entrepreneurship in Bosnia and Herzegovina: Opportunities and constraints. *Economics, Entrepreneurship and Management Research*, *1*(1), 1–19.

Vukovic, M., & Bulatovic, J. (2016). Needs analysis of social enterprises in Montenegro. Retrieved from https://crnvo.me/wp-content/uploads/2021/03/Analysis-of-needs-of-social-enterprises-in-Montenegro.pdf. Accessed on January 11, 2023.

Weerawardena, J., & Mort, G. S. (2006). Investigating social entrepreneurship: A multidimensional model. *Journal of World Business*, *41*(1), 21–35.

Wry, T., & Zhao, E. Y. (2018). Taking trade-offs seriously: Examining the contextually contingent relationship between social outreach intensity and financial sustainability in global microfinance. *Organization Science*, *29*(3), 507–528.

Zahra, S. A., Gedajlovic, E., Neubaum, D. O., & Shulman, J. M. (2009). A typology of social entrepreneurs: Motives, search processes and ethical challenges. *Journal of Business Venturing*, *24*(5), 519–532.

Zahra, S. A., & Wright, M. (2011). Entrepreneurship's next act. *Academy of Management Perspectives*, *25*(4), 67–83.

Žarković Rakić, J., Aleksić Mirić, A., Lebedinski, L., & Vladisavljević, M. (2017). Welfare state and social enterprise in transition: Evidence from Serbia. *Volunta*, *28*(6), 2423–2448.

Chapter 4

Green Entrepreneurship and Firm Performance: The Case of Albania

Gadaf Rexhepi, Hyrije Abazi-Alili, Selajdin Abduli, Sadudin Ibraimi and Rasim Zuferi

Abstract

Green entrepreneurship is gaining more attention as the interest in sustainability is growing. This is mainly because consumer awareness is rising and thus many regulations have been implied and several research are proving positive relationship from the use of green entrepreneurship. Using enterprise data for the Republic of Albania (ALB), this study examines the effects of green entrepreneurship on firm performance. Our findings when we investigate the determinants of firm performance, the green entrepreneurship, certification, innovation activities, foreign ownership, and monitoring energy appear to have a positive impact on firm performance, while the effect of direct export is negative.

Keywords: Green entrepreneurship; performance; certification; innovation; foreign ownership; Albania.

1. Introduction

Environmental issues for many years have been a big concern of humanity. They are gaining more attention due to many negative impacts that have been done as a result of harming the environment from many organizations, mainly in their attempt to increase the organizations' profitability (Suki, Suki, Sharif, Afshan, & Rexhepi, 2022). This has led to several kinds of research in the field of sustainability, which is analyzing different topics from many perspectives, mainly under the name green (Chen, Hu, Razi, & Rexhepi, 2022). The most impact in this

Entrepreneurship Development in the Balkans: Perspective from Diverse Contexts, 69–80

Published under exclusive licence by Emerald Publishing Limited
doi:10.1108/978-1-83753-454-820231004

direction has been made from the presentation of the Sustainable Development Goals Agenda 2030, the green deal, and the Paris Agreement which influenced many researchers to study and contribute to the field of sustainable development (Sepasi, Rexhepi, & Rahdari, 2021). With the main aim to find innovative ways of meeting the present needs, without compromising or jeopardizing the future generation in satisfying their needs. The issues and terms surrounding the research are broad and complex. Sustainability is a ubiquitous term and means anything from saving the planetary natural environment to making profits for the foreseeable future as a result of a competitive position (Porter, 2008; Rahdari et al., 2020).

Sustainable entrepreneurship is related to creating value and benefits for three parts, the entrepreneur, other people, and society. Entrepreneurs can generate economic wealth for themselves, but their impact on overall development can be much greater. They can also generate benefits for others, of an economic, environmental, and social nature. In the literature, these benefits are known as the triple-bottom line, shown in Fig. 1.

Sustainable entrepreneurship is about value and quality for all actors: to achieve more value with less environmental impact (Al-Abrrow et al., 2021; Ramadani, Agarwal, Caputo, Kumar Dixit, & Agrawal, 2022; Rexhepi & Berisha, 2017). According to many researchers, sustainable entrepreneurship has a triple effect on society that can be divided into three broad overlapping areas, such as social, economic, and environmental dimensions (Rexhepi, Kurtishi, & Bexheti, 2013):

- *Social dimension* – the social criteria are often neglected by many organizations. This particular category highlights the significance of social indicators and that they are as important in all organizations in the business and social sectors, if not more so. The social dimension includes a wide variety of issues

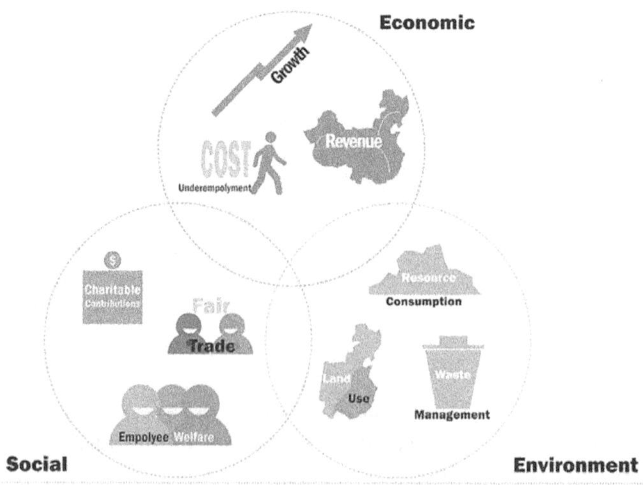

Fig. 1. Triple-bottom Line. *Source*: Wikimedia/Triplebotline.

such as stakeholder management, socially responsible investing, social inclusion and equality, labor and human rights, outreach through community development and philanthropy, and transparency of social performance (Sepasi, Rahdari, & Rexhepi, 2018).

- *Economic dimension* – addresses issues that are related to jobs, ethical training standards, and product value. They can be related also to the creation of opportunities for employment, the provision of better-quality products and services, the increase of the standard in the countries where entrepreneurs operate, as well as increasing revenues in the state budget (Ramadani & Schneider, 2013).
- *Environmental dimension* – the environmental dimension is much highlighted in most of organizations with a focus on sustainability. The environmental dimension entails environmental management (environmental management systems, water–energy efficiency, services, and supply chain), natural preservation (climate change mitigation efforts, biodiversity, waste, and emission reduction), and general categories (risk assessment, transparency of environmental performance, and outreach through participating in nature conservation efforts) (Rexhepi, Ramadani, & Ratten, 2018; Sepasi, Rahdari, & Rexhepi, 2018).

Sustainability entrepreneurship and green entrepreneurship are topics in which success depends mainly on the entrepreneur who is the founder of the organization. Small organizations are usually faced with difficulties, thus in many cases, they are more focused on gaining more economic benefits. Shepherd, Patzelt, and Baron (2013) in their study of 83 entrepreneurs, found that even though most of the entrepreneurs had positive attitudes toward the environmental impact and harming the environment, many times they left aside these values to pursue an opportunity that, however, they knew it will have caused harm to the natural environment (Shepherd et al., 2013). However, this and much other research provide data for many benefits that organizations are gaining from their orientations toward green entrepreneurship (Mohsen, Ramadani, & Dana, 2020).

The structure of this chapter is as follows. The first section is summarized the relevant literature review related to green entrepreneurship. Section 2 elaborates on the sample and data used for the empirical analysis, that is, BEEPS 2019 consisting of 377 companies in the Republic of Albania. It then continues with the methodology and the empirical estimations using Ordinary Least Square (OLS) technique, following by the interpretation of the results. The chapter ends with a conclusion, recommendation, and limitation of the research.

2. Literature Review

2.1. Green Entrepreneurship: An Overview

The increased environmental challenges in the world led organizations to increase their sustainability business activities. "Going green" is becoming a very important environmental issue in more and more contemporary business practices worldwide (Weng, Chen, & Chen, 2015). Resource limitations, consumer preferences, societal pressures, internal pressure, and regulatory policies have pushed organizations into a much more balanced approach to economic growth and environmental sustainability (Tang, Walsh, Lerner, Fitza, & Li, 2018). Weng et al. (2015) found that pressure from competitors, the government, and employees had significant and positive effects on green innovation practices. Some sectors show a much more need for more rapid change and are more under public pressure. In the automotive industry, for example, the pressure is much higher because of a more environmental impact compared to other sectors (Albort-Morant, Leal-Millán, & Cepeda-Carrión, 2016).

This influenced the growth of public concern and stakeholders about the natural environment and the transformation of the competitive landscape, by influencing organizations to adopt more green innovation strategies (Wang, 2019). Green entrepreneurship has been one of the new concepts used as a new strategic orientation of organizations in this context. Green entrepreneurship is a relatively new concept, but it has been one of the most researched areas in the past two decades, from different perspectives. Green entrepreneurship has been related to other terms such as green innovation, eco-innovation, eco-entrepreneurship, environmental entrepreneurship, etc.

Green entrepreneurship deals with an environmental problem or needs through the realization of entrepreneurial ideas including risk, which has a net positive effect on the environment, but at the same time secures financial sustainability for organizations (Koester, 2001). It aims to offer products and services which secure financial gain without harming the environment and does not have a negative effect on the society. This effect can result from (Mohsen et al., 2020):

- Providing products or services, the consumption of which leads to a change in consumer behavior, reducing the negative effect on the environment.
- Balancing the ecological and economic goals of the company.
- Introducing innovative ecological solutions to problems related to the production and consumption of products and services.
- Identification of business models that, when implemented, can lead to sustainable economic development.
- Identification of new opportunities in the market which are related to the demand and the new way of life of the society.

Green entrepreneurship is mainly related to green innovation or eco-innovation which mainly deals with the environmental issues related to energy saving, pollution prevention, waste recycling, and eco-design (Bocken et al., 2014). It is also related to green products and green processes that creates and modifies existing product and new products and services in order to reduce the negative impact on the environment (Chen, Lai, & Wen, 2006). Green innovation and therefore green entrepreneurship is very closely dependent on the level of knowledge, expertise, and commitment of organizational members to delivering new values (Mohsen et al., 2020).

2.2. Green Entrepreneurship and Performance

Current research relating to green entrepreneurship and related terminology is deficient on whether the motivation for firms to adopt and implement green processes and offer green products to the markets is internally driven or if this is as a result of stakeholder pressure (Singh, Giudice, Jabbour, Latan, & Sohal, 2022). Thus, organizations need more research related to this topic in order to increase the use of green entrepreneurship and the related topic. In the study, Chen et al. (2006) found that the performances of green entrepreneurship, including green product innovation and green process innovation were positively correlated to corporate competitive advantage. Much other research offers similar results, the use of green entrepreneurship including green innovation increases the overall firm performance. This includes the offer of a new form of green supply chain management, new product and service development, new production processes, increase resource productivity, and enables firms to more sustainable competitive advantage (de Burgos-Jiménez et al., 2013; Singh et al., 2022). Therefore, green entrepreneurship and related topic contribute offer for the more significant benefits to the environmental performance and suggest that processes and product innovations significantly enhance a firm's market and financial performance (Chiou, Chan, Lettice, & Chung, 2011; Hsu, Quang-Thanh, Chien, Li, & Mohsin, 2021; Singh et al., 2022; Tseng, Wang, Chiu, Geng, & Lin, 2013).

However, there is other research that points to different results than those previously presented, several kinds of research have found mixed findings. There is still some un-clarity on the relationship between firm performance, and environmental orientation of firms, and making sure that they are not harming the environment. Some research found that there has not been an increase in financial performance with the use of green entrepreneurship and related topics, since green entrepreneurship and innovation influenced an increase in the total cost of the firms (Driessen, Dieperink, Van Laerhoven, Runhaar, & Vermeulen, 2012; Singh et al., 2022). These results are related to some other research mainly from the traditional economics perspective that green innovation is costly and that environmental management causes inefficiencies and productivity loss, which results in a negative or null impact on firm performance (Palmer, Oates, & Portney, 1995). Some research also points to the partial positive implication of green entrepreneurship and related topics. Tang et al. (2018), in their research of 188 manufacturing firms in China, found that firm performance when managers had managerial concern for the environment, firms compound the positive effect of green process innovation on firm performance – but not product innovation.

2.3. Challenges Facing Green Entrepreneurship

From all presented above, it is obvious that the use of green entrepreneurship, green innovation, and related topics depends on internal forces and the external factors such are governmental regulations, consumers, environmental constraints, etc. Environmental regulations are a collection of policies or initiatives enacted by the government to protect the environment (Hsu et al., 2021), that might have a crucial impact on the success of green entrepreneurship and related topics. The more the pressure from both sides the results of the green entrepreneurship will be higher. With the rise of the acknowledgment and the significance shown by firms for environmental management have made it an integral part of their corporate objectives, practices, and strategies, as a result of the influence of consumer concerns and governmental environmental regulations. In the literature review, we saw different results from the implementation of green entrepreneurship and related topic. This could be for many reasons, different environmental strategies or practices could result in different results (Tseng et al., 2013). Findings also indicate that organizations can improve their capacity for more use of green innovations and have a more significant positive impact by focusing on three predictors of green business advantage: acquisition, assimilation, and transformation (Gluch, Gustafsson, & Thuvander, 2009). The results also depend on the management views and employee pressure, green HRM indirectly through green innovation also has a significant impact on a firm's environmental performance (Singh, Giudice, Chierici, & Graziano, 2020).

3. Methodology

This section presents the source of data that are employed for the empirical analysis of this chapter (Abazi-Alili, Ramadani, & Hughes, 2023; Wooldridge, 2020). Business Environment Enterprise Performance Surveys (BEEPS), a joint project of the European Bank for Reconstruction and Development (EBRD) and the World Bank Group (World Bank), gathers information from firms in transition countries on the impact of various aspects of their environment on their performance. BEEPS firm-level data of 2019 is used in this chapter, which consists of 377 companies in the Republic of Albania and questions that allow us to specify the variables which are used in the theoretical framework. Specifically, this round contains questions on (i) strategic objectives mentioning environmental or climate change issues; (ii) having a manager responsible for environmental or climate issues; and (iii) monitoring its energy consumption and others.

Table 1 gives a description of the variables employed in the model.

In this part are presented the variables and their specification according to the questionnaire. Table 2 provides the description of the variables employed in the model, for both: (i) continuous and (ii) dichotomous variables.

This chapter is applied the OLS estimator for the empirical investigation of the relationship between green entrepreneurship and productivity. The general model is presented below:

$$\begin{aligned}\log(productivity) = \beta_0 + \beta_1 Innovact + \beta_2 green\_ent + \beta_3 size + \\ \beta_4 size\_sq + \beta_5 foreign + \beta_6 monitorenergy + \\ \beta_7 Direct\_export + \beta_8\ Certification + \\ \beta_9 ISIC\_prodcode + u_i\end{aligned} \tag{1}$$

Table 1 Description of the Variables.

Variable Name	Variable Definition	BEEPS Question
Productivity	*Sales/labor*	
green_ent	*Green entrepreneurship*	*Dummy variable = 1 if new product/new process=1 and customers require certifications or adherence to some environmental standards?*
Size	*Number of employees*	*No. of permanent, full-time employees of this firm at the end of last fiscal year*
Direct exports	*Percentage of establishment direct exports*	*What percentage of the establishment's sales were: Direct exports?*
Foreign ownership		*What percentage of this firm does the foreign owner(s) own?*
Innov_act		*Dummy variable = 1 if new product/new process=1*
Sales	*Last year's total annual sales*	*In the last fiscal year, what was this establishment's total annual sales?*
Certification		*Does the establishment have an internationally-recognized quality certification?*
monitor_energy		*Over the last 3 years, did this establishment monitor its energy consumption?*
env_obj		*In the last FY, strategic objectives mention environmental or climate change issues*
ISIC_prodcode		*Main product/service ISIC (Rev. 3.1) code*

Dependent variable: The dependent variable in the model is the performance variable measured as labor productivity. The values are logarithmic.

Independent variable: The independent variable employed is firm characteristics and green entrepreneurship components. The interaction term of innovation and environmental standards fulfilled by the new product presents the green entrepreneurship variable.

Table 2. Summary Statistics of the Variables.

Variables	Obs	Mean	Std. Dev.	Min	Max
		(i) Continuous variables			
Direct_export	374	22.30	38.98	0	100
Foreign	375	7.981333	26.32	0	100
Concentration	375	72.77	26.72	2	100
		(ii) Dichotomous variables			
Innov_act	377	24.40	75.60		
Green_ent	372	5.11	94.89		
Monitor_energy	372	53.23	46.77		
Certification	369	23.85	76.15		

Source: Author's own calculations based on data from BEEPS 2019 Albania.

4. Regression Results

The results of the OLS are presented in Table 3.

This study found significant coefficients for innovation activities, green entrepreneurship, foreign ownership, monitoring energy, and certification, which can be interpreted as follows:

- The coefficient of the innovation activities is positive and statistically significant. This indicates that companies that undertake innovation activities are 67% more likely to have better performance compared to non-innovating companies, and this effect is statistically significant.
- The coefficient of green entrepreneurship is positive and statistically significant. This indicates that companies that consider customer environmental standards in their innovation activities are 30.7% more likely to have better performance compared to companies that do not consider customer environmental standards in their innovation activities, and this effect is statistically significant.
- The relationship between performance and size is found to be a statistically significant and non-linear U-shaped relationship. Labor performance of firms initially falls with the size of the firm, to a turning point when it turns positive as indicated by the squared variable size.
- Companies that monitor energy are 33% more likely to perform better than those that do not, and this finding is statistically significant at a 10% level of significance.
- The coefficient of the variable direct exports is negative indicating that an increase in direct export will tend to reduce the performance of companies and this effect is found to be statistically significant at a 10% level of significance.
- The variable indicating the certification of the companies is positive and statistically significant. This indicates that companies that have certification are 71.1% more likely to have better performance compared to companies that do not have certification, and this effect is statistically significant at a 1% level of significance.

Table 3. The OLS Productivity Model.

Method	**OLS**	
	Dependent variable: LNLP	
Independent variables	**Coeff.**	**St. Err.**
Innov_act	0.670***	(0.250)
green_ent	0.307*	(0.293)
size	−0.0161***	(0.00325)
size_sq	1.08e−05***	(3.13e−06)
foreign	0.00861**	(0.00397)
monitor_energy	0.333*	(0.195)
Direct_export	−0.00571*	(0.00323)
Certification	0.711***	(0.236)
ISIC_prodcode	0.000112	(7.44e-05)
Constant	15.28***	(0.394)
Observations	331	
R-squared	0.211	

Notes: Robust standard errors in parentheses.

*** $p < 0.01$, **$p < 0.05$, and *$p < 0.1$.

5. Conclusions

Taking into consideration that this is a new field of investigation, there is a lot of room for recommendations. For the purpose of this study, we will highlight only recommendations based on the empirical investigation. The first key enablers for the sustainability transition are set to be, education, science, technology, research, and innovation, as prerequisites for achieving the SDGs and a sustainable economy, creating a sustainability culture and mindset, and ensuring that the transition will lead to an increase in our wellbeing. Empirical investigation showed that establishments that consist of elements of the green component have better productivity. Furthermore, studies show that green entrepreneurship contributes to job creation, fostering growth, energy efficiency, etc. (Corbett & Montgomery, 2017).

Some recommendations can be outlined as follows:

- Making this contribution more visible and more recognized both in the field of higher education itself and also at policy levels.
- Targeting funds for renewable resources, investments, etc.
- Prepare the graduates with the necessary knowledge to operate under the legal aspect and regulations required by the business sector in the European Union.
- More interinstitutional collaboration and engagement including governments, non-governmental organizations, and businesses.

Further research directions should be focused on applying measures in the field to enable data creation as the lack of data was the main limitation of this research.

References

Abazi-Alili, H., Ramadani, V., & Hughes, M. (2023). Green entrepreneurship and productivity: Firm-level evidence from the BEEPS Survey in the Republic of North Macedonia. In *Proceedings dedicated to Academician Alajdin Abazi on the occasion of the 80th anniversary of his birth*. Skopje: Macedonian Academy of Science and Arts.

Al-Abrrow, H., Fayez, A. S., Abdullah, H., Khaw, K. W., Alnoor, A., & Rexhepi, G. (2021). Effect of open-mindedness and humble behavior on innovation: Mediator role of learning. *International Journal of Emerging Markets*. https://doi.org/10.1108/IJOEM-08-2020-0888

Albort-Morant, G., Leal-Millán, A., & Cepeda-Carrión, G. (2016). The antecedents of green innovation performance: A model of learning and capabilities. *Journal of Business Research*, *69*(11), 4912–4917.

Bocken, N.M., Short, S.W., Rana, P., & Evans, S. (2014). A literature and practice review to develop sustainable business model archetypes. *Journal of Cleaner Production*, *65*, 42–56.

Chen, J., Hu, X., Razi, U., & Rexhepi, G. (2022). The sustainable potential of efficient air-transportation industry and green innovation in realising environmental sustainability in G7 countries. *Economic Research-Ekonomska Istraživanja*, *35*(1), 3814–3835.

Chen, Y. S., Lai, S. B., & Wen, C. T. (2006). The influence of green innovation performance on corporate advantage in Taiwan. *Journal of Business Ethics*, *67*(2), 331–339.

Chiou, T. Y., Chan, H. K., Lettice, F., & Chung, S. H. (2011). The influence of greening the suppliers and green innovation on environmental performance and competitive advantage in Taiwan. *Transportation Research Part E: Logistics and Transportation Review*, *47*(6), 822–836.

Corbett, J., & Montgomery, A. W. (2017). Environmental entrepreneurship and interorganizational arrangements: A model of social-benefit market creation. *Strategic Entrepreneurship Journal*, *11*(4), 422–440.

de Burgos-Jiménez, J., Vázquez-Brust, D., Plaza-Úbeda, J. A., & Dijkshoorn, J. (2013). Environmental protection and financial performance: An empirical analysis in Wales.. *International Journal of Operations & Production Management*, *33*(8), 981–1018.

Driessen, P. P., Dieperink, C., Van Laerhoven, F., Runhaar, H. A., & Vermeulen, W. J. (2012). Towards a conceptual framework for the study of shifts in modes of environmental governance–experiences from the Netherlands. *Environmental Policy and Governance*, *22*(3), 143–160.

Gluch, P., Gustafsson, M., & Thuvander, L. (2009). An absorptive capacity model for green innovation and performance in the construction industry. *Construction Management and Economics*, *27*(5), 451–464.

Hsu, C. C., Quang-Thanh, N., Chien, F., Li, L., & Mohsin, M. (2021). Evaluating green innovation and performance of financial development: Mediating concerns of environmental regulation. *Environmental Science and Pollution Research*, *28*(40), 57386–57397.

Koester, E. (2001). *Green entrepreneur handbook: The guide to building and growing a green and clean business*. Boca Raton: CRC Press.

Mohsen, A., Ramadani, V., & Dana, L. P. (2020). Green entrepreneurship prospects and challenges: The context of Afghanistan. In *Research Handbook on entrepreneurship in emerging economies*. London: Routledge.

Palmer, K., Oates, W. E., & Portney, P. R. (1995). Tightening environmental standards: The benefit-cost or the no-cost paradigm? *Journal of Economic Perspectives*, *9*(4), 119–132.

Porter, M. E., (2008). The five competitive forces that shape strategy. *Harvard Business Review*, *86*(1), 78.

Rahdari, A., Sheehy, B., Khan, H. Z., Braendle, U., Rexhepi, G., & Sepasi, S. (2020). Exploring global retailers' corporate social responsibility performance. *Heliyon*, *6*(8), e04644.

Ramadani, V., Agarwal, S., Caputo, A., Kumar Dixit, J., & Agrawal, V. (2022). Sustainable competencies of social entrepreneurship for sustainable development: Exploratory analysis from a developing economy. *Business Strategy and the Environment*, *31*(7), 3437–3453.

Ramadani, V., & Schneider, R. (2013). *Entrepreneurship in the Balkans: Diversity, support and prospects*. Heidelberg: Springer.

Rexhepi, G., & Berisha, B. (2017). The effects of emotional intelligence in managing changes: An entrepreneurial perspective. *World Review of Entrepreneurship, Management and Sustainable Development*, *13*(2–3), 237–251.

Rexhepi, G., Kurtishi, S., & Bexheti, G. (2013). Corporate social responsibility (CSR) and innovation: The drivers of business growth? *Procedia-Social and Behavioural Sciences*, *75*(2), 532–541.

Rexhepi, G., Ramadani, V., & Ratten, V. (2018). TQM techniques as an innovative approach in sport organisations management: Toward a conceptual framework. *International Journal of Business and Globalisation*, *20*(1), 18–30.

Sepasi, S., Rahdari, A., & Rexhepi, G. (2018). Developing a sustainability reporting assessment tool for higher education institutions: The University of California. *Sustainable Development*, *26*(6), 672–682.

Sepasi, S., Rexhepi, G., & Rahdari, A. (2021). The changing prospects of corporate social responsibility in the decade of action: Do personal values matter? *Corporate Social Responsibility and Environmental Management*, *28*(1), 138–152.

Shepherd, D., Patzelt, H., & Baron, R. (2013). 'I Care about nature, but…': Disengaging values in assessing opportunities that cause harm. *Academy of Management Journal*, *56*(5), 1251–1273.

Singh, S. K., Giudice, M. D., Chierici, R., & Graziano, D. (2020). Green innovation and environmental performance: The role of green transformational leadership and green human resource management. *Technological Forecasting and Social Change*, *150*(1), 119–762.

Singh, S. K., Giudice, M. D., Jabbour, C. J. C., Latan, H., & Sohal, A. S. (2022). Stakeholder pressure, green innovation, and performance in small and medium-sized enterprises: The role of green dynamic capabilities. *Business Strategy and the Environment*, *31*(1), 500–514.

Suki, N. M., Suki, N. M., Sharif, A., Afshan, S., & Rexhepi, G. (2022). Importance of green innovation for business sustainability: Identifying the key role of green intellectual capital and green SCM. *Business Strategy and the Environment*.

Tang, M., Walsh, G., Lerner, D., Fitza, M. A., & Li, Q. (2018). Green innovation, managerial concern and firm performance: An empirical study. *Business Strategy and the Environment*, *27*(1), 39–51.

Tseng, M. L., Wang, R., Chiu, A. S., Geng, Y., & Lin, Y. H. (2013). Improving performance of green innovation practices under uncertainty. *Journal of Cleaner Production*, *40*(1), 71–82.

Wang, C. H. (2019). How organizational green culture influences green performance and competitive advantage: The mediating role of green innovation. *Journal of Manufacturing Technology Management*, *30*(4), 666–683.

Weng, H. H., Chen, J. S., & Chen, P. C. (2015). Effects of green innovation on environmental and corporate performance: A stakeholder perspective. *Sustainability*, *7*(5), 4997–5026.

Wooldridge, J. M. (2020). *Introductory econometrics: A modern approach*. Mason, OH: South-Western Cengage Learning.

Chapter 5

Entrepreneurship Ecosystem in Bosnia and Herzegovina: Perspectives and Challenges

Ramo Palalić, Ognjen Riđić, Tomislav Jukić, Abdul Wahab Aidoo, Goran Riđić and Mohammad Rezaur Razzak

Abstract

Similar to other countries of former Yugoslavia, Bosnia and Herzegovina (BiH) is still regarded to be a transitional economy, both from the social, political, and economic perspectives. In this regard, it is important to note that political agendas and economic strategies are still not satisfactory for the development of entrepreneurial activities. There are serious deficiency issues in regard to entrepreneurship ecosystem in BiH. This chapter describes 10 elements of the entrepreneurial ecosystem (EES) and their implications on the EES outlook of BiH.

Keywords: Entrepreneurial ecosystem; entrepreneurship; government; innovations; challenges; Bosnia and Herzegovina

1. Introduction

Modern communication and information technology caused the appearance of new rules in terms of market and industry games. Hence, unlike before, today all parts of the world are potential market opportunities and potential sources of competition. It used to be that one region is a safe heaven and very much protected from outside players, which secured their sustainable competitive advantage. Nowadays, it has substantially changed. Companies from the Far East can compete with Western competitors easily, and without hesitation, they can take over each other in their mutual competition.

Entrepreneurship Development in the Balkans: Perspective from Diverse Contexts, 81–93

Published under exclusive licence by Emerald Publishing Limited
doi:10.1108/978-1-83753-454-820231005

What has been changed so that now competitors can be from any part of the world in one place?! Well, it should first be noted that the game has always been set up according to an internal "system" that recently, as modern communication and information technology has been deployed, has changed its power due to globalization. It was the "stick" and "carrot" at the same time, shaping businesses' behavior. Such a system that ruled the way of gameplay in a specific region is known as the entrepreneurship ecosystem. Each country has its own entrepreneurship ecosystem setting while trying to accommodate the free flow of people, goods, and capital.

Second, chasing the best option to reduce the cost of doing business and finding a talented, skilled, knowledgeable, and educated but cheap labor force, it opened the door for globalization that goes beyond the local rules of the entrepreneurship ecosystem.

And third, today's local entrepreneurship ecosystem should be in line with globalization's rules otherwise local businesses will not have a chance to get and sustain their competitive advantage. Thus, the local entrepreneurship ecosystem becomes part of the overall global entrepreneurship system that will allow local businesses to exploit this opportunity to play fairly in the local as well as in the global markets. Yet, the national economy's performance will depend on how much is open to foreign direct investment (FDI), and how many and how strong local businesses exit locally, which contribute to the overall national economy.

Considering the content above, this section portrays a general view of the entrepreneurship ecosystem and its importance.

1.1. Introduction to the EES

The term EES appeared in the 1980s as an alternative to the current "individualistic" approach of entrepreneurship, to give a wider span of perspective constituted of social, cultural, and economic forces, which are crucial in the overall entrepreneurship process (Stam & Spiegel, 2016). Moreover, Stam and Spiegel (2016) in their discussion paper analyzed the term EES. They observed that "entrepreneurial has root in defining the process in which firms try to achieve competitive advantage in terms of profitability and scalability." These types of firms are pursuing high growth like fast-growing small and medium enterprises (gazelles) (Palalic & Durakovic, 2018), whose performance is based on innovative products wanted in the market. However, the term of ecosystem is an application of the biological approach of the bio-ecosystem, which represents a symbiotic life in which all creatures live together in harmony. Furthermore, following a biological perspective of the ecosystem by Tansley (1935) and a more economical perspective described by Moore (1993), researcher Dana formulated a definition, whereby "the entrepreneurial ecosystem represents a setup of actors in the form of individuals, groups, private and public institutions, and organizations." Similarly, Palalić, Knezović, and Dana (2020) defined the EES broadly, as

> a setup of actors like individuals, groups, private and public institutions, and organizations, integrated into legal and cultural

> outlook, mutually interconnected and whose role influences entrepreneurial activity and gives its positive or negative output in one country. (p. 25)

All of them are integrated into legal and cultural outlooks. They are mutually interconnected. Finally, their role influences the entrepreneurial activity and provides the positive or negative output in any given country or geographical territory. As such, it represents the symbiotic type of life (Dana, 2001).

In the last two decades of discussion on the entrepreneurship ecosystem brought a new horizon to be observed. This implies that entrepreneurs if they want to be successful, factors that surround them should be favorable in a broader perspective. In other words, the entrepreneurship process will not depend on entrepreneurs' capabilities and core competencies, but on other factors that influence the whole entrepreneurial process of creating and delivering innovative products and services. Additionally, the degree of harmony created by the surroundings will affect in either way the whole entrepreneurship process. Therefore, it is important to have a favorable EES in the market that would easier help entrepreneurship development to flourish.

Discussion on this matter goes on and there is no perfect EES that can accommodate all challenges imposed by globalization effects, rather it is subject to national or regional settings.

In the case of BiH, it is important that the country moves on in regard to a favorable EES, which will suit the local entrepreneurial firms as well as foreign investors. The case of women's EES was discussed recently by Palalic, Knezović, et al. (2020). According to all players in the current EES in BiH, it can be observed that is not developed yet to attract foreign investors and to motivate local entrepreneurs to contribute to the overall social and economic development of the country.

1.2. Importance of Entrepreneurship Ecosystem

As previously mentioned, the importance of the EES is crucial in developing entrepreneurial activities, and society as a whole. Being part of the global market, it is necessary that the local EES paves the way for a solid development of entrepreneurship. If the EES is favorable, it will be an important variable in the function of socioeconomic development.

How to balance between EES pillars is a matter of the system that already exists. As the EES is highly complexed (Stephens, McLaughlin, Ryan, Catena, & Bonner, 2022), it is important to note that each country's EES is subject to its own pillars and the balance among those pillars. Each of the ecosystem pillars should be thoroughly studied in order to identify "outliers" which do not benefit the favorable business surroundings. Or, they can be enhanced in order to comply with the harmony that will produce a great outcome in the local business environment. Nonetheless, the EES is truly important for the development of national economies which will produce a better life for the society.

In the case of BiH, no need to mention how much the ESS is important because BiH is going through a political and economic transition for the last three decades. Yet, recent migration is constantly evaporating a pool of talents (individuals) as one of the pillars of the EES, which causes brain drain (Palalić, Duraković, Ramadani, & Ferreira, 2021, Turulja et al., 2020). Consequently, it erodes and weakens the current EES. Hence, the voice of should be raised to the current political and economic establishment of BiH, to understand the importance of the favorable EES.

The next section discusses an overview of entrepreneurship in BiH.

2. Overview of Entrepreneurship in BiH

2.1. Entrepreneurial Activities in BiH

As the other countries of former Yugoslavia, BiH is still regarded to be a transitional economy, both from the social, political, and economic perspectives. In this regard, it is important to note that political agendas and economic strategies are still not satisfactory for the development of entrepreneurial activities. There are serious deficiency issues in regard to the entrepreneurship ecosystem in BiH. However, the early stages of research could be traced back to researchers Dana (1999), Dana and Dana (2003), and Ramadani and Dana (2013). These pioneering researchers discussed the first steps of entrepreneurial development in this country. In them, small businesses were created by entrepreneurial-spirited individuals who never desired governmental assistance. There is also a disparity in entrepreneurial activities between men and women. Due to cultural, social, economic, and political issues, the women were not sufficiently involved in the process of entrepreneurial creation following the end of the Bosnian war in 1995. During that period majority of women were tackling home-related issues. In this context, it is important to mention some extraordinary women who initiated small business entrepreneurial activities in addition to trading agricultural products at local marketplaces (Bičo, Aydin, Smajić, & Knezović, 2022; Dabić, Vlajčić, & Novak, 2016; Tekin, Ramadani, & Dana, 2021).

Dana (2010) and Palalić, Dana, and Ramadani (2018a) accurately described entrepreneurship, as a private sector activity, which was poorly recognized and promoted by the socialist state of Yugoslavia, which was in existence from 1945 to 1992. It is critical to note that entrepreneurship was generally regarded as an individualistic, materialistic, and capitalistic activity. As such it needed to be discouraged and closely controlled and monitored by the one-party existing communist government. According to Palalić et al. (2018b), individual entrepreneurship was severely restricted in this sense an individual entrepreneur was allowed to employ a maximum of three employees in the period from 1945 to 1965. This number increased to five employees in the period stemming from 1965 to 1983. Finally, an individual entrepreneur was allowed to employ up to 10 employees in the period from 1983 to still countries dissolution in 1992. To a large extent, the entrepreneurial activities in the former Socialist Federative Republic of Yugoslavia (SFRJ) and the Socialist Republic of BiH, as one of its six composing republics, were found in blacksmith hardware producing businesses in addition to hospitality, food, souvenir, and crafts shops (Palalic, Knezović, et al., 2020; Ramadani et al., 2020).

There are numerous reasons as to why particular individuals become entrepreneurs. Some reasons are connected to personality traits. For example, self-confident, curious, ambitious, communicative, innovative, and risk-taking individuals predominantly take necessary actions to start working for themselves instead of working for others. This unique kind of individual tends to envision an opportunity and utilize it to their advantage. Another view filtered from the extensive literature review states that entrepreneurship is not connected to personality traits and that is connected to a national culture. Dominantly individualistic cultures, like the one in the United States of America, promote entrepreneurial behavior, while the others more collectivistic do not to a large extent (Palalić, Duraković, Branković, & Riđić, 2016). Furthermore, cultures which are ranked on uncertainty avoidance encourage entrepreneurial activities. The situation for new entrepreneurs has improved to a certain extent following the end of the Bosnian War in 1995. Capitalist market economy and political pluralization have replaced the one-party socialist society and system which was in existence for 45 years. Unfortunately, the entrepreneurs in the post-war period in BiH are still suffering from several issues, which are detrimental to their entrepreneurial activities. These issues stem from non-existent or poor-quality entrepreneurial education, in addition to high taxation and credit-extending issues. On a positive note, the number of entrepreneurial activities is moderately rising in BiH, and the composition of new entrepreneurs is being enriched with college and university students and women of all ages. The entrepreneurial orientation is composed of several dimensions which make business more competitive. Furthermore, entrepreneurial orientation is self-sustainability in the long run. In this context, it is important to remember that entrepreneurial orientation is composed of three main dimensions, which are defined as proactiveness, innovativeness, and risk-taking. Innovativeness represents the main foundation of the entrepreneurial activity. As such it brings the flexibility of mindset. Proactiveness enables the first mover ability in the highly competitive market and this type of productivity increases a positive effect on the performance of the businesses. Finally, the ability to take risks is the third critical element of the entrepreneurial orientation. A complete and educated entrepreneur is taught to be knowledgeable about the three composing elements of the entrepreneurial orientation in order to be better prepared for entrepreneurial challenges in the future (Petković, Jäger, & Sašić, 2016).

2.2. Comparison of Entrepreneurship Development with Balkan Countries

The extensive review of literature seeking to compare the entrepreneurial development between BiH and surrounding Balkan countries must mention a very important and rather rare publication titled "Entrepreneurship in the Balkans: diversity, support and prospects," co-edited by Ramadani and Schneider (2013).

Their research postulates death of free enterprise system is not predominantly the result of the transfer of ownership of existing firms. In contrast to that entrepreneurs in BiH are rebuilding the economy by identifying niches, flexible and dynamic business structures. Interviewed entrepreneurs stated that the government appears to be less active comparing to other countries in the promotion of entrepreneurship. In this regard, the majority of entrepreneurial promotion is organized by and paid for by external/non-governmental sources. In that spirit, in 2002, United Nations Development Program assisted the youth enterprise program in the Brčko district. This program focuses when encouraging entrepreneurial activities among young people between 18 years and 30 years. This program provides three critical areas for the future entrepreneurial activities of young entrepreneurs, such as training, business mentoring and advisory services, and micro-credit financing. The training and business advisory services were provided free of charge while mentoring and financing activities operated on a cost-recovery basis.

In comparison to BiH, the government's attitude was shaped in Albania during the 1999 Kosovo crisis. At that time, Albania was utilized by the North Atlantic Treaty Organization as a supply base. Albanian government developed and launched a growth-oriented program of reform, which was based on free market economic principles, law, and order. This reform was assisted by utilizing cooperation with the International Monetary Fund. Albania's increasing disposable incomes have boosted consumer demand (Ramadani & Schneider, 2013).

3. Entrepreneurship Ecosystem in BiH

The EES represents an important concept in order to understand the overall context of entrepreneurship at the organizational macro-level. It is composed of a variety of interdependent factors. These factors, at the same time, promote and constrain the entire entrepreneurial activity inside a defined geographical territory. Even though the EES is gaining in popularity, it still remains loosely defined and assessed. Entrepreneurial scholars are being increasingly worried regarding the quality and quantity of entrepreneurial activity. Thus, there is a need to utilize the EES as a complex system of interrelated elements, which are conducive to enabling productive entrepreneurship. The first part of the term signifies that something is being "entrepreneurial" when it is one process thereby there are opportunities to produce new goods and services. On the other hand, the second part signifies the term "ecosystem," which is used in the science of biology, is an ecological system being composed in the form of a biotic community, its physical environment and a variety of possible interactions among/between "complex living and nonliving elements" (Stam & van de Ven, 2019). Fig. 1 depicts the key elements of the EES model. These are (a) *formal institutions*, which make rules of the game in the society (indicated by corruption, rule of law, government effectiveness and voice and accountability), (b) *entrepreneurship culture* implies how much is the entrepreneurship is valued in the region (indicated by a number of new firms registered per 1,000 inhabitants), (c) *physical infrastructure* represents the physical infrastructure and position in the region (indicated by accessibility via road, accessibility via railroad, accessibility via airports (indicated by a number of passenger flights within 90 minutes drive), (d) *demand* explains the potential in market demand (measured by purchasing power per capita, regional product, total human population), (e) *networks* describes connectedness of businesses for new value creation (measured by percentage of firms in the business population that collaborate for innovation), (f) *leadership* implies guidance for and direction of collective action (measured by prevalence of innovation project leaders per 1,000 businesses), (g) *talents* represents talented individuals with high level of human capital (indicated by percentage of higher-educated in the adult population), (h) *finance* describes accessibility and supply of loans to new firms (percentage of SMEs that have applied for bank loans and also received this.), (i) new *knowledge* implies how much is investing in new knowledge (percentage of gross domestic product invested in R&D (by public and private organizations), and (j) *intermediate services* describes the supply and accessibility of intermediate business services (percentage of business service firms in the business population) (Stam & van de Ven, 2019, p. 814). The recent study by Palalić Knezović, et al. (2020) tackled the EES that impacts women's entrepreneurial activities in BiH. The model was examined through the prism EES developed by Stam (2018) and Stam and van de Ven (2019). Their study encompassed almost all elements shown in Fig. 1.

In the context of the EES in BiH, it is important to note that it is constantly evolving from the humbling beginnings during the socialist one-party system transferring into the capitalistic and multi-party system after the last war in the period 1992–1995. Léo-Paul Dana, as an academic authority in this area, defined former Yugoslavia as a nationalized and state-owned economy where entrepreneurs were under a strict taxation regimen (Dana, 2010). Formally this form of the privately owned company did exist. However, it was highly constrained by the regulatory mechanism of the socialist and one-party system, which was supposed to promote all-encompassing equality, even though this proved to be highly idealistic and impossible to reach. The overall philosophy toward such an entrepreneurial form of business was predominantly negative. As such, it was regarded as an extension of the individualistic, self-centered, non-social, and greedy approach with the ruling party barely tolerated and highly limited by the number of employees allowed to be employed by any individual entrepreneur spanning from three to a maximum of ten employees – all the way up to the breakup of the socialist block in Eastern Europe following the fall of the Berlin Wall in 1989 (Knezović, Riđić, & Chambas, 2020).

The post-war period following 1995 was usually described as the process of physical, economic, and social reconstruction. The entrepreneurial trend started to take hold together with the need for qualified, competent and workforce. There was a big increase in willingness to start a new business. Legally self-employed entrepreneurs could either be registered as sole proprietors or were even not registered at all. Discussion on the EES in BiH could not be complete without *yeah noesis* of various sources of obstacles entrepreneurs face to start and operate the business. These obstacles range from insufficient *knowledge* to limited financing access. All of these are reflected in the inability to make a business plan, the inability to productively run business administration, issues with incompetent staff, non-favorable credit conditions, and lack of knowledge of the regulatory framework. In that spirit, Doing Business Report (2019) ranks BiH 60th out of 190 countries measuring the weight and ease of how to obtain loans. Support for entrepreneurial activities comes from the multitude of sources, in the form

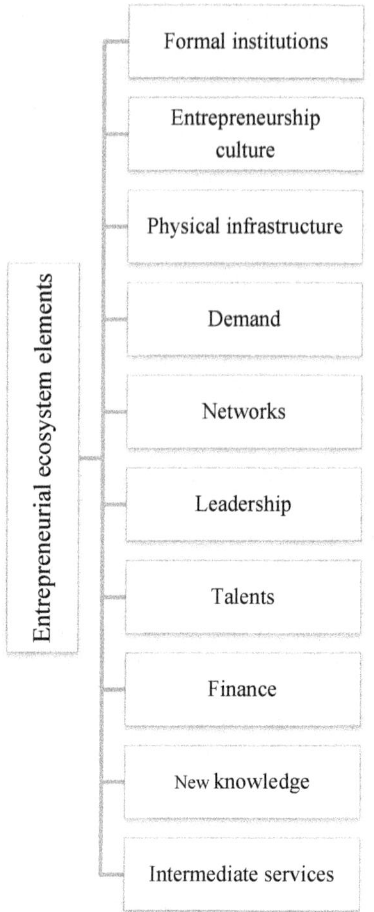

Fig. 1. Composing Elements of the EES. *Source*: Based on Stam and van de Ven (2019, p. 814).

of governmental and non-governmental domestic and foreign institutions and donors. At the state level, policy for entrepreneurial activities of small and medium enterprises is under the umbrella responsibility of the sector for economic development and entrepreneurship being part of the Ministry of foreign trade and economic relations. At the entity level, for example, in the federation entity of BiH, there is the Ministry of Development, Entrepreneurship, and Crafts. This ministry is responsible to develop the action plan tasks to promote the development of entrepreneurship. In the entity Republic of Srpska (RS), there is the corresponding Ministry of Industry, Energy, and Mining which produced the strategy for the development of entrepreneurship with the support of German Technical Assistance (GIZ). There is also Chambers of Commerce at the entity, cantonal, and municipal levels which offer assistance in starting a new business.

In addition to these, there are numerous international donors which are extending support to BiH in addition to NGOs. The entrepreneurship centers have been opened at the state Faculty of Economics in Sarajevo, Tuzla, and Banja Luka.

Currently, as far as *physical infrastructure* is concerned, this is the basic infrastructure that every country needs, including roads, railroads quantity of passenger flights within a 90-minute drive, etc. The Federation of BiH entity developed the 2017–2020 strategy to build certain routes into fast roads and motorways. The next ecosystem element is demand. *Demand* signifies the potential market demand, which is composed of three distinctive components one purchasing power per capita, regional product, and total human population. The purchasing power per capita of 11,500 US dollars from the year 2018 is relatively low in comparison to developed countries. Furthermore, the regional product is not comparable with the aggregate human population. Imports outweigh exports by almost 50% according to State Agency for Statistics in 2019. There is a long way to start leveling *innovative leadership* in BiH. There is the detrimental summary effect of numerous, often contradicting laws and regulations, which restrict good initiatives in the areas of innovation and entrepreneurship. As far as *talent* is concerned, there is a positive development that BiH is developing above-average talents, which to a large extent choose to migrate to Western Europe (Palalić et al., 2021) or even overseas in a search of a better job, quality of life and opportunities. In this regard, the country's talent is diminishing and the red alarm has been plaguing BiH for more than two decades. As far as *finance* is concerned potential entrepreneurs have difficulties in obtaining the necessary capital. This is especially true when it comes to receiving loans from banks. There is a positive development that shows the private business growth exceeding 20% from the year 2001. In conclusion, the *intermediate service* to existing entrepreneurial businesses has received a relatively acceptable grade. The service sector is growing rapidly, and this especially includes tourism all those situations are far from desirable. There is a room for immediate and long-term improvement.

In regard to *formal institutions* that create the rules for the market game, it can be observed that improvements are fewer because BiH is still in 184th place in the ranking for starting a new business out of 190 countries (Doing Business Report, 2019). In terms of procedures to start a new business, time, cost, and capital is still below average, which indicates a red alarm for the Bosnian government to work on. *Networks* exist but in line with innovative businesses available for collaboration. This element will depend on innovative businesses available in the country and once it is improved the network will follow up in improvement. Being under the system in which entrepreneurship was not supported by the government for five decades (Palalić et al., 2018b), it is no surprise that entrepreneurial culture in this region is not popular and yet a normal way of life among residents. Objectively, an entrepreneurial mindset exists (Palalić, Bičo, Ramadani, & Dana, 2020; Palalić, Branković, & Bičo, 2020), however, new talents (educated youth) are migrating to new places in Western Europe (Palalić et al., 2021) and settling where they expect to have better sunsets and sunrises, unfortunately. Nevertheless, this region of BiH has entrepreneurial potential, because it is the country of talents and an educated workforce that can help in developing the society.

4. Concluding Remarks

4.1. BiH at a Glance

Doing Business Report (2019) reported that the population of BiH is 3,323,929 million, which is subject to accuracy since there is a huge migration trend from the country. According to a recent report by Trading Economics (2023), the GDP growth rate is 1.4 in the first quarter of 2023, which is less than 0.2 from the same period of the previous year. The GDP growth annual rate in the first quarter of 2023 is 2.6 which has dropped by 3.2 in comparison to the same period in 2022. However, the full-year GDP growth year in 2022 is 6.5, which is doubled in comparison to the previous year (2021). GDP per capita is $5862 recorded in the first quarter of 2023, which is higher than the same period of 2022. The unemployment rate is more less the same in the last two years (31.12%). Wages in overall are growing, while wages in manufacturing are less than the average wage in BiH. Annual wage growth is 14.44%, however, this growth is less than the annual inflation rate (14.8%). This spark of the inflation rate is due to global crises recently in the European Peninsula. Export is less than import which is reflected in the overall country's deficit. The corruption index is quite high (34), which puts BiH in 110th place of the corruption rank.

4.2. The Current EES in BiH

Based on the above statistics, it can be concluded that BiH has a lot to work to improve the current state of the EES. All aspects are critical and important to improve. We believe if the country improves at least one of the elements so the EES, like formal institutions, rapid development in entrepreneurship will be noticed. If we rely on premise that entrepreneurship is an "engine of national economy" (Fayolle, 2007), then improvement in this EES will help other elements to be improved. As discussed in earlier sections, some of them are recording improvements, but still far less than the regional or global average.

4.3. The Future

Many, major obstacles plague the socioeconomic growth of BiH. Yet everything tied to it makes the situation worse. For instance, the overall socioeconomic development is difficult and slow due to the concurrent political, economic, and demographic challenges.

Challenge 1–EU membership. BiH struggled to join the EU but failed to address the post-war problems that prevented it from moving forward and setting standards that would have accelerated and enhanced the EU membership process. All other tenets upon which this administration is based are slowed down by this problem, and no substantial advancements were seen. Although the EU proposed BiH receive "EU Candidate Status" at the end of 2022, not much has happened since then. The elections in October 2022 are one of the significant barriers preventing BiH from becoming an EU candidate. While other EU membership requirements are put on hold, establishing a new government has been and continues to be difficult. Establishing a government that will wisely strive toward EU membership by bringing the country's present socioeconomic conditions up to EU norms will help BiH advance. This strategy will help to address two issues – the nation's declining population (demographics) and the development of a favorable business environment (EES).

Challenge 2–Demographics. The population of BiH is rapidly changing. There were 3.4 million Bosnians in the last census in 2013. However, this number is quickly shrinking. Some of the factors that led to this decline include migration over the previous 10 years, COVID-19, and additional migration in the wake of the pandemic. Being a small nation, BiH's demographic composition is crucial to its development. As previously mentioned, since they do not see a promising future in this country, young individuals and entire families are moving from BiH to countries in Western Europe without hesitation. Demographics will probably improve if the first concern is substantially addressed. The present and future governments must also "populate" the nation by offering significant financial and other incentives to families (couples with three children or more) to keep them in the country. Even "yesterday" was a warning sign that demanded action right away. Government should create a stable and family-friendly atmosphere to discourage individuals from moving to other nations. Thus, demographics will be positively altered by both strategies (EU membership and populating the country).

Challenge 3–EES–Status Quo (economic outlook). The current state of BiH's EES is only impacted by the country's tumultuous political environment, which slows down all beneficial initiatives started in 1995, including the EES. Formal institutions are a good place to start when improving the EES because they are currently underdeveloped due to unfavorable political conditions in the nation. Governmental bodies must understand that it is essential to stop the demographic movement of Bosnians to other nations. Bosnians will continue to migrate as long as those institutions fail to function or hinder the creation of a suitable economic climate. For sure, people would not need to leave the country if entrepreneurial components are properly put up. Instead, they will be content to participate in society's growth and progress.

The *final question* is – which problem should be overcome first? We advise focusing initially on the EES. Because it does not discriminate against anyone based on their gender, nationality, religion, or other characteristics. Instead, it opens the door to a "symbiotic" life in which everyone will be happy together forever. This can be done by any government, at State, Federal, Cantonal, or Municipal level, governed by any political party.

References

Bičo, A., Aydin, Š., Smajić, H., & Knezović, E. (2022). Entrepreneurial and intrapreneurial intentions: Analyzing the premise of distinct constructs with different determinants. *Periodicals of Engineering and Natural Sciences*, *10*(3), 5–22.

Dabić, M., Vlajčić, D., & Novak, I. (2016). Entrepreneurial management education needs in the Republic of Croatia, Poland and the United Kingdom. *International Journal of Educational Management, 30*(6), 738–755.

Dana, L. P. (1999). Business and entrepreneurship in Bosnia-Herzegovina. *Journal of Business and Entrepreneurship, 11*(2), 105–110.

Dana, L. P. (2001). The education and training of entrepreneurs in Asia. *Education + Training, 43*(8–9), 405–415.

Dana, L. P. (2010). *When economies change hands: A survey of entrepreneurship in the emerging markets of Europe from the Balkans to the Baltic States*. New York, NY: Routledge.

Dana, L. P., & Dana, T. (2003). Management and enterprise development in post-communist economies. *International Journal of Management and Enterprise Development, 1*(1), 45–54.

Doing Business Report. (2019). Report. Retrieved from https://www.doingbusiness.org/content/dam/doingBusiness/media/Annual-Reports/English/DB2019-report_web-version.pdf. Accessed on February 15, 2023.

Fayolle, A. (2007). Entrepreneurship and New Value Creation the Dynamic of the Entrepreneurial Process, 1st ed., Cambridge University Press.

Knezović, E., Riđić, O., & Chambas, A. I. (2020). *Human capital and innovation: An analysis of Western Balkans*. Cham: Springer.

Moore, J. F. (1993). Predators and prey: A new ecology of competition. *Harvard Business Review, 71*(3), 75–83.

Palalić, R., Bičo, A., Ramadani, V., & Dana, L. P. (2020). Human capital and entrepreneurial intentions in Bosnia and Herzegovina. *Studies on Entrepreneurship, Structural Change and Industrial Dynamics* (pp. 117–136). Cham: Springer.

Palalić, R., Branković, A., & Bičo, A. (2020). Entrepreneurial mindset and SMEs' sustainability. In J. Leitao (Ed.), *Organizational mindset of entrepreneurship* (pp. 53–77). Cham: Springer.

Palalić, R., Dana, L. P., & Ramadani, V. (2018a). *Entrepreneurship in former Yugoslavia: Diversity, institutional constraints and prospects*. Cham: Springer.

Palalić, R., Dana, L. P., & Ramadani, V. (2018b). Entrepreneurship in former Yugoslavia: Toward the Future. In R. Palalić, L. P. Dana, & V. Ramadani (Eds.), *Entrepreneurship in former Yugoslavia: Diversity, institutional constraints, and prospects* (pp. 147–151). Cham: Springer,

Palalic, R., & Durakovic, B. (2018). Does transformational leadership matter in gazelles and mice: Evidence from Bosnia and Herzegovina? *International Journal of Entrepreneurship and Small Business, 34*(3), 289–308.

Palalić, R., Duraković, B., Branković, A. & Riđić, O. (2016). Students' entrepreneurial orientation intention, business environment and networking: Insights from Bosnia and Herzegovina. *International Journal of Foresight and Innovation Policy, 11*(4), 240–255.

Palalić, R., Duraković, B., Ramadani, V., & Ferreira, J. J. M. (2021). Human capital and youth emigration in the "new normal". *Thunderbird International Business Review, 65*(1), 49–63. doi:10.1002/tie.22250

Palalić, R., Knezović, E., Branković, A., Bičo, A. (2020). Women's Entrepreneurship in Bosnia and Herzegovina. In R. Palalić, E. Knezović & L. P. Dana (Eds.), *Women's entrepreneurship in former Yugoslavia* (pp. 11–15). Contributions to Management Science. Springer, Cham. https://doi.org/10.1007/978-3-030-45253-7_2

Palalić, R., Knezović, E., & Dana, L. P. (2020). Women entrepreneurship in Bosnia and Herzegovina. In R. Palalić, E. Knezović, & L. P. Dana (Eds.), *Women's entrepreneurship in former Yugoslavia*. Cham: Springer.

Petković, S., Jäger, C., & Sašić, B. (2016). Challenges of small and medium sized companies at early stage of development: Insights from Bosnia and Herzegovina. *Management: Journal of Contemporary Management Issues*, *21*(2), 45–76.

Ramadani, V., & Dana, L. P. (2013). The state of entrepreneurship in the Balkans: Evidence from selected countries. In V. Ramadani, & R. C. Schneider (Eds.), *Entrepreneurship in the Balkans: Diversity, support and prospects*. Berlin: Springer. https://doi.org/10.1007/978-3-642-36577-5_12 pp. 217-250

Ramadani, V., Memili, E., Palalić, R. & Chang, E. P. C. (2020). *Entrepreneurial Family Businesses*, Switzerland, AG: Springer Nature

Ramadani, V., & Schneider, R. C. (2013). *Entrepreneurship in the Balkans: Diversity, support and prospects*. Berlin: Springer.

Stam, E. (2018). Measuring entrepreneurial ecosystems. *Entrepreneurial Ecosystems*, *38*(1), 173–197.

Stam, F. C., & Spigel, B. (2016). Entrepreneurial Ecosystems. Working Papers 16-13, Utrecht School of Economics.

Stam, E., & van de Ven, A. (2019). Entrepreneurial ecosystem elements. *Small Business Economics*, *56*(3), 809–832.

Stephens, S., McLaughlin, C., Ryan, L., Catena, M., & Bonner, A. (2022). Entrepreneurial ecosystems: Multiple domains, dimensions and relationships. *Journal of Business Venturing Insights*, *18*(1), e00344.

Tansley, A. J. (1935). The use and abuse of vegetational concepts and terms. *Ecology*, *16*(2), 284–307.

Tekin, E., Ramadani, V., & Dana, L. P. (2021). Entrepreneurship in Turkey and other Balkan countries: Are there opportunities for mutual co-operation through internationalisation? *Review of International Business & Strategy*, *31*(2), 297–314.

Trade Economics. (2023). https://tradingeconomics.com/bosnia-and-herzegovina/indicators. Accessed January 2023.

Turulja, L., Veselinović, L. J., Agić, E., & Pašić-Mesihović, A. (2020). Entrepreneurial intention of students in Bosnia and Herzegovina: What type of support matters? *Economic Research-Ekonomska Istraživanja*, *33*(1), 2713–2732.

Chapter 6

Entrepreneurial Implementation Intentions Among Bulgarian STEM Students: Facilitators and Constraints

Desislava I. Yordanova, Albena Pergelova, Fernando Angulo-Ruiz and Tatiana S. Manolova

Abstract

Despite the important role of entrepreneurial implementation intentions for closing the intention-behavior gap, empirical evidence on their drivers and mechanisms is scant and inconclusive. In the case of college students' technology-driven entrepreneurship, the objective of the present study is to examine whether implementation intentions are contingent on the university environment in which the progression from entrepreneurial intentions to subsequent actions unfolds. The sample for this study is composed of 299 Bulgarian STEM students, who reported technology-based entrepreneurial intentions. A binary logistic regression is applied to examine four specific mechanisms that facilitate or impede the students' actual implementation intentions. Findings suggest that students enrolled in universities that provide greater concept development support are more likely to have formed specific implementation intentions, while students in more research-intensive universities are less likely to do so. Practitioner implications and recommendations for future research are provided.

Keywords: Technology-based entrepreneurship; implementation intentions; concept development support; research-intensive universities; STEM students; Bulgaria

Entrepreneurship Development in the Balkans: Perspective from Diverse Contexts, 95–112

Published under exclusive licence by Emerald Publishing Limited
doi:10.1108/978-1-83753-454-820231006

1. Introduction

The literature on entrepreneurial intentions has increased significantly during the last decades. The premise of this literature is that entrepreneurial intentions are a good predictor of subsequent entrepreneurial action and that intentions can provide an understanding of entrepreneurial behavior without witnessing it. Thus, models of intentions and their antecedents are useful frameworks for studying entrepreneurial behavior (Krueger & Carsrud, 1993; Krueger, Reilly, & Carsrud, 2000). However, several authors highlight that the link between entrepreneurial intentions and behavior may not be so straightforward. For example, Krueger (2009) argues that there is no guarantee that a person's intentions for starting a business will be actually implemented, while Krueger et al. (2000) stress that even when intentionality is present, the timing of the creation of the new venture might be relatively unplanned and even sudden. Other authors point out that "it may be a relatively long or short time after intent develops before a new venture opportunity is even identified" (Shook, Priem, & McGee, 2003, p. 383). In fact, the meta-analytic study of Armitage and Conner (2001) reports that intentions account for only 27% of the variance in behavior, and Schlaegel and Koenig (2014) put that number somewhat, but not much, higher, at 37%. Thus, it is critical to shed light on the mechanisms and contingencies that help (or impede) the translation of entrepreneurial intentions into entrepreneurial action.

To better understand the link between entrepreneurial intentions and entrepreneurial behavior, we leverage the body of knowledge on implementation intentions, more specifically the Rubicon model of action phases (Adam & Fayolle, 2015; Gollwitzer, 1999). Implementation intentions specify the sub-steps of how to achieve a goal (Frese, 2009; Gielnik et al., 2014; Gollwitzer, 1999). By detailing "when, where, and how to act" (Sniehotta et al., 2005, p. 567), implementation intentions facilitate goal attainment and thus provide a critical link between intentions and subsequent actions. A growing body of work has offered theoretical treatments and empirical accounts of the role of implementation intentions as a mediator or moderator of the intention-action link (Adam & Fayolle, 2015, 2016; Gielnik et al., 2014, 2015; Gollwitzer & Sheeran, 2006; van Gelderen, Kautonen, Wincen, & Biniari, 2018). Less clear is whether implementation intentions themselves are contingent on the environment in which the progression from entrepreneurial intentions to subsequent actions unfolds. This is the research gap that our study addresses. We focus on the specific context of university students' technology-based entrepreneurship in transition economies, and ask, *Does the university environment in transition economies support students' entrepreneurial implementation intentions in technology-based entrepreneurship*?

Universities are important hubs in the development of entrepreneurship ecosystems (Audretsch, 2014; Isenberg, 2010), partners in the commercialization of university knowledge (Politis et al., 2012), enhancers of students' entrepreneurial intentions (Bae, Qian, Miao, & Fiet, 2014; Liñan et al., 2011), and supporters of nascent entrepreneurship thorough accelerator programs, mentoring, and network platforms (Nielsen & Lassen, 2012). Yet, when it comes to the role of universities as facilitators of their entrepreneurially minded students' transition from intention to action, empirical evidence is scant and inconclusive. While a large-scale study of over 70,000 students in 34 countries reported a significant positive effect (Shirokova, Osiyevskyy, & Bogatyreva, 2016), another large-scale study across 41 European universities reported that the actual establishment of a new firm is less dependent on the university context (Bergmann et al., 2016). The inconclusive findings warrant a closer look at the nature of the university environment, particularly in the context of technology-based entrepreneurship in the transition economies of Central and Eastern Europe. Under the socialist regime, universities in these economies focused on the generation of fundamental knowledge, staying away from technology commercialization. During the transition period, the economies were gradually integrated into the institutional framework of the European Union, and universities needed to step into new and unfamiliar roles. Recent research documents that the mechanisms of university research commercialization in transition economies do not mirror what has been found in developed economies (Belitski et al., 2019; Carayannis et al., 2016). We surmise that, similarly, universities in transition economies will operate in distinct ways in supporting their students' entrepreneurial initiatives.

The chapter is structured as follows. In the next section, we review the literature on goal and implementation intentions and the Rubicon model of action phases and formulate hypotheses on university-related facilitators and constraints to students' technology-based entrepreneurial implementation intentions. We then report on our methods and empirical findings. We conclude by discussing our findings and outlining the practitioner implications of the study, as well as its boundaries, limitations and possible extensions for future research.

2. Background and Hypotheses

2.1. Goal and Implementation Intentions and the Rubicon Model of Action Phases

The Rubicon model of action phases takes a temporal view of the course of action and conceptualizes goal pursuit as a consequence of four different action phases (predecisional, postdecisional or preactional, actional, and postactional) (Gollwitzer, 1990, 2012). Each of these phases involves solving a distinct task and is linked to a different mindset (Gollwitzer, 1990, 2012). During the predecisional phase, some wishes are selected based on the criteria of feasibility and desirability and are transformed into goals. The formation of goal intentions involves "turning the selected wish or desire into a chosen goal" (Gollwitzer & Brandstätter, 1997, p. 186). Such intentions exhibit the structure of "I intend to pursue x," where x indicates a desired outcome or behavior (Gollwitzer, 1993, p. 150; 1999, p. 494). In other words, "<g>oal intentions specify a certain end point that may be either a desired performance or an outcome" (Gollwitzer, 1999, p. 494). Although the formation of goal intentions favors goal pursuit and promotes goal achievement, goal realization may be delayed or hampered, as "<s>uccessful goal attainment requires that problems associated with getting started and persisting until the goal is reached are effectively solved" (Gollwitzer, 1999, p. 493). The transition from wishes to binding goals represents crossing the Rubicon (Gollwitzer, 1990).

Our study is situated in the second phase of the Rubicon model. The second phase (called postdecisional/preactional) poses the task of getting started with goal-directed behaviors (Gollwitzer, 2012). It involves effective planning about when, where and how to act aiming to promote the initiation of relevant actions. Implementation intentions are viewed as "subordinate to goal intentions" (Gollwitzer, 1999, p. 494) and their role is to solve conflicts between different potential routes to implementation (Gollwitzer, 1993). They specify when, where and how implementation will start and what course the goal pursuit will follow (Gollwitzer, 1993). Implementation intentions link a certain goal-directed behavior with an anticipated situational context (Gollwitzer, 1993) and have the structure of "When situation x arises, I will perform response y!" (Gollwitzer, 1999, p. 494). People who complement their goal intentions with implementation intentions are more successful in goal realization (Gollwitzer, 1993). The actional phase is characterized by relevant actions to effectively achieve the desired outcomes. Gollwitzer (2012, p. 527) argues that "this is best achieved by determined and persistent pursuit of goal completion." During the evaluative phase comparisons between the desired and achieved outcomes are made, and decisions on whether or not further attempts to realize the goal are necessary are taken.

Empirical research highlights the role of implementation intentions for goal attainment (Gollwitzer & Sheeran, 2006), focusing mainly on the link between implementation intentions, entrepreneurial action and business creation. This research has documented that action planning and implementation intentions contribute to the transformation of entrepreneurial intentions into actions (Adam & Fayolle, 2016; Gielnik et al., 2014, 2015; van Gelderen et al., 2018). For example, van Gelderen et al. (2018) showed that implementation intentions mediate the effects of goal intentions on entrepreneurial action and the mediation effect is stronger for individuals with strong entrepreneurial intentions. Other authors built and tested moderation models, in which action planning moderates the effect of entrepreneurial goal intentions on entrepreneurial action (Gielnik et al., 2015) and new venture creation (Gielnik et al., 2014). Adam and Fayolle (2016) found that the formation of implementation intentions increases the probability and the speed of becoming an entrepreneur, while Delanoë-Gueguen and Fayolle (2019) demonstrated that after crossing the entrepreneurial Rubicon, entrepreneurial intentions no longer matter. As the academic interest in the development of implementation intentions in the entrepreneurial process is relatively recent, it is not surprising that there is still a lack of understanding of the mechanisms that impede or facilitate implementation intentions. Therefore, in this study, we specifically focus on how university-related factors such as entrepreneurship education, concept development support, research intensity, and industry ties affect the likelihood of forming implementation intentions.

2.2. University Antecedents of Implementation Intentions

2.2.1. Entrepreneurship Education. A large volume of empirical research investigates the entrepreneurship education – entrepreneurial intentions link. Several quantitative reviews of research on this topic find a significant correlation between entrepreneurship education and entrepreneurial intentions (Bae et al., 2014; Dickson, Solomon, & Weaver, 2008; Martin, McNally, & Kay, 2013). Martin et al. (2013) reported that entrepreneurship education and training affect positively entrepreneurship-related knowledge and skills and entrepreneurial attitudes and perceptions. Further, Rideout and Gray (2013) identified several rigorous empirical studies confirming the link between entrepreneurship education and entrepreneurial behavior (Charney & Libecap, 2000; Kolvereid & Moen, 1997; Menzies & Paradi, 2002), entrepreneurial capabilities (Thursby, Fuller, & Thursby, 2009), entrepreneurial competencies (Sanchez, 2011), and opportunity identification (DeTienne & Chandler, 2004).

In the specific context of entrepreneurship education in the STEM field, entrepreneurship education allows STEM students to acquire entrepreneurship-related knowledge and skills, entrepreneurial competencies and capabilities, abilities to identify opportunities, and to plan and perform entrepreneurial activities. Previous research demonstrates that prior knowledge affects the recognition of entrepreneurial opportunities resulting from technological change (Shane, 2000). Specific knowledge about entrepreneurship gleaned from entrepreneurship education may thus enhance the opportunity-identification abilities of students (Souitaris, Zerbinati, & Al-Laham, 2007), while relevant information might allow for reducing risk and the barriers to the new firm formation (Mukhtar, Oakey, & Kippling, 1999). Entrepreneurship-related human capital such as knowledge and skills may be especially valuable for entrepreneurs in technology sectors where technology challenges in the environment are often on the technological frontier, and business survival and growth depend on the implementation of a reliable innovation strategy (Park, 2005).

Previous research has documented that entrepreneurship curricula and pedagogical methods used in entrepreneurship education have a significant effect on implementation intentions (Sherkat & Chenari, 2020). For example, Haddoud, Onjewu, Nowinski, and Alammari (2020) found that entrepreneurship education affects positively students' implementation intentions by regulating students' emotions such as inspiration, passion and optimism. Therefore, we argue that participation in entrepreneurship education may stimulate students to formulate implementation intentions:

H1. Participation in entrepreneurship education increases the likelihood of entrepreneurial implementation intentions among STEM students.

2.2.2. Concept Development Support for Entrepreneurship. Entrepreneurship support programs can increase students' awareness about self-employment and encourage them to become entrepreneurs by providing access to critical resources, extra-curricular training, counseling, financial support, contacts facilitating opportunity exploration, and access to experts (Walter, Parboteeah, & Walter, 2013). A positive university environment and support will provide both tangible (finance, know-how) and intangible resources (motivation, self-confidence, awareness) needed for an entrepreneurial career (Trivedi, 2016). Thus, contextual support factors influence significantly the entrepreneurial intentions of STEM students (Lüthje & Franke, 2003), both directly (Minola, Donina, & Meoli, 2016) and indirectly (Trivedi, 2017). Shirokova et al. (2016) reported that the university entrepreneurial environment reinforces the link between entrepreneurial intentions and the scope of start-up activities that student entrepreneurs are engaged in, while Arrighetti, Caricati, Landini, and Monacelli (2016) showed that perceptions of university support influence positively both the perceived likelihood of being an entrepreneur and the propensity to start a new venture among students.

One important type of university support is concept development support (Kraaijenbrink, Groen, & Bos, 2010). Concept development support may enhance students' awareness and motivation to choose an entrepreneurial career, especially during the early stages of the entrepreneurial process in which opportunity recognition and development occurs (Mustafa et al., 2016). Saeed, Yousafzai, Yani De Soriano, and Muffatto (2015) find that concept development support significantly influences students' entrepreneurial self-efficacy and entrepreneurial intentions. Students with technopreneurial goal intentions in universities providing concept development support may be more likely to gain confidence (Kraaijenbrink et al., 2010) and to overcome problems associated with getting started and problems associated with planning about when, where and how a new technology venture will be started. Therefore, we suggest that:

> *H2*. Concept development support increases the likelihood of entrepreneurial implementation intentions among STEM students.

2.2.3. University Research Intensity. Universities provide a rich source of technological opportunities that can be exploited for creating new technology ventures (Rasmussen & Borch, 2010). Reynolds, Miller, and Maki (1995, p. 391) argue that "where information is readily available and innovation and creativity flourish, the formation rate of new firms is enhanced." More research-oriented universities may be more likely to provide students with superior knowledge and skills to create and commercialize complex ideas (Walter et al., 2013). This is because university research is seen as an important resource for aspiring entrepreneurs resulting in new knowledge and technologies that can be eventually commercialized (Walter et al., 2013). Students with more knowledge about a domain or industry will be able to identify viable market openings to introduce new products and services, obtain resources, and recombine resources to create feasible and viable ventures (Hisrich & Ramadani, 2018; Jarvis, 2016). Beyhan and Findik (2018) argued that universities with high-quality research and better knowledge production provide a supportive environment for their students to acquire tacit knowledge about conducting research, to explore information gaps, to exploit new knowledge, and to develop technological innovations. Not surprisingly, the research excellence of universities is associated with higher entrepreneurial activity (Barbosa & Faria, 2020; Beyhan & Findik, 2018; Bonaccorsi, Colombo, Guerini, & Rossi-Lamastra, 2014; Di Gregorio & Shane, 2003; Van Looy et al., 2011).

However, an alternative view suggests that because students at research-intensive universities may be more likely to have access to advanced knowledge, skills, latest advancements, innovations, and new technologies, they may be more likely to postpone entrepreneurial activities in the short run in order to pursue an academic research career or to get a highly paid STEM job at an existing company. There is empirical evidence suggesting that the research orientation of the university is negatively associated with students' self-employment intentions (Walter et al., 2013). This may be particularly the case in transition economies, the context of our research, where universities are still redefining their role in supporting students' entrepreneurial endeavors. We surmise that students in research intensive universities will be presented with a host of promising opportunities other than entrepreneurship, which may delay their entrepreneurial implementation intentions. Therefore, we suggest that:

H3. University research intensity decreases the likelihood of entrepreneurial implementation intentions among STEM students.

2.2.4. Industry Ties. It has been acknowledged that networking and interaction with industry play an important role in university entrepreneurship by offering positive entrepreneurial role models and informal forums, both of which are important intangible factors for the development of technological entrepreneurship (Rothaermel, Agung, & Jiang, 2007). Positive entrepreneurial role models may help students perceive the entrepreneurial challenge as feasible, while informal forums provide opportunities for exchanging ideas and real entrepreneurial learning (Venkataraman, 2004).

Entrepreneurial role models are an important factor for the development of the entrepreneurial university (Guerrero & Urbano, 2012), while the lack of entrepreneurial role models within the university is identified as a key barrier to the establishment of an entrepreneurial university (Philpott, Dooley, O'Reilly, & Lupton, 2011). In addition, the commercialization of research and the entrepreneurial behavior of students and researchers is affected positively by the presence of entrepreneurial role models on campus (Cunningham & Harney, 2006).

Walter et al. (2013) found that industry ties positively influence the self-employment intentions among students and concluded that intensive connections between universities and industry partners inspire potential entrepreneurs. Further, non-academic contacts among early-stage academic entrepreneurs are important for academic spin-off development (Hayter, Lubynsky, & Maroulis, 2016). In support of these arguments, Fischer, Schaeffer, Vonortas, and Queiroz (2018) demonstrated that the content of university-industry collaboration has a strong effect on academic entrepreneurial activity. Therefore, we suggest that

H4. Industry ties increase the likelihood of entrepreneurial implementation intentions among STEM students.

3. Research Methodology

This study utilizes proprietary data on technology-based entrepreneurship among STEM students collected through a survey administrated in 15 Bulgarian universities over the 2015–2016 period. STEM students were selected for the empirical analysis because they have the potential to start technology ventures (Souitaris et al., 2007). In this study, a technology-based business is defined as a business whose products or services depend largely on the application of scientific or technological knowledge (Allen, 1992). A quota sampling technique, based on the total number of STEM students enrolled in each university, was adopted for data collection. Enrollments were obtained from the Ministry of Education and Science. The sample for this study comprises 299 STEM students, who indicated their technology-based entrepreneurial intentions, in that they indicated they would start a technology business, but were at the time of the survey neither business owners, nor in the process of starting a business (Krueger, 1993; Peterman & Kennedy, 2003). More than 80% of the respondents in the sample were undergraduate students. Female students represented less than 41% of the sample. The great majority of the respondents (81.9%) were full-time students.

Rise, Thompson, and Verplanken (2003) emphasize that although most studies measuring implementation intentions have induced implementation intentions experimentally, it is worth exploring implementation intentions as a measured construct in a survey context. Previous studies of implementation intentions have focused on the "how," "when," and "where" aspects of implementation intentions (Gollwitzer & Brandstätter, 1997; Orbell, Hodgldns, & Sheeran, 1997; Rise et al., 2003; Sheeran & Orbell, 1999; Verplanken & Faes, 1999). Following Rise et al. (2003), we provided respondents with specific questions covering the "when," "where," and "how" of implementation intentions. As suggested by Rise et al. (2003), respondents were asked three different questions, that is, if they already know where, when, and how they will start a technology business. The respondents were requested to answer 'yes' or 'no' and the scores were summed (Rise et al., 2003). In the present study, the dependent variable is collapsed into a binary variable. The variable takes a value of "1" if the respondent has answered "yes" to at least two of the three questions above, and takes a value of "0" otherwise.

The study employs several independent variables. *Entrepreneurship education* takes a value of "1" if the respondent was/is enrolled in an entrepreneurship course within the university and a value of "0" otherwise. A perceptual measure of *concept development support* is adopted. It has been suggested that although universities can support concept development with objective measures, it is important to take into account the extent to which such objective measures can influence students by evaluating students' perceptions of concept development support provided by the university (Kraaijenbrink et al., 2010). The variable is measured by a four-item 7-point Likert-type scale developed by Kraaijenbrink et al. (2010), which reveals students' perceptions of the support for business concept development by the university beyond teaching. The scale exhibits high reliability (Cronbach's alpha = 0.925). *University research intensity* is measured with the Scopus *H*-index of the university in the scientific field of study of the respondent. *Industry ties* are measured by a two-item 7-point Likert scale and indicate students' perceptions of the frequency of lectures and presentations held by industry partners at the university (Walter et al., 2013). Cronbach's alpha is 0.915.

The study employs several control variables, which have been identified as significant predictors of entrepreneurial intentions in the literature (Krueger et al.,

2000; Liñán & Fayolle, 2015). Perceived new technology venture *feasibility* captures how feasible technology entrepreneurship is for the respondents. It is measured by an index composed of four items measured on a 7-point Likert-type scale (Drennan, Kennedy, & Renfrow, 2005; Krueger, 1993; Krueger et al., 2000). Cronbach's alpha for feasibility is 0.616, which exceeds the minimum acceptable level of 0.6 (Hair, Anderson, Tathan, & Black, 1998). Perceived new technology venture *desirability* indicates how desirable technology entrepreneurship is for respondents. It is measured with an index composed of three items measured on a 7-point Likert-type scale (Drennan et al., 2005; Krueger, 1993; Krueger et al., 2000). Cronbach's alpha for desirability is 0.702, which exceeds the minimum acceptable level of 0.6 (Hair et al., 1998). The variable *willingness to take risks* (Risk) indicates students' willingness to take risks and is measured by four items adopted from Gomez-Mejia and Balkin (1989) (Cronbach's alpha = 0.736). Entrepreneurial *role models* (Role Models) take a value of "1" if the respondent has at least one entrepreneur among parents, relatives, friends, or acquaintances whose success gave her/him a positive impression of entrepreneurship (Walter et al., 2013) and value of "0" if otherwise. Support from *social networks* takes a value of "1" if the respondent can count on support from family, partner, friends, and acquaintances if s/he becomes entrepreneur after his/her studies (Walter et al., 2013), and "0" otherwise. *Gender* takes a value of "1" if the respondent is male and a value of "0" if the respondent is female. *Previous experience* in a technology company takes a value of "1" if the respondent has previous experience in a technology company and "0" otherwise. Age indicates the *age* of respondents in years.

Taking into account the objectives of this study and the properties of the data, we apply a binary logistic regression analysis (Greene, 1997). Logistic regression is a more robust method for several reasons (Greene, 1997). The dependent variable needs not to be normally distributed. There is no assumption about a linear relationship between the dependent and the independent variables. The dependent variable needs not to be homoskedastic for each level of the independent variable(s). Normally distributed error terms are not assumed. Independent variables can be categorical. Logistic regression does not require independent variables to be interval or unbounded. The application of non-parametric techniques is adequate when the independent variables are predominantly categorical. The use of the maximum likelihood approach is recommended when sample selection bias is possible (Nawata, 1994). The correlations between independent variables in the study are below 0.35, which indicates the absence of multicollinearity problems (Hair et al., 1998). For more details see the Appendix (Table A1).

4. Empirical Findings

The results of the study are reported in the Appendix (Table A2). The model is significant at the 99% confidence level according to Chi-square statistics. Therefore, the null hypothesis that all coefficients (except the constant) are zero can be rejected. The variance inflation factors for the variables in the regression indicate that there are no serious multicollinearity problems, as they are all well within the acceptable limits (less than 4). The overall predictive ability of the model to correctly classify students by their technology-based entrepreneurial implementation intentions is 71.6%.

As reported in Table A2, entrepreneurship education is not statistically significant. Participation in entrepreneurship education is not related to the likelihood of technology-based entrepreneurial implementation intentions (0.251, p-value = 0.376). This result does not support *H1* that participation in entrepreneurship education increases the likelihood of entrepreneurial implementation intentions among STEM students.

Concept development support affects positively the odds of technology-based entrepreneurial implementation intentions. STEM students with technology-based entrepreneurial goal intention enrolled in universities that provide greater concept development support are more likely to exhibit entrepreneurial implementation intentions (0.200, p-value = 0.020), in support of *H2*.

University research intensity negatively influences the odds of technology-based entrepreneurial implementation intentions. STEM students with technology-based entrepreneurial goal intention in research-oriented universities are less likely to exhibit entrepreneurial implementation intentions (−0.076, p = 0.002). This result supports *H3* in that that university research intensity decreases the likelihood of entrepreneurial implementation intentions among STEM students.

Industry ties have no effect on the dependent variable (0.042, p-value = 0.578). STEM students with technology-based entrepreneurial goal intentions in universities with better industry ties are not more likely to have entrepreneurial implementation intentions.

Of the control variables, role models, desirability and feasibility exert a significant influence on the likelihood of technology-based entrepreneurial implementation intentions. The likelihood of technology-based entrepreneurial implementation intentions is not associated with gender, age, risk, previous experience in a technology company, or support from social networks.

5. Discussion

A large number of studies have focused on students' entrepreneurial goal intentions to gain an understanding of their future entrepreneurial behavior. Drawing upon implementation intention theory (Gollwitzer, 1999), this study examines four specific mechanisms that facilitate or constrain technology-based entrepreneurial implementation intentions in a sample of 299 Bulgarian STEM students.

As hypothesized, students perceiving greater concept development support are more likely to exhibit technology-based entrepreneurial implementation intentions. This finding provides support to previous empirical evidence about the role of universities for building entrepreneurial intentionality among students (Arrighetti et al., 2016; Kraaijenbrink et al., 2010; Mustafa et al., 2016; Saeed et al., 2015; Trivedi, 2016). It seems that students in universities providing greater concept development support may gain confidence (Kraaijenbrink et al., 2010) to overcome problems associated with getting started with a venture and problems associated with formulating simple plans about when, where, and how a new technology venture will be started.

As expected, students in more research-intensive universities are less likely to exhibit technology-based entrepreneurial implementation intentions. These results are in line with previous findings that university research orientation influences negatively students' self-employment intentions (Walter et al., 2013). Perhaps, students at such universities are encouraged to consider an academic career and may postpone their entrepreneurial careers (Walter et al., 2013). Although they may postpone making plans about when, where, and how to start a technology business, they may establish such plans in the future. Previous research demonstrates that technology entrepreneurs often have "research" background (Jones-Evans, 1995).

In our study, students' participation in entrepreneurship education is not related to the likelihood of technology-based entrepreneurial implementation intentions. This result supports the view that entrepreneurial intentions and knowledge generated by entrepreneurship education might not necessarily lead to entrepreneurial behavior, in our study context, which suggests the need for a specific framework to facilitate the transformation process (Manning, 2018). The results also raise the question about what content and teaching methods are used in the entrepreneurship courses and to what extent they are conductive for the formation of entrepreneurial implementation intentions. Previous studies conceive entrepreneurial learning as an experiential process (Secundo, Del Vecchio, Schiuma, & Passiante, 2017). Hence, entrepreneurship education should go beyond promoting awareness and providing knowledge (Ahmed, Chandran, & Klobas, 2017) and should focus on experimentation and experiential learning (Joensuu-Salo, Varamäki, & Viljamaa, 2015) in order to enhance entrepreneurial implementation intentions and behavior.

Somewhat surprisingly, industry ties are not related to technology-based entrepreneurial implementation intentions of STEM students. These results are in line with the previous empirical evidence about the limited extent of collaboration between universities and industry in Central and Eastern Europe (Stojčić, 2021). In addition, students' perceptions of guest speakers referring to the difficulty of running a venture (Kirkwood, Dwyer, & Gray, 2014) may also influence negatively the development of technology-based entrepreneurial implementation intentions.

6. Contributions and Future Research Lines

Our study on the mechanisms that facilitate or impede technology-based entrepreneurial implementation intentions among Bulgarian STEM students extends the literature in several ways. First, our study makes a theoretical contribution to entrepreneurial intentionality models by specifying some of the boundaries of implementation intentions – concept development support and university research intensity – as critical factors affecting the links between entrepreneurial intentions and actions. Second, we contribute to the literature on technology entrepreneurship, by exploring the pre-venture process and identifying some of the significant determinants of implementation intentions in students' technology-based entrepreneurship (Gollwitzer, 1999). Finally, this study contributes to the literature on technology entrepreneurship, by offering a context-specific understanding of the pre-venture processes, and by identifying significant determinants of entrepreneurial implementation intentions for STEM students in a post-transition economy.

The reported empirical findings open several new directions for future research. First, future research could provide a greater understanding of the impact of various educational variables related to entrepreneurship education such as teaching methods, learning outcomes, educator teaching beliefs, etc. on students' entrepreneurial implementation intentions. Second, future studies need to identify effective entrepreneurship support services and activities that stimulate the transformation of students' entrepreneurial goal intentions into implementation intentions. Third, future research should test theoretically justified determinants of the translation of entrepreneurial goal intentions into implementation intentions using different samples (not only students) from different countries and contexts. Future research with longitudinal design is necessary to provide insights into different levels of mechanisms that contribute or constrain the transformation of entrepreneurial goal intentions into implementation intentions.

This study has several limitations. The data were collected through a self-reported survey and thus may be subjected to cognitive biases and errors. The findings might also be influenced by specific features of the Bulgarian cultural and institutional environment and therefore may not be applicable to other contexts.

The present research has practical implications for policymakers and higher education instructions. The insights from our study inform university leaders and public policymakers in transition economies on ways to promote technology-based entrepreneurship via support for concept development and more tightly linking basic research with feasible avenues for technology commercialization, including student-initiated new ventures.

References

Adam, A. F., & Fayolle, A. (2015). Bridging the entrepreneurial intention–behaviour gap: The role of commitment and implementation intention. *International Journal of Entrepreneurship and Small Business*, *25*(1), 36–54.

Adam, A.-F., & Fayolle, A. (2016). Can implementation intention help to bridge the intention–behaviour gap in the entrepreneurial process? An experimental approach. *The International Journal of Entrepreneurship and Innovation*, *17*(2), 80–88.

Ahmed, T., Chandran, V. G. R., & Klobas, J. (2017). Specialized entrepreneurship education: Does it really matter? Fresh evidence from Pakistan. *International Journal of Entrepreneurial Behavior & Research*, *23*(1), 4–19.

Allen, J. C. (1992) *Starting a technology business*. London: Pitman.

Armitage, C. J., & Conner, M. (2001). Efficacy of the theory of planned behaviour: A meta-analytic review. *British journal of social psychology*, *40*(4), 471–499.

Arrighetti, A., Caricati, L., Landini, F., & Monacelli, N. (2016). Entrepreneurial intention in the time of crisis: A field study. *International Journal of Entrepreneurial Behavior & Research*, *22*(6), 835–859.

Audretsch, D. B. (2014). From the entrepreneurial university to the university for the entrepreneurial society. *The Journal of Technology Transfer*, *39*, 313–321.

Bae, T. J., Qian, S., Miao, C., & Fiet, J. O. (2014). The relationship between entrepreneurship education and entrepreneurial intentions: A meta-analytic review. *Entrepreneurship Theory and Practice*, *38*(2), 217–254.

Bergmann, H., Hundt, C., & Sternberg, R. (2016). What makes student entrepreneurs? On the relevance (and irrelevance) of the university and the regional context for student start-ups. *Small Business Economics*, *47*, 53–76.

Beyhan, B., & Findik, D. (2018). Student and graduate entrepreneurship: Ambidextrous universities create more nascent entrepreneurs. *The Journal of Technology Transfer*, *43*, 1346–1374.

Belitski, M., Aginskaja, A., & Marozau, R. (2019). Commercializing university research in transition economies: Technology transfer offices or direct industrial funding?. *Research policy*, *48*(3), 601–615.

Bonaccorsi, A., Colombo, M. G., Guerini, M., & Rossi-Lamastra, C. (2014). The impact of local and external university knowledge on the creation of knowledge-intensive firms: Evidence from the Italian case. *Small Business Economics*, *43*, 261–287.

Barbosa, N., & Faria, A. P. (2020). The effect of entrepreneurial origin on firms' performance: the case of Portuguese academic spinoffs. *Industrial and Corporate Change*, *29*(1), 25–42.

Carayannis, E. G., Cherepovitsyn, A. Y., & Ilinova, A. A. (2016). Technology commercialization in entrepreneurial universities: the US and Russian experience. *The Journal of Technology Transfer*, *41*, 1135–1147.

Charney, A., & Libecap, G. (2000). *The impact of entrepreneurship education: An evaluation of the Berger Entrepreneurship Program at the University of Arizona 1985–1999*, Report prepared for the Kauffman Center for Entrepreneurial Leadership. The Ewing Marion Kauffman Foundation, Kansas City, MO.

Cunningham, J. A., & Harney, B. (2006). *Strategic management of technology transfer: The new challenge on campus*. Oxfordshire: Oak Tree Press.

Delanoë-Gueguen, S., & Fayolle, A. (2019). Crossing the entrepreneurial Rubicon: A longitudinal investigation. *Journal of Small Business Management*, *57*(3), 1044–1065.

DeTienne, D. R., & Chandler, G. N. (2004). Opportunity identification and its role in the entrepreneurial classroom: A pedagogical approach and empirical test. *Academy of Management Learning and Education*, *3*(3), 242–257.

Dickson, P. H., Solomon, G. T., & Weaver, K. M. (2008). Entrepreneurial selection and success: does education matter?. *Journal of Small Business and Enterprise Development*, *15*(2), 239–258.

Di Gregorio, D., & Shane, S. (2003). Why do some universities generate more start-ups than others?. *Research Policy*, *32*(2), 209–227.

Drennan, J., Kennedy, J., & Renfrow, P. (2005). Impact of childhood experiences on the development of entrepreneurial intentions. *International Journal of Entrepreneurship and Innovation*, *6*(4), 231–238.

Fischer, B. B., Schaeffer, P. R., Vonortas, N. S., & Queiroz, S. (2018). Quality comes first: University–industry collaboration as a source of academic entrepreneurship in a developing country. *The Journal of Technology Transfer*, *43*(2), 263–284.

Frese, M. (2009). Towards a psychology of entrepreneurship—an action theory perspective. *Foundations and Trends® in Entrepreneurship*, *5*(6), 437–496.

Gielnik, M. M., Barabas, S., Frese, M., Namatovu-Dawa, R., Scholz, F. A., Metzger, J. R., & Walter, T. (2014). A temporal analysis of how entrepreneurial goal intentions, positive fantasies, and action planning affect starting a new venture and when the effects wear off. *Journal of Business Venturing*, *29*(6), 755–772.

Gielnik, M. M., Frese, M., Kahara-Kawuki, A., Wasswa Katono, I., Kyejjusa, S., Ngoma, M., … Oyugi, J. (2015). Action and action-regulation in entrepreneurship: Evaluating a student training for promoting entrepreneurship. *Academy of Management Learning & Education*, *14*(1), 69–94.

Gollwitzer, P. M. (1990). Action phases and mind-sets. In E. T. Higgins & R. M. Sorrentino (Eds.), *Handbook of motivation and cognition: Foundations of social behavior* (Vol. 2, pp. 53–92). New York, NY: Guilford Press.

Gollwitzer, P. M. (1993). Goal achievement: The role of intentions. *European Review of Social Psychology*, *4*(1), 141–185.

Gollwitzer, P. M. (1999). Implementation intentions: Strong effects of simple plans. *American Psychologist*, *54*(7), 493–503.

Gollwitzer, P. M. (2012). Mindset theory of action phases. In P. van Lange (Ed.), *Handbook of theories of social psychology* (pp. 526–545). Thousand Oaks, CA: Sage.

Gollwitzer, P. M. & Brandstätter, V. (1997). Implementation intentions and effective goal pursuit. *Journal of Personality and Social Psychology*, *73*(1), 186.

Gollwitzer, P. M., & Sheeran, P. (2006). Implementation intentions and goal achievement: A meta-analysis of effects and processes. *Advances in Experimental Social Psychology*, *38*, 69–119.

Gomez-Mejia, L. R., & Balkin, D. B. (1989). Effectiveness of individual and aggregate compensation strategies. *Industrial Relations*, *28*(3), 431–445.

Greene, W. H. (1997), *Econometric analysis*. Saddle River, NJ: Prentice Hall.

Guerrero, M., & Urbano, D. (2012). The development of an entrepreneurial university. *The Journal of Technology Transfer*, *37*(1), 43–74.

Haddoud, M. Y., Onjewu, A. K. E., Nowinski, W., & Alammari, K. (2020). Assessing the role of entrepreneurship education in regulating emotions and fostering implementation intention: evidence from Nigerian universities. *Studies in Higher Education*, *47*(2), 1–19.

Hair, F. J., Anderson E. R., Tathan L. R., & Black C. (1998). *Multivariate data analysis* (5th ed.). Saddle River, NJ: Prentice Hall.

Hayter, C., Lubynsky, R., & Maroulis, S. (2016). Who is the academic entrepreneur? The role of graduate students in the development of university spinoffs. *The Journal of Technology Transfer*, *42*, 1237–1254.

Hisrich, R. D., & Ramadani, V. (2018). *Entrepreneurial marketing: A practical managerial approach*. Cheltenham: Edward Elgar.

Isenberg, D. J. (2010). How to start an entrepreneurial revolution. *Harvard Business Review*, *88*(6), 40–50.

Jarvis, L. C. (2016). Identification, intentions and entrepreneurial opportunities: An integrative process model. *International Journal of Entrepreneurial Behavior & Research*, *22*(2), 182–198.

Joensuu-Salo, S., Varamäki, E., & Viljamaa, A. (2015). Beyond intentions-what makes a student start a firm?. *Education & Training*, *57*(8–9), 853–873.

Jones-Evans, D. (1995). A typology of technology-based entrepreneurs: A model based on previous occupational background. *International Journal of Entrepreneurial Behavior & Research*, *1*(1), 26–47.

Kirchhoff, B. A., Newbert, S. L., Hasan, I., & Armington, C. (2007). The influence of university R & D expenditures on new business formations and employment growth. *Entrepreneurship Theory and Practice*, *31*(4), 543–559.

Kirkwood, J., Dwyer, K., & Gray, B. (2014). Students' reflections on the value of an entrepreneurship education. *The International Journal of Management Education*, *12*(3), 307–316.

Kolvereid, L., & Moen, O. (1997). Entrepreneurship among business graduates: Does a major in entrepreneurship make a difference?. *Journal of European Industrial Training*, *21*(4), 154–160.

Kraaijenbrink, J., Bos, G., & Groen, A. (2010). What do students think of the entrepreneurial support given by their universities?. *International Journal of Entrepreneurship and Small Business*, *9*(1), 110–125.

Krueger, N. F. (1993). The impact of prior entrepreneurship exposure on perception of new venture feasibility and desirability. *Entrepreneurship Theory and Practice*, *18*, 5–21.

Krueger, N. F. (2009). Entrepreneurial intentions are dead: Long live entrepreneurial intentions. In A. L. Carsrud & M. Brännback (Eds.), *Understanding the entrepreneurial mind* (pp. 51–72). New York, NY: Springer.

Krueger, N., & Carsrud, A. (1993). Entrepreneurial intentions: Applying the theory of planned behaviour. *Entrepreneurship & Regional Development*, *5*, 315–330.

Krueger, N., Reilly, M., & Carsrud, A. (2000). Competing models of entrepreneurial intentions. *Journal of Business Venturing*, *15*(5–6), 411–432.

Liñán, F., Rodríguez-Cohard, J. C., & Rueda-Cantuche, J. M. (2011). Factors affecting entrepreneurial intention levels: a role for education. *International Entrepreneurship and Management Journal*, *7*, 195–218.

Liñán, F., & Fayolle, A. (2015). A systematic literature review on entrepreneurial intentions: Citation, thematic analyses, and research agenda. *International Entrepreneurship and Management Journal*, *11*(4), 907–933.

Lüthje, C., & Franke, N. (2003). The 'making' of an entrepreneur: testing a model of entrepreneurial intent among engineering students at MIT. *R&D Management*, *33*(2), 135–147.

Manning, L. (2018). Enabling entrepreneurial behaviour in a land-based university. *Education+Training*, *60*(7–8), 735–748.

Martin, B. C., McNally, J. J., & Kay, M. J. (2013). Examining the formation of human capital in entrepreneurship: A meta-analysis of entrepreneurship education outcomes. *Journal of Business Venturing*, *28*(2), 211–224.

Menzies, T. V., & Paradi, J. C. (2002). Encouraging technology-based ventures: Entrepreneurship education and engineering graduates. *New England Journal of Entrepreneurship*, *5*(2), 57–64.

Minola, T., Donina, D., & Meoli, M. (2016). Students climbing the entrepreneurial ladder: Does university internationalization pay off?. *Small Business Economics*, *47*(3), 565–587.

Mukhtar, S. M., Oakey, R., & Kippling, M. (1999). Utilisation of science and technology graduates by the small and medium-sized enterprise sector. *International Journal of Entrepreneurial Behavior & Research*, *5*(3), 126–143.

Mustafa, M. J., Mustafa, M. J., Hernandez, E., Hernandez, E., Mahon, C., Mahon, C., & Chee, L. K. (2016). Entrepreneurial intentions of university students in an emerging economy: The influence of university support and proactive personality on students' entrepreneurial intention. *Journal of Entrepreneurship in Emerging Economies*, *8*(2), 162–179.

Nielsen, S. L., & Lassen, A. H. (2012). Identity in entrepreneurship effectuation theory: A supplementary framework. *International Entrepreneurship and Management Journal*, *8*, 373–389.

Nawata, K. (1994). Estimation of sample selection bias models by the maximum likelihood estimator and Heckman's two-step estimator. *Economics Letters*, *45*(1), 33–40.

Orbell, S., Hodgldns, S., & Sheeran, P. (1997). Implementation intentions and the theory of planned behavior. *Personality and Social Psychology Bulletin*, *23*(9), 945–954.

Park, J. S. (2005). Opportunity recognition and product innovation in entrepreneurial hi-tech start-ups: A new perspective and supporting case study. *Technovation*, *25*(7), 739–752.

Peterman, N., & Kennedy, J. (2003). Enterprise education: Influencing students' perceptions of entrepreneurship. *Entrepreneurship Theory and Practice*, *28*(2), 129–144.

Philpott, K., Dooley, L., O'Reilly, C., & Lupton, G. (2011). The entrepreneurial university: Examining the underlying academic tensions. *Technovation*, *31*(4), 161–170.

Politis, D., Gabrielsson, J., & Shveykina, O. (2012). Early-stage finance and the role of external entrepreneurs in the commercialization of university-generated knowledge. *Venture Capital*, *14*(2–3), 175–198.

Rasmussen, E., & Borch, O. J. (2010). University capabilities in facilitating entrepreneurship: A longitudinal study of spin-off ventures at mid-range universities. *Research Policy*, *39*(5), 602–612.

Reynolds, P. D., Miller, B., & Maki, W. R. (1995). Explaining regional variation in business births and deaths: US 1976–88. *Small Business Economics*, *7*(5), 389–407.

Rideout, E. C., & Gray, D. O. (2013). Does entrepreneurship education really work? A review and methodological critique of the empirical literature on the effects of university-based entrepreneurship education. *Journal of Small Business Management*, *51*(3), 329–351.

Rise, J., Thompson, M., & Verplanken, B. (2003). Measuring implementation intentions in the context of the theory of planned behavior. *Scandinavian Journal of Psychology*, *44*(2), 87–95.

Rothaermel, F. T., Agung, S. D., & Jiang, L. (2007). University entrepreneurship: A taxonomy of the literature. *Industrial and Corporate Change*, *16*(4), 691–791.

Saeed, S., Yousafzai, S. Y., Yani De Soriano, M., & Muffatto, M. (2015). The role of perceived university support in the formation of students' entrepreneurial intention. *Journal of Small Business Management*, *53*(4), 1127–1145.

Sanchez, J. C. (2011). University training for entrepreneurial competencies: Its impact on intention of venture creation, *International Entrepreneurship and Management Journal*, *7*, 239–254.

Schlaegel, C., & Koenig, M. (2014). Determinants of entrepreneurial intent: A meta-analytic test and integration of competing models. *Entrepreneurship Theory and Practice*, *38*(2), 291–332.

Secundo, G., Del Vecchio, P., Schiuma, G., & Passiante, G. (2017). Activating entrepreneurial learning processes for transforming university students' idea into entrepreneurial practices. *International Journal of Entrepreneurial Behavior & Research*, *23*(3), 465–485.

Shane, S. (2000). Prior knowledge and the discovery of entrepreneurial opportunities. *Organization Science*, *11*(4), 448–469.

Sheeran, P., & Orbell, S. (1999). Implementation intentions and repeated behaviour: Augmenting the predictive validity of the theory of planned behaviour. *European Journal of Social Psychology*, *29*(23), 349–369.

Sherkat, A., & Chenari, A. (2020). Assessing the effectiveness of entrepreneurship education in the universities of Tehran province based on an entrepreneurial intention model. *Studies in Higher Education*, *47*(1), 1–19.

Shirokova, G., Osiyevskyy, O., & Bogatyreva, K. (2016). Exploring the intention–behavior link in student entrepreneurship: Moderating effects of individual and environmental characteristics. *European Management Journal*, *34*(4), 386–399.

Shook, C. L., Priem, R. L., & McGee, J. E. (2003). Venture creation and the enterprising individual: A review and synthesis. *Journal of management*, *29*(3), 379–399.

Sniehotta, F. F., Scholz, U., & Schwarzer, R. (2005). Bridging the intention–behaviour gap: Planning, self-efficacy, and action control in the adoption and maintenance of physical exercise. *Psychology & Health*, *20*(2), 143–160.

Souitaris, V., Zerbinati, S., & Al-Laham, A. (2007). Do entrepreneurship programmes raise entrepreneurial intention of science and engineering students? The effect of learning, inspiration and resources. *Journal of Business Venturing*, *22*(4), 566–591.

Stewart, W. H., Jr, & Roth, P. L. (2001). Risk propensity differences between entrepreneurs and managers: A meta-analytic review. *Journal of Applied Psychology*, *86*(1), 145–153.

Stojčić, N. (2021). Collaborative innovation in emerging innovation systems: Evidence from Central and Eastern Europe. *The Journal of Technology Transfer*, *46*(2), 531–562.

Thursby, M. C., Fuller, A. W., & Thursby, J. (2009). An integrated approach to educating professionals for careers in innovation. *Academy of Management Learning & Education*, *8*(3), 389–405.

Trivedi, R. (2016). Does university play significant role in shaping entrepreneurial intention? A cross-country comparative analysis. *Journal of Small Business and Enterprise Development*, *23*(3), 790–811.

van Gelderen, M., Kautonen, T., Wincent, J., & Biniari, M. (2018). Implementation intentions in the entrepreneurial process: concept, empirical findings, and research agenda. *Small Business Economics*, *51*(4), 923–941.

Van Looy, B., Landoni, P., Callaert, J., Van Pottelsberghe, B., Sapsalis, E., & Debackere, K. (2011). Entrepreneurial effectiveness of European universities: An empirical assessment of antecedents and trade-offs. *Research Policy*, *40*(4), 553–564.

Venkataraman, S. (2004). Regional transformation through technological entrepreneurship. *Journal of Business Venturing*, *19*(1), 153–167.

Verplanken, B., & Faes, S. (1999). Good intentions, bad habits, and effects of forming implementation intentions on healthy eating. *European Journal of Social Psychology*, *29*(56), 591–604.

Walter, S. G., Parboteeah, K. P., & Walter, A. (2013). University departments and self-employment intentions of business students: A cross-level analysis. *Entrepreneurship Theory and Practice*, *37*(2), 175–200.

Appendix

Table A1. Descriptive Statistics and Correlations (n = 299).

		Mean	SD	1	2	3	4	5	6	7	8	9	10	11	12
1	Technology-based implementation intentions	0.50	0.50	1											
2	Gender	0.60	0.49	0.03	1										
3	Age	22.64	4.58	0.05	0.18**	1									
4	Risk	3.49	1.30	−0.08	0.02	0.12*	1								
5	Previous experience in a technology company	0.33	0.47	0.08	0.27**	0.30*	0.09	1							
6	Role models	0.42	0.49	0.12	0.00	0.01	−0.05	−0.09	1						
7	Support from social networks	0.82	0.39	−0.03	0.05	0.02	0.06	0.02	−0.07	1					
8	Desirability	5.89	0.92	0.22**	−0.06	−0.1	−0.15**	0.01	0.05	0.08	1				
9	Feasibility	3.69	0.99	0.32**	0.01	0.03	0.00	−0.02	0.03	0.10	0.06	1			
10	Entrepreneurship education	0.44	0.50	0.12*	−0.19**	−0.19**	−0.10	0.03	0.00	0.07	0.03	0.16**	1		
11	Concept development support	3.84	1.70	0.24**	−0.12*	−0.11*	0.00	0.07	−0.03	0.01	0.13**	0.24**	0.16	1	
12	University research intensity	9.04	5.72	−0.21**	0.01	−0.12*	−0.12*	−0.05	0.09	0.05	0.04	−0.15*	−0.08	−0.09	1
13	Industry ties	2.99	1.85	0.09	0.02	0.13*	−0.03	0.05	−0.05	0.02	0.06	0.13*	0.14*	0.22*	0.03

**$p < 0.01$ and * $p < 0.05$.

Table A2. Results from a Binary Logistic Regression (Dependent Variable = Technology-based Implementation Intentions).

Variables	*B*	St. Error	Sig.
Control variables			
Gender	0.145	0.294	0.623
Age	0.029	0.032	0.377
Risk	−0.150	0.107	0.160
Previous experience in a technology company	0.481	0.308	0.119
Role models	0.553	0.273	0.043
Support from social networks	−0.351	0.352	0.318
Desirability	0.530	0.157	0.001
Feasibility	0.634	0.152	0.000
Main variables			
Entrepreneurship education	0.251	0.284	0.376
Concept development support	0.200	0.086	0.020
University research intensity	−0.076	0.025	0.002
Industry ties	0.042	0.075	0.578
Constant	−6.084	1.513	0.000
Model Chi-square	76.948***		
Nagelkerke *R* square	0.303		
−2 Log likelihood	337.550		
Percentage of correct predictions	71.6		

*** $p < 0.001$.

Chapter 7

Social Entrepreneurship: Perspective of Croatia

Marko Kolaković, Mladen Turuk and Ivan Turčić

Abstract

The purpose of this chapter is to present and review: (a) the development of social entrepreneurship in Croatia over the last 10 years; (b) the current state and perspective of the development of social entrepreneurship; and (c) strategic documents related to social entrepreneurship with an emphasis on the Strategy for the Development of Social Entrepreneurship 2015–2020 which was an essential document for the promotion and financing of social entrepreneurship. At the beginning of the chapter, the historical reasons for the emergence of the concept of social entrepreneurship are briefly described. Next, entrepreneurship is defined, then entrepreneur, and later the concepts of social entrepreneurship and social entrepreneur are introduced with an emphasis on the differences between commercial and social entrepreneurship. After the basic concepts have been explained, the chapter focusses on social entrepreneurship in Croatia: (a) the types of legal forms in which a social enterprise can be initiated, are listed due to the absence of a separate legal form in Croatian legislation; (b) several examples of positive practices were presented; and (c) the Social Entrepreneurship Development Strategy was analysed by comparing planned and executed activities and allocated and implemented resources. Unfortunately, the strategy did not achieve the expected effect and boosted social entrepreneurship's development, which slowed growth. Social entrepreneurship in Croatia is still in its initial development phase, and a colossal opportunity has been missed. The government and other stakeholders must make additional efforts to develop social entrepreneurship in Croatia.

Keywords: Development strategy; perspective of social entrepreneurship; social entrepreneurship; social enterprise; Croatia; social entrepreneurship ecosystem; WISE; positive practice; national strategy

Entrepreneurship Development in the Balkans: Perspective from Diverse Contexts, 113–130

doi:10.1108/978-1-83753-454-820231007

1. Introduction

In the last 30 years, a significant increase in entrepreneurship studies has been evident, emphasising the purely economic aspect of entrepreneurship. However, recent researches are focussed on entrepreneurship in not-for-profit and public sectors, collective entrepreneurship aspects, and ways of creating sustainable and responsible businesses. That has led to organisational structures, individual incentives, and social movements, known under the umbrella term social entrepreneurship.

Analysis of this social phenomenon's historical formation shows its connection with the formation and destruction of the welfare state, reaffirming neoliberalism's free market and creating a 'third-way' policy. After Second World War (Roper & Cheney, 2005, pp. 96–97) until the early 1970s, governments of Western countries have been maintaining the Keynesian model of social democracy, wherein the system of fixed exchange rates (Bretton Woods), low inflation, and full employment, the country has taken care over satisfying social services. This stability was disturbed by the oil crisis in the early 1970s and high inflation. Many of these countries traverse to free market neoliberalism already in the 1980s. The government participates in the economic sector as little as possible; there are deregulation, privatisation, and marketisation which means that a considerable part of social services is left to the market and individual need satisfaction, which were organised collectively before. The government has withdrawn from its function in the welfare system, lowered taxes, and left individuals responsible for their own welfare. Otherside, significant processes of globalisation have manifested in free financial capital movement and the globalisation of financial markets. In such conditions, the necessary negative appearance of uncontrolled spreading of the market principles in the public sector and civil society has occurred. More social inequalities within individual national countries (globally between developed countries and countries in transition) have led to a compromised model of economic and social development, which is known as the 'third way'. The neoliberal model was rejected, but not the market mechanism. The tendency is to compromisingly conciliate the market economy with a more substantial influence on equality, solidarity, and reciprocity. Social services want to be ensured a new relationship between civil society and the state and the strongest influence of various types of community operations on the insurance of social welfare. Therefore, interest in the theoretical elaboration of social entrepreneurship was born, as well as empirical researches on this phenomenon.

2. What is Social Entrepreneurship and Who is a Social Entrepreneur?

The question is, what is social entrepreneurship? The answer is complex because there is no general definition of social entrepreneurship or classic (commercial) entrepreneurship. In the traditional sense, entrepreneurship is connected with business and profit activities, and the definitions mainly consist of the profit component. However, versatile analysis of entrepreneurial activities goes behind only earning profit (Wickham, 2006, pp. 180–181) and shows the following:

- 'entrepreneurship is a style of management;
- entrepreneurs are managers who are very effective at pursuing opportunity and creating change;
- entrepreneurship is a social as well as an economic activity; and
- the motivations of the entrepreneur are varied and go beyond a desire to make money; they also involve a desire to create a new and better world'.

Hence, the term *entrepreneurship* can also be derived from activities outside the strictly economic field and motives of creating money. What is typical for entrepreneurship, no matter the field? There are three elements (Thompson, Alvy, & Less, 2000, p. 330):

- 'a vision;
- someone with leadership skills who can operationalise the vision – which often involves finding a suitable partner, engaging the support of a range of, sometimes voluntary, helpers, and dealing with inevitable setbacks (the vision may be that of the social entrepreneur who starts the venture or one which is "bought-in"; and
- a will to build something which will grow and endure'.

These terms can also be presented if we mention some essential entrepreneurship functions that differ from classic management. Mostly they are innovation and risk takeover because entrepreneurs start proactive actions in which they bear the risk and implement innovations. The next entrepreneurship function is to take these actions before competitors so that they can create a vision of market opportunities for an entrepreneurial venture. Proactive entrepreneurs are the ones who create or control the situation as causes of events and do not react to what had previously happened. A typical entrepreneur's function is network expansion. There can be a formal network towards individual stakeholders and an informal network (friends, informal business contacts, and family). Spreading the network is not just a tool for generating profit; it also creates social capital representing an intangible network of all kinds, which helps society to accept changes easier. Social capital is an essential resource in the social economy. The next significant entrepreneurship function is team building and building the organisation by getting necessary resources, technology, personnel, etc. Entrepreneurship functions can be shown as degrees of certain processes (Thompson, 2002, p. 415):

- 'Envisioning – clarifying a need, gap, and opportunity.
- Engaging – engaging the opportunity with a mind to doing something about it.
- Enabling – ensuring something happens by acquiring the necessary resources, such as people and money and, if necessary, premises.
- Enacting – championing and leading the project to a satisfactory conclusion.'

From the following entrepreneurship functions, we can derive the necessary attributes of a successful entrepreneur. He is innovative, oriented towards searching the opportunities, who has the resources, and generates value. More detailed

(Zimmerer & Scarborough, 2005, pp. 4–5), entrepreneurs' characteristics are as follows:

- '*Willingness for responsibility*. Entrepreneur feels deep responsibility for started venture. He wants to control his own resources and use them to achieve wanted goals.
- *Readiness on medium risk*. Entrepreneurs do not want high risk but are ready to accept medium, calculated one.
- *Trust in his ability to succeed*. Entrepreneurs often have enormous trust in own ability to succeed. They tend to be optimistic towards their opportunities to succeed.
- *Want for immediate reaction*. Entrepreneurs enjoy handling their business and want to know the majority to independently make business decisions.
- *High energy level*. Entrepreneurs are more energetic than usual men. This energy can be critical factor for starting their own enterprises.
- *Orientation towards future*. Entrepreneurs have a good defined feeling to search for the opportunities. They look forward and are less laden with yesterday and focus more on tomorrow.
- *Organizational skill*. Entrepreneurs know how to connect men for accomplishing certain duties. Effectively men and job combining allow them to transform their vision in reality.
- *Willingness for success before the money*. It is not true that entrepreneurs only search for the money. Moreover, their willingness for success is on the first place, and the money is the way to evaluate this achievement.'

We can differentiate entrepreneurial management from conventional by defining *entrepreneurship* as a management style. Namely, entrepreneurial management is focussed on changes, not preserving continuity; it deals with the whole organisation, not only specific divisions, and searches for new opportunities but does not want to conserve current resources.

After mentioning basic principles about entrepreneurs and entrepreneurship, we can define social entrepreneurship and social entrepreneur. The critical difference is that social entrepreneurs aim to create positive social change, not only money. Social entrepreneurs search for the opportunity to make society better, and concerning that, they overtake actions. They have a clear conscious about their social mission, they are searching for new and better ways to create social values, and their primary goal is to make the world a better place to live. Social entrepreneurs are bearers of society changes by (Dees, Emerson, & Economy, 2001, p. 5):

- '*Adopting a mission to create and sustain social value*. For social entrepreneurs, the mission of social improvement is critical, and it takes priority over generating profits. Instead of going for the quick fix, social entrepreneurs look for ways to create lasting improvements.
- *Recognizing and relentlessly pursuing new opportunities to serve that mission*. Where others see problems, entrepreneurs see opportunities. Social

entrepreneurs have a vision of how to achieve their goals, and they are determined to make their vision work.

- *Engaging in a process of continuous innovation, adaptation, and learning.* Social entrepreneurs look for innovative ways to assure that their ventures will have access to needed resources funding as long as they are creating social value.
- *Acting boldly without being limited to resources currently in hand.* Social entrepreneurs are skilled at doing more with less and at attracting resources from others. They explore all resource options, from pure philanthropy to the commercial methods of the business sector, but they are not bound by norms and traditions.
- *Exhibiting a heightened sense of accountability to the constituencies served and for the outcomes created.* Social entrepreneurs take steps to assure they are creating value. They seek to provide real social improvements to their beneficiaries and their communities as well as an attractive social and/or financial return to their investors.'

Defining *entrepreneurship* as a wanted skill of management emphasises creation and vision governance, transferring the skill to others, motivating the people to operate concerning their vision, and possessing of leader skills – it points to a common attribute of all entrepreneurial ventures, no matter whether they are in the private, public or not-for-profit sector. Although many social entrepreneurs have skills and attributes which can associate with commercial entrepreneurs, they have primary operation community place, and are more preoccupied with worry and help, than generating money (Thompson, 2002). One of the most accepted definitions of *social entrepreneurship* is mentioned by Mort, Weerawardena, and Carnegie (2003, p. 76):

> A multidimensional construct involving the expression of entrepreneurially virtuous behaviour to achieve the social mission, a coherent unity of purpose and action in the face of moral complexity, the ability to recognise social-value creating opportunities, and key decision-making characteristics of innovativeness, proactiveness, and risk-taking.

However, if we want to strictly differentiate social entrepreneurs from classical ones, we have to take various criteria for differentiating personal motivation, sector activity, and ethical judgement (Table 1).

Borders of different sectors in which entrepreneurial ventures are accepted are mostly undefined. This is a consequence of the gap in satisfying social services in which society was founded, and for which had previously taken care welfare state. Therefore, we can find examples of social entrepreneurship in the private, public, and not-for-profit sectors. For example, in the private sector that searches for profit, we can find examples of how that business has specific liabilities to do well and help the society to keep the environment with its strategies and financial donations. A similar example we can find in enterprises in this sector that have important social skills and lend money and knowledge to not-for-profit

Table 1. Social and Commercial Entrepreneurs – Similarities and Differences

	Commercial Entrepreneur	**Social Entrepreneur**
Motivation	Motivated to maximise own wealth	Motivated to maximise social impact and values
Sector	Commercial/profit oriented	Public/non-profit/NGOs
Organisational form	Entrepreneur as a leader in a traditional hierarchy	Egalitarianism before efficiency in non-traditional business form
Strategies	Aggressive competition; focussed on maximised return for him/herself	Evade competition; focussed on social value maximisation
Relationship with stakeholders	Relationship with investors are seen as critical, while those with customers as means to end	Stakeholders are considered as wide and broad groups
Social environment interactions	Aspire narrow social legitimacy	Aspire general social legitimacy from several parties
Ethical issues	Self-interested above all; altruism is not a strong part. Unethically oriented or ethically neutral?	Altruism before self-interest. Ethically oriented?

Source: Based on Wickham (2006, p. 184).

organisations. On the contrary, not-for-profit organisations can have branches that generate profit for the social goals of those organisations. Mentioned examples of social entrepreneurship in hybrid forms between private, public, and not-for-profit sectors show that all types of entrepreneurship have something familiar, and these are some basic ways of operating and behaving in their entrepreneurial ventures because they behave entrepreneurial no matter the sector.

3. Social Entrepreneurship in Croatia

Interest in social entrepreneurship in Croatia has increased over the past 10 years. At the beginning of the 2000s, most social enterprises in Croatia operate within civil society organisations – either by establishing a separate legal entity, usually a cooperative or a company, which returns its profits to the civil society organisation that founded it; or by organising an initiative for social entrepreneurship within the organisation's own work (Government of the Republic of Croatia, 2012).

Currently, no specific law defines or regulates a social enterprise as a separate legal entity. However, the legal acts related to the operations of social entrepreneurs within the framework of Croatian legislation are as follows: Act on Croatian Veterans of the Homeland War and Members of Their Families (Official Gazette 121/17, 98/19, 84/217), Act on Credit Institutions (Official Gazette 159/13, 19/15, 102/15, 15/18), Act on Professional Rehabilitation and Employment of Persons with Disabilities (Official Gazette 157/13, 152/14, 39/18, 32/20), Act on Accounting of Non-Profit Organizations (Official Gazette 121/14), Act on Commercial Companies (Official Gazette 152/11, 111/12), Act on Associations (OG 74/14), Act on Institutions (OG 76/93, 29/97, 47/99, 35/08), Act on Cooperatives (Official Gazette 34/11, 125/13, 76/14), and Act on Foundations (Official Gazette 36/95, 64/01).

Accordingly, social entrepreneurship can be carried out through associations, cooperatives, institutions, foundations, companies, and protective and integrative workshops that are not separate legal units, but can operate within cooperatives, trading companies, or institutions and are subject to the Act on Professional Rehabilitation and Employment Person With Disability. According to the law mentioned above (2013), an integrative workshop is defined as

> an institution or company established to employ persons with disabilities who cannot be employed on the open labour market ... and employs at least 40% of persons with disabilities in relation to the total number of employees.

A protective workshop is defined as

> an institution or commercial company that is established to employ persons with disabilities who cannot be employed in integrative workshops, ..., and employs at least 51% of persons with disabilities in relation to the total number of employees, exclusively in protective workplaces.

The forms of social enterprises operating on the market of the Republic of Croatia with subtypes within each category are listed in Fig. 1.

Vidović and Baturina (2016, 2021) reported in their research the division of social enterprises in the Republic of Croatia into three types that differ regarding the motivation or purpose of starting a social enterprise and its management: (a) *social enterprises driven by the purpose of employment* – social enterprises driven by people, (b) *social enterprises driven by financial sustainability goals* – social enterprises guided by earned income, and finally (c) *social enterprises driven by the search for innovative solutions* – social enterprises driven by innovations.

Social enterprises driven by the purpose of employment – any form of social enterprise in which vulnerable groups with limited access to the regular labour market are employed, most often people with disabilities, ethnic minority groups, older women, etc. (Vidović & Baturina, 2016). They are often organised as cooperatives, but this social enterprise also includes protective and integrative workshops and social enterprises for work integration (Work Integration Social Enterprise – WISE). The latter companies help to include mostly disabled people in work

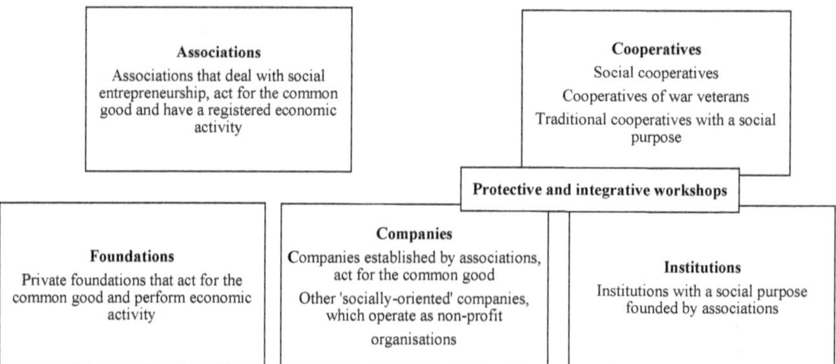

Fig. 1. Spectrum of Forms of Social Enterprises in the Republic of Croatia. *Source*: European Commission (2019).

and social integration by allowing them to enter the labour market (Marković, Baturina, & Babić, 2017), and their main goal is to help low-skilled unemployed people who are threatened with permanent exclusion from the labour market (Defourny & Nyssens, 2006).

Social enterprises driven by financial sustainability goals – this type usually appears as limited liability companies in already established civil society organisations/NGOs that have utilised donated financial funds. They are forced to start economic activities in order to fulfil their social goals (Vidović & Baturina, 2016).

The last type of social enterprise is based on social innovation. The motivation lies in implementing an innovative response to a need that the social system does not satisfy. This sort of enterprise tends to be very innovative in developing new business models, services or products with good potential for growth and spreading influence to the region or even the whole world (Vidović & Baturina, 2021). This group's most frequent organisation and legal forms are some hybrid forms that join a non-profit organisation and a subsidiary company or spin-off enterprise (Vidović & Baturina, 2016).

Vuković, Kedmenec, and Detelj (2017) identified three types of social entrepreneurs: *actors of the civil sector* – they are related to associations and the specific needs of association members, social entrepreneurship for therapeutic work, training for the labour market, employment of people with disabilities, etc., commitment to social goals and reliance on external sources of financing; *those who act as professional managers* – a professional approach to leading and managing a social enterprise, previous work experience in the field of expertise, sustainability as a goal of a social enterprise; and *those who act as entrepreneurs* – identify with traditional and social entrepreneurship, balancing between social and business (economic) goals.

The exact number of enterprises that can be considered social enterprises is not known in Croatia. The reason for this is the lack of records of social enterprises (Kolaković, Turuk, & Turčić, 2018), which would greatly facilitate monitoring the number, growth, and development of social enterprises. However, domestic scholars have researched to determine and/or estimate the number of social enterprises. The number of social enterprises is estimated between 40 and 210 according to the social enterprise mapping project for the European Commission (ICF Consulting Services, 2014), while Šimleša, Puđak, Majetić, and Tonković (2015) estimate the number at 90 legal entities that meet the criteria according to the Social Entrepreneurship Development Strategy. The latest research indicates about 70 active social enterprises and about five hundred potential social enterprises (WYG Consulting, 2021). Lists of all surveys that estimate the number of active and potential (in brackets) social enterprises in the Republic of Croatia are presented in Table 2.

Vidović states in the report on social entrepreneurship and the ecosystem a number of 526 social enterprises operating in the Republic of Croatia (that is

Table 2. Estimated Number of Social Enterprises in the Republic of Croatia According to Previous Research

Year of the Conducted Research	Estimated Number of (Potential) Social Enterprises	Source
2012	40	Online database of social enterprises, Slap Association, portal pomakonline.com according to Šimleša et al. (2015)
2013	(147) 56	Research by CEDRA HR (Cluster for Eco-Social Innovation and Development) according to Turza (2014) and the European Commission (2019)
2013	95	Institute of Social Sciences 'Ivo Pilar', iPRESENT Project, according to Šimleša et al. (2015)
2013	40–210	A map of social enterprises and their eco-systems in Europe – Country Report Croatia (ICF Consulting Services, 2014)
2014	90	Project iPRESENT, Institute of Social Sciences 'Ivo Pilar' (Šimleša et al., 2015)
2017	105	Mapping Social Entrepreneurs, ACT Group for Internal Use by WYG Consulting (2021)
2018	(526)	Country report about Croatia – Social enterprises and their ecosystems in Europe, according to European Commission (2019)
2020	86	European Social Enterprise Monitor, research for Croatia, ACT Grupa (Dupain et al., 2021)

Source: Based on WYG Consulting (2021).

estimated according to the EMES criteria). Of these are (ordered by type of social enterprise from the largest to the smallest number):

> associations that deal with social entrepreneurship, act for the common good (environmental protection, sustainable development, social care, health care, childcare, and education, etc.) and have registered economic activity – 346 enterprises; companies founded by associations, and acting for the common good – 50 enterprises; veterans' cooperatives – 35 enterprises; cooperatives with a social purpose – 33 enterprises; social cooperatives – 25 enterprises; institutions with a social purpose owned by associations – 15 enterprises; other companies with a social purpose, which operate as non-profit organisations – 10 enterprises and protective workshops – 7 enterprises; private foundations that act for the common good and perform the economic activity – 5 enterprises. (European Commission, 2019)

In the last recent survey conducted in 2020 by the Initiative of Euclid Network under the name European Social Enterprise Monitor (ESEM) in seven countries of the European Union and the United Kingdom, 86 social enterprises participated in the research from the Republic of Croatia gave. According to the legal form, the largest share was made by limited liability companies (29%), with a share of 9% of simple limited liability companies making a share in the sample of almost 40%. The following most represented forms were associations with 27% and cooperatives with 23%. The rest was made up of institutions with 7%, joint-stock companies with 3%, and all other forms with 3%. The sample from Croatia, according to the main activity and the sector in which the analysed companies operate, mostly accounted for other service activities (member organisations: other personal services) 20%, then education 19% and art, entertainment, and recreation 16% (Dupain et al., 2021).

There is a broad spectrum of activities that social enterprises are engaged in the Republic of Croatia: from strictly social and social activities such as social welfare services, social and health work activities; education and training: social cooperatives through activities related to agriculture, forestry, and fishing; ecological/environmental activities such as sustainable tourism, renewable energy, sustainable waste management; up to activities that at first glance cannot be connected with social entrepreneurship; accounting and other administrative services, wholesale and retail trade, metal industry, cosmetics industry, urban planning, and construction, art, entertainment and recreation, IT industry and others (ACT Group, 2017 according to WYG Consulting, 2021; Šimleša et al., 2015; Vidović & Baturina, 2016).

3.1. The Positive Practice of Social Entrepreneurship in Croatia

Association for Creative Development Slap deals with development projects which encourage social employment of young people and other marginalised groups in the labour market. The Association acknowledges the importance on Croatian local products, tradition, and culture. As a part of its projects, it provides microcredit lines, marketing services, and professional assistance to social entrepreneurs. So far it successfully participated in several projects, including the Ethno brand project through which handmade artefacts based on traditional values and motives were woven into the modern and practical items. Products are made by unemployed women and are sold through web stores. Project EcoCompetitive aimed to promote the competitiveness of manufacturers of organic foods from Slavonia and Baranja counties. The project enabled access to microcredits to entrepreneurs in order to start their own organic production. All the participants visited Belgium where they could also acquire the necessary knowledge and skills for organic farming from the local producers. In addition to the above projects, the Association through its training centre held workshops and consultations for all interested civil society organisations with various topics such as the development of social entrepreneurship, market positioning, access to finance, sustainability, etc. The Association is mainly financed by offering consulting and marketing services and through European funds. Income earned is mainly directed to programmes of social employment (Slap Association, n.d.).

The activities of the Hands cooperative include farming seasonal fruits and vegetables in greenhouses and represent one of the most significant examples of social entrepreneurship in Croatia. Its production includes women victims of domestic violence, most often financially dependent, under-educated, and without enough work experience. In order to include them in the activities of the Cooperative, women are undergoing non-formal education for the production of vegetables in the greenhouse. In addition to growing fruits and vegetables, Cooperative empowers women to become carers of elderly and sick people. Although the Cooperative is mainly funded independently from its revenues, it is also financed through local and regional authorities, government programmes, and European funds. Cooperative reinvests its revenues in new employment programmes (Ruke Cooperative, n.d.).

ACT Printlab is a design, visual communication, and web development studio. The enterprise is democratically organised and every employee and member of the management has one vote in the decision-making process. ACT Printlab is a profitable enterprise that reinvests its profit in various social projects (ACT Printlab, n.d.). ACT Accounting is a profitable enterprise as well, specialised in providing accounting and tax advisory services to non-profit organisations and social enterprises. In addition to the involvement of marginalised groups of society through the employment of people with disabilities, the enterprise also reinvests its profits for the benefit of the local community (ACT Konto, n.d.).

Social Entrepreneurs Forum (SEFOR, n.d.) project is used to create a stimulating environment for social employment in Croatia by encouraging a higher level of sustainability of non-profit organisations. The tasks of the Forum are to develop national networks, create a forum of support, gather local social entrepreneurs, map capacity and creation of a database, and organise informational seminars, conferences, etc. It aims to ensure the sustainability of non-profit organisations, and provide a safer workplace to their employees. Furthermore, the project aims to increase the employment of marginalised population groups in the labour market and improve the capacity of social entrepreneurs in order to increase their competitiveness. The target groups are social entrepreneurs who need assistance strengthening their capacity to manage and better position their companies. In addition, 30–50 organisations involved in social employment become SEFOR members and receive information and education through web magazines, manuals, and other supporting activities. It is estimated that the targeted 40 social entrepreneurs will employ at least 200 people. These companies currently provide at least 100 jobs through their social employment projects but have the potential for employment of at least 100 new people (SEFOR, n.d.).

Social cooperative Humana Nova was founded in 2011. The vision of social cooperative Humana Nova is to become a leader of social entrepreneurship, recognised in the wider region, and to actively and directly contribute to building a society of tolerance, cooperation, and assistance to socially excluded individuals and their families, and to improve their self-esteem and quality of life. The Cooperative was founded as part of the ESCO 'Education for Social Co-operatives – New Opportunities for Persons with Disabilities' project which was started with the purpose to provide people with disabilities new employment opportunities. Thirty-eight people attended its educational activities. The main objective of the project was to increase employment opportunities for people with disabilities in Medimurje county, promote social inclusion and raise awareness of the employment opportunities of people with disabilities, and to develop sustainable models at a local and national level. Eight people successfully completed the course for office administrator while five completed a course for web administrators. Nine people are reclassified to accountants, and eight people are reclassified to tailors. Today Cooperative employs 45 people – 25 of whom are disabled, and 13 are members of other marginalised groups whose work at Humana Nova changes their lives. As can be seen, Humana Nova encourages the employment of people with disabilities and other socially excluded people through the production and sale of high-quality and innovative textile products of ecological and recycled materials for domestic and overseas markets. According to Cooperative, 2,000 tons of clothing and footwear were collected so far through its work. In addition, Cooperative actively and directly contributes to building a society of tolerance and cooperation and helps socially excluded individuals and their families to improve their self-esteem and quality of life. Humana Nova actively contributes to the sustainable development of local communities, poverty reduction, and environmental protection (Humana Nova Cooperative, n.d.).

3.2. The Perspective of Social Entrepreneurship

Term social entrepreneurship for the first time is mentioned in one strategic national document in Croatia – 'National Strategy for Creating a Stimulating Environment for the Development of Civil Society (for the period 2006–2011)', but Vincetić, Babić, and Baturina (2013) consider that the mentioned concept

> is not a definition, but rather a framework that is defined as follows: social or non-profit entrepreneurship occurs in different forms and through different subjects of income acquisition, striving to achieve economic, social and ecological effects at the same time.

In 'National strategy of creating a stimulating environment for the development of civil society 2012–2016' (Government of the Republic of Croatia, 2012), the concept of social entrepreneurship is defined in more detail as

> a way of solving social problems by applying the entrepreneurial method, taking into account sustainable development and applying a system of democratic decision-making (with solidarity and mutual aid) and defined activities aimed at the development of non-profit, social entrepreneurship.

According to the Strategy for the Development of Social Entrepreneurship in the Republic of Croatia from 2015 to 2020 (Government of the Republic of Croatia, 2015), social entrepreneurship has for the first time official definition. It is defined as 'a business based on the principles of social, environmental, and economic sustainability, in which generated profit is entirely or largely reinvested for the benefit of the community'. However, Kolaković et al. (2018, p. 133) emphasise that

> the concept of social entrepreneurship in Croatia is defined more broadly due to the lack of a clear definition of the sector (non-profit, business or government sector) in which social entrepreneurship can occurs.

The criteria for recognising social entrepreneurs are also for the first time defined in Croatia in the Social Entrepreneurship Development Strategy (Government of the Republic of Croatia, 2015, p. 8):

- A social entrepreneur achieves a balance of social, environmental, and economic business goals.
- A social entrepreneur carries out the activity of production and trade of goods, provision of services, or performs an artistic activity that generates income on the market and that has a favourable impact on the environment, contributes to the improvement of the development of the local community and society as a whole.
- A social entrepreneur creates new value and ensures financial sustainability in such a way that, in the three-year period of operation, at least 25% of the annual income is planned to be realized or realized through the performance of its entrepreneurial activity.
- A social entrepreneur invests at least 75% of the annual profit, i.e. the excess income generated by the performance of his activity, in the realization and development of business objectives, that is, activities.

- A social entrepreneur is characterized by voluntary and open membership and the autonomy of business, that is, activity.
- The Republic of Croatia, a unit of local and regional (regional) self-government or public authority cannot be the sole founder of a social entrepreneur.
- A social entrepreneur is characterized by a democratic way of decision-making (involvement of stakeholders in transparent and responsible management), that is, decision-making is not exclusively related to ownership shares or membership roles, but includes key stakeholders: workers, members, users, or consumers, and cooperative organizations.
- The social entrepreneur monitors and evaluates his social, economic, and environmental effects and impact, as well as the results of the evaluation of benefits in planning his further business and taking care of their improvement.
- In the event that a social entrepreneur ceases to carry out his activity, his general acts have a defined obligation to transfer his remaining assets, after covering liabilities to creditors and covering losses from the previous period, to the ownership of another social entrepreneur with the same or similar business goals, or to the ownership of a unit.

It is visible from the above criteria that they are aligned with the criteria stated in the EMES European research network. Despite the progress made in the sphere of social entrepreneurship, the aforementioned strategy did not achieve the set goals. A significant part of the planned activities was not implemented. According to the final report on the evaluation of the Social Entrepreneurship Development Strategy (WYG Consulting, 2021, p. 24)

> out of a total of 31 activities planned within the framework of the five measures of the Social Entrepreneurship Development Strategy, only one activity was implemented, while 10 activities were partially implemented, with limited achieved indicators and impact on the achievement of goals Strategies for the development of social entrepreneurship and with a minimal contribution to the development of a stimulating environment for the development of social entrepreneurship in the Republic of Croatia. 65% of the planned activities were never initiated, even though funds were allocated for this within the Social Entrepreneurship Development Strategy.

Failure to initiate the planned activities directly affected the development of the social entrepreneurship ecosystem in the Republic of Croatia, resulting in its slowdown. For example, the planned Register of Social Enterprises, based on which social enterprises would apply for tenders and grants for financing, was never established, although it was planned to be established in the second quarter of 2016 (Kolaković et al., 2018).

Furthermore, in the evaluation report (WYG Consulting, 2021, p. 27) were published information and amounts on planned funds based on Social Entrepreneurship Development Strategy compared with allocated funds for the published call for proposals and direct award and with contracted funds:

> Within the Operational program Effective Human Potential 2014 - 2020 for the operations of the specific objective 9.v.1,[1] a total of HRK 286,117,648.00 (EUR 37,974,337.78) is planned, for the published call for proposals and one direct award a total of HRK 112,517,433.15, (EUR 14,933,629.72) was allocated which represents less than 40% of the planned funds at the level of specific objective 9.v.1. Taking into account the cut-off period until December 31, 2020, 69 projects are being implemented (HRK 70,894,306.63 – EUR 9,409,291.48), which represents 63% of the total allocation for published calls and direct allocation, i.e. only 24.8% of the total planned amount of funds for all interventions within the SC 9.v.1.

The reasons for the low share of contracted funds in relation to the total planned funds can primarily be found in delays with direct allocations, announcements of new calls, evaluation of submitted project proposals and contracting of projects (WYG Consulting, 2021). However, the Ministry of Labour, Pension System, Family and Social Policy, which was in charge of implementing tenders from the Strategy, decided in 2021 on additional financing of 43 projects with a total value of approx. HRK 46,000,000 (EUR 6,105,249.19) as part of the Call for proposals 'Strengthening the business of social entrepreneurs – phase I' whereby, despite the delay, all the allocated funds of that call were contracted (ESF, n.d.).

Social entrepreneurship, unfortunately, did not get the expected growth in its evolution despite the adopted strategy and plans for its development. The Social Entrepreneurship Development Strategy is no longer actual, and a significant opportunity has been missed. Vidović emphasises in the report for the European Commission that the main culprit behind such a lack of development of social entrepreneurship is the inertia and lack of political will of state institutions (European Commission, 2019).

The 'National Development Strategy of the Republic of Croatia until 2030' is the only national strategic document that mentions social entrepreneurship and must be the new cornerstone for the development of social entrepreneurship. Social entrepreneurship is listed within two strategic goals (Government of the Republic of Croatia, 2021):

(a) Goal 1 Competitive and innovative economy – a priority area of public policies 'Development of entrepreneurship and crafts' – support for the development

---

[1]European Social Fund – Operational Program Effective Human Resources 2014–2020; priority axis 2 'Social inclusion' – investment priority 9.v: 'Promotion of social entrepreneurship and professional integration in social enterprises and the social and solidarity economy in order to facilitate access to employment – Specific objective 9.v.1 Increasing the number and sustainability of social enterprises and their employees'. This objective also represents a strategic framework for the development of social entrepreneurship.

of social entrepreneurship is one of the prominent priorities of public policy implementation that will contribute to the development of entrepreneurship and crafts

(b) Goal 5 Healthy, active, and quality life – a priority area of public policies 'Social solidarity and responsibility' – social inclusion, social entrepreneurship, social innovation, employment and greater competitiveness on the labour market will be encouraged and investment in housing for the most vulnerable will be encouraged.

The European Commission (2020) divided countries according to the level of acceptance of the concept of social enterprises in its comparative report on social enterprises and their ecosystem in Europe. Countries were analysed according to the degree of presence in the legal and political framework of various social enterprises and the degree of acceptance of these forms by the enterprises themselves. It was determined that Croatia is in a group of countries where, despite the recognition of the concept of social enterprises by legal and political frameworks, there is insufficient recognition by the social enterprises themselves – the level of self-recognition among organisations is relatively low. Also, the above report analysed the existence of a strategic and legal framework. The Republic of Croatia is in the group of countries with a developed strategic but not developed legal framework.

4. Conclusion

Social entrepreneurship is a commendable concept aimed at community development and solving social problems. Social entrepreneurs strive to maximise social benefit and achieve social goals, and profit maximisation is not primarily important to them. The facts presented in this chapter, about the absence of an exact number of social enterprises, low level of recognition, unclear forms and variations of social enterprises in the Croatian discourse despite the adopted strategic documents, indicate that social entrepreneurship in the Republic of Croatia is still in its initial phase. Furthermore, the potential based on the strategic development document was not used, and not all planned activities were implemented in the period from 2015 to 2020 (only 35% of the planned activities were implemented, while slightly less than 25% of the planned funds were contracted in time duration of the strategy, which is an insufficient figure). It is also negative that there is no continuation of the strategy after 2020, although social entrepreneurship is mentioned in the National Development Strategy of the Republic of Croatia until 2030.

It is necessary to stimulate even more strongly the establishment of social enterprises and to focus on education programmes about and for social entrepreneurship at all educational levels, especially in the domain of higher education and lifelong education. Despite the positive practice of social enterprises and educational programmes for social entrepreneurs, more needs to be done for social entrepreneurship to reach its full potential, develop to an appropriate level and reach the countries of Western and Central Europe. Failure is the government's responsibility as the leading policymaker and other related institutions, which must advocate for social entrepreneurship, and not just declaratively 'on paper' by adopting a strategy. Therefore, it is necessary to adopt a new strategy for developing social entrepreneurship for the upcoming period. However, lessons should be learned from the past period, and the prescribed activities should be implemented on time. It is also necessary to create a Register of Social Enterprises that would help in the development of the social entrepreneurship ecosystem, and in the next step, to develop and adopt the first Act on social enterprises.

References

ACT Konto Ltd. (n.d.). Retrieved from https://act-konto.hr/#onama

ACT Printlab Ltd. (n.d.). Retrieved from http://www.printlab.hr/web/hr/

Dees, J. G., Emerson, J., & Economy, P. (2001). *Enterprising nonprofits: Tools for social entrepreneurs*. New York, NY: John Wiley & Sons, Inc.

Defourny, J., & Nyssens, M. (2006). Defining social enterprise. In M. Nyssens (Ed.), *Social enterprise – At the crossroads of market, public policies and civil society* (pp. 3–26). London: Routledge.

Dupain, W., Pilia, O., Wunsch, M., Hoffmann, P., Scharpe, K., Mair, J. … Bosma, N. (2021). The state of social enterprise in Europe – European Social Enterprise Monitor 2020–2021. Retrieved from https://knowledgecentre.euclidnetwork.eu/download/european-social-enterprise-monitor-report-2020-2021/#

ESF. (n.d.). Retrieved from http://www.esf.hr/natjecaji/socijalno-ukljucivanje/poziv-na-dostavu-projektnih-prijedloga-jacanje-poslovanja-drustvenih-poduzetnika-faza-i/

European Commission. (2011). *Social business initiative: Creating a favourable climate for social enterprises, key stakeholders in the social economy and innovation*. Brussels: European Commission

European Commission. (2019). Social enterprises and their ecosystems in Europe. Updated country report: Croatia. Retrieved from https://www.euricse.eu/social-enterprises-and-their-ecosystems-in-europe-mapping-study/

European Commission. (2020). Social enterprises and their ecosystems in Europe. Comparative synthesis report. Retrieved from https://europa.eu/!Qq64ny

Government of the Republic of Croatia. (2012). National strategy for creating a stimulatory environment for civil society from 2012–2016. Retrieved from https://udruge.gov.hr/UserDocsImages/UserFiles/File/%20strategija%20stvaranja%20poticajnog%20okruženja%20za%20razvoj%20civilnog%20društva%202012-2016.pdf

Government of the Republic of Croatia. (2015). Strategy for the development of social entrepreneurship in the Republic of Croatia for the period from 2015 to 2020. Retrieved from http://www.esf.hr/wordpress/wp-content/uploads/2015/02/Strategija-razvoja-dru%C5%A1tvenog-poduzetni%C5%A1tva-u-RH-za-razdoblje-2015-2020.pdf

Government of the Republic of Croatia. (2021). Croatian National Development Strategy until 2030. Retrieved from https://hrvatska2030.hr/wp-content/uploads/2021/02/Nacionalna-razvojna-strategija-RH-do-2030.-godine.pdf

Humana Nova Cooperative. (n.d.). Retrieved from http://www.humananova.org/hr/home/

ICF Consulting Services. (2014). A map of social enterprises and their eco-systems in Europe, Country Report: Croatia. Retrieved from http://ec.europa.eu/social/BlobServlet?docId=12991&langId=en

Kolaković, M., Turuk, M., & Turčić, I. (2018). Social entrepreneurship: Strategic development in Croatia. *Zagreb International Review of Economics & Business*, *21*(2), 129–143. https://doi.org/10.2478/zireb-2018-0018

Marković, L., Baturina, D., & Babić, Z. (2017). Socijalna poduzeća za radnu integraciju (WISE) u postsocijalističkim zemljama. *Hrvatska revija za rehabilitacijska istraživanja*, *53*(1), 139–158. https://doi.org/10.31299/hrri.53.1.11
Mort, G. S., Weerawardena, J., & Carnegie, K. (2003). Social entrepreneurship: Towards conceptualisation. *International Journal of Non-profit and Voluntary Sector Marketing*, *8*(1), 76–88.
Official Gazette 121/14. Act on accounting of non-profit organisations.
Official Gazette 74/14. Act on associations.
Official Gazette 152/11, 111/12. Act on commercial companies.
Official Gazette 34/11, 125/13, 76/14. Act on cooperatives.
Official Gazette 159/13, 19/15, 102/15, 15/18. Act on credit institutions.
Official Gazette 121/17, 98/19, 84/217. Act on Croatian veterans of the homeland war and members of their families.
Official Gazette 36/95, 64/01. Act on foundations.
Official Gazette 76/93, 29/97, 47/99, 35/08. Act on institutions.
Official Gazette 157/13, 152/14, 39/18, 32/20. Act on professional rehabilitation and employment of persons with disabilities.
Roper, J., & Cheney, G. (2005). The meanings of social entrepreneurship today. *Corporate Governance*, *5*(3), 95–104.
Ruke Cooperative. (n.d.). Retrieved from http://www.pomakonline.com/content/view/619/29/
Šimleša, D., Puđak, J., Majetić, F., & Tonković, A. B. (2015). *Mapping New Horizons – Report on the state of social entrepreneurship in Croatia*. Institute of Social Science Ivo Pilar.
Slap Association. (n.d.). Retrieved from http://www.slap.hr/
Social Entrepreneurs Forum (SEFOR). (n.d.). Retrieved from http://www.pomakonline.com/content/view/624/32/
Thompson, J., Alvy, G., & Less, A. (2000). Social entrepreneur – A new look at the people and the potential. *Management Decision*, *38*(5), 328–338.
Thompson, J. L. (2002). The world of the social entrepreneur. *International Journal of Public Sector Management*, *15*(5), 412–431.
Turza, B. (2014). *Social Entrepreneurship in Croatia: Survey and Analysis of the Results*. Osijek: SLAP
Vidović, D., & Baturina, D. (2016). *Social enterprise in Croatia: Charting new territories*. ICSEM Working Paper No. 32 (pp. 1–24). Retrieved from https://www.iap-socent.be/sites/default/files/Croatia%20-%20Vidovic%20%26%20Baturina_0.pdf
Vidović, D., & Baturina, D. (2021). Social enterprise in Croatia: Charting new territories. In J. Defourny & M. Nyssens (Eds.), *Social enterprise in central and eastern Europe theory, models and practice* (pp. 40–55). London: Routledge. https://doi.org/10.4324/9780429324529-4
Vincetić, V., Babić, Z., & Baturina, D. (2013). Definiranje područja i potencijal razvoja socijalnog poduzetništva Hrvatske u komparativnom kontekstu. *Ekonomski pregled*, *64*(3), 256–278.
Vuković, K., Kedmenec, I., & Detelj, K. (2017). Discourse of social entrepreneurs in Croatia. In M. K. Veysel (Ed.), *Conference proceedings of 5th RSEP social science conference* (pp. 13–19). Ankara: Sanat Kırtasiyecilik Reklamcılık Ltd. Şti.
Wickham, P. A. (2006). *Strategic entrepreneurship*. Hoboken, NJ: Prentice Hall.
WYG Consulting. (2021). Završno izvješće o provedenom vrednovanju - Vrednovanje djelotvornosti, učinkovitosti i učinka Operativnog programa Učinkoviti ljudski potencijali 2014 – 2020, Grupa 7: Vrednovanje društvenog poduzetništva. Retrieved from http://www.esf.hr/wordpress/wp-content/uploads/2021/11/Zavrs%CC%8Cnoizvjes%CC%8Cc%CC%81e_vrednovanje-dru%C5%A1tvenog-poduzetni%C5%A1tva.pdf?msclkid=6fa4274cc80e11ecb50fbe011954a5d2
Zimmerer, T. W., & Scarborough, N. M. (2005). *Essentials of entrepreneurship and small business management*. Hoboken, NJ: Prentice Hall.

Chapter 8

Digital Entrepreneurship and Disruptive Innovation in the Greek Maritime Industry: the Case of Harbor Lab

Daphne Halkias, Mark Esposito, Tatiana Harkiolakis, Jordi Diaz and Nicholas Mmaduabuchi Ikpogu

Abstract

The global shipping industry has been rocked by a wave of disruptive innovation driven by a thriving ecosystem of digital technology start-ups that have emerged in the last few years and set up offices in Greece. After the appearance of COVID-19, entrepreneurial leadership has grown in importance for guiding commercial shipping through times of exceptional circumstances. The problem is that there is a lack of understanding of the experiences of Greek digital entrepreneurs launching their tech start-ups within the maritime sector – from the initial vision to a real-world innovative business disruptor. We aim to answer the questions of who the Greek digital entrepreneur in the maritime sector is and how their entrepreneurial actions contribute to a growing knowledge base of digital entrepreneurship for future theoretical research and professional practice. This single-subject, archival case study demonstrates the social and commercial value of the "who" and "how" of digital entrepreneurship in the maritime sector through the case of Harbor Lab, an Athens-based start-up that disrupted the maritime industry through innovative use of emerging technologies to calculate disbursements (port expenses) and through the establishment of a horizontal, empathetic, open workplace culture. The outcomes of this study contributed a fresh perspective of scholarly knowledge on digital entrepreneurship for future theoretical research and professional practice.

Keywords: Digital entrepreneurship; disruptive innovation; Greece; maritime industry; Harbor Lab; workplace culture; disbursements

---

Entrepreneurship Development in the Balkans: Perspective from Diverse Contexts, 131–150

Published under exclusive licence by Emerald Publishing Limited
doi:10.1108/978-1-83753-454-820231008

1. Introduction

The global shipping industry has been rocked by a wave of disruptive innovation driven by a thriving ecosystem of digital technology start-ups based in Greece that has emerged in the last few years (Papachristou, 2022; Powered by Harbor Lab, 2022). Tech start-ups with solutions that can upscale maritime shipping have blossomed in the local entrepreneurial sector in Greece (OECD, 2020). The total goods of cargo loaded globally totaled 11.076 million tons in 2019 alone, making maritime shipping one of the keystones of the worldwide economy (United Nations Conference on Trade and Development, 2020). In addition to Singapore, Japan, Hong Kong, and China, Greece is one of the five big ship-owning nations, with maritime shipping a crucial pillar of the local Greek economy. Holding about 54% of the European Union (EU)-controlled tonnage and more than 20% of the global tonnage, Greece holds the title of the biggest shipowning nation in the world (Hellenic Shipping News, 2020).

Business and technology models are being altered through digital transformation, which acts as a disruptive innovation in organizations that yields opportunities and challenges for start-ups and established companies in the shipping industry (Raza, Woxenius, Vural, & Lind, 2023; Simplilearn, 2023). The digital transformation of the national economy has reached remarkable progress in the Greek ecosystem, which has had a notably positive impact on innovation in start-ups by Greek digital entrepreneurs (Karagiorgos, 2022). In just 1 year (2018), Athens ascended 28 places higher in the "Founders Choice" category as ranked by founders of a start-up in their picks of foundation country of choice among EU countries, being a crucial breeding ground for innovation in start-ups and ranking among other major European capitals; Greece as a whole nation climbed higher in the ranking as well (Gavalas, 2020).

After the appearance of COVID-19, entrepreneurial leadership has grown in importance for guiding commercial shipping through times of exceptional circumstances (Vasilopoulos & Tsitsakis, 2023). Thanks to growing trends such as digitalization/automation and sustainability (Cyprus Shipping News, 2022), it is more pertinent to analyze the digital entrepreneur's role as a leader in the maritime sector (Elnavi Monthly Shipping Review, 2023). A new kind of transformational leadership is required to foster innovation and adaptation in tech start-ups and is sought at all levels in the current maritime industry environment (Karekla, Pollalis, & Angelopoulos, 2021).

Greece is one of the popular destinations for digital entrepreneurs across industry sectors (Splash, 2022). Nevertheless, how Greek digital entrepreneurs developed and continue to grow their tech start-ups within the maritime sector is considered critical policy information for the future of the Greek economy. Nevertheless, Greece's digital ecosystem remains an understudied research topic in the scholarly literature (Gavalas, 2020). The problem is that there is a lack of understanding of the experiences of Greek digital entrepreneurs launching their tech start-ups within the maritime sector – from the initial vision to a real-world innovative business disruptor.

With full consideration of such a gap in the entrepreneurship, technology, and maritime literature, the purpose of this archival case study is to describe how one Greek digital entrepreneur and his team launched a tech start-up within the maritime sector – from the initial vision to become an innovative, profitable business disruptor in the Greek maritime sector. In doing so, we intend to specify three critical components of digital entrepreneurship a business model, disruption through technology, and disruption through workplace culture. We aim to answer the questions of who the Greek digital entrepreneur in the maritime sector is and how their entrepreneurial actions contribute to a growing knowledge base of digital entrepreneurship for future theoretical research and professional practice. This single-subject, archival case study will demonstrate the social and commercial value of the "who" and "how" of digital entrepreneurship in the maritime sector as an ongoing phenomenon in the global digital economy.

1.1. Background

The maritime logistics industry can barely be defined as a leader in digitalization; nevertheless, it has a crucial role in trade at the regional and global levels (Mallas, 2022; Nguyen, My Tran, Duc, & Thai, 2022). The result of all the challenges the industry faces is poor predictability, challenges which include brutal inter-industry rivalries from competing freight transport modes, low visibility and transparency, high fragmentation, and expensive manual processes, in addition to the common factors of environmental regulations, volatile fuel prices, outdated customer interfaces, and demand uncertainties (Raza et al., 2023). Several independent actors are involved in a door-to-door or port-to-port voyage, with up to 40 actors involved in some cases, leading to a network-centric industry. Poor reliability, longer transit times, an increased cost of maritime logistics services, and delays all result from these maritime logistics actors lacking seamless coordination and using manual processes (Papadakis & Kopanaki, 2022).

Digital transformation yields vital opportunities to improve stakeholders' economic and environmental maritime logistics performance; it has been defined as the needed transformations propelling digitalization between and within organizations based on a specific digital strategy (Kavussanos, Strandenes, & Thanopoulou, 2022). As of late, the applied discourse of maritime informatics has used the critical role of digitalization in maritime logistics operations. The digital transformation of various sections of maritime logistics needs particular attentiveness, even though freight forwarders, rail operators, shipping companies, seaports and inland terminal operators, and road haulers are just some of the many actors involved in the maritime logistics industry (Papageorgiou, 2022; Roblek, Meško, Pušavec, & Likar, 2021).

The digitalization of the shipping industry requires a focused analysis because the demand for shipping services sparks the demand from these networks (Raza et al., 2023). The maritime sector is reluctant to increase innovation and utilize emerging digital technologies despite digital transformation's assured benefits. Maritime logistics industry policymakers and policymakers have gained interest and put forward efforts relevant to digital transformation. However, digital transformation in maritime logistics as a topic in academic research is currently emerging. The pressing demand for more empirical research to achieve more in-depth insights regarding the maritime sector's digital awareness has been stressed by scholars such as Tijan, Jović, Aksentijević, and Pucihar (2021).

1.2. Theoretical Framework

Disruptive Innovation Theory. Although the concept of disruption was first put forth 20 years ago, it can still make a difference between one organization and another today, and it has remained an enduring framework model in the business literature. Professor Clayton Christensen popularized the concept of disruption in his book *The Innovator's Dilemma* in 1997. Twenty years ago, he talked about a new way of innovating by introducing sophisticated technologies to optimize processes and make a difference compared to other organizations. At that time, Christensen emphasized the need to incorporate disruption in the company's daily operations, processes, stakeholder relationships, and communication channels. King and Baatartogtokh (2015) interpreted Christensen's original notion of "the innovator's dilemma," which eventually morphed into a theory of disruptive innovation (Christensen, Raynor, & McDonald, 2015) by stating that disruptive innovation concepts are "new to the world products" or "business model innovations" not just technical innovations (Diaz & Halkias, 2022).

Following this path of disruptive innovation in digital start-ups has accelerated by the exponential enhancement of technology and digital capabilities (Feng, Qin, Wang, & Zhang, 2022). Papathomas and Konteos (2022) used Christensen et al.'s (2015) disruptive innovation as a process whereby entrants with fewer resources can successfully disrupt incumbents by offering a value proposition based on digital technology and a value network utilizing an exponential price-performance trajectory to explain the digital transformation in the Greek banking system. Karekla et al. (2021) also commented on how industry innovation in the Greek marketplace has driven start-ups known for their innovation and industry disruption.

Diffusion of Innovations Framework. Rogers's (2003) theory has provided a foundation for developing many models to elucidate the factors contributing to whether individuals and organizations adopt and share an innovation. According to Rogers (2003), "diffusion is the process by which an innovation is communicated through different channels within a certain time period among the members of a social system" (p. 5). As expressed in this definition, *innovation, communication channels, time, and social systems* are the four critical components of the diffusion of innovations. Rogers (1995), in his seminal theoretical work on the diffusion of innovations, proposes that *relative advantage, compatibility, complexity, observability, and trialability are essential attributes of innovation for its wider acceptance*.

Contemporary economists expect the development of digital entrepreneurship across nations to be modern, contemporary, and inclusive (Goyal, Sergi, & Esposito, 2019). Noninclusive economic and technological development ignites conflicts between rich and poor, rural and urban, educated and uneducated, upper and lower social classes, and indigenous and modern societies (Esposito, 2022). Social values must support innovation diffusion to propel regional economic development in impoverished regions, and local stakeholders drive such changes (Santos & Halkias, 2021).

Acceptance and diffusion of innovation within an industry in a country such as Greece must also be driven by its compatibility with the existing social and cultural norms and a good fit with the specific context's needs, demand, resources, available skills, local entrepreneurial knowledge, and modern financing methods (Ramadani & Schneider, 2013; Sidiropoulos, 2017; Vasilopoulos & Tsitsakis, 2023; Vlados, Katimertzopoulos, & Blatsos, 2018). In their research, Tsolakidis, Mylonas, and Petridou (2020) conducted survey research on 486 start-up owners operating in Greece, where 289 responses were received with findings demonstrating the influence of management and entrepreneurial skills on the development and diffusion of innovation.

Digital Entrepreneurship. Digital entrepreneurship is a term that encompasses online businesses that individuals create and run, including those that have recently adopted metaverse applications (Weking, Desouza, Fielt, & Kowalkiewicz, 2023). Sussan and Acs's (2017) definition of digital entrepreneurship includes the combination of digital infrastructure, digital platforms, and entrepreneurial agents that use computing power on universal public networks are known as digital technologies. The development of digital platforms and related entrepreneurial environments has spearheaded a contemporary perspective on entrepreneurship (Raza et al., 2023; Volkmann & Gavrilescu, 2022).

The advent of innovative and potent digital technologies, platforms, and infrastructures has considerably disrupted innovation and entrepreneurship (Paul, Alhassan, Binsaif, & Singh, 2023). However, the benefits of digital platforms to tech entrepreneurs and the associated technological disruptions leading to digital entrepreneurship remain understudied in the extant entrepreneurship literature (Erkut & Esenyel, 2022). In the post-pandemic era, researchers and practitioners have targeted four critical benefits of digital transformation and digital entrepreneurship: scalability, adaptability, accessibility to global markets, products and customers, and profitability due to a fast virtual presence to grow the steady customer base (Esposito, Lanteri, & Tse, 2021; Ramadani, Istrefi-Jahja, Zeqiri, & Ribeiro-Soriano, 2022; Spyropoulos & Varsakelis, 2023).

2. Literature Review

2.1. Maritime Shipping Digitization

Digital connectivity drives change across the maritime industry; ships can rely on connectivity to collect data, analyze vessel performance, and monitor compliance with environmental regulations (Newsroom, 2021; Nguyen et al., 2022). Digital technology drives growth and development and supports trade creation, efficiency, and access to the market by facilitating data movement across borders. Adopting updated technologies is a significant driver of change in the operations management strategies in many fields, such as automation and industrial manufacturing, supply chain management, agile manufacturing, lean production, and total quality management (Endeavor, n.d.; Goyal et al., 2019).

Blockchain technology provides unchangeable, decentralized, and time-stamped record-keeping attributes critical to enhancing efficiency and improving performance if adopted in the maritime industry (Diaz, Smith, Bertagna, & Bucci, 2023). Maritime shipping digitization uses disruptive technologies to reduce transportation costs, shape global trade prospects and give companies a higher competitive advantage (Georgiou, 2022). Maritime informatics is a new research stream, and scholars contribute to this research gap by analyzing the acceptance of updated digital technologies for logistical and security operations within the maritime sector (Ikpogu, 2021). Digital tools are increasing operational efficiencies, helping to decrease fossil fuel consumption, and reducing the number of port visits for maintenance and repairs. Digitalization is a foundational strategy for meeting the maritime industry's decarbonization goals. With this rapidly evolving digital landscape, connectivity is about doing more and using digital products for smarter workflow, seamless communications, and sustainable environment-friendly processes (Yang, 2019).

Using outdated technology in the industry lowers port performance from cargo handling operations, contributing to port congestion and increasing ship operators' costs (Ikpogu, 2021). The inadequacy of ship repair and maintenance facilities contributes to the high cost of ship repairs and ship abandonment due to the high cost of transporting to a foreign ship repair facility. Digital technology provides a wide range of maritime logistics and electronic data exchange applications from ship to ship, land to ship, and ship to land. These applications can transform traffic, port logistics, and just-in-time shipping, improving navigation and communication efficiency, safety, and data security (Yang, 2019).

Rasvanis and Tselios (2023) argued that digital technologies reduce business operations costs by creating a global digital infrastructure that eliminates intermediaries. Traditional jobs are broken down into tasks and assigned to qualified and low-cost bidders across the globe. Digital platforms provide significant potential for improving, monitoring, controlling, and planning port operation processes to improve sea-land logistics and operational efficiency in the port's networks. Blockchain technology application such as the blockchain documentation transaction system (BDTS) provides a smart bill of lading (B/L) that is extremely fast, safe, reliable, and cost-effective for processing shipping documents across the globe. BDTS creates trust and interaction among issuers, carriers, importers, exporters, and other stakeholders (Papadakis & Kopanaki, 2022).

2.2. Digital Transformation and Disruptive Innovation in the Maritime Industry

Yang (2019) defined the concept of maritime shipping digitization as using disruptive technologies to reduce transportation costs, shape global trade prospects and provide companies with a higher degree of competitive advantage. Maritime informatics is a new research stream, and scholars contribute to this research gap by analyzing the acceptance of updated digital technologies for logistical and security operations within the maritime sector (Ikpogu, 2021).

Technology advances create uncertainty, technostress, and loss of control among employees; thus, resistance and lack of support represent a major behavioral challenge to technology acceptance (Harkiolakis & Komodromos, 2023). Human capabilities to use technology are essential to adopting new processes as new technology's practical knowledge may enhance its acceptance. Ensuring that the workforce has the essential competency for technology use will require an effective workforce and information technology. Learning capabilities are essential for innovating and adopting new technologies, so organizational learning capabilities (OLC) should consider organizational commitment, system perspective, openness, experimentation, transfer, and integration in technology adoption strategies (Esposito, 2022)

Trust and privacy concerns contribute to technology diffusion (Rogers, 2003). For example, mobile commerce (m-commerce) technology provides services such as asset tracking, directory and city guides, emergency services, entertainment, navigation, location-sensitive billing, location-based advertising services, risk- and safety-related services, and traffic updates. There are also security and privacy concerns when the computing power has enormous power to modify the data and when the participating individual wishes to remove his data. A cyber-attack or failure in the system leads to privacy leakages and other vulnerabilities. Stakeholders' interests, an intricate logistics system, and institutional diversity contribute to the identified challenges to technology acceptance, which include the high cost of licensing fees for software and consultancy services, information and communication technologies (ICT) training, lack of trust, government legislation, organizational size, and infrastructural deficits (Gavalas, 2020).

The contemporary digital era of shipping, also known as Shipping 4.0, comprises the Internet of Things (IoT) technology, Big Data Analytics, and cloud computing (Aiello, Giallanza, & Mascarella, 2020; Stamoulis, 2022). This new technology requires four factors to ensure its success: technology availability and robustness, organizations expected benefits and support, enabling environment and favorable policies, and technology infrastructure security. Virtual reality technology, an interactive, immersive, and intuitive learning environment in metaverse-enabled enterprises, is making inroads in various industries such as logistics and transport, manufacturing, product design, and construction (Jović, Tijan, Vidmar, & Pucihar, 2022; Weking et al., 2023).

The high cost of developing, implementing, and maintaining digital systems contributes to blockchain technology challenges in the maritime industry. Papadakis and Kopanaki (2022) identified other challenges: the poor internet connectivity at offshore facilities, out-of-touch decision-makers, the organization's technology-oriented culture, the lack of investment initiatives, the low level of blockchain diffusion through the supply chain, and risk aversion. OLC factors must ensure successful technology acceptance, top management commitment, the shared perspective of shared identity and clear objectives, knowledge transfer and collective learning from individuals and organizations, and an open mindset to test new ideas. Digital facilitation of maritime logistics can provide shipping companies, port operators, freight forwarders, shipping agencies, and other maritime shipping supply chain operators with real-time cargo status tracking (Gavalas, 2020).

2.3. Digital Entrepreneurship and Disruptive Innovation in the Greek Maritime Sector

Greek entrepreneurs, investors, and companies have been driven to explore and re-design opportunities for digitalization in their operations by the European Commission's business requirements. Communication, data exchange, traceability, analysis, and information modeling are among the many solutions disruptive digital innovations offer in the shipping industry and other sectors. In recent years, many young entrepreneurs have set up shop in Athens, Greece, offering a widening range of digital tech services to shipping companies (Great Place to Work, n.d.). Made-in-Greece software is heading far beyond the country's borders, from vessel monitoring to electronic procurement, crewing, and billing.

Recent achievements for digital entrepreneurship in the Greek maritime sector were recently published in *Economia.gr* by Touchtidou (2022) and included the following statistics:

- 2021 was a record year for the Greek Tech scene. Fundraising hit a new full-year record, exceeding $1 billion in equity and debt raised by Greek start-ups, representing an approximately 110% jump compared with 2020.
- The number of full-time equivalent (FTE) employees at Greek start-ups and scale-ups grew by 82%, reaching the all-time high record of 12,785 full-time employees globally, 66% of whom are based in Greece.
- 138 international companies in different stages, from start-ups to big-tech, have set up tech teams in Greece totaling 8,650 employees in tech positions.
- Greek start-ups are becoming key drivers of job creation as the total number of full-time jobs from start-ups in Greece (8,536) is on a par with the full-time jobs created by the international tech companies that have a Greek presence (8,650).
- The research has identified 17 Greek-founded start-ups at Unicorn status (valued at more than $1 billion), 10 of which reached Unicorn status in 2021 (p. 1).

Sustainability has long been a goal of the Greek maritime industry, driven by a desire to reduce the industry's carbon footprint, and digital technologies play a critical role in executing this strategy. As zero-carbon fuels are predicted to be widely adopted over the next decade, all actors involved in the maritime industry, from lenders to charterers to shipowners to cargo owners, are getting ready for a low-carbon future as Greek entrepreneurs lead the world in maritime start-ups.

Continuing digitalization in the supply chain, ports, and other areas will propel efficiency and aid this transition. Emerging business models will propel the transition as maritime clusters and cities lead the industry in this green shift and cope with such global transformations by creating unique strategies. Cities compete to attract the best tech start-ups and the most talented people in today's world, particularly in the maritime industry. Athens is evolving as a city, launching disruptive innovations supported by cutting-edge technologies that are set to transform shipping, and industry experts suggest the capital city of Greece will continue to be one of the leading maritime centers worldwide. Greek digital enterprises continue to innovate with new technologies and services to maintain a competitive edge and retain its best and brightest people through shipping companies' internship and mentoring programs. With the support of the Hellenic Shipping Chamber and the Chamber of Commerce of Piraeus in cooperation with the maritime cluster and incubator hubs such as Piraeus University, competitions and investments by funds and shipping companies to maritime continue to support tech start-ups in the Greek maritime sector.

3. Research Method: The Archival Case Study Design

This study applies an archival case study design (Yin, 2017) to describe and investigate. With full consideration of such a gap in the entrepreneurship, technology, and maritime literature, the purpose of this archival case study is to describe how one Greek digital entrepreneur and his team launched 2020 a tech start-up to become an innovative, profitable business disruptor in the Greek maritime sector. A qualitative approach allows the researcher to gather much richer, in-depth data than quantitative approaches using secondary data or qualitative approaches such as open-ended surveys that only provide limited findings (Halkias, Neubert, Thurman, & Harkiolakis, 2022). The researcher considered various qualitative research methods ranging from ethnographies to document analysis but decided to use an archival case study design because this study aimed to look at "how" the company was launched, adapted to the specific business environment of the maritime sector and at "how" stakeholders perceived this, which ideally fulfills the conditions for an archival case study design (Ellet, 2007; Yin, 2017).

Using the case study research design, investigators can rely on archival data to study organizational practices (Halkias & Neubert, 2020). Ventresca and Mohr (2017) noted that archival research methods allow investigators to study historical data to explore company practices at different times. Archival research has been defined as a systematic form of knowledge inquiry used to search, analyze, and draw inferences from archival data. Investigators could use archival research methods to answer new research questions, evaluate existing conclusions, discover emerging issues, and strengthen findings' transferability by aggregating archival data from multiple sources (Corti, 2004).

Case study design generally allows the researcher to be more flexible when examining contemporary issues, given that, in this case, the researcher cannot control behavioral events (Halkias & Neubert, 2020). At the same time, case study design enables the researcher to clarify aspects of the study's social complexities (Yin, 2017). In archival studies, data collection sources include company annual reports, historical documents, websites, financial reports, and organizational resources. While interview and observation approaches are the most commonly applied methods in qualitative research, a case study design based on archival data offers rich information and valid evidence to support research findings (Corti & Bishop, 2020).

Halkias and Neubert (2020) argued that a case study design is a valuable research tool to understand the links between the personal, social, behavioral, psychological, organizational, cultural, and environmental factors that guide organizational strategy.

Single-subject cases, such as this one on the tech start-up *Harbor Lab*, are used to confirm or challenge a theory or intervention or represent a unique case (Yin, 2017). Unlike group designs, single-case research designs follow an inductive approach, where researchers formulate general principles based on results from particular sets of results and data.

Finally, the research design incorporated investigator triangulation in the content analysis process to strengthen confidence in the findings (Farquhar, Michels, & Robson, 2020). The investigator triangulation team included subject matter experts from disruptive innovation, digital entrepreneurship, and the technology sector of the maritime industry. Each investigator examined the results and findings. We compared results between investigators to develop a broader and more in-depth understanding of how the different investigators viewed the issue and confirmed the trustworthiness of our qualitative data results (Schippling, 2017). This approach will allow us to convey and discuss this qualitative, archival case study purpose methodologically rigorously and meaningfully (Yin, 2017).

4. The Case of Harbor Lab: Digital Entrepreneurship and Disruptive Innovation in the Greek Maritime Industry

4.1. Harbor Lab's Founder: The Journey of a Greek Digital Entrepreneur

From the time he was a child, Antonis Malaxianakis had always dreamed of working in the maritime industry. He began working in his family's business in 2005 while getting an undergraduate degree in statistics from the University of Piraeus. After living through the dark years of Greece's economic crisis from 2008 onwards, Malaxianakis decided to finally pursue his dream and get started in the shipping industry, which remained unaffected by domestic economic conditions. In 2013, he began his first internship at a shipping company, producing performance indicators for a fuel supply office.

As he moved forward with employment in the maritime industry, Malaxianakis began dealing with port expenses, known as disbursements. Port expenses include all expenses incurred by the agent on behalf of the operators of the shipping company while the ship is in port, such as towing and berthing fees. Port expenses are the second-largest expense for shipping companies, reaching approximately 120 billion dollars a year. At that time, the port expenses at this company were dealt with as hardcopy paper invoices stored in a large box. Eventually, they developed internal software to help the company better manage port charges. In 2018, Malaxianakis moved to another shipping company where he took on the role of port expenses supervisor and closely observed the company's tankers involved in the spot market.

Malaxianakis's experience with the industry's inefficient, outdated methods of dealing with port expenses inspired him to start designing a smart expense management software. He first began by communicating with other companies in the industry to see if they faced similar problems. He hired a software designer in 2019, and the software was completed in late 2019 – early 2020. Malaxianakis began slowly introducing it to the industry, where it was very well received; this positive feedback gave him the final push to resign from the shipping company he was employed. The software, named *Harbor Lab*, officially went live on March 10, 2020. At its founding, Malaxianakis raised 150,000 euros for *Harbor Lab* from angel investors, including one of his former employers. The same day it was founded, his first customer was another former employer, reinforcing showing belief in Malaxianakis' vision.

Two days later, however, Greece went into its first lockdown amidst the coronavirus pandemic, interrupting Malaxianakis's plans to sell the software abroad. The shipping industry has traditionally been network-centric and family-controlled, being slower to adopt digitalization and other innovations than other industries such as retail, telecommunications, and banking. Greek shipowners, in particular, have a reputation for being conservative in their business dealings. Adapting to the pandemic situation, Malaxianakis introduced *Harbor Lab* to the Greek domestic market. To his surprise, the software was a rapid success among Greek shipping companies. Initially, Malaxianakis aimed to have 20 ships on the platform by the end of 2020; instead, they ended up with 220.

In 2022, *Harbor Lab* received one of the largest amounts of funding during a seed round for a start-up in the shipping field, totaling 6.1 million euros. The funding round was led by *Speedinvest* and *VentureFriends*. Many additional investors followed, including *Charge VC, Signal Ocean, DOCK, TecPier, Motion Ventures, Innoport*, and others. Prominent tech entrepreneurs also made investments, including the founder of apartment rental agency *Blueground.*

Malaxianakis is among many Greek digital entrepreneurs joining the nation's growing wave of maritime start-ups. Although the shipping industry has been slow to transform digitally, current trends, including a pressing need to lower the industry's carbon footprint, are driving more digital and data-based solutions. Athens is currently one of the leading maritime innovation centers in the world, thanks to the primacy of the shipping industry in the local economy and a wide range of competitions, investments, and grants into maritime start-ups by institutions such as the Hellenic Shipping Chamber, the Chamber of Commerce of Piraeus, Piraeus University, and Athens municipality. Even the notoriously conservative Greek shipowners began seeing value in digital solutions like *Harbor Lab.*

4.2. Habor Lab as a Disruptor in the Maritime Industry

Disruption Through Technology. Shipping companies are taking the first steps toward experimenting with artificial intelligence, blockchain, programmable application interfaces, IoT, and other technologies to improve efficiency and save costs in operations. Shipping companies vary in their level of digital maturity; the intricacy of individual organizations and shipping processes hinder many organizations from implementing digital solutions. Logistics, accounting, and finance tend to be among the least digitally developed segments of shipping companies. Digital strategies in these segments tend to be underdeveloped, and management is skeptical of the value of advanced digital solutions, especially in the face of many companies' tight budgets.

Harbor Lab is the first software-as-a-service on the market that uses cloud-based technology to analyze port expenses, particularly by calculating port charges against port invoices. The software is aimed at shipowners, ship managers, and charterers and is available for desktops and mobile devices. The platform consists of four sections: DA (Disbursement accounting) tool, position list, cost estimator, and port directory. The DA tool analyzes port costs, offers a streamlined process for booking appointments with agents, allows users to request a quote on husbandry services and coordinate launches, and includes a bespoke approval flow and other business intelligence tools and comprehensive reports tailored to the end user. The position list allows users to track vessels and obtain data on their fleet and operations with an organizational operations tool, vessel tracking and weather monitoring features, and data insights and reports. The cost estimator automatically estimates port expenses within moments, with instant rough estimates and a customized, detailed cost analysis based on each vessel's weight, length, and other features.

The uniqueness of the platform lies in two functions: port analysis and request functionality. In port analysis, the platform automatically calculates berthing costs based on the collection of updated prices, analyzing costs for the individual port. Behind the analysis is a team of people who talk directly to port authorities worldwide, get the tariff, and determine how each output is calculated at each port, terminal, and berth, which often represents a different pricing policy.

When a shipping company registers with *Harbor Lab*, the shipping company loads data into the platform, such as the relevant ship's name and IMO ID. Whenever a ship travels to a specific port, the platform makes an appointment with a shipping agent, who enters their details into the platform and submits a pre-invoice. The *Harbor Lab* team receives the document from the agent, splits it into outputs, and writes an algorithm for calculating each output. The algorithm gives the shipping company all the necessary details of the costs they have to pay, including if the agent has overcharged them.

Meanwhile, request functionality refers to the process by which, when a ship docks in a port, the shipping company can request multiple quotes from port agents for various services. When the agents submit the cost, the user from the shipping company presses a button, and a comparison table is instantly created, showing which agent is the cheapest. The user can negotiate the prices and book an appointment with the agent through the platform. In this case, two options are available: the shipping company can get the software in-house if they have the right staff to use it effectively, or outsource the service to *Harbor Lab*, which handles the negotiations on their behalf. In the first option, *Harbor Lab* has a global monopoly; in the second option, it faces competition from two other companies based in India.

Malazianakis's goals for *Harbor Lab* were to reduce the slow, bureaucratic process of calculating port expenses, streamline the process into one integrated solution with as few clicks and windows open as possible, and bring greater transparency to the shipping industry. In doing so, it demonstrates to managers in shipping companies that it promises enormous value as a business tool. It speeds up the process of making appointments, dealing with other processes incurred at ports, and receiving relevant documents, putting their users a step ahead of their competition.

Whereas one operator on their own can only manage six to eight ships, they can reach up to 40 ships with the platform. The platform reduces office administration by 75%, management by 500%, and printed paper use. The DA tool section can save operators $2,000 per port call when the vessel operated in the spot market and $1,500 when time chartered; overall, operators can save up to 6% per call and save on average seven times the amount they spend on the software (which consists of a fixed fee per port call). Shipmangement companies have also reported savings of about 5% compared to the original amounts submitted by agents. The platform's average return on investment is 1 in 9 for commercial management and 1 in 16 for technical management, one of the biggest returns on investment (ROIs) for a shipping company from a digital platform or software.

Disruption Through Workplace Culture. Beyond disrupting the Greek and international shipping industry with the first smart platform to manage port expenses, Malaxianakis also created one of the next generations of humane, horizontal workplaces in Greece. Organizational culture remains a considerable obstacle preventing shipping companies from embracing digital transformation and innovation. A strong hierarchal orientation, dedication to legacy systems, and working in silos prevent individuals in traditional shipping companies from proposing digital solutions out of fear of job loss or disturbing the status quo.

Like many digital ventures abroad, *Harbor Lab* disrupted this model by building a horizontal organization where communication between employees and management is encouraged. From the start, Malaxianakis wanted to create a company where people were the cornerstone of its operations, and transparency thrived in the software and the relationships between employees and management. The company's motto is "Lead by example, lead with empathy." The *Harbor Lab* workplace is where employees are always asked for their opinion on critical decisions, especially those that could impact the company's future. Employees and independent reviewers describe the *Harbor Lab* workplace as one of trust, respect, and cooperation. In 2022, *Harbor Lab* also hired its first People & Culture Director, a rare step for a start-up.

The average lifecycle of an employee in a shipping company often leads to companies being filled with older employees who have specialized in traditional skills, further hampering the innovation possible at these organizations. Shipping company employees tend to be transferred to office work after working for years as master mariners onboard vessels training in traditional skills, in contrast to a younger labor force with digital skills needed to move forward with digital transformation. Younger employees with the required digital skills tend to be difficult to attract in shipping companies.

Harbor Lab, in contrast, attracts employees across the lifespan, focusing on building a healthy, flexible, balanced working environment. Employees are given flexible working hours and can start and end the workday whenever they like, as long as they complete the required daily working hours. They also have the option to work from home and leave early on some days of the week, such as Fridays, and new mothers are given a flexible daily schedule. All employees are entitled to up to 30 days of leave per year, with the possibility of additional days per year for new mothers and new fathers, for birthdays or name days, and for illness (without providing supporting documents), as well as additional days of leave without pay. The company offers yoga sessions twice a week and life coaching sessions once a week, and it has a ping-pong table and access to healthy snacks in its office.

Harbor Lab also helps cultivate digital competencies and nurture young talent through its *HarborLab Academy* online course, which teaches users about disbursement account analysis for those who want to specialize in the field. Available for professionals, students, and other interested individuals, the course covers all aspects of disbursement accounting and port expenses, such as appointments and requests for quotes, proforma and final disbursement accounts, evaluating disbursement accounts, standard forms of voyage and time charter parties and their clauses, and different kinds of port charges and supporting documents needed for disbursements accounts. The course also utilizes case studies to help students apply the knowledge they have gained in practice.

Harbor Lab's collaboration and open communication culture also comes through in its partnerships with other companies emphasizing information sharing and data transparency. In 2022, they integrated with fleet management and operations systems software to share data between the two systems and save their clients the inconvenience of making double entries into the programs. The company is also partnering with all the Enterprise Resource Planning and Voyage Estimation Systems already used by shipping companies and continues to seek new partnerships as it develops and grows.

4.3. Looking Toward the Future

Today, *Harbor Lab* has a turnover of around 2.5 million euros annually and has implemented over 10,000 port calls. The company has 52 employees and 750 participating ships from the Greek and international shipping community, with a ratio of one employee for 40 steamers. As well as its head office in Athens, the company now has offices in London and will soon expand to Singapore and Copenhagen. Harbor Lab's clients include prominent names in the Greek and international shipping industry, including both of Malaxianakis's former employers and *Blue Seas Shipping, Kyklades Maritime, Pleiades Shipping, Golden Union, Queensway Navigation, SwissChemGas, TMA Bulk*, and *Olam*, among others.

With Malaxianakis's 6.1 million euro funding, he aims to streamline further the process of a company joining the platform without providing massive amounts of data and develop the algorithms to the point where all procedures can be automated with a single reading of the .pdf file of the expense report. Malaxianakis also aims to hire specialized personnel to develop the software further, expand the company's reach to North American and Asian markets, and eventually have a ratio of one employee to 200 steamers.

Malaxianakis received the Next Generation award in the shipping industry in the recent Lloyd's List Greek Shipping Awards 2022. *Harbor Lab* has also been awarded for its innovative approach to workplace culture. *Harbor Lab* was certified as a "Great Place to Work" for November 2022 – November 2023 in

Greece. Great Place to Work is an independent organization in Greece that certifies workplaces in Greece and internationally based on five dimensions: reliability, respect, justice, pride, and companionship. In *Harbor Lab*'s Great Place to Work certification, 84% of its employees considered it an ideal working environment. Great Place to Work also certified *Harbor Lab* as one of the Best Workplaces Hellas 2022; it was the only maritime-affiliated company to make the ranking for the small-sized businesses section of the list (workplaces with 20–49 employees), where it ranked fourth on the list.

Malaxianakis's business idea to simplify and digitize a complex, bureaucratic, unglamorous part of the shipping process disrupted an entire industry lagging in digital transformation. In doing so, he created one of the first digital native organizations targeting the shipping industry. Harnessing the power of data analytics and artificial intelligence, *Harbor Lab* offers shipping companies massive time and money savings and immense digital value. However, an integral part of a digital native organization is a workplace with a collaborative, horizontal form of governance, unencumbered by traditional, hierarchal work models.

Malaxianakis is one of the pioneers in bringing artificial intelligence, data analytics, and cloud computing to the shipping industry. In the years to come, data-driven solutions will continue to gain prominence in this industry, and the demand for talent with data competencies will grow. Malaxianakis predicts that new talent will seek financial compensation and transparent, fair workplaces where employees' voices are heard and valued. These demands – for more data-based solutions and more humane workplaces – caused *Harbor Lab* to disrupt the maritime industry and pave the way for more digital disruption and innovation in this sector.

5. Conclusion

In this decade, digital connectivity between ships and shore will be driven by digital entrepreneurship that will drive operational efficiency and automation, safety and security issues, and reduce the environmental impact of shipping activities. Further scholarly insight is needed into how the digital entrepreneur has transformed into a leader in the maritime sector today, given emerging trends such as sustainability and Industry 4.0. Greece is one of the popular destinations for digital entrepreneurs across industry sectors. Nevertheless, how Greek digital entrepreneurs developed and continue to grow their tech start-ups within the maritime sector is considered critical policy information for the future of the Greek economy. Extant literature searches revealed a lack of understanding of the experiences of Greek digital entrepreneurs launching their tech start-ups within the maritime sector – from the initial vision to a real-world innovative business disruptor.

With full consideration of such a gap in the entrepreneurship, technology, and maritime literature, the purpose of this archival case study is to describe the case of *Harbor Lab*, a tech start-up, and how its founder, a Greek digital entrepreneur, and his team-led one of the most commercially successfully a tech start-up within the maritime sector – from the initial vision to become an innovative, profitable business disruptor in the Greek maritime sector. Through *Harbor Lab*'s story, this single-subject, archival case study presented three critical components of digital entrepreneurship: a business model, technology disruption, and workplace culture. The outcomes of this study contributed a fresh perspective of scholarly knowledge on digital entrepreneurship for future theoretical research and professional practice. This single-subject, archival case study demonstrated the social and commercial value of the "who" and "how" of digital entrepreneurship in the maritime sector has launched a growing phenomenon in the global digital economy.

References

Aiello, G., Giallanza, A., & Mascarella, G. (2020). Towards shipping 4.0. A preliminary gap analysis. *Procedia Manufacturing*, *42*, 24–29.

Christensen, C. M., Raynor, M., & McDonald, R. (2015). What is disruptive innovation? *Harvard Business Review*. Retrieved from https://hbr.org/2015/12/what-is-disruptive-innovation

Corti, L. (2004). Archival research. In M. S. Lewis-Beck, A. Bryman, & T. F. Liao (Eds.), *The SAGE encyclopedia of social science research methods* (pp. 20–21). Thousand Oaks, CA: Sage. doi:10.4135/9781412950589

Corti, L., & Bishop, L. (2020). Ethical issues in data sharing and archiving. In Ron Iphofen (Ed.), *Handbook of research ethics and scientific integrity* (pp. 403–426). Cham: Springer.

Cyprus Shipping News. (2022, July 1). Harbor lab recognised by best workplaces and appoints people and culture director. Retrieved from https://cyprusshippingnews.com/2022/07/01/harbor-lab-recognised-by-best-workplaces-and-appoints-people-culture-director/

Diaz, J., & Halkias, D. (2022, September 1). E-healthcare service innovation at SaludAbierta: A teaching case study on improving access to healthcare in Peru. http://dx.doi.org/10.2139/ssrn.4206533

Diaz, R., Smith, K., Bertagna, S., & Bucci, V. (2023). Digital transformation, applications, and vulnerabilities in maritime and shipbuilding ecosystems. *Procedia Computer Science*, *217*, 1396–1405. https://doi.org/10.1016/j.procs.2022.12.338

Ellet, W. (2007). *The case study handbook: How to read, discuss, and write persuasively about cases*. Brighton, MA: Harvard Business Press.

Elnavi Monthly Shipping Review. (2023, February). Harbor lab innovates and evolves experience in port call. Retrieved from https://www.flipsnack.com/elnavimagazine/590-e-paper-february-2023/full-view.html

Endeavor. (n.d.). Harbor lab. Retrieved from https://www.endeavor.org.gr/companies/harbor-lab. Accessed on February 26, 2023.

Erkut, B., & Esenyel, V. (2022). What's "next"? On the future of digital entrepreneurship. In B. Erkut & V. Esenyel (Eds.), *Next generation entrepreneurship* (pp. 1–12). London: IntechOpen.

Esposito, M. (2022). Applied sustainability in the real world: A roadmap between SDGs and circularity. In *Excellence in pedagogy electives – Spring 2022* (pp. 16–17). Dijon: Burgundy School of Business.

Esposito, M., Lanteri, A., & Tse, T. (2021). Building the strategic architecture of the post pandemic corporate landscape. *LSE Business Review*. Retrieved from https://blogs.lse.ac.uk/businessreview/

Farquhar, J., Michels, N., & Robson, J. (2020). Triangulation in industrial qualitative case study research: Widening the scope. *Industrial Marketing Management*, *87*, 160–170.

Feng, L., Qin, G., Wang, J., & Zhang, K. (2022). Disruptive innovation path of start-ups in the digital context: The perspective of dynamic capabilities. *Sustainability*, *14*(19), Article 12839. https://doi.org/10.3390/su141912839

Gavalas, P. (2020). *Onboard vessels digital disruption through ICT technologies: Strategic incentives, anew perils and adoption tendencies. Focusing on the Greek maritime shipping sector* (Publication No. 29296197). Doctoral dissertation, University of Piraeus. ProQuest Dissertations Publishing.

Georgiou, G. (2022, December 29). Brain regain με μοχλό τις ναυτιλιακές start-ups [Brain regain with the lever of shipping start-ups]. *Naftemporiki*. Retrieved from https://www.naftemporiki.gr/maritime/1422517/brain-regain-me-mochlo-tis-naytiliakes-startups/

Goyal, S., Sergi, B. S., & Esposito, M. (2019). Literature review of emerging trends and future directions of e-commerce in global business landscape. *World Review of Entrepreneurship, Management and Sustainable Development*, *15*(1–2), 226–255. https://doi.org/10.1504/WREMSD.2019.098454

Great Place to Work. (n.d.). Harbor lab. Retrieved from https://www.greatplacetowork.gr/certified-company/harbor-lab/. Accessed from February 26, 2023.

Halkias, D., & Neubert, M. (2020). Extension of theory in leadership and management studies using the multiple-case study design. *International Leadership Journal*, *12*(2), 48–73. https://doi.org/10.2139/ssrn.3586256

Halkias, D., Neubert, M., Thurman, P. W., & Harkiolakis, N. (2022). *The multiple case study design: Methodology and application for management education*. London: Routledge.

Harkiolakis, T., & Komodromos, M. (2023). Supporting knowledge workers' health and well-being in the post-lockdown era. *Administrative Sciences*, *13*(2), 49–55. https://doi.org/10.3390/admsci13020049

Hellenic Shipping News. (2020, September 9). Greek shipping and economy 2020: The strategic and economic role of Greek shipping. Retrieved from https://www.hellenicshippingnews.com/greek-shipping-and-economy-2020-the-strategic-and-economic-role-of-greek-shipping/. Accessed on February 26, 2023.

Ikpogu, N. M. (2021). *Barriers to technology adoption among maritime industry stakeholders in Nigeria*. ProQuest Publishing.

Jović, M., Tijan, E., Vidmar, D., & Pucihar, A. (2022). Factors of digital transformation in the maritime transport sector. *Sustainability*, *14*(15), Article 9776. https://doi.org/10.3390/su14159776

Karagiorgos, L. (2022, December 8). Greek start-up harbor lab: Secures $6.1M in funding for 'harbor disbursement' calculation software. *Economic Post*. Retrieved from https://www.ot.gr/2022/12/08/english-edition/greek-startup-harbor-lab-secures-6-1m-in-funding-for-harbor-disbursement-calculation-software/

Karekla, M., Pollalis, Y., & Angelopoulos, M. (2021). Key drivers of digital transformation in Greek businesses: Strategy vs. technology. *Central European Management Journal*, *29*(2), 33–62. Retrieved from https://doi.org/10.7206/cemj.2658-0845.45

Kavussanos, M., Strandenes, S. P., & Thanopoulou, H. (2022). Special issue: Ends of eras and new beginnings: Twenty-first century challenges for shipping [Editorial]. *Maritime Economics & Logistics*, *24*(2), 347–367. https://doi.org/10.1057/s41278-021-00207-5

King, A., & Baatartogtokh, B. (2015). How useful is the theory of disruptive innovation? *MIT Sloan Management Review*, *57*(1), 77–90. Retrieved from http://mitsmr.com/1LezH20

Malaxianakis, A. (2022, March 24). Signal ventures ecosystem stories: Harbor lab and disbursements. *signal.* Retrieved from https://www.thesignalgroup.com/newsroom/signal-ventures-ecosystem-stories-harbor-lab-and-disbursements

Mallas, D. (2022, December 8). *Harbor Lab:* Μια από τις *μεγαλύτερες* αρχικές χρηματοδοτήσεις ναυτιλιακού *start-up* [Harbor Lab: One of the largest initial financings of a shipping start-up]. CNN. Retrieved from https://www.cnn.gr/oikonomia/epixeiriseis/story/340795/harbor-lab-mia-apo-tis-megalyteres-arxikes-xrimatodotiseis-naftiliakoy-startup

Nguyen, T. T., My Tran, D. T., Duc, T. T. H., & Thai, V. V. (2022). Managing disruptions in the maritime industry–A systematic literature review. *Maritime Business Review*. Advanced online publication. Retrieved from https://doi.org/10.1108/MABR-09-2021-0072

Newsroom. (2021, July 16). Harbor lab greets 300th vessel to utilize its service. *Ekathimerini*. Retrieved from https://www.ekathimerini.com/economy/1164613/harbor-lab-greets-300th-vessel-to-utilize-its-service/

OECD. (2020). *Financing SMEs and entrepreneurs 2020. An OECD scoreboard.* Retrieved from https://www.oecd-ilibrary.org/sites/0f52ae26-en/index.html?itemId=/content/component/0f52ae26-en

Papachristou, H. (2022, May 30). Greek shipping's new digital in-crowd eyes global markets. *TradeWinds*. Retrieved from https://www.tradewindsnews.com/business-focus/greek-shipping-s-new-digital-in-crowd-eyes-global-markets/2-1-1218043

Papadakis, M. N., & Kopanaki, E. (2022). Innovative maritime operations management using blockchain technology & standardization. *Journal of ICT Standardization*, *10*(4), 469–508. Retrieved from https://doi.org/10.13052/jicts2245-800X.1041

Papageorgiou, M. (2022, December). Digital transformation in the shipping industry is here. *NAFS Magazine*, *138*, 50–52. Retrieved from https://issuu.com/duken/docs/nafs_138

Papathomas, A., & Konteos, G. (2022). Digital transformation journey for incumbent banks: The case study of Greece. *International Journal of Marketing Studies*, *14*(2), 1–13. Retrieved from https://doi.org/10.5539/ijms.v14n2p13

Paul, J., Alhassan, I., Binsaif, N., & Singh, P. (2023). Digital entrepreneurship research: A systematic review. *Journal of Business Research*, *156*, Article 113507. Retrieved from https://doi.org/10.1016/j.jbusres.2022.113507

Powered by Harbor Lab. (2022, May 9). Harbor Lab: Συνεργασία και επικοινωνία [Harbor Lab: Collaboration and communication]. *Kathimerini*. Retrieved from https://www.kathimerini.gr/economy/business/561844204/harbor-lab-synergasia-kai-epikoinonia/

Ramadani, V., Istrefi-Jahja, A., Zeqiri, J., & Ribeiro-Soriano, D. (2022). COVID-19 and SMEs digital transformation. *IEEE Transactions on Engineering*. Retrieved from https://doi.org/10.1109/TEM.2022.3174628

Ramadani, V., & Schneider, R. (2013). *Entrepreneurship in the Balkans: Diversity, support and prospects*. Heidelberg: Springer.

Rasvanis, E., & Tselios, V. (2023). Do geography and institutions affect entrepreneurs' future business plans? Insights from Greece. *Journal of Innovation and Entrepreneurship*, *12*(1), Article 3. https://doi.org/10.1186/s13731-023-00266-3

Raza, Z., Woxenius, J., Vural, C. A., & Lind, M. (2023). Digital transformation of maritime logistics: Exploring trends in the liner shipping segment. *Computers in Industry*, *145*, Article 103811. https://doi.org/10.1016/j.compind.2022.103811

Roblek, V., Meško, M., Pušavec, F., & Likar, B. (2021). The role and meaning of the digital transformation as a disruptive innovation on small and medium manufacturing enterprises. *Frontiers in Psychology*, *12*, Article 592528. https://doi.org/10.3389/fpsyg.2021.592528

Rogers, E. M. (2003). *Diffusion of innovations*. New York, NY: Free Press.

Rogers, E. M. (1995). Diffusion of Innovations: Modifications of a model for telecommunications. In M.-W. Stoetzer & A. Mahler (Eds.), *Die diffusion von innovationen in der telekommunikation* (pp. 25–38). Berlin: Springer.

Santos, É., & Halkias, D. (2021). Diffusion of innovations and labor market challenges: A multiple case study from Angola. *Journal of Enterprising Communities*, *15*(2), 204–227. https://doi.org/10.1108/JEC-12-2020-0198

Schippling, A. (2017). Investigator triangulation in the data interpretation process. An almost untouched research area. *La Critica sociologica*, *51*(203), 87–100.

Sidiropoulos, Z. (2017). The development of start-up entrepreneurship in Greece supported by modern financing methods. In *Proceedings of the 7th international conference of ASECU youth* (pp. 379–408). Thessaloniki: Association of Economic Universities of South and Eastern Europe and the Black Sea Region (ASECU).

Simplilearn. (2023, February 14). What is digital disruption and the top five digital disruptors to watch out for in 2023? Retrieved from https://www.simplilearn.com/digital-disruption-article

Splash. (2022, June 8). Athens as a maritime start-up hotbed. Retrieved from https://splash247.com/athens-as-a-maritime-start-up-hotbed/

Spyropoulos, T. S., & Varsakelis, N. (2023). Business opportunity ontology. *KnE Social Sciences*, *8*(1), 148–171. https://doi.org/10.18502/kss.v8i1.12645.

Stamoulis, D. S. (2022). Managerial issues in the adoption of digital twins by shipping companies in Greece. *European Journal of Engineering and Technology Research*, *7*(5), 27–31. https://doi.org/10.24018/ejeng.2022.7.5.2879

Sussan, F., & Acs, Z. J. (2017). The digital entrepreneurial ecosystem. *Small Business Economics*, *49*, 55–73. https://doi.org/10.1007/s11187-017-9867-5

Tijan, E., Jović, M., Aksentijević, S., & Pucihar, A. (2021). Digital transformation in the maritime transport sector. *Technological Forecasting and Social Change*, *170*, 120879. https://doi.org/10.1016/j.techfore.2021.120879

Touchtidou, S. (2022). The Greek brand has never been stronger." Panagiotis Karampinis, managing director of Endeavor Greece, does not hide his enthusiasm. "We have regained trust," he says. "Anyone who wants to participate in the Greek digital ecosystem and invest in the Greek economy knows what they do will have results. *Economia*. Retrieved from https://www.economia.gr/the-greek-digital-ecosystem-grows-stronger-2/?cv=1

Tsolakidis, P., Mylonas, N., & Petridou, E. (2020). The impact of imitation strategies, managerial and entrepreneurial skills on start-ups' entrepreneurial innovation. *Economies*, *8*(4), Article 81. https://doi.org/10.3390/economies8040081

United Nations Conference on Trade and Development. (2020). *Trade and development report 2020*. United Nations. Retrieved from https://unctad.org/system/files/official-document/tdr2020_en.pdf

Vasilopoulos, A., & Tsitsakis, C. (2023). How start-up ecosystem in Greece is recovering from the effects of the COVID-19 pandemic. *KnE Social Sciences*, *8*(1), 324–334. https://doi.org/10.18502/kss.v8i1.12654

Ventresca, J. M., & Mohr, W. J. (2017). Archival research methods. In J. Baum (Ed.), *The Blackwell companion to organizations* (pp. 805–828). Hoboken, NJ: Blackwell. doi:10.1002/9781405164061.ch35

Vlados, C., Katimertzopoulos, F., & Blatsos, I. (2018). Towards an holistic innovation conception (the Stra.Tech.Man approach): The case of small and medium (SMEs) enterprises in Greece. In *3rd international conference of development and economy* (pp. 1–7). Kalamata, Greece: Technological Educational Institute (TEI) of Peloponnese. Retrieved from https://pure.unic.ac.cy/en/publications/towards-an-holistic-innovation-conception-the-stratechman-approac

Volkmann, C., & Gavrilescu, I. (2022). The context of digital entrepreneurship. New Technologies between evolution and revolution. In A. M. Dima & M. Kelemen

(Eds.), *Digitalization and big data for resilience and economic intelligence: 4th international conference on economics and social sciences, ICESS 2021, Bucharest, Romania* (pp. 109–120). Cham: Springer.

Weking, J., Desouza, K. C., Fielt, E., & Kowalkiewicz, M. (2023). Metaverse-enabled entrepreneurship. *Journal of Business Venturing Insights*, *19*, Article e00375. https://doi.org/10.1016/j.jbvi.2023.e00375

Yang, C. S. (2019). Maritime shipping digitalization: Blockchain-based technology applications, future improvements, and intention to use. *Transportation Research Part E: Logistics and Transportation Review*, *131*, 108–117. https://doi.org/10.1016/j.tre.2019.09.020

Yin, R. K. (2017). *Case study research and applications: Design and methods* (6th ed.). Thousand Oaks, CA: Sage.

Chapter 9

Informal Entrepreneurship in Kosovo: An Institutionalist Approach

Isa Mustafa, Justina Pula-Shiroka, Besnik A. Krasniqi, Veland Ramadani and Liridon Kryeziu

Abstract

Informal entrepreneurship challenges sustainable economic performance and is a barrier to productive entrepreneurship. In this context, the level of development of formal and informal institutions and their impact on informal entrepreneurship is crucial. This chapter examines the informal sector entrepreneurship in Kosovo using institutional theory lenses. Using a survey with 500 owners/managers of private companies, the study finds that the service industry has the highest participation in the informal economy compared to other sectors. On average small firms, compared to larger ones, report a higher percentage of unreported incomes. Our findings also suggest that when informal entrepreneurs perceive penalties for tax avoidance from tax authorities as high, they tend to have higher compliance with reporting their income. In addition, our findings indicate that the higher the vertical (trust in formal institutions) and horizontal distrust (trust in business partners), the higher the involvement in the informal economy. The chapter concludes with some policy implications for tackling the informal economy in Kosovo and similar institutional contexts.

Keywords: Informal entrepreneurship; institutions; vertical and horizontal trust; sustainable economic performance; productive entrepreneurship; tax avoidance

Entrepreneurship Development in the Balkans: Perspective from Diverse Contexts, 151–169

Published under exclusive licence by Emerald Publishing Limited
doi:10.1108/978-1-83753-454-820231009

1. Introduction

There is a growing scholarly interest in informal entrepreneurship (Williams & Horodnic, 2015; Williams & Kosta, 2019; Williams & Krasniqi, 2018; Williams & Youssef, 2013) as well as the integration of institutions in examining informal entrepreneurship (Autio & Fu, 2015; Krasniqi, 2012; Thai & Turkina, 2014; Williams & Krasniqi, 2018). Informal entrepreneurship refers to business activities outside formal institutions' rules and within informal institutions' boundaries (Webb, Bruton, Tihanyi, & Ireland, 2013). The field of informal entrepreneurship has received increased attention and recognition due to its distinctive characteristics and practical relevance (Salvi, Belz, & Bacq, 2022). This attention of scholarly interest is also related to the high percentage of informal entrepreneurial activities in developing and transition economies (Autio & Fu, 2015; Bruton, Ireland, & Ketchen, 2012).

The source of informal entrepreneurship relates to how "the rules of the game" in society are adequately defined in a country. Thus, scholars relying on the lenses of institutional theory examined informal entrepreneurship. The institutional approach allows us to explain the factors that lead entrepreneurs into the informal sector and the extent to which institutional and structural factors influence the degree of their formalisation (Williams & Shahid, 2016). Scholars examined informal entrepreneurship by relying on three waves of institutional theory and, within them, examining vertical and horizontal trust (Williams & Kosta, 2019; Williams & Krasniqi, 2017, 2018). Several studies examined informal entrepreneurship, focussing on the impact of institutional quality. These studies maintain that the level of institutional quality has a relationship with the level of informal entrepreneurship, suggesting that countries with a low level of institutional quality determine the level of informal entrepreneurial activities within the country (De Castro, Khavul, & Bruton, 2014; Elgin & Oztunali, 2014; Krasniqi & Desai, 2016; Salvi et al., 2022; Williams, Plakoyiannaki, & Krasniqi, 2022).

Despite the growing body of literature, scholars maintain that there is a need for more studies on informal entrepreneurship. Focussing on informal entrepreneurs and examining the factors why entrepreneurs underreport sales (Williams & Krasniqi, 2018). Likewise, focussing on the three waves of institutional theory would shed more light on informal entrepreneurship and horizontal and vertical trust (Williams & Kosta, 2019; Williams & Shahid, 2016). This study focusses on Kosovo as a transition economy facing formal structural and institutional challenges that negatively reflect the business environment and informality. The reason is the need for consistent institutional reforms, discouraging entrepreneurs from engaging in informal entrepreneurial activities and making formal entrepreneurial activities more attractive (Hashi & Krasniqi, 2011; Krasniqi, 2007). Kosovo has widespread informality, and the informal sectors in many sectors reduce budget revenues, are a barrier to investments and development of private firms, and consequently are the main barrier to economic growth (European Bank for Reconstruction and Development (EBRD), 2022). Based on previous estimates, firms do not report 34.4% of their income to tax authorities (Riinvest Institute, 2013). The origins of informality can be traced back to formal and formal institutional settings. Concerning the presence of informality, factors related to formal institutional settings are corruption, an inefficient judiciary system, and a weak rule of law (Krasniqi & Branch, 2020; Williams & Krasniqi, 2018). These also present obstacles to doing business for formal entrepreneurial firms and influence their growth and development. The failure of formal institutions to create a favourable business environment has also negatively influenced the entrepreneurs' trust in institutions and created distrust within the sector among entrepreneurs (Williams & Krasniqi, 2018). Therefore, the purpose of this chapter is to examine unreported sales of entrepreneurs and horizontal and vertical trust in the case of Kosovo.

The structure of this chapter is as follows: The next section reviews the literature on informal entrepreneurship, institutions, and horizontal and vertical trust: the third section method and findings and the last section discusses policy implications and limitations and future suggestions.

2. Literature Review

This section reviews the literature on institutional theory and informal entrepreneurship in transition economies. To examine informal entrepreneurship in the case of Kosovo, we rely on institutional theory as the most suitable theoretical framework. Institutions are defined as the

> rules of the game in a society, or, more formally, are the humanly devised constraints that shape human interaction … they structure incentives in human exchange, whether political, social, or economic. (North, 1990, p. 1)

According to North, institutions are formal and informal and define the rules of the game in a society. Relying on institutional theory lenses, many scholars maintain that the differences between poor and rich countries and the failure to "catch up" are related to the inability of governments to reform institutional settings and provide rules of the game in a given society (Acemoglu, 2006; Acemoglu, Johnson, & Robinson, 2002; Acemoglu & Robinson, 2010; Aron, 2000; Efendic & Pugh, 2007; North, 1990). Scholars maintain that institutional theory is the most suitable theoretical framework to examine the characteristics of institutional context, its impact on informal entrepreneurship, and how informal entrepreneurs operate outside the boundaries of formal institutions (Ramadani & Schneider, 2013; Webb et al., 2013; Williams & Krasniqi, 2019).

Failure to provide "rules of the game" in society has a negative impact on a country's economic performance and a negative impact on doing business. The business environment in the case of Kosovo, the context of this study, has improved over the years, but the lack of consistent reform packages has created uncertainty among private sector businesses (Coşkun, Kryeziu, & Krasniqi, 2022; Kryeziu & Coşkun, 2018; Kryeziu, Coşkun, & Krasniqi, 2022). As a result, firms face various barriers to growth derived from institutional settings (Hashi & Krasniqi, 2011; Krasniqi, 2007; Krasniqi & Mustafa, 2016). Therefore, firms are motivated to engage in informal entrepreneurial activities when they face barriers derived from formal institutional settings and additional business costs. This is due to the rapid policy change that created institutional voids in formal and informal institutions, generating new opportunities in the informal economy (Webb et al., 2013). Below, we review the literature on informal entrepreneurship and institutions and how these two interact in transition economies in the context of this study in Kosovo.

2.1. Informal Entrepreneurship

There is a growing scholarly interest in the informal economy, particularly informal entrepreneurship (Fadahunsi & Rosa, 2002; Friman, 2001; Ramadani, Dana, Ratten, & Bexheti, 2019; Williams & Horodnic, 2019; Williams & Nadin, 2010). The informal economy is evident in many national contexts, emphasising the importance of understanding the social context within entrepreneurship and institutional theoretical frameworks (Webb, Ireland, & Ketchen, 2014). Several studies maintain that the informal economy is related to the low economic performance of a country (Elgin & Oztunali, 2014; Hayat & Rashid, 2020; Khuong, Shabbir, Sial, & Khanh, 2021). Elgin and Birinci's (2016) study shows an inverted-U relationship between the informal sector's size and GDP per capita growth. This study shows that small and large sizes of the informal economy are related to a low level of development, while medium levels and the size of the informal economy are associated with a high level of growth. The "informal economy" can be defined as firms that operate outside of formal institutional settings within the boundaries of informal institutional settings. In the informal economy, there are different types of entrepreneurs: those seeking to replace their current incomes to improve their lifestyles and entrepreneurs committed to growing their firms by competing in the informal sector (Webb et al., 2014). Scholars maintain that there are several consequences of the informal economy, among which is that it negatively influences a country's economic performance in the short and long term (Radwan & Daoud, 2022; Thai & Turkina, 2014), resulting in lower entrepreneurial productivity at the national level (Fredström, Peltonen, & Wincent, 2021).

Countries in the early stages of development tend to have a high level of informality in the entrepreneurial sector. In cases where a country's economy experiences growth, it influences informal entrepreneurial firms as their business costs rise due to high wages and competition. In this case, when a country's economy is advanced, formal entrepreneurship dominates over informal entrepreneurial activities (Thai & Turkina, 2014). Furthermore, Autio and Fu (2015) maintained that informal entrepreneurship mitigates poverty at the individual level and preserves economic inefficiency at the national level. As a result, creating a business environment for individuals with entrepreneurial intentions is critical to reducing poverty and combating informality. This is important, considering that besides the consequences mentioned above, the informal economy produces unstable working conditions, uncertainty in finding jobs, and working conditions that are not decent. As a result, this influences the country's ability to achieve sustainable economic growth and performance (Estevão, Lopes, & Penela, 2022). The following section reviews the literature on institutions and informal entrepreneurship.

2.2. Institutions and Informal Entrepreneurship

As mentioned in the previous section, a country's low economic performance is related to informal entrepreneurship at the national level. The main determining factor is the quality of formal institutions at the national level. Studies maintain that the low GDP per capita associated with informal entrepreneurship is related to the quality of formal institutions (Elgin & Oztunali, 2014). This is due to the constraints formal institutions impose on entrepreneurs, forcing them to enter the informal economy and exploit resources (Autio & Fu, 2015; Salvi et al., 2022; Webb et al., 2013). Thereby, entrepreneurs operating in the informal economy may undertake several strategies to improve resource availability and react to resource constraints, which in most cases derive from formal institutions (Webb et al., 2013). This is due to the causality in the institutional and entrepreneurial choice relationship, where institutions shape economic actions. This leads to individuals entering the informal economy and growing their ventures outside formal institutional rules (Autio & Fu, 2015; Krasniqi & Williams, 2020).

De Castro et al. (2014) and Webb et al. (2013) investigated the relationship between institutional quality and informal entrepreneurship because these institutions influence entrepreneurial processes. Thai and Turkina's (2014) studies show that the quality of governance matters in encouraging formal entrepreneurship and affects the level of informal entrepreneurship. According to de Mello, de Moraes, and Fischer's (2022) study, the extent to which institutional voids are addressed at the country level in response to unproductive entrepreneurship and to encourage productive entrepreneurial activities is related to the quality of institutions and productive entrepreneurship. Similarly, Fredström et al.'s (2021) study maintains that the larger the size of informal entrepreneurship, the lower the entrepreneurial activities at the country level. Thereby, the higher the quality of economic and political institutions, the lower the level of informal entrepreneurs (Santos, Fernandes, & Ferreira, 2019).

The quality of formal and informal institutions drives and complements the transition of entrepreneurs from informal to formal entrepreneurial activities (Autio & Fu, 2015). This is due to the quality of institutional settings in countries with high corruption levels and weak legal institutions, which present barriers for entrepreneurs to get contracts, access resources, and grow their businesses (Urban & Ndou, 2019). This is due to clear rules, policies, laws, and regulations to build and foster competitive economic activities (Webb et al., 2013). Scholars suggest that improving institutional quality reduces the size of the informal economy, leading to a country's better economic performance. Similarly, in addition to the quality of formal institutions, particular emphasis has been placed on the quality of informal institutions, which play a significant role in entrepreneurs' decisions to continue operating in the informal economy (Hayat & Rashid, 2020). Therefore, besides improving formal institutions, which likely will reduce informal entrepreneurship (Salvi et al., 2022) and encourage productive entrepreneurial activities (Autio & Fu, 2015; Thai & Turkina, 2014), informal institutions are of crucial importance.

2.3. Horizontal and Vertical Trust and Informal Entrepreneurship

Scholars contend that institutional settings have a variety of responses to lower informal entrepreneurial activity. Among them are improving credit access, the tax system, and investor protection (Estevão et al., 2022). These are essential reactions, as firms in countries with a high informality face these barriers. The motive to enter informal activity is to substitute formal institutional incentives with high incomes through tax evasion or other forms of informality. Thereby, informality is related to legality because businesses operate outside "the rules of the game," and informal institutions play an essential role in determining how entrepreneurs operate outside the rules of the game. Likewise, it is vital to raise the question in this context of how these entrepreneurs that operate in informality can grow their firms despite working outside the game's rules (Webb et al., 2014). An essential answer to this question is the failure of the government to provide a better business environment through functioning institutional settings (Estevão et al., 2022).

Scholars argued that in explaining informal entrepreneurship, it is crucial to examine it from three lenses of institutional theory (Mustafa, Shiroka-Pula, & Krasniqi, 2022; Williams & Kosta, 2019; Williams & Krasniqi, 2018; Williams & Shahid, 2016). Understanding the informal economy in general and informal entrepreneurship, in particular, requires a thorough understanding of formal and informal institutional settings and how they function within a given society. Scholars focussed on institutional theory to understand how formal and informal institutions interact and influence informal entrepreneurship and how the latter emerges in weak and inefficient institutional settings. This paper evaluates three waves of an institutional theory that have variously explained participation in informal sector entrepreneurship. The first wave of institutional theory explains informal entrepreneurship resulting from formal institutional failures. This second wave of theory explains it as resulting from an asymmetry between the laws and regulations of formal institutions and the unwritten, socially shared rules of informal institutions. Finally, a third wave of theory resulting from a lack of vertical and horizontal trust explains informal entrepreneurship (Williams & Kosta, 2019; Williams & Krasniqi, 2018).

The first wave of institutional theory focusses on how informal entrepreneurship results from the failure of formal institutional settings. The second wave of institutional theory is related to the asymmetry between laws and regulations derived from formal institutions and social norms and rules, which are mainly unwritten and come from informal institutions. In addition, the third wave of institutional theory results from a lack of vertical and horizontal trust, which explains informal entrepreneurship. Vertical trust, or institutional asymmetry, relates to the asymmetry between the government and its citizens (or entrepreneurs) and its relationship with their participation in informal entrepreneurship. In this context, studies have mainly focussed on vertical trust, and little has been done to examine horizontal trust. Horizontal trust refers to the relationship between participation in informal entrepreneurship and the level of trust between entrepreneurs. In this vein, in cases where entrepreneurs perceive that sales are underreported in their country, they perceive that underreported sales are widespread in society and tend to avoid paying taxes. This is due to their belief that there are no sanctions from laws and regulations, and thereby, entrepreneurs believe that they can underreport their sales as many other entrepreneurs do (Williams & Kosta, 2019; Williams & Krasniqi, 2018).

Several studies have examined informal entrepreneurship relying on waves of institutional entrepreneurship, including horizontal and vertical trust. For example, the Williams and Krasniqi (2018) study reports that 35.7% of sales of small and medium-sized enterprises are underreported and small and older firms owned by men significantly underreport their sales compared to others. This study also suggests no correlation between formal institutional failure and underreported sales and no statistically significant relationship between the levels of vertical and horizontal trust and underreported sales. Another study by Williams and Kosta (2019) shows that 30% of turnover is underreported in Albania, and the percentage is higher in small firms. This study shows a relationship between underreported turnover, red tape dealing with tax administration, and the frequency of visits from tax inspectors. This study also indicates that both vertical and horizontal trust are associated with participation in informal entrepreneurship in the case of Albania. Similar findings in other studies have been found (Kosta & Williams, 2020; Williams & Youssef, 2013), including cross-country studies (Williams, 2020), as well as the importance of institutional trust for social and economic activities through reducing uncertainty and leading the economy from unproductive to productive entrepreneurial activities (Khlystova, Kalyuzhnova, & Belitski, 2022).

3. Methodology

3.1. Data and the Sample

The data used in the analysis are based on a survey of 500 owners/managers. The Kosovo Academy of Sciences and Arts conducted the survey in December 2019. The interviews were conducted by trained enumerators, third-year students of the Faculty of Economics at the University of Prishtina. The interviews were conducted with key decision-makers or informants in the company, mainly company owners/managers. The study uses random stratified sampling to construct samples representative of the Kosovo firms' population. The sample is drawn from the business register of Kosovo's companies kept at the Agency of Business Registration in Kosovo. The critical component of the questionnaire, "informal business," is constructed based on the concepts of productive, unproductive, and destructive entrepreneurship (Baumol, 1990), assessment of "deviance" or "departure from norms" within organisations (e.g., Warren, 2003) and empirical studies of tax evasion in various settings (e.g., Aidis & Van Praag, 2007; Fairlie, 2002; Feld & Schneider, 2010; Webb et al., 2013). We assess the amount of informal business activity by asking entrepreneurs to estimate the degree of underreporting of business income (net profits). Also, the survey contained questions related to institutional trust and business trust, entrepreneur-level and firm-level variables such as education, gender, firm size, firm age, and perceived degree of penalties for tax non-compliance.[1] Descriptive statistics of the sample are reported in the Appendix.

3.2. Empirical Analysis

In this section, we estimate the factors associated with the firm's involvement in the informal economy using econometric analysis based on a series of linear regression models, given that the dependent variable is a continuous variable that reports the percentage of unreported sales. The following section briefly explains the variables and principal component analysis (PCA) used to identify clusters of factors related to institutional and business trust.

3.3. Dependent Variable

To estimate the factors associated with the firm's involvement in informal entrepreneurship, we use the dependent variable extracted from the question, "Based on your experience, what is the approximate estimation of unreported sales from similar firms in your industry?" The indirect way of measuring unreported sales is the standard method in similar studies of informality (Abdixhiku, Krasniqi, Pugh, & Hashi, 2017; Mustafa et al., 2022; Williams & Krasniqi, 2018). Thus, the dependent variable is a continuous variable reporting the percentage of a firm's unreported sales.

3.4. Independent Variables

To analyse the hypotheses regarding the levels of informal entrepreneurs across firms in Kosovo, the study tests the following hypotheses:

- Firm age (natural logarithm): firms' years in operation.
- Firm size (natural logarithm): natural logarithm of the number of employees at the beginning of the survey year.
- Gender: a dummy variable with a value 1 for male entrepreneurs and 0 otherwise.
- Sector dummies for retail and services with a value of 1 and 0 for manufacturing and other sectors as a reference category.
- Age of the entrepreneur: a continuous variable for the age.
- Education: a categorical variable for the educational level with a value of 1 university education and zero for secondary and primary education as a reference base category.
- Penalty: a Likert scale variable with a value of 1 to 5 (1 – Nothing serious; 2 – A small fine, 3 – A serious fine that would affect the competitiveness of the company, 4 – A serious fine that would put the company at risk of insolvency, and 5 –The company would be forced to cease operations.

---

[1]For details on sampling and methodology, see Mustafa et al. (2019).

- Institutional trust: measures the trust of firms in formal institutions.
- Business trust measures the trust of businesses in business partners (customers, suppliers, and employees).

3.5. Principal Component Analysis

To analyse hypotheses related to the institutional quality of firms' participation in the informal economy, we examine the trust in government institutions such as tax and customs authorities, municipalities, and courts and related variables deemed necessary in each explanation. Furthermore, entrepreneurs were asked about their trust in their customers, suppliers, and staff. In the context of our study of horizontal and business trust, we carried out a PCA, discussed in the next section, to provide a more detailed analysis of institutional and business trust.

The rationale for employing PCA analysis is that the institutional trust variables are highly correlated, violating the assumption of independent variables' linear independence. The PCA is a critical analysis tool to examine whether the data from the real world confirm the relationships between constructs as predicted by theories (Bağış et al., 2022; Krasniqi & Desai, 2016; Lajqi & Krasniqi, 2017). The score was based on factor weights of seven variables to uncover the common variance of quality institutional variables across all firms in the sample. In addition, an exploratory factor analysis using Varimax rotation with Kaiser normalisation was conducted. The rotated matrix produced a three-factor solution with satisfactory results (Kaiser–Meyer–Olkin measure of sampling adequacy = 0.789, $p < 0.00$).

Table 1 shows that the central government trust has the highest loading on the first factor, which explains the most institutional quality. The "local government"

Table 1. Rotated Component Matrix.

Variables	**Component**	
	Institutional Trust (Vertical Trust)	**Business Trust (Horizontal Trust)**
Central government	0.815	
Local government	0.821	
Courts	0.770	
Customs and tax administration	0.530	
Costumers		0.743
Suppliers		0.751
Company staff		0.676

Note: Extraction method: PCA. Rotation method: Varimax with Kaiser normalization.

[a]Rotation converged in three iterations. Kaiser–Meyer–Olkin measure of sampling adequacy 0.789. Bartlett's test $p < 0.000$. Cumulative explained variance: 75.60%.

ranks second highest, courts rank third and "customs and tax administration" fourth in loading on the first factor. These variables were named under "institutional trust" or "vertical trust." The second factor grouped variables ranging from highest such as "customers," "suppliers," and "company staff." We refer to this factor as "business trust" or "horizontal trust." Factor analysis scores from PCA are used as independent variables in regression analysis.

3.6. Econometric Model

To estimate the factors influencing the firm's involvement in the informal economy, we use econometric analysis based on a series of linear regression models, given that the dependent variable is a continuous variable that reports the percentage of the firm's involvement in the informal economy.

The first and second model specifications include firm-level variables and variables related to entrepreneurs such as age, gender, and education; the third specification includes penalties; the fourth model includes institutional and business trust variables extracted from the factor analysis to capture the effect of both horizontal and vertical trust – trust on government and tax authority and trust on business partners and employees. All the models significantly improve the explanatory power of models. The final econometric model takes the following form:

$$Unreported\ sales = \beta_0 + \beta_1 X_i + \ldots + \beta_n n + \varepsilon i$$

where β_0 is the intercept, *Xi* represents the vector of independent variables and εi is the error term. *Xi* consists of three groups of factors associated with informal entrepreneurship.

4. Results

Before discussing econometric results, we show statistical diagnostic testing. The diagnostics show the presence of heteroscedasticity. We used the "robust standard error" technique based on the Huber–White sandwich to deal with this problem. According to Hamilton (2006, p. 239), the Huber–White sandwich estimation option does not assume identically distributed error terms.[2] We tested for multicollinearity using the Variable Inflated Factor (VIF) in STATA, which suggested that multicollinearity was not a problem in our estimations. The VIF mean

[2]Literature maintains that this is a common procedure when facing minor problems derived from heteroscedasticity or non-normality or large residuals in variations because the OLS regression tends to fit outliers at the expense of the rest of the sample. Doing the robust standard error option is an advantage in cases where estimates of the coefficients are exactly the same as OLS; the standard errors take account of heterogeneity and the lack of normality (Hamilton, 2006, p. 239).

VIF=1.20, which is lower than the threshold of 10. In addition, the correlation matrix confirms this, as the correlations between individual variables are generally very low (<0.49). The explanatory power, as indicated by *R*-squared, ranges from 3.7% (basic model) to 14% (full model), which explains more than 14% of the variation in the dependent variable, which is usual in this type of cross-section data in transition economies (Table 2).

Examining whether there is a significant association between individual and entrepreneur variables and firms' participation in the informal economy, we found that firm size and age have a statistically significant and negative relationship with the informal economy. More particularly, for each one-percent increase in age, firms' involvement in the informal economy decreases by 3.4 points (Model 1) and 3.01 points (Model 4). On average, a 1% increase in the company's size decreases the informal economy by 3.2 points (see Models 1 and 4).

From sector dummy variables, findings suggest that the service industry exhibits more informal entrepreneurial activities than manufacturing as a reference base. The possible explanation is that firms in the service sector are more likely to underreport their findings and operate in the informal economy. Results suggest that the dummy for retail is not statistically significant. Firms in the service sector have, on average, 6.8 percentage points more unreported sales than their manufacturing sector counterparts.

The findings show that perceived penalties' effect on firms' tendency to engage in deliberate misreporting is consistent with the predictions of rational choice models, that is, the higher the perceived penalties, the lower the amount of tax evasion and misreporting. The penalty effect stands out as a particularly effective deterrent to informal activity. On average, a one-unit change in the perception of the higher penalty on a Likert scale from 1 to 5 decreases the informal economy of firms by 4.8 points. This evidence suggests a possible policy tool for reducing the size of the informal economies, namely increasing the penalties for misreporting. Williams and Krasniqi (2018) indicate that penalties may be essential policy mechanisms to discourage entrepreneurs from engaging in the informal economy. At the same time, Williams and Franic's (2016) study suggests no relationship between undeclared work and the perceived level of penalties and risk detection. This study maintains that participation in undeclared work and the level of tax morale have a strong relationship.

Finally, the institutional trust variables are found to be statistically significant. The higher the institutional distrust, the higher the firms' involvement in informal economic activity. These findings are in line with previous studies suggesting that even entrepreneurs lack trust in formal institutions, manifested in a perception that public sector corruption acts as a barrier to their businesses and that the level of the shadow economy or under-reporting is significantly higher (Krasniqi & Williams, 2018; Williams & Shahid, 2016). This has been propounded by second-wave institutionalist thought, a lack of which refers to this as "vertical trust," that is, an asymmetry between formal and informal institutions. None of the entrepreneur-related variables (university education, entrepreneur's age, and gender) is statistically significant.

Table 2. Regression Results: Determinants of Firms' Involvement in Shadow Activity.

Variables	**(1)**	**(2)**	**(3)**	**(4)**
	Model 1	**Model 2**	**Model 3**	**Model 4**
Firm and individual-level variables				
Lnage (natural log)	−3.471**	−2.778	−2.553	−3.013
	(1.727)	(2.035)	(2.036)	(2.102)
Lnsize (natural log)	−3.175***	−4.036***	−3.843***	−3.167*
	(1.118)	(1.436)	(1.459)	(1.611)
gender		−0.858	−1.091	−1.614
		(3.258)	(3.369)	(3.543)
EntreAge		−0.0897	−0.0440	0.0151
		(0.114)	(0.113)	(0.117)
UniEdu		−1.504	−1.680	−1.705
		(2.464)	(2.487)	(2.612)
services		5.560**	5.636**	6.765**
		(2.814)	(2.816)	(3.011)
retail		−2.820	−3.167	−2.030
		(3.019)	(3.047)	(3.072)
Penalty for non-compliance				
Perceived penalty			−5.918**	−4.818*
			(2.376)	(2.562)
Institutional and business trust				
Institutional distrust				3.248***
				(1.206)
Business distrust				3.361***
				(1.238)
Constant	47.22***	50.19***	51.27***	48.38***
	(3.952)	(6.505)	(6.707)	(7.184)
Observations	414	351	343	304
R-squared	0.037	0.065	0.084	0.140

Note: Robust standard errors in parentheses.

*** $p < 0.01$, ** $p < 0.05$, and * $p < 0.1$.

5. Conclusions and Implications for Policymakers

The informal economy is a challenge for the transition economy. Informal entrepreneurship has become a challenge for governments, and mechanisms to reduce the presence of entrepreneurs in the informal economy are weak in transitional economies. This present study examines informal entrepreneurship in the case of Kosovo. This study investigated firms' participation in the informal economy based on age and size. Likewise, this study also analyses the extent to which penalties reduce the presence of firms in the informal economy. Furthermore, to clearly understand informal entrepreneurship, we analysed horizontal and vertical trust as essential factors for firm participation in the informal sector. In doing so, we measured firms' involvement in the informal sector by asking what percentage of firms in a similar industry underreport their incomes. This study also responded to various calls by scholars to examine informal entrepreneurship in multiple contexts (Salvi et al., 2022; Thai & Turkina, 2014; Webb et al., 2009). Furthermore, scholars call for more empirical studies on vertical and horizontal trust (Williams & Kosta, 2019; Williams & Krasniqi, 2018).

We used regression analysis to identify the critical influencing factors of the firm's involvement in the informal economy. Findings suggest that younger and smaller companies reported a higher percentage of unreported income than other firms. Results indicate that firm size and age significantly negatively affect the informal economy. For a 1% increase in age, firms decrease their involvement in informal entrepreneurial activities. Furthermore, our regression analysis suggests that 3.2 percentage points on an average decrease in the informal economy when 1% of the firm's size decreases. In terms of industry, we find that firms in the service industry have higher participation in the informal economy compared to the retail sector. More particularly, our findings suggest that, on average, 6.8 points of firms in the service industry underreport sales compared to their counterparts in the manufacturing sector.

Our study also examined the perceived penalties and the tendency of firms to engage in the informal sector. As penalties are an essential indicator, firms that perceive that the penalties may be high may decide to pursue their entrepreneurial activities in the formal sector. Our findings suggest that when entrepreneurs perceive penalties as high, their informal entrepreneurial activities, namely the informal economy, decrease by 4.8 points. These findings confirm scholars' arguments for implementing penalties as a policy tool to react to the informal sector (Ihrig & Moe, 2004; Williams & Krasniqi, 2018).

Besides perceived penalties, our study focussed on institutional and business trust, namely, vertical and horizontal trust. Our findings suggest that intuitional and business trust variables are statistically significant. Results indicate that the higher the institutional distrust, the higher the firms' involvement in informal economic activity. These findings are in line with previous studies suggesting that even entrepreneurs lack trust in formal institutions, manifested in a perception that public sector corruption acts as a barrier to their businesses and that the level of the informal economy or under-reporting is significantly higher (Williams,

2020; Williams & Krasniqi, 2018; Williams & Shahid, 2016). This has been supported by second-wave institutionalist thought, a lack of which refers to this as "vertical trust," that is, an asymmetry between formal and informal institutions. None of the entrepreneur-related variables (university education, entrepreneur's age, and gender) is statistically significant. These findings contribute to studies on vertical and horizontal trust, empirical studies, and discussions (Horodnic et al., 2021; Williams, 2020; Williams & Krasniqi, 2018).

Policymakers can use these results to combine "sticks" and "carrots" against informal entrepreneurial activities. This policy tool, for policymakers, may be necessary, taking into consideration that, until currently, policymakers used either "sticks" against the informal economy or "carrots" as incentives to encourage entrepreneurs to formalise their business activities (Williams, 2015; Williams & Franic, 2015). Furthermore, our study also supports scholars' arguments on the importance of formal enforcement mechanisms to lower the informal economy. Through better policies, regulatory and government agencies encourage entrepreneurs to transition into the formal economy (Webb, Tihanyi, Ireland, & Sirmon, 2009). This can be done by improving governance systems and relaxing regulations to lower barriers for new entrants in the economy (Thai & Turkina, 2014).

Furthermore, our findings indicate that vertical and horizontal trust are important determining factors. As a result, decreasing the asymmetry between formal and informal institutions may result in lower informal entrepreneurs (Williams & Shahid, 2016). Governments need to focus on building intuitional trust to change the perception of entrepreneurs, which influences their incentives to formalize their business activities. This is important as government through consistent policy incentives, tax systems and other forms to create trust between the private sector and institutions.

6. Limitations and Future Suggestions

The major limitation of this study is that it only evaluated the firm size, age, sector, penalties, and horizontal and vertical trust based on unreported sales. Future research needs to replicate our study's findings in other contexts, as we do not know whether these findings may be replicated in different institutional and cultural contexts. Second, this study employed a cross-sectional design; thus, it is worth examining informal entrepreneurship in transition and developing economies from a longitudinal perspective. Third, we recommend investigating entrepreneurs' characteristics, values, and motivations in the informal economy. This topic may be worth examining in different intuitional and cultural contexts. These informal entrepreneurs may interact differently with their own in-groups and societal groups when they operate in formal or informal sectors (Salvi et al., 2022). In addition, we recommend conducting a longitudinal comparative analysis of the determining factors of formal and informal entrepreneurship (Thai & Turkina, 2014).

References

Abdixhiku, L., Krasniqi, B., Pugh, G., & Hashi, I. (2017). Firm-level determinants of tax evasion in transition economies. *Economic Systems*, *41*(3), 354–366.

Acemoglu, D. (2006). A simple model of inefficient institutions. *The Scandinavian Journal of Economics*, *108*(4), 515–546.

Acemoglu, D., Johnson, S., & Robinson, J. A. (2002). Reversal of fortune: Geography and institutions in the making of the modern world income distribution. *The Quarterly Journal of Economics*, *117*(4), 1231–1294.

Acemoglu, D., & Robinson, J. (2010). The role of institutions in growth and development. *Review of Economics and Institutions*, *1*(2), 1–33.

Aidis, R., & Van Praag, M. (2007). Illegal entrepreneurship experience: Does it make a difference for business performance and motivation?. *Journal of Business Venturing*, *22*(2), 283–310.

Aron, J. (2000). Growth and institutions: A review of the evidence. *The world Bank Research Observer*, *15*(1), 99–135.

Autio, E., & Fu, K. (2015). Economic and political institutions and entry into formal and informal entrepreneurship. *Asia Pacific Journal of Management*, *32*(1), 67–94. https://doi.org/10.1007/s10490-014-9381

Bağış, M., Kryeziu, L., Kurutkan, M. N., Krasniqi, B. A., Hernik, J., Karagüzel, E. S., Karaca, V., Ateş, Ç. (2022). Youth entrepreneurial intentions: A cross-cultural comparison. *Journal of Enterprising Communities: People and Places in the Global Economy*. Vol. ahead-of-print No. ahead-of-print. https://doi.org/10.1108/JEC-01-2022-0005

Baumol, W. J. (1990). Entrepreneurship: Productive, unproductive and destructive. *Journal of Political Economy*, *98* (5), 893–921.

Bruton, G. D., Ireland, R. D., & Ketchen, D. J. Jr. (2012). Toward a research agenda on the informal economy. *Academy of Management Perspectives*, *26*(3), 1–11.

Coşkun, R., Kryeziu, L., & Krasniqi, B. A. (2022). Institutions and competition: Does internationalisation provide advantages for the family firms in a transition economy? *Journal of Entrepreneurship and Public Policy*, *11*(2/3), 253–272. https://doi.org/10.1108/JEPP-01-2022-0010

De Castro, J. O., Khavul, S., & Bruton, G. D. (2014). Shades of grey: How do informal firms navigate between macro and meso institutional environments? *Strategic Entrepreneurship Journal*, *8*(1), 75–94.

de Mello, L. P., de Moraes, G. H. S. M., & Fischer, B. B. (2022). The impact of the institutional environment on entrepreneurial activity: An analysis of developing and developed countries. *Journal of Entrepreneurship and Public Policy*, *11*(1), 1–22. https://doi.org/10.1108/JEPP-09-2021-0113

Efendic, A., & Pugh, G. (2007). Institutions and economic performance: An overview of empirical research with the main focus on transition economies. *South East European Journal of economics and business*, *2*(1), 25–30.

Elgin, C., & Birinci, S. (2016). Growth and informality: A comprehensive panel data analysis. *Journal of Applied Economics*, *19*(2), 271–292.

Elgin, C., & Oztunali, O. (2014). Institutions, informal economy, and economic development. *Emerging Markets Finance and Trade*, *50*(4), 145–162.

Estevão, J., Lopes, J. D., & Penela, D. (2022). The importance of the business environment for the informal economy: Evidence from the Doing Business ranking. *Technological Forecasting and Social Change*, *174*(1), 121288.

European Bank for Reconstruction and Development (EBRD). (2022). *Kosovo country diagnostic: Private investment challenges and opportunities 2022*. Brussels: EBRD.

Fadahunsi, A., & Rosa, P. (2002). Entrepreneurship and illegality: Insights from the Nigerian crossborder trade. *Journal of Business Venturing*, *17*(2), 397–429.

Fairlie, R. W. (2002). Drug dealing and legitimate self-employment. *Journal of Labor Economics*, *20*(3), 538–567.

Feld, L. P., & Schneider, F. (2010). Survey on the shadow economy and undeclared earnings in OECD countries. *German Economic Review*, *11*(2), 109–149.

Fredström, A., Peltonen, J., & Wincent, J. (2021). A country-level institutional perspective on entrepreneurship productivity: The effects of informal economy and regulation. *Journal of Business Venturing*, *36*(5), 106002.

Friman, H. R. (2001). Informal economies, immigrant entrepreneurship and drug crime in Japan. *Journal of Ethnic and Migration Studies*, *27*(2), 313–333.

Hamilton, L (2006). *Statistics with Stata*. Belmont, CA: Thomson Brooks.

Hashi, I., & Krasniqi, B. A. (2011). Entrepreneurship and SME growth: Evidence from advanced and laggard transition economies. *International Journal of Entrepreneurial Behavior & Research*, *17*(5), 456–487. https://doi.org/10.1108/13552551111158817

Hayat, R., & Rashid, A. (2020). Exploring legal and political-institutional determinants of the informal economy of Pakistan. *Cogent Economics & Finance*, *8*(1), 1782075.

Horodnic, I. A., Williams, C. C., Maxim, A., Stoian, I. C., Ţugulea, O. C., & Horodnic, A. V. (2021). Knowing and unknowing purchases of undeclared healthcare goods and services: The role of vertical and horizontal trust. *International Journal of Environmental Research and Public Health*, *18*(21), 11561.

Ihrig, J., & Moe, K. S. (2004). Lurking in the shadows: The informal sector and government policy. *Journal of Development Economics*, *73*(2), 541–557.

Khlystova, O., Kalyuzhnova, Y., & Belitski, M. (2022). Towards the regional aspects of institutional trust and entrepreneurial ecosystems. Vol. ahead-of-print No. ahead-of-print. *International Journal of Entrepreneurial Behavior & Research*. https://doi.org/10.1108/IJEBR-02-2022-0108

Khuong, N. V., Shabbir, M. S., Sial, M. S., & Khanh, T. H. T. (2021). Does informal economy impede economic growth? Evidence from an emerging economy. *Journal of Sustainable Finance & Investment*, *11*(2), 103–122.

Kosta, B., & Williams, C. C. (2020). Evaluating the effects of the informal sector on the growth of formal sector enterprises: Lessons from Italy. *Journal of Developmental Entrepreneurship*, *25*(3), 2050019.

Krasniqi, B. A. (2007). Barriers to entrepreneurship and SME growth in transition: The case of Kosova. *Journal of Developmental Entrepreneurship*, *12*(1), 71–94.

Krasniqi, B. A. (2012). *Entrepreneurship and small business development in Kosova*. Hauppauge, NY: Nova Science Publishers, Incorporated.

Krasniqi, B. A., & Branch, D. (2020). Institutions and firm growth in a transitional and post-conflict economy of Kosovo. *Journal of Entrepreneurship in Emerging Economies 12*(2), 187–204.

Krasniqi, B. A., & Desai, S. (2016). Institutional drivers of high-growth firms: Country-level evidence from 26 transition economies. *Small Business Economics*, *47*(4), 1075–1094.

Krasniqi, B. A., & Mustafa, M. (2016). Small firm growth in a post-conflict environment: The role of human capital, institutional quality, and managerial capacities. *International Entrepreneurship and Management Journal*, *12*(4), 1165–1207.

Krasniqi, B. A., & Williams, N. (2019). Migration and intention to return: Entrepreneurial intentions of the diaspora in post-conflict economies. *Post-Communist Economies*, *31*(4), 464–483.

Krasniqi, B. A., & Williams, C. (2020). Does informality help entrepreneurs achieve firm growth? Evidence from a post-conflict economy. *Economic research-Ekonomska istraživanja*, *33*(1), 1581–1599.

Kryeziu, L., & Coşkun, R. (2018). Political and economic institutions and economic performance: Evidence from Kosovo. *South East European Journal of Economics and Business*, *13*(2), 84–99.

Kryeziu, L., Coşkun, R., & Krasniqi, B. (2022). Social networks and family firm internationalisation: Cases from a transition economy. *Review of International Business and Strategy*, *32*(2), 284–304.

Lajqi, S., & Krasniqi, B. A. (2017). Entrepreneurial growth aspirations in challenging environment: The role of institutional quality, human and social capital. *Strategic Change*, *26*(4), 385–401.

Mustafa, I., Shiroka-Pula, J., & Krasniqi, B. (2022). *Ekonomia në hije: trajtim teorik dhe empirik*. Prishtinë: Akademia e Shkencave dhe e Arteve e Kosovës.

Mustafa, I., Shiroka-Pula, J., Krasniqi, B, Sauka, A., Berisha, B., Pula, L., …, & Jaha, A. (2019). *Analysis of the shadow economy in Kosova*. Prishtina: Kosovo Academy of Sciences and Arts.

North, D. C. (1990). *Institutions, institutional change and economic performance*. Cambridge: Cambridge University Press.

Radwan, L., & Daoud, Y. (2022). Entrepreneurship–growth nexus: Does the size of the informal economy matter? *Journal of Sustainable Finance & Investment*, *12*(1), 169–194.

Ramadani, V., Dana, L. P., Ratten, V., & Bexheti, A. (2019). *Informal ethnic entrepreneurship: Future research paradigms for creating innovative business activity*. Cham: Springer.

Ramadani, V., & Schneider, R. (2013). *Entrepreneurship in the Balkans: Diversity, support and prospects*. Heidelberg: Springer.

Riinvest Institute. (2013). *A business perspective of informality in Kosovo: To pay or not to pay*. Retrieved from https://www.riinvestinstitute.org/uploads/files/2016/October/17/BUSINESS_INFORMALITY_5mm_bleed_no_inside_ENG_FINALV_3139643857314766930005.pdf

Salvi, E., Belz, F. M., & Bacq, S. (2022). Informal entrepreneurship: An integrative review and future research agenda. *Entrepreneurship Theory and Practice*, 0(0) 1–3. doi:10.1177/10422587221115365.

Santos, E., Fernandes, C. I., & Ferreira, J. J. (2019). The role of political and economic institutions in informal entrepreneurship. *World Journal of Entrepreneurship, Management and Sustainable Development*, *15*(4), 366–383.

Thai, M. T. T., & Turkina, E. (2014). Macro-level determinants of formal entrepreneurship versus informal entrepreneurship. *Journal of Business Venturing*, *29*(4), 490–510.

Urban, B., & Ndou, B. (2019). Informal entrepreneurship: A focus on South African township entrepreneurs. *Journal of Developmental Entrepreneurship*, *24*(4), 1950021.

Warren, D. E. (2003). Constructive and destructive deviance in organizations. *Academy of Management Review*, *28*(4), 622–632.

Webb, J. W., Bruton, G. D., Tihanyi, L., & Ireland, R. D. (2013). Research on entrepreneurship in the informal economy: Framing a research agenda. *Journal of Business Venturing*, *28*(5), 598–614.

Webb, J. W., Ireland, R. D., & Ketchen, D. J. (2014). Toward a greater understanding of entrepreneurship and strategy in the informal economy. *Strategic Entrepreneurship Journal*, *8*(1), 1–15.

Webb, J. W., Tihanyi, L., Ireland, R. D., & Sirmon, D. G. (2009). You say illegal, I say legitimate: Entrepreneurship in the informal economy. *Academy of Management Review*, *34*(3), 492–510.

Williams, C. (2020). Evaluating public administration approaches towards tax non-compliance in Europe. *Administrative Sciences*, *10*(3), 43.

Williams, C. C. (2015). Tackling entrepreneurship in the informal sector: An overview of the policy options, approaches and measures. *Journal of Developmental Entrepreneurship*, *20*(1), 1550006.

Williams, C. C. (2020). Tackling informal entrepreneurship in east-central Europe: From a deterrence to preventative approach. *Journal of Developmental Entrepreneurship, 25*(4), 2050024.

Williams, C. C., & Franic, J. (2015). Tackling the propensity towards undeclared work: Some policy lessons from Croatia. *South East European Journal of Economics and Business, 10*(1), 18–31.

Williams, C. C., & Franic, J. (2016). Beyond a deterrence approach towards the undeclared economy: Some lessons from Bulgaria. *Journal of Balkan and Near Eastern Studies, 18*(1), 90–106.

Williams, C. C., & Horodnic, I. (2015). Self-employment, the informal economy and the marginalisation thesis: Some evidence from the European Union. *International Journal of Entrepreneurial Behavior and Research, 21*(2), 224–242.

Williams, C. C., & Horodnic, I. A. (2019). Evaluating working conditions in the informal economy: Evidence from the 2015 European Working Conditions Survey. *International Sociology, 34*(3), 281–306.

Williams, C. C., & Kosta, B. (2019). Evaluating institutional theories of informal sector entrepreneurship: Some lessons from Albania. *Journal of Developmental Entrepreneurship, 24*(2), 1950009.

Williams, C. C., & Krasniqi, B. (2017). Evaluating the individual-and country-level variations in tax morale: Evidence from 35 Eurasian countries. *Journal of Economic Studies, 44*(5) 816–832. https://doi.org/10.1108/JES-09-2016-0182.

Williams, C. C., & Krasniqi, B. (2018). Explaining informal sector entrepreneurship in Kosovo: An institutionalist perspective. *Journal of Developmental Entrepreneurship, 23*(2), 1850011.

Williams, C. C., & Nadin, S. (2010). Entrepreneurship and the informal economy: An overview. *Journal of Developmental Entrepreneurship, 15*(4), 361–378.

Williams, C. C., & Shahid, M. S. (2016). Informal entrepreneurship and institutional theory: Explaining the varying degrees of (in) formalisation of entrepreneurs in Pakistan. *Entrepreneurship & Regional Development, 28*(1–2), 1–25.

Williams, C. C., & Youssef, Y. (2013). Evaluating the gender variations in informal sector entrepreneurship: Some lessons from Brazil. *Journal of Developmental Entrepreneurship, 18*(1), 1–16.

Williams, N., Plakoyiannaki, E., & Krasniqi, B. A. (2022). When forced migrants go home: The journey of returnee entrepreneurs in the post-conflict economies of Bosnia & Herzegovina and Kosovo. *Entrepreneurship Theory and Practice.* , 47(2), 430–460 doi:10.1177/10422587221082678

Appendix: Descriptive Statistics of the Sample

Variable	Obs	Mean	Std. Dev.	Min	Max
lnage	455	2.32	0.65	0.00	3.93
lnsize	464	1.19	0.97	0.00	5.75
gender	495	0.84	0.37	0.00	1.00
EntreAge	413	43.30	11.41	18.00	75.00
UniEdu	499	0.38	0.49	0.00	1.00
services	499	0.35	0.48	0.00	1.00
retail	499	0.33	0.47	0.00	1.00
Penalty	481	0.61	0.49	0.00	1.00

Chapter 10

Multi-Context Analysis of the Environment for the Development of Entrepreneurship in Montenegro

Boban Melović and Dragana Ćirović

Abstract

This chapter provides an overview of entrepreneurship in Montenegro, through various aspects of the analysis. The chapter begins with an analysis of the role and importance of the development of entrepreneurship in Montenegro, followed by an analysis of the institutional and strategic framework for supporting the development of entrepreneurship. In this sense, a significant segment of the chapter is the analysis of various strategic documents, with a special focus placed on the role of the entrepreneurship development strategy, as well as the institutions responsible for the creation and implementation of entrepreneurship policies in Montenegro. The study also includes state measures, that is, support programs for the development of entrepreneurship, and thus the overall Montenegrin economy, which belongs to the group of less developed countries. In addition, the chapter indicates the importance of entrepreneurial learning in the development of entrepreneurial activity. The analysis shows that entrepreneurship is a concept that is increasingly used in Montenegrin economic theory, but also that it is increasingly present in everyday life, which is confirmed by numerous examples from practice. Therefore, through a multi-context analysis, the study depicts the environment for entrepreneurship development in Montenegro, including an overview of the state support, the influence of various factors, as well as certain forms of entrepreneurship that are current, and those that may be promising. The chapter ends with recommendations and guidelines for the further development of entrepreneurship in this country. With this regard, the key elements for increasing entrepreneurial activity are recognized in multiple support for a

Entrepreneurship Development in the Balkans: Perspective from Diverse Contexts, 171–195

Published under exclusive licence by Emerald Publishing Limited
doi:10.1108/978-1-83753-454-820231010

greater number of people to get involved in business, as well as in the improvement of a favorable business environment through the strengthening of institutional and infrastructural support.

Keywords: Entrepreneurship; institutional framework; strategy; entrepreneurial support; Montenegro; multi-context analysis

1. Analysis of the Role and Importance of Entrepreneurship Development in Montenegro

In today's modern business conditions, the role of entrepreneurship is undeniable. Entrepreneurship manifests itself through the implementation of innovations that renew, transform, and encourage the development of the economy around the world, and it is necessary for every country to provide the conditions for the development of this phenomenon. Therefore, entrepreneurship must be grounded in the overall social system in order to ensure its effective functionality and development. The success of entrepreneurship lies in the ability of the entrepreneurial process to create a purposeful cohesive social and economic system that will be able to support the creation and growth of business ventures, which positively affects the economic growth of the entire country (Raut, Veljković, Melović, Ćelić, & Nikolić, 2022).

Encouraging innovation and entrepreneurship development in Montenegro significantly contributes to the overall economic growth of the country (Government of Montenegro, 2018). The development of entrepreneurship can absorb unemployment to a certain extent, increase the employment rate, and ensure the inclusiveness of different social groups. Additionally, the development of entrepreneurship leads to greater innovation and contributes to a more dynamic economy and strengthening competitiveness. This is also recognized in Montenegro, where entrepreneurship has been strongly promoted as an important factor of economic development in the last 10 years.

The available statistical data indicate the transformation of the economy of Montenegro through the transition from traditional industrial to service sectors, and in such circumstances, small- and medium-sized enterprises (SMEs) play a more significant role (OECD, 2019), which is also of great importance when it comes to entrepreneurship development. According to the data of the Revenue and Customs Administration of Montenegro, the number of micro-, small-, and medium-sized enterprises and employees is continuously growing (Ministry of Economic Development, 2022). However, despite such data and the significant progress achieved by this sector, entrepreneurship still does not represent a key option for young people in Montenegro (OECD, 2019). Accordingly, adequately focused entrepreneurial training is needed to improve the development of young people in this regard, which is confirmed by studies conducted on entrepreneurship in other countries as well (Ashoka & Duggappa, 2014; Klandt & Volkmann, 2006).

In small economic systems, such as the Montenegrin one, entrepreneurship is considered a crucial driver of economic growth, creation of new jobs, and encouragement of innovation (Melović & Mitrović, 2013). Through the analysis of entrepreneurial traits, the research of the Montenegrin Academy of Sciences and Arts – MASA showed that the citizens of Montenegro possess attributes that highlight a tendency toward entrepreneurial behavior (Ministry of Economic Development and Tourism of Montenegro, 2020). Considering the fact that entrepreneurs reflect the fundamental characteristics of the environment in which they live, the most significant entrepreneurial traits that have been singled out are innovativity, self-confidence, as well as tendency to take risks (OECD, 2019). In today's time, which is characterized by rapid changes and the continuous development of technology, these traits gain even more importance.

In order to foster entrepreneurial activity, it is necessary to improve the entire ambiance for its development, where the environment, infrastructure, and support are especially highlighted. Support for entrepreneurship growth through the development of institutional infrastructure and the provision of various support services aimed at entrepreneurs is continuously implemented in Montenegro (Ministry of Economic Development and Tourism of Montenegro, 2019). Continuous and dedicated institutional support for the development of entrepreneurship, in addition to the constant improvement of the framework conditions for the business of micro-, small-, and medium-sized enterprises, is a strategic commitment of the Government of Montenegro and other competent institutions (Government of Montenegro, 2021). Adequately selected mechanisms and programs to support entrepreneurship development can determine the degree of effectiveness and efficiency of micro-, small-, and medium-sized enterprises and potentially have a multiplied effect on the degree of their competitiveness. Numerous activities have been carried out so far, in order to create a stimulating environment for the development of entrepreneurship. Three business incubators, three local and regional business centers, and the entrepreneurial impulse center "Tehnopolis" have been developed, which support entrepreneurship development through the provision of information, advice, the organization of training cycles, and the provision of support in writing and implementing projects, with the aim to foster entrepreneurial activity (Ministry of Economic Development and Tourism of Montenegro, 2019).

The progress in the area of SMEs policy within the framework of Montenegro's accession to the European Union (EU) should be particularly highlighted, with an emphasis placed on the opening of negotiation Chapter 20 – Entrepreneurship and Industrial Policy in 2013. In the Report of the European Commission on the progress of Montenegro for the year 2020 (European Commission, 2020), in the part related to entrepreneurship, it was pointed out that Montenegro achieved a good level of readiness, which indicates significant institutional efforts made in the previous period. The achieved progress is reflected in the improvement of the business environment for the development of entrepreneurship, better and easier availability of financial resources, the introduction of entrepreneurial competencies in education, the promotion of entrepreneurship through the strengthening of the role of women and young people in business, support for beginners in business, access to information, etc. (Government of Montenegro, 2018).

Namely, in the period 2019–2022, Montenegro has achieved progress in the implementation of the Small Business Act (SBA), where it achieved the highest average scores in the following areas: entrepreneurial learning and female entrepreneurship; institutional and regulatory framework for creating SME policy; support services for SMEs; and public procurement and SMEs in the green economy. These scores exceed the average of the countries of the Western Balkans (OECD, 2022).

It can be stated that Montenegro has embarked on the path of capacity building in order to achieve a growth model based on innovation and entrepreneurship (European Commission, 2020), but it is necessary to continue with strong promotion and encouragement of entrepreneurial learning and entrepreneurial orientation, as a priority professional choice for young people (OECD, 2019).

2. Institutional and Strategic Framework of Entrepreneurship Development Support

The creation and implementation of policies and programs for entrepreneurship development is the responsibility of several state institutions in Montenegro. It is carried out continuously, through activities that include a significant number of incentives, subsidies, loans, and various types of education, which are made available to the economy through various financial and non-financial support programs. Key institutions that provide support to entrepreneurship are line ministries in charge of the economy, science, agriculture and rural development, sustainable development, and tourism, followed by the Investment and Development Fund of Montenegro, Chamber of Commerce, etc. It is necessary to point out the role of the Ministry of Economy and Tourism as an institution whose responsibility includes the process of creation and implementation of the policy aimed at providing support to entrepreneurship development as well as support to SMEs. The creation and implementation of entrepreneurship development policies are defined as priorities within the competence of the line ministry for economic development, and one of the strategic priorities defined for the upcoming period relates to the improvement of the existing infrastructure and the networking of the entrepreneurial (institutional) infrastructure. In its structure, the Ministry established the directorate for investments, development of SMEs, and management of EU funds, which represents a unique "one-stop-shop" for SMEs and entrepreneurs. This directorate provides business entities with information and inputs on all programs aimed at encouraging business development, as well as with information regarding opportunities for business improvement and connection with other departmental institutions at the state and local levels (Government of Montenegro, 2018). Also, the Ministry of Economy is part of the European Entrepreneurship Network. The European Entrepreneurship Network helps entrepreneurs, micro, small, and medium-sized enterprises, characterized by European and international ambitions, to make the most of business opportunities in the EU and beyond, which is of great importance for Montenegro as well.

Besides that, support for the development of entrepreneurship is also provided by the Employment Institute of Montenegro, the Investment and Development Fund of Montenegro, the Ministry of Agriculture and Rural Development, the Ministry of Tourism and Sustainable Development, the Ministry of Science, Local Secretariats for Entrepreneurship Development, regional/local business centers, business incubators and innovation-entrepreneurial centers, business associations, universities, international organizations, and others. Therefore, there is a clearly defined institutional framework for providing support to entrepreneurship in Montenegro, which is recognized as essential for the continuous development of micro-, small-, and medium-sized enterprises. However, there is an impression that novice entrepreneurs are not sufficiently familiar with the competencies of certain institutions, which opens up space for improving promotion and communication strategies. Digital marketing channels, which young people especially prefer, can be of great importance here. With this regard, the creation of an online platform where all relevant information related to the encouragement and support of entrepreneurial activities would be combined is of extreme importance.

There are two important aspects of the strategic framework for supporting entrepreneurship in Montenegro, that intertwine with each other, and are important for the analysis – namely the national and regional, that is, the European support framework. When analyzing the availability and content of specific program lines with the aim of supporting entrepreneurship, it can be noted that the goals and priorities set in specific programs and strategies are intertwined and in mutual correlation.

The Strategy for the Development of Micro-, Small-, and Medium-Sized Enterprises in Montenegro 2018–2022 represents a key strategy at the national level, which defines key measures needed for improving the framework of entrepreneurship development in Montenegro and promoting competitiveness. The strategic directions for the development of entrepreneurship are set in this strategy, while measures needed for their realization are defined and innovated, with the aim to promote the conditions necessary for the growth and development of entrepreneurship. These measures primarily refer to the creation and improvement of a favorable business and regulatory environment, the construction and strengthening of sustainable infrastructure, and institutions that provide and implement programs of financial and non-financial support (Government of Montenegro, 2018). The need to establish this strategy arose from the framework conditions defined by the umbrella strategic development documents of Montenegro, the need to align with the policy and principles of encouraging entrepreneurship development in the EU, as well as from the identified new needs of Montenegrin companies (Government of Montenegro, 2018). Strategy for the Development of Micro-, Small- and Medium-Sized Enterprises in Montenegro 2018–2022, in addition to other measures to encourage SMEs, is also based on guidelines for improving entrepreneurial infrastructure and strengthening entrepreneurial knowledge and skills. However, it should be noted that there are many other strategic documents dealing with this issue.

One of these documents is the Industrial Policy of Montenegro 2019–2023, which is a strategic document aimed at improving the competitiveness of the Montenegrin economy based on changes in the business environment and improvement of access to development resources, in order to promote the internal performance of companies, primarily SMEs in priority sectors (Ministry of Economic Development and Tourism of Montenegro, 2019). Within the framework of designing measures and activities for innovation and entrepreneurship, this document also foresees the promotion of entrepreneurship and entrepreneurial culture for innovation and stable economic growth, as well as increasing productivity and employment.

Furthermore, *the Regional Development Strategy 2014–2020* defines the achievement of more even socio-economic development of all local self-government units and regions, based on competitiveness, innovation, and employment (Ministry of Economy, 2014). This strategy defines a set of priorities and measures. Among them, those that are related to entrepreneurship include: strengthening the competitiveness of SMEs and promotion of entrepreneurship; strengthening the quality infrastructure for the development of entrepreneurship; and supporting for beginners in business – start-ups.

Strategy of Scientific Research Activity 2017–2021 introduces new measures and instruments aimed at better research quality, access to modern technologies and large infrastructures, as well as those aimed at encouraging a more competitive economy based on knowledge, through the partnership of scientific research institutions and economic entities (Ministry of Education, 2018). One of the strategic goals of this document is to create a more favorable environment for innovative entrepreneurship and financial support for R/D activities and entrepreneurship.

In addition to the above, it is important to point out the importance of the *National Strategy for Sustainable Development of Montenegro by 2030*, which establishes the principles, strategic goals, and measures for achieving the long-term sustainable development of Montenegrin society, taking into account the current situation and assumed international obligations (Ministry of Sustainable Development and Tourism, 2016). The aforementioned strategy defines numerous goals that are complementary to the Strategy for the Development of Micro-, Small- and Medium-Sized Enterprises in Montenegro 2018–2022, and which encourage sustainable development and entrepreneurship. They refer to improving the state of human resources, supporting values, norms, and patterns of behavior important for the sustainability of society, preserving natural capital, introducing a green economy, and improving management for sustainable development (Ministry of Sustainable Development and Tourism, 2016).

Furthermore, the *National Strategy for Lifelong Entrepreneurial Learning of Montenegro 2020–2024* and the *Smart Specialization Strategy of Montenegro 2019–2024* are key documents for entrepreneurial learning, which is important for strengthening the development of entrepreneurial activity. Within the Strategy for Development of Lifelong Entrepreneurial Learning 2020–2024, a coordination concept specific to the development of entrepreneurial learning and entrepreneurial competencies was analyzed – "National Partnership." This concept represents a partnership between public authorities, the academic community, representatives of the economy, and the non-governmental sector which, with their common goals, strive for coherence and connection in various areas of the national policy of education, employment, and economy (Ministry of Economic Development and Tourism of Montenegro, 2020). National Strategy for Lifelong Entrepreneurial Learning 2020–2024 sets a clear vision and strives to provide support and resources for carrying out the tasks that are supposed to be realized by National Partnership. In other words, this document provides advices to decision-makers in its full capacity and coordinately raises awareness of the need for a stronger influence of entrepreneurial education at all levels of formal and of informal education. It also aims to ensure the safe dissemination of examples of good practice and to support the coordination of cooperation between successful educational institutions and those that are just introducing entrepreneurial learning (Ministry of Economic Development and Tourism of Montenegro, 2020). On the other hand, the Smart Specialization Strategy of Montenegro 2019–2024 places emphasis on investment and development of innovation and research potential in selected priority areas, which will create new opportunities for entrepreneurial activities and the development of the knowledge-based economy (Ministry of Education, 2019).

The next document that is correlated with entrepreneurship is the *Strategic Guidelines for the Development of SMEs 2018–2021*, which presents an analysis of the implementation of the SME policy in the previous period and the achieved effects on the development of the SME sector (Government of Montenegro, 2018). Improving the entrepreneurial infrastructure and strengthening entrepreneurial knowledge and skills is one of the main priorities of this document, which is a starting point for the creation of the Strategy for the Development of MSMEs in Montenegro 2018–2022. In addition to the aforementioned document, this strategy also relied heavily on the Strategy for Lifelong Entrepreneurial Learning 2015–2019, the Strategy for Gender Equality 2021–2025, and the Strategy for the Development of Female Entrepreneurship in Montenegro 2021–2024 (in the segment related to the promotion of female entrepreneurship, social entrepreneurship, and support for young people in this area).

In addition to the previously mentioned documents, international business expertise is combined with local knowledge to help entrepreneurs bring their innovations to the European and international markets. The relevant framework for formulating the Strategy for the Development of Micro-, Small-, and Medium-Sized Enterprises in Montenegro 2018–2022, which represents a key strategy at the national level, stems from the need for strategic alignment with policy and the application of best practices in the EU. In this context, certain EU documents were also considered, such as the EU 2020 Strategy, the Southeast Europe Strategy 2020, the Adriatic-Ionian Strategy, and the Danube Strategy, as well as strategic documents that are directly aimed at supporting the development of entrepreneurship and SMEs in the EU – SBA for Europe and the EU Entrepreneurship 2020 Action Plan, as well as specific support programs such as COSME or HORIZON 2020 (Government of Montenegro, 2018).

In order to eliminate the barriers faced by entrepreneurs and to strengthen the development of entrepreneurship, the European Commission formulated the Entrepreneurship 2020 Action Plan, which highlights the following important areas (European Commission, 2013): entrepreneurial education and training to support growth; removing existing administrative barriers and supporting entrepreneurs in key stages of the business life cycle; and raising the culture of entrepreneurship in Europe and fostering a new generation of entrepreneurs.

In addition to the above, the SBA is a strategic document that defines a set of principles and policies that have a significant impact on improving the overall framework and conditions for encouraging the development of entrepreneurship (Government of Montenegro, 2018).

It is also important to mention the EU Program for Competitiveness of Entrepreneurship and SMEs (COSME), which defines key goals such as improving framework conditions for competitiveness, encouraging entrepreneurial culture, improving access to finance, and improving access to the market. Besides that, another important program is the "HORIZON 2020" – Program for Research and Innovation, as the largest program of the EU, which aims to provide financial support for transnational research for entrepreneurs and SMEs, who want to innovate and improve their competitiveness by increasing investment in research activities (Government of Montenegro, 2018).

After gaining insight into a significant number of strategies and policies that recognize the importance of strengthening entrepreneurship in Montenegro, it can be concluded that all the aforementioned policies and strategies focus on creating stimulating business frameworks for creating added value, improving knowledge, innovation, and digitalization of business processes, all that with the ultimate goal to stimulate competitiveness.

3. State Measures – Financial and Non-financial Programs to Support the Entrepreneurship Development

Entrepreneurship relies mainly on micro-, small-, and medium-sized enterprises whose primary goal is to make the best use of their own and/or other people's knowledge and experience, own or borrowed funds, available equipment, personnel potential, and everything else that is necessary to start certain business ventures (Martinović & Tanasković, 2013). Therefore, there are numerous factors that can affect the success of entrepreneurial ventures, and certainly, one of the key ones that can potentially have multiplied effects on the competitiveness of companies is state support and adequate programs to support entrepreneurship. The role of governments and other state institutions is to provide the economy with the easiest possible access to capital, new technologies, various markets, and information, through the creation of an economic framework and adequate financial and non-financial incentive programs for entrepreneurship development (Cvjetković, 2017; Novaković, Stošković, & Nikolić, 2011). Also, numerous authors emphasize the extremely important role of state support programs for the development of entrepreneurship in transitional conditions (Cvjetković, 2017; Novaković et al., 2011). One of the biggest challenges for entrepreneurs is how to find and provide the financial resources necessary for starting a business, how to acquire the necessary resources, and maintain the liquidity of ongoing investment projects, all with the aim of achieving business growth and development. Bank loans are generally expensive and difficult for entrepreneurs to access, which is why this problem becomes even more important. Hence, financial support programs for SMEs by various state institutions can serve to them as an alternative to bank loans (Ravić & Obradović, 2017).

Various programs of financial and non-financial support for the development of entrepreneurship in Montenegro were created in the previous period by relevant ministries and state institutions, with the aim of stimulating entrepreneurial activities, that is, the competitiveness of micro-, small-, and medium-sized enterprises. Financial support was created and implemented in the last few years by the line ministries for the economy, science, agriculture and rural development, tourism, and sustainable development, in cooperation with competent state institutions, as well as the domain of the Investment and Development Fund for the area of credit arrangements. The state-owned investment and development fund plays a key role in facilitating lending. The classification of programs can be done as follows:

- Entrepreneurship development support programs of competent ministries and non-credit state institutions, which are focused on encouraging competitiveness.
- Entrepreneurship development support programs of the Investment and Development Fund, banks, and microcredit financial institutions.
- Non-financial support programs for entrepreneurship, that is, support programs of business associations and organizations for the development of entrepreneurship in Montenegro.

Continuous monitoring of the demands of the economy and the directing of budget funds to support those activities, that is, micro-, small-, and medium-sized enterprises for which the highest need is expressed (all with the aim of strengthening their competitiveness, productivity, innovation, flexibility, and recognition on the wider international market) is imperative for creators of economic policies aimed at providing support to the entrepreneurship development.

The Ministry of Economy continuously implements a different range of programs and program lines aimed at supporting entrepreneurship and encouraging competitiveness. In 2019, it adopted the "Program for the Improvement of the Competitiveness of the Economy" which united all previous program lines for supporting enterprises. It continued with this practice in 2020 with the adoption of a new program which, in addition to the previous ones, added new and improved existing program lines (Government of Montenegro, 2020).

Another important source of support to entrepreneurial efforts is the Ministry of Science, which in 2017 announced the first call for financing entrepreneurial projects based on innovation. In 2018, it received a 60% increase in the budget for financing entrepreneurial projects for innovation, with the aim to continue its support. However, it is of great importance to continue efforts in the direction of the development of the scientific community and its relations with the factors within the ecosystem (European Commission, 2019). Also, a very important program that can be analyzed in the context of supporting entrepreneurship in the field of agriculture is the IPARD-like project (Investment and Development Fund of Montenegro, 2022), under the jurisdiction of the Ministry of Agriculture.

Furthermore, non-financial support is provided by the Innovation and Entrepreneurship Center Tehnopolis (Tehnopolis, n.d.). This center creates and provides consulting services, and organizes training, workshops, and seminars, all with the aim to improve knowledge, and skills and support the adoption of new tools, which are needed for better management, that is, starting a new business. Besides that, this center connects tenants with partners and associates from the region, in order to improve their business performance. Similarly, the Business Start-Up Center Bar (n.d.) provides support for the development and survival of new companies and entrepreneurs during the first years of business, as well as support for increasing the competitiveness of existing companies, which makes an important contribution to reducing the number of unsuccessful business entities.

Innovation and Entrepreneurship Center Tehnopolis is the most important center for the development of startup companies and entrepreneurship in Montenegro. It officially started operating in 2014, and its founder and owner (100%), is the Government of Montenegro. The Ministry of Science and Technological Development is responsible for the supervision of Tehnopolis, while the partners of this center are: the Ministry of Agriculture, Forestry and Water Management, the Investment and Development Fund of Montenegro, and the Municipality of Nikšić.

As one of the key actors in the creation and reshaping of the innovation ecosystem, Technopolis provides a series of infrastructure and support measures that enable the opening of new companies and the development of business based on new, innovative ideas and technologies. Through its activities and cooperation with more than 150 partners, it supports the improvement of the innovation system and infrastructure for the overall sustainable economic development of Montenegro (ICT Cortex, 2021).

Services and Products (Tehnopolis, n.d.):

Business incubator – provides support to development of teams, startups and already registered companies with high growth potential, that is, whose business is based on scientific and research work, development and implementation of new technologies.

Biotechnology Laboratory – BioLab Tehnopolis – provides support to agricultural producers and encourages the development of agriculture, both through the provision of its own services and through the connection of the academic and business sectors in order to encourage the transfer of knowledge and innovation, which will lead to the creation of new products, as well as the improvement of the quality of existing ones.

Laboratory for Industrial Design – TechLab Tehnopolis – it is available to academic community and all innovative SMEs, innovators and startups, which are the part of the IPC Tehnopolis support system, all with the aim of introducing new technologies and implementing innovative solutions in the development of new products and improvements of the existing ones.

Data Center Tehnopolis – provides support for the development of start-up companies in Montenegro and supports the overall digitization of the operations of micro-, small-, and medium-sized enterprises. In addition to support, the Data Center also provides commercial services.

Program activities include the creation of content that is adapted and harmonized with the policies of the state, and their goal is to create an entrepreneurial and innovative ecosystem, as well as its empowerment through various types of financial and non-financial support.

Example: *Innovation and Entrepreneurship Center Tehnopolis*[1]

Support programs for the development of entrepreneurship are also provided by the Innovation Fund of Montenegro, which represents a specialized institution that gathers internal and external experts from the fields of research and development, technology transfer, EU funds, financial management, and evaluation (Innovation Fund of Montenegro, 2022). It also deals with the monitoring of projects necessary for the implementation of government programs that contribute to increasing the technological capacities of Montenegrin companies. The role of the fund is reflected in encouraging the transfer of technologies and the commercialization of innovations. The numerous programs of the fund contribute to more efficient cooperation between the academic community and the private sector and encourage the private sector to innovate more. The Innovation Fund is the umbrella state institution in charge of the implementation of innovation policy measures and programs intended for micro-, small-, and medium-sized entrepreneurship, as well as for the transfer of technologies from scientific and research institutions (Innovation Fund of Montenegro, 2022).

Furthermore, the University of Montenegro realizes *Training for Beginners in Business*, in which the emphasis is placed on strengthening the awareness of young people, predominantly students, about entrepreneurship and business (University

[1]Information used in this example are mostly obtained from websites of the ICT Cortex Company and the Innovation and Entrepreneurship Center Tehnopolis.

of Montenegro, 2022). The mentioned training covers key topics from this field, through a combination of theoretical and applied teaching methods.

In addition to the above, the European Bank for Reconstruction and Development – EBRD in Montenegro provides advisory services through various forms of non-financial support. More precisely, this organization enables the transfer of expertise and knowledge of local and international consultants in the following areas: strategy, marketing, information technology, engineering solutions, quality management, financial management, energy efficiency, and environmental protection (European Bank for Reconstruction and Development, 2021).

All previously stated reveals that progress is evident in the provision of business support services, where the number and scope of support programs for the development of entrepreneurship in Montenegro have increased. In this sense, grants, export-finance support, information and communication technologies (ICT), and resource efficiency training are now available to entrepreneurs (OECD, 2022).

Based on the presented available support programs, it can be concluded that there is a wide range of well-designed support mechanisms aimed at creating preconditions for entrepreneurship development in Montenegro. However, as it was recognized for the previously analyzed entrepreneurship support programs, it is necessary to provide financial and non-financial support to a significantly larger number of entrepreneurs, so that the effects of the implementation of the aforementioned programs can become more significantly reflected in a higher degree of competitiveness on the local, regional, and international markets.

4. The Importance of Entrepreneurial Learning in the Development of Entrepreneurial Activity in Montenegro

Research confirms that educational programs in the field of entrepreneurship have a positive effect on the development of entrepreneurial activities, strengthen the entrepreneurial intentions of students and young people, and represent the foundation for entrepreneurship development (Subotić, Mitrović, Melović, & Nikolić, 2018). According to OECD data (OECD, 2016; OECD, 2022), Montenegro has a leadership position in the field of entrepreneurial learning in the Western Balkans and is an example of good practice in the region, with the SBA – SME Policy Index 2022 score of 4.61, compared to the average of 3.33.

Table 1 shows the grades for entrepreneurial learning for Montenegro in the period 2016–2022, where Montenegro's progress in this area is evident.

Activities in the field of entrepreneurial learning have been taking place since 2008 (in vocational education since 2004), and Montenegro has decided to have a clear direction in its formal and informal education system toward the comprehensive application of entrepreneurial learning (Ministry of Economic Development and Tourism of Montenegro, 2020). With its involvement, the national partnership significantly contributed to the development of entrepreneurial learning and the successful implementation of the Strategy for Lifelong Entrepreneurial Learning of Montenegro 2020–2024, which further contributed to Montenegro becoming an example of good practice in the region.

Table 1. Results for Entrepreneurial Learning of Montenegro for the Period 2016–2022.

Dimension	Year		
	2016	**2019**	**2022**
Entrepreneurial learning	2.83	4.08	4.61

Source: Author's view based on available OECD reports SME Policy Index: Western Balkans and Turkey for years 2016, 2019 and 2022 (OCED, 2016; OECD, 2019, OECD, 2022).

Entrepreneurship is seen as the key to creating new jobs and employing the young population. Today, the entrepreneurial potential is a phenomenon that should be nurtured and encouraged through the education system, socialization, and training programs (Subotić et al., 2018).

By accepting a broader concept in the formulation and implementation of entrepreneurial learning, key requirements are being created in Montenegro on how to manage and develop schools and faculties, how to modernize the teaching profession and the learning process, promoting entrepreneurship within every component of the learning system (from primary education to universities, as well as through the adult education system), where it is objectively possible, with a clear need to build the entrepreneurial learning outcomes on the results of earlier learning (Ministry of Economic Development and Tourism of Montenegro, 2020). Montenegro stands out among the countries of the Western Balkans, with a curriculum from primary to professional education that clearly develops the key competencies of entrepreneurship, which are reflected in related learning outcomes in the areas of the curriculum (OECD, 2022)

When it comes to higher education, where most economies show independent programs or ad hoc initiatives which are not available to all students, Montenegro introduced mandatory practical teaching for all students, providing the opportunity to orient this practice toward the explicit development of entrepreneurial competencies (OECD, 2022). In accordance with the above, the University of Montenegro is currently implementing the project *Strengthening Capacities for the Implementation of Dual Education in Montenegro Higher Education (DUALMON),* which refers to the development of dual higher education in Montenegro. The goal of this project is to create conditions for the development of dual education and the improvement of the competencies of graduate students in Montenegro, in order to increase the motivation of students to study while simultaneously acquiring practical competencies, that is, acquiring more relevant knowledge and skills by combining formal education with training at the workplace (internship). The above indicates that human resources, education, and improvement of knowledge and skills are one of the key priorities that should be fulfilled in order to promote entrepreneurship development (Dualmon, 2021).

5. Case Study – The Success of Young People from Montenegro at the Prestigious EUROSKILLS Competition

EuroSkills is a competition in various disciplines in which hundreds of talented young people take part. It is the largest European skills competition, held every other year, while its participants are selected through national competitions and selection processes. Competitors can be up to 25 years old in the year of the competition and can only compete once (WorldSkills Europe, n.d.). During the EuroSkills competition, international partners from the economic sector, government institutions, and educational institutions gather. The goals of organizing the EuroSkills competition are to raise standards in skills, promote professional education in Europe, and develop an awareness of the importance of knowledge and professional education for the development of the EU. Besides that, special focus is placed on making the connection between the economy and education, which is one of the main reasons for the existence of this association.

Montenegro became the first country from the region to participate in the EuroSkills competition without being a member of the EU. At previous Euroskills competitions, Montenegro competed in the following disciplines: entrepreneurship, mobile robotics, cooking, and catering and hairdressing services. The institution that represents Montenegro in the WorldSkills Europe association is the Center for Vocational Education. In this study, we particularly point out the success of the students of the Faculty of Economics of the University of Montenegro at the Euroskills competition.

Namely, Euroskills 2016 was held in Gothenburg (Sweden) with more than 480 competitors from 28 European countries, who competed in 44 disciplines (WorldSkills Europe, 2016). Students of the Faculty of Economics, Damjana Katnić, and Bojan Pejović, under the mentorship of professor Boban Melović, won first place in the field of entrepreneurship. The task that the contestants were given was related to one of the 17 global goals of the United Nations (Good Health). Based on the given task, through 10 modules, the contestants made a detailed elaboration of the business project "EUREKA" – a former sport (wo) men company.

At the following competition, Euroskills Europe (2018) held in Budapest (Hungary), about 500 competitors from 28 European countries and 15 competitors from 4 guest countries outside Europe (India, UAE, Japan, Korea) that are members of the WorldSkills International association took part (WorldSkills Europe, 2018). A team from the Faculty of Economics – contestants Aleksandra Jovanović and Nikola Martinović took part in the *Entrepreneurship – Business Development* discipline, while colleague Bojan Pejović and professor Boban Melović played the role of mentors – experts in the preparation of the contestants. The team of the Faculty of Economics won second place and a silver medal. The task that the contestants received in Budapest was related to one of the 17 global goals of the United Nations and was in the area of waste management, that is, responsible consumption.

In addition to the mentioned successes of young people in Montenegro and another proof of the importance of entrepreneurial learning at the level of higher education, the Faculty of Economics was an honorary participant of WorldSkills Russia 2019 in November 2019, where it represented Montenegro in the discipline *entrepreneurship*. The competition included 51 disciplines and brought together hundreds of competitors from more than 80 educational institutions, that is, universities. Professor Boban Melović, associate Bojan Pejović, and students Marina Vojinović and Andrija Pavićević made a team of the Faculty of Economics. After detailed preparations, the team of the Faculty of Economics presented itself with a business idea – the online learning platform one-clicksolutions.com, and according to the criteria of the jury, it was ranked among the most successful presented business ideas, thus once again confirming the quality of the education that Faculty of Economics provides in the field of entrepreneurship and business.

6. Female Entrepreneurship as a Growing form of Entrepreneurial Activity in Montenegro

The development of female entrepreneurship is important for all economies, especially for those that are going through transition and have high unemployment rates. By encouraging the development of female entrepreneurship, society gets better utilization of all resources. However, in the current period, national statistics on the entrepreneurial activity of women in Montenegro have not been developed at an appropriate level. However, it is evident that deeply rooted patriarchal attitudes of men and women in Montenegro represent a significant barrier to female entrepreneurship development (Popović, 2013). Namely, gender inequality manifests itself through the low level of representation of women in leadership and decision-making positions, insufficient political participation of women, as well as through economic inequality, the feminization of certain professions, the segregation of educational profiles, the difference in earnings for the jobs of the same value, property ownership, and unequal division of obligations in the family (Melovic & Djurisic, 2020). Women entrepreneurs face significant obstacles when starting a business due to cultural and traditional perceptions toward women in Montenegro because according to these perceptions, women should stay at home and take care of their families (Dinc & Hadzic, 2018). Despite these obstacles, some personality traits of women, such as innovativeness, risk-taking, and self-confidence, encourage their entrepreneurial intention to start a business (Dinc & Hadzic, 2018). The future of the modern woman lies precisely in entrepreneurship (Dautović, Omerhodžić, & Lekić, 2019). However, it should be noted that numerous activities are implemented in Montenegro with the aim of achieving gender equality and economic empowerment of women.

In April 2020, the Expert Group for the Economic Empowerment of Women was established, whose purpose was strengthening the coordination of strategic documents related to the economic empowerment of women, with special reference to the Strategy for the Development of Women's Entrepreneurship in Montenegro (Ministry of Economic Development, 2021a). In the aforementioned Strategy, digitization is highlighted as a driver of female entrepreneurship and it builds on previous work in the sectors of the digital, green, and creative economy, along with plans to improve the digital literacy of women in business (Ministry of Economic Development, 2021a; OECD, 2022).

According to OECD data (OECD, 2022), Montenegro has a leadership position in the field of female entrepreneurship among the Western Balkans countries and is an example of good practice in the region, with the SBA – SME Policy Index 2022 score of 4.26 (compared to the average of 3.73). Table 2 shows the ratings for female entrepreneurship in Montenegro in the period 2016–2022, where the significant progress of this country in the mentioned area is evident.

The aforementioned progress is the result of the efforts of the Government of Montenegro, which has taken an important step in order to establish coordination in women's entrepreneurship at the system level and to improve mechanisms of evaluation in this field. The strategy for the development of female entrepreneurship in Montenegro 2021–2024 encourages the continuous improvement of this type of entrepreneurship, with a 4.6% increase in the share of women business owners from the year 2018 to 2020, and a 10% increase in the share of self-employed women in the same period (OECD, 2022).

Almost all entrepreneurial activities of women in Montenegro are based on projects conducted in coordination and cooperation with numerous institutions from the private sector,[2] non-governmental organizations,[3] and government institutions, and with the support of numerous international donor programs.[4] Furthermore, support for female entrepreneurship is also reflected in specialized credit lines designed by the Investment and Development Fund of Montenegro, as well as through the programs of the Employment Agency, which provide training and financial support to certain categories of unemployed women.

It should be noted that incentives for women-led businesses have been increased in recent years and that they are included in the government's financial programs for small investments, which resulted in an increased rate of financial grant intervention from 50% to 80% for businesses that are owned by at least 50% of women

Table 2. Results for Female Entrepreneurship in the Period 2016–2022.

Dimension	**Year**		
	2016	**2019**	**2022**
Women's entrepreneurship	2.50	3.46	4.26

Source: Author's view based on available OECD reports SME Policy Index: Western Balkans and Turkey for years 2016, 2019 and 2022 (OCED, 2016; OECD, 2019, OECD, 2022).

[2]The Chamber of Commerce of Montenegro and the Union of Employers of Montenegro.

[3]Institute for Entrepreneurship and Economic Development, Business Women Association of Montenegro, Association of Entrepreneurs of Montenegro, and Business Start-Up Center Bar.

[4]United Nations Development Program (UNDP), EU, EBRD, and World Bank.

(Ministry of Economic Development, 2021b). Also, the fact that Montenegro is working intensively on the realization and implementation of the Strategy for the Development of Women's Entrepreneurship in this area, thereby actively working to empower women in business, is very encouraging. As women in Montenegro makeup slightly more than half of the population and thus, represent a significant potential for economic development, this kind of encouragement of female entrepreneurship is one of the ways to valorize that potential (Melovic & Djurisic, 2020).

Although good practice can be seen in initiatives funded by international partners, and future actions are identified in the new strategy, there is still insufficient evaluation at the program level and a general lack of gender-disaggregated statistical data (OECD, 2022). In this regard, it is necessary to work on developing a systematic approach to monitoring female entrepreneurship in the future, with special reference to the inclusion of gender indicators in accordance with international standards. The above should be implemented in coordination with the Statistical Office of Montenegro. Namely, if the entrepreneurial activity of women can be measured, it will be easier to understand how and to what extent women entrepreneurs contribute to the economy and society (Meunier, Krylova, & Ramalho, 2017). However, in addition to determining gender indicators, as an important segment of the improvement of female entrepreneurship in Montenegro, the creation of a unique portal for female entrepreneurship can be singled out, which would unite all relevant information and resources and thus increase the visibility and availability of support for this area. Namely, not all women have equal access to information about existing support services, so connecting all relevant information about access to finances, training, mentoring, and networking would be extremely useful.

The United Nations Development Program (UNDP), in cooperation with the Ministry of Economic Development, created the website www.zenskibiznis.me, intended for all women in Montenegro who want to start or improve an existing business, educate themselves and inform about business opportunities and support programs, achieve mutual cooperation, and strengthen ties with the public sector.

Aware of the opportunities offered to women entrepreneurs and their position in the market, the platform was created to follow digitization trends and, thus, support the economic empowerment of women in Montenegro and provide support to those who are already in business, as well as those who want to implement a business idea.

Women make up 51% of the population of Montenegro, but they are still not sufficiently represented in economic life. Nevertheless, there is a noticeable increase in women entrepreneurs, compared to the period 10 years ago, when there were only 9.6% of female business owners. Today, 32% of entrepreneurs are women. However, this is still below the world and European average (UNDP Montenegro, 2022).

Taking into account previously mentioned, the goal of the www.zenskibiznis.me platform is precisely to contribute to women being more productive in the digital revolution by helping them to improve their knowledge and digital literacy, and to take advantage of as many opportunities as possible. All registered users will have access to trainings on the platform, which will be organized online, through video modules and presentations. The platform enables female entrepreneurs to receive education in all necessary areas – from establishing and running a business, through marketing, financial and human resource management, to business development and internationalization of business.

Additionally, the platform will contribute to strengthening cooperation with the public sector in order to create new policies that will enable a better position of women in the market. The national platform was created for the needs of the Government of Montenegro, that is, the Ministry of Economic Development, in accordance with the government Strategy for the Development of Women's Entrepreneurship in Montenegro for the period 2021–2024, within the project named "Acceleration of Digital Management," implemented and financed by UNDP in Montenegro (UNDP Montenegro, 2022).

Example: *UNDP Created a Site Intended for Women in Business*[5]

7. Specific Forms of Entrepreneurship – A Chance or Limitation of Further Development

Montenegrin society is characterized by the presence of various types of entrepreneurial activity, which are developed to a greater or lesser extent. This section provides a brief overview of some of the specific forms of entrepreneurship that are current and those that may be promising.

7.1. Social Entrepreneurship

Social entrepreneurship as a process includes an innovative entrepreneurial approach that combines limited resources with the purpose of using opportunities and generating changes in society, in order to meet social needs (Katsikis &

[5]Information used in this example are mostly obtained from the official website of UNDP Montenegro.

Kyrgidou, 2016, p. 94). It is of exceptional importance when it comes to Montenegro. This form of entrepreneurial activity is significantly determined by social policies as guidelines aimed at creating, maintaining, and positively changing the living conditions of members of a certain local community (Melović et al., 2020). Instead of profit, success through the prism of social entrepreneurship can be viewed as an increased level of employment, economic growth, and increased quality of life for vulnerable groups. This means that the primary goal of this type of entrepreneurship is to solve certain social problems, while the economic effects are of secondary importance (Pärenson, 2011, p. 41).

In the last decade, numerous activities have been initiated in Montenegro, especially by the non-governmental sector, which strives to ensure greater inclusion of vulnerable groups and thereby stimulate the development of social entrepreneurship. However, the report of the European Commission (2020b) states that the level of development of social entrepreneurship in Montenegro is at a low level, which is also the result of the lack of the Law on Social Entrepreneurship and corresponding national strategies in this area (European Commission, 2020b). Nevertheless, regardless of the fact that there is no special law governing this area in Montenegro, practice confirms that an increasing number of non-governmental organizations are engaged in the production of certain products and the provision of services from the domain of social entrepreneurship, which makes this area inclusive, philanthropic and promising in the long term.

7.2. Immigrant Entrepreneurship and Digital Nomads as a Form of Entrepreneurial Activity in Montenegro

Based on the fact that entrepreneurship is a powerful driver of economic growth and job creation, decision-makers aim to support an environment that is attractive to all its forms. Thus, in recent years, the topic of the connection between migrants and entrepreneurship has become more and more relevant, which is becoming the focus of scientific and professional publications (Predojević-Despić & Lukić, 2018). Migrations, which have multiple economic and social repercussions, are associated with the phenomenon known as "brain drain," but also as a factor that can stimulate the development of entrepreneurship.

On the other hand, the rise of telecommuting opportunities and the influence of social media has increased interest in the lifestyle of digital nomads. Digital nomads, that is, those who travel while working, are becoming more and more numerous globally. Consequently, in 2021, the Ministry of Public Administration, Digital Society, and Media adopted the Program for Attracting Digital Nomads in Montenegro until 2025 (Ministry of Public Administration, Digital Society and Media, 2021). The goal of this program, along with the proposed action plan and set of measures, is to improve the environment for the longest possible stay of digital nomads in Montenegro and to make Montenegro an attractive destination for the work and life of digital nomads.

It can be stated that, in recent years, Montenegro has become an increasingly popular destination for starting a business for companies whose owners are foreign nationals. The observation of the situation in Montenegro shows that the number of companies, whose owners are foreigners, is growing year by year. Thus, according to available data for the year 2022, the largest number of active business entities in foreign ownership (based on the owner's country of origin) was from Turkey (3,772 or 25.7%), Russia (2,645 business entities or 18%), Serbia (2,122 or 14.5%), and Ukraine (764 business entities, i.e. 5.2%) (Investitor, 2022). Foreign entrepreneurs who start a business in Montenegro are mostly related to the trade, hospitality, construction, and IT sectors.

7.3. Economic Citizenship as a Form of Stimulating Entrepreneurship

The Citizenship by Investment Program in Montenegro attracts successful investors and entrepreneurs who are needed for state progress and who contribute to the economy, connect Montenegro with the world, invest in Montenegro, help accelerate its development, and enable the creation of new jobs. A significant beneficiary of this program is the Innovation Fund of Montenegro, whose primary goal is to stimulate the economic growth and competitiveness of Montenegro by increasing the innovativeness of the Montenegrin economy. Namely, thanks to this program, the fund will be able to receive and distribute between 30 and 40 million euros, which will enable the government to, among other things, implement various projects, such as financing start-up companies for Montenegrin entrepreneurs in various fields (Bankar.me, 2022).

Although the interest from foreign entrepreneurs is significant and enviable results are being achieved in terms of investment, there are also different opinions when it comes to the Citizenship by Investment Program. Thus, criticism can be heard from relevant addresses (such as the European Commission), from which it is pointed out that the economic citizenship scheme should be abolished for investors due to the risks it presents, such as money laundering, tax evasion, financing of terrorism, corruption, and the infiltration of organized crime (Bankar.me, 2023).

8. Recommendations and Suggestions for Further Development of Entrepreneurship in Montenegro

In addition to the activities and steps already implemented, the development of entrepreneurship in Montenegro requires continuous efforts aimed at creating a favorable business environment. In other words, it is necessary to work intensively on the development of infrastructure facilities and ensure the inclusiveness of different social groups, in order to create an environment that is simulative for entrepreneurship development. Besides that, the formation of a strong advisory and supervisory board with numerous experts (mentors) from the mentioned field, using a lot of university resources, stands out as a valid proposal that can have significant positive effects on promoting entrepreneurial activity. The diverse expertise stands out as one of the key factors that contribute to the development of quality assistance both for beginners and young people, as well as for those who are already implementing entrepreneurial activities. An adequate list of mentors, that is, experts from both the public and private sectors, should be constantly updated and expanded, in order to sufficiently respond to the business needs of entrepreneurs. Mentors should have relevant theoretical and practical knowledge of various aspects of business, emphasizing marketing, finance, and product development.

Those who engage in entrepreneurship for the first time need to be provided with adequate and suitable conditions and numerous incentives for the implementation of innovations. These incentives can be provided in various forms, including issuing licenses, providing financial support, facilitating the importation of equipment, etc. Support should be particularly provided to those entrepreneurs who are planning or are already engaged in research and innovation activities. Also, the support of the government in the marketing and promotion of their ventures/products is considered to be of great importance.

Although there are numerous training programs for entrepreneurs that are available in Montenegro, it is necessary to constantly work on their improvement and updating, so that the entrepreneurs can be prepared to realize their entrepreneurial activities in a successful way. Training and mentoring programs should encourage innovative ideas and find a way to create demand for new products/services. For those who have already passed one of the offered training, after a certain time, it is necessary to organize courses where they would refresh their knowledge and solve the doubts and problems they faced up to that moment. Also, training programs should be adequately promoted, in order to attract as many unemployed persons and other specific (vulnerable) social groups as possible and encourage them to entrepreneurship.

Therefore, it is necessary to significantly improve marketing and communication, especially through digital marketing channels, in order to raise awareness about entrepreneurship and attract the right candidates. In addition to numerous training, it is also necessary to provide adequate literature in this area and distribute it adequately. The aforementioned literature should be recent and contain all adequate information, incentives, steps, support programs, and guidelines on how to prepare proposals for investments and how to use the offered funding grants as efficiently as possible. Also, it is desirable to include the stories of successful entrepreneurs, stating their experiences and the problems they faced, as well as the ways in which they solved them. The mentioned literature can be distributed in printed form or by creating a website where all relevant information from this field would be combined.

Another important step that should be taken is related to making law and all legal provisions prescribed for entrepreneurship as simple, logical, rational, and practical as possible, in order to encourage and foster potential entrepreneurs to carry out entrepreneurial activities. Also, the financial sector should be even more cooperative with entrepreneurs and listen to their needs.

The analysis of modern ways of doing business reveals the need to create or strengthen an entrepreneurial ecosystem in Montenegro at the national and local level, which includes the academic and business community, state institutions and companies, agencies, and non-governmental organizations, in order to synergistically provide support for digital transformation, that is, to increase the level of digital maturity of entrepreneurs through strengthening digital skills and providing adequate digital infrastructure. It is also necessary to encourage Montenegrin entrepreneurs to initiate green innovations and rely on sustainable business models. All these aforementioned recommendations and suggestions should be incorporated into various economic policies, in order to create a synergy effect during their implementation. Although it is obvious that there is significant room for improvement of support directed toward entrepreneurship development, all previously stated indicates that the efforts that were made in Montenegro in this direction so far have given really encouraging results.

References

Ashoka, M., & Duggappa, M. C. (2014). Prospects of entrepreneurial development towards economic development. *South Asian Journal of Marketing & Management Research*, *4*(8), 98–105.

Bankar.me. (2022). Why the economic citizenship program should continue. Retrieved from https://www.bankar.me/2022/12/23/zasto-program-ekonomskog-drzavljanstva-treba-da-se-nastavi/. Accessed on February 7, 2023.

Bankar.me. (2023). Pisonero: EC again recommended Montenegro to abolish the economic citizenship scheme as soon as possible. Retrieved from https://www.bankar.me/2023/01/13/pisonero-ek-ponovo-preporucila-crnoj-gori-da-sto-prije-ukine-semu-ekonomskog-drzavljanstva/. Accessed on February 5, 2023.

Business Start-Up Center Bar. About business incubator. (n.d.). Retrieved from https://www.bscbar.org/. Accessed on January 25, 2023.

Cvjetković, M. (2017). *Analiza ključnih faktora unapređenja poslovanja i konkurentnosti preduzeća*. Doctoral dissertation, University of Novi Sad, Serbia.

Dautović, E., Omerhodžić, N., & Lekić, S. (2019). Analysis of women entrepreneurship in Montenegro. *KNOWLEDGE – International Journal*, *31*(5), 1251–1257.

Dinc, M. S., & Hadzic, M. (2018). The mediating impact of personality traits on entrepreneurial intention of women in Northern Montenegro. *International Journal of Entrepreneurship and Small Business*, *33*(3), 400–416.

DUALMON. (2021). Beginning of the DUALMON project – Strengthening capacities for the implementation of dual education in Montenegro higher education. Retrieved from https://www.dualmon.ucg.ac.me/2021/04/23/pocetak-projekta-dualmon-jacanje-kapaciteta-za-implementaciju-dualnog-obrazovanja-u-crnogorskom-visokom-obrazovanju/. Accessed on February 1, 2023.

European Bank for Reconstruction and Development. (2021). Advice for small businesses. Retrieved from https://www.ebrd.com/work-with-us/advice-for-small-businesses/overview.html. Accessed on February 4, 2023.

European Commission. (2013). Entrepreneurship 2020 action plan. Retrieved from https://www.eesc.europa.eu/en/our-work/opinions-information-reports/opinions/entrepreneurship-2020-action-plan. Accessed on January 17, 2023.

European Commission. (2019). Montenegro 2019 report. Retrieved from https://neighbourhood-enlargement.ec.europa.eu/system/files/2019-05/20190529-montenegro-report.pdf. Accessed on January 25, 2023.

European Commission. (2020a). Montenegro 2020 report. Retrieved from https://neighbourhood-enlargement.ec.europa.eu/system/files/2020-10/montenegro_report_2020.pdf. Accessed on January 30, 2023.

European Commission. (2020b). Social enterprises and their ecosystems in Europe – Comparative synthesis report. Retrieved from https://ec.europa.eu/social/main.jsp?catId=738&langId=en&pubId=8274. Accessed on February 5, 2023.

EuroSkills Europe. (2018). EuroSkills Budapest 2018. Retrieved from https://www.worldskillsuk.org/skills/international-competition/euroskills-budapest-2018/. Accessed on January 15, 2023.

Government of Montenegro. (2018). Strategy for the development of micro, small and medium enterprises in Montenegro 2018–2022. Retrieved from https://javnepolitike.me/wp-content/uploads/2020/06/Strategija-razvoja-MMSP-2018-2022.pdf. Accessed on February 9, 2023.

Government of Montenegro. (2020). Proposal of a programme for improving the competitiveness of the economy for 2020. Retrieved from https://wapi.gov.me/download/38fcea70-188a-4ba1-bb61-03e3c8408b80?version=1.0. Accessed on February 7, 2023.

Government of Montenegro. (2021). Montenegro economic reform programme 2021–2023. Retrieved from https://wapi.gov.me/download/993f6bc7-bace-4ec7-b49a-f58419ec9804?version=1.0. Accessed on January 29, 2023.

ICT Cortex. (2021). Innovation and Entrepreneurship Center Tehnopolis. Retrieved from https://ictcortex.me/clanica/inovaciono-preduzetnicki-centar-tehnopolis/. Accessed on January 15, 2023.

Innovation Fund of Montenegro. About the Fund. (2022). Retrieved from https://fondzainovacije.me/o-fondu/. Accessed on January 30, 2023.

Investitor. (2022). Most foreign companies in Montenegro owned by Turkish citizens. Retrieved from https://investitor.me/2022/07/22/najvise-stranih-kompanija-u-crnoj-gori-u-vlasnistvu-je-drzavljana-turske/. Accessed on February 2, 2023.

Investment and Development Fund of Montenegro. (2022). Investment loans for agricultural development: IPARD. Retrieved from https://www.irfcg.me/me/2014-03-10-14-49-50/program-podrske-razvoju-poljoprivrede-ipard.html. Accessed on January 28, 2023.

Katsikis, I. N., & Kyrgidou, L. P. (2016). Social policy and social entrepreneurship: Between the public and the private. In *Innovation and entrepreneurship in education*. Retrieved from https://doi.org/10.1108/S2051-229520160000002005. Accessed on December 9, 2016.

Klandt, H., & Volkmann, C. (2006). Development and prospects of academic entrepreneurship education in Germany. *Higher Education in Europe*, *31*(2), 195–208.

Martinović, M., & Tanasković, Z. (2013). Entrepreneurship and its influence on the enterprises of the 21st century. *Trendovi u poslovanju*, *1*(2), 11–15.

Melovic, B., & Djurisic, V. (2020). Women's entrepreneurship in Montenegro. In R. Palalić, E. Knezović & L. P. Dana (Eds.). *Women's entrepreneurship in former Yugoslavia: Historical framework, ecosystem, and future perspectives for the region* (pp. 83–111). Switzerland: Springer Cham.

Melović, B., & Mitrović, S. (2013). Istraživanje preduzetničkih stavova mladih u Crnoj Gori. *Economics & Economy*, *1*(1), 175–184.

Melović, B., Radević, I., Backović-Vulić, T., & Haček, M. (2020). Social entrepreneurship and development of local self-governments: Evidence from Montenegro. *Lex Localis*, *18*(4), 855–883.

Meunier, F., Krylova, Y., & Ramalho, R. (2017). Women's entrepreneurship: how to measure the gap between new female and male entrepreneurs? *World Bank Policy Research Working Paper No. 8242*.

Ministry of Economic Development. (2022). Programme for improving the competitiveness of the economy for 2022. Retrieved from https://wapi.gov.me/download/fa2b4f1b-5331-4df8-bee2-ecf6c2ca7a55?version=1.0. Accessed on February 3, 2023.

Ministry of Economic Development and Tourism of Montenegro. (2019). Industrial policy of Montenegro 2019–2023. Retrieved from https://wapi.gov.me/download/af22514f-712a-4fb8-8ab5-acfa8e083c4c?version=1.0. Accessed on February 1, 2023.

Ministry of Economic Development and Tourism of Montenegro. (2020). Strategy for lifelong entrepreneurial learning of Montenegro 2020–2024. Retrieved from https://wapi.gov.me/download/59a998e8-af01-4e54-a205-fc81584163f8?version=1.0. Accessed on February 5, 2023.

Ministry of Economic Development. (2021a). Women entrepreneurship development strategy 2021–2024. Retrieved from https://wapi.gov.me/download/0a95b4be-c3f4-4f9b-8c36-964d9684c885?version=1.0. Accessed on January 23, 2023.

Ministry of Economic Development. (2021b). Programme for improving the competitiveness of the economy for 2021. Retrieved from https://wapi.gov.me/download/2dd06bd7-cda2-4635-961c-d84cffe4a3eb?version=1.0. Accessed on January 29, 2023.

Ministry of Economy. (2014). Strategy for regional development of Montenegro 2014–2020. Retrieved from https://javnepolitike.me/wp-content/uploads/2020/07/5.-Strategija-regionalnog-razvoja-Crne-Gore-za-period-2014-2020-godina.pdf. Accessed on January 15, 2023.

Ministry of Education. (2018). Strategy of scientific research activities 2017–2021. Retrieved from https://wapi.gov.me/download/20080ae6-11e9-45d6-9a4e-7f452cbb1ae4?version=1.0 Accessed on January 18, 2023.

Ministry of Education. (2019). Smart specialization strategy of Montenegro 2019–2024. Retrieved from https://wapi.gov.me/download/ea1d661e-922a-4d42-af8d-ae55bc53988e?version=1.0. Accessed on January 17, 2023.

Ministry of Public Administration, Digital Society and Media. (2021). Programme for attracting digital nomads in Montenegro until 2025 with the action plan for 2022. Retrieved from https://wapi.gov.me/download/580ee5de-36c7-4133-9b7b-e80cf4941ae9?version=1.0. Accessed on February 6, 2023.

Ministry of Sustainable Development and Tourism. (2016). National Strategy for Sustainable Development of Montenegro. Retrieved from https://faolex.fao.org/docs/pdf/mne180387.pdf. Accessed on January 17, 2023.

Novaković, V., Stošković, M., & Nikolić, M. (2011). *Mala privreda i preduzetništvo* (p. 27). Belgrade: AGM knjiga d.o.o.

OECD. (2016). SME policy index: Western Balkans and Turkey 2016. Retrieved from https://www.oecd.org/countries/republicofnorthmacedonia/sme-policy-index-western-balkans-and-turkey-2016-9789264254473-en.htm. Accessed on February 2, 2023.

OECD. (2019). SME policy index: Western Balkans and Turkey 2019. Retrieved from https://www.oecd.org/publications/sme-policy-index-western-balkans-and-turkey-2019-g2g9fa9a-en.htm. Accessed on February 2, 2023.

OECD. (2022). SME Policy Index: Western Balkans and Turkey 2022. Retrieved from https://www.oecd.org/countries/republicofnorthmacedonia/sme-policy-index-western-balkans-and-turkey-2022-b47d15f0-en.htm. Accessed on February 2, 2023.

Pärenson, T. (2011). The criteria for a solid impact evaluation in social entrepreneurship. *Society and Business Review*, *6*(1), 39–48.https://doi.org/10.1108/17465681111105823

Popović, M. (2013). Rodna dimenzija razvoja preduzetništva u postsocijalističkoj Crnoj Gori. In *Sociološka luča* (pp. 40–43). Nikšić: Filozofski fakultet.

Predojević-Despić, J., & Lukić, V. (2018). Migrant entrepreneurship in the light of public policies. *Zbornik Matice srpske za drustvene nauke*, *167*, 607–618.https://doi.org/10.2298/ZMSDN1867607P.

Raut, J., Veljković, S. M., Melović, B., Ćelić, Đ., & Nikolić, D. (2022). Preduzetnički ekosistem kao novi koncept preduzetništva. In *XXVIII Skup TRENDOVI RAZVOJA: "Univerzitetsko obrazovanje za privredu"*, Kopaonik.

Ravić, N., & Obradovic, I. (2017). Programi finansijske podrške malim i srednjim preduzećima u Republici Srbiji od strane nebankarskih institucija. *Trendovi u poslovanju, 1*(9), 25–32.

Subotić, M., Mitrović, S., Melović, B., & Nikolić, D. (2018). Preduzetničko obrazovanje kao važan faktor privrednog razvoja. In *XXIV Skup Trendovi Razvoja: "Digitalizacija visokog obrazovanja"*, Kopaonik.

Tehnopolis. About Tehnopolis (n.d.). Retrieved from http://www.tehnopolis.me/online/mne/o-tehnopolisu/. Accessed January 25, 2023.

UNDP Montenegro. (2022). UNDP created a site intended for women in business. Retrieved from https://www.undp.org/cnr/montenegro/press-releases/undp-kreirao-sajt-namijenjen-%C5%BEenama-u-biznisu. Accessed on February 1, 2023.

University of Montenegro. (2022). Training for beginners in business. Retrieved from https://www.ucg.ac.me/objava/blog/1024/objava/44-obuka-za-pocetnike-u-biznisu. Accessed on February 5, 2023.

WorldSkills Europe. (n.d.). What we do? Retrieved from https://worldskillseurope.org/index.php/what-we-do. Accessed February 3, 2023.

WorldSkills Europe. (2016). EuroSkills 2016: Medals, medals medals! Retrieved from https://worldskillseurope.org/index.php/media/press-releases/euroskills-2016-medals-medals-medals. Accessed on February 1, 2023.

Chapter 11

Sustainable Entrepreneurship in North Macedonia: Challenges and Perspectives

Marsela Thanasi-Boçe, Selma Kurtishi-Kastrati, Veland Ramadani and Rasim Zuferi

Abstract

Entrepreneurship is a mechanism that generates economic benefits. However, due to the emergence of the concept of sustainable development as an urgent issue that is affecting the globe, it is emphasized that entrepreneurship should generate sustainable wealth rather than just wealth. Therefore, the sustainable entrepreneurship (SE) notion has received rising interest lately. Nowadays, many business organizations in the Balkan region are moving toward sustainable solutions and there is a need to share knowledge on the best practices of SE. This chapter provides a detailed description of sustainable entrepreneurship drivers and outcomes with a focus on the challenges and perspectives of sustainable entrepreneurship in North Macedonia (NM). The case of Ecolog discussed in the chapter is an excellent example of its leadership in sustainable entrepreneurship and its positive impact on the community and wider. Lessons from challenges and best practices of sustainable ventures in NM are provided together with suggestions for these practices to be adopted in other countries associated with the actions required for implementation.

Keywords: North Macedonia; sustainable entrepreneurship; social entrepreneurship; innovation; collaboration; organizational governance

1. Introduction

In the last decade, entrepreneurship has been considered a solution to social inequality and environmental degradation rather than a possible threat of them (Muñoz & Cohen, 2018). Growing concerns among policymakers and academia,

Entrepreneurship Development in the Balkans: Perspective from Diverse Contexts, 197–211

Published under exclusive licence by Emerald Publishing Limited
doi:10.1108/978-1-83753-454-820231011

in this regard, have led to the development of sustainable entrepreneurship (SE) as a connection between entrepreneurship, society, and the environment (Cohen & Winn, 2007) bringing forth attention to finding ways how to attain sustainable development (Haldar, 2019).

SE also known in the literature as social or environmental entrepreneurship, is developed as an approach that supports the creation of environmental, social, and economic values (Anderson, 1998), which focuses on guaranteeing the future welfare of the society (Binder & Belz, 2015).

The SE discourse is segmented into topical streams addressing different subfields, notably corporate social responsibility (CSR), and environmental management, while an integrated SE perspective that looks at all three dimensions (the social, environmental, and economic) is still fairly new (Dyllick & Muff, 2016; Ramadani, Agarwal, Caputo, Agrawal, & Dixit, 2022). To date, academic research has failed to effectively advise management about sustainable development practices. There is a disconnect between micro-level improvement and macro-level decline that requires a comprehensive analysis of drivers of business sustainability along with the business practice. The SE debate is mainly taking place on a micro-level while sustainable development discussions are focused on a macro-level including the economy and the society (Ramadani & Schneider, 2013; Tregidga, Kearins, & Milne, 2013). Different authors have concluded that the focus of SE research is usually on the organization and how it can profit from SE with less consideration for the environment or society failing to provide new insights and asking significant questions about the sustainability issues the world is facing (Bansal & Gao, 2006). Approaches that effectively link both levels are needed (Whiteman, Walker, & Perego 2013) and an integrated SE focus would help considerably to respond adequately to complex and interconnected sustainability issues.

The proliferation of studies on SE has resulted in a lack of theoretical framework, so this field needs to be analyzed, organized, and synthesized to bring clarity (Terán-Yépez, Marín-Carrillo, Casado-Belmonte, & Capobianco-Uriarte, 2020). Shepherd and Patzelt (2011) emphasized the significance of SE research to examine the impact of entrepreneurial action for sustaining nature and ecosystems while providing economic and non-economic gains for investors, entrepreneurs, and societies in general.

Nowadays, businesses in developing countries are raising claims to manage sustainably, but not all of them are contributing to sustainable development mainly due to the difficulties they face in developing innovative green products and services (Vasilescu, Dimian, & Gradinaru, 2023).

Especially in NM reports show that, although good progress has been achieved in certain development areas, there is still room for improvement. Therefore, this chapter addresses two questions: What are the main challenges toward sustainability in NM? What actions can a business in NM take in its journey to becoming truly sustainable?

This study contributes to the existing SE literature theoretically by providing a comprehensive SE framework that incorporates drivers and outcomes of SE at the micro- and macro-level, and by providing practical knowledge for entrepreneurs on the importance of integrating the framework into their strategies and business models toward becoming sustainable businesses.

In addition, the study provides a theoretical understanding of SE and suggests practical implications for entrepreneurs in their journey toward sustainability-driven entrepreneurship.

This chapter is organized as follows: it starts with a review of the SE concept and definition, followed by a discussion on the drivers of SE. The fourth section is focused on the challenges of adopting sustainable solutions in NM, followed by the analysis of the case of Ecolog company as an example of excellence in SE. Managerial implications are further discussed and a future research agenda on SE is provided.

2. Sustainable Entrepreneurship: Concept and Definition

Sustainability-oriented entrepreneurship is rooted back in the 1950s when the concept of "social responsibility" was introduced into the discourse of modern literature on CSR (Bowen, 1953). CSR emphasizes actions taken by businesses beyond the requirements of law and highlights that a business has certain responsibilities to society which extend beyond economic and legal obligations (Sharma, 2019). Although the evolving concept of CSR tackles the organization's strategic impact on social and environmental performance (Greco & De Jong, 2017), it is mainly oriented toward adjusting firms' actions in line with business standards, norms, regulations, and stakeholder demands for CSR rather than being intentionality and consciousness driven.

Meanwhile, SE is a wide-ranging concept wherein corporate leaders are driven by environmental and social awareness to set up and run businesses to produce environmental, economic, and social value right from the inception rather than complying with standards and legal regulations/norms (Haldar, 2019).

Many explanations of SE can be found in the literature. As a more comprehensive definition is the one provided by Shepherd and Patzelt (2011) who noted that the aim of SE is

> to preserve nature, life support, and community in the pursuit of perceived opportunities to bring into existence future products, processes, and services for gain, where the gain is broadly construed to include economic and non-economic gains to individuals, the economy, and society. (p. 137)

Dyllick and Muff (2016) introduced the concept of truly sustainable business that shifts the SE perspective from seeking to minimize its negative impacts to understanding how it can create a significant positive impact in critical and relevant areas for society and the planet. Hockerts and Wüstenhagen (2010) stated that sustainable entrepreneurial behavior exists when a balance is created between economic health, social equity, and environmental resilience.

A sustainable business identifies critical challenges in the external environment, which need to be overcome, and translates them into business opportunities making "business sense" of societal and environmental concerns.

2.1. What Should Sustainable Entrepreneurship Sustain and Develop?

According to Shepherd and Patzelt (2011), SE should sustain nature, sources of life support, and communities:

- Nature refers to the phenomena of the physical world and includes the earth, biodiversity, and ecosystems. There is a direct link between human health and exposure to naturally green places (Adams, 2019). Nature can be sustained if individuals, organizations, and nations can act in ways to preserve the earth, biodiversity, and ecosystems.
- Sources of life support are found in the environment as a source of resources that supports human lives and can be sustained through preserving and protecting the environment, natural resources, and ecosystem services.
- Communities refer to relationships developed between individuals sharing values, norms, meanings, history, and identity. Individuals can protect their identities only when they are capable of preserving their culture within the larger society. SE can contribute to sustaining communities. Especially in developing countries, the engagement of community members as entrepreneurs can have a positive impact on reducing poverty while preserving the natural environment.

Apart from the economic profit related to the advancement of individuals' socioeconomic status, SE provides some non-economic gains to people and society that include child survival, life expectancy, education, equity, and equal opportunity (Hummels & Argyrou, 2021).

Non-economic gains to society are related to the level of happiness of citizens and their security from threats (Jayaratne, Mort, & D'Souza, 2019). Moreover, the well-being of a society is reflected in the strong social ties and interpersonal relationships developed between individuals.

At the micro-level, organizations gain tangible benefits from embracing a sustainable business approach in the form of reduced costs and risks of doing business, as well as through intangible benefits in the form of increased brand reputation, increased attractiveness to talent, and increased competitiveness (Rosário, Raimundo, & Cruz, 2022).

Organizations' reports show an increasing commitment to sustainability addressing sustainable actions that preserve ecosystems, reduce climate change impact and environmental degradation and deforestation, improve agricultural practices and freshwater supply, and maintain biodiversity (Dean & McMullen, 2007).

At a larger scale, SE has a positive impact on the economy and society especially in developing countries as it contributes to productivity, socioeconomic status, physical health, education, and self-reliance of individuals and societies (Shepherd, Patzelt, Shepherd, & Patzelt, 2017).

3. Drivers of Sustainable Entrepreneurship

Koe et al. (2014) identified a few characteristics of a sustainable entrepreneur running small- and medium-sized enterprises (SMEs) such as a sustainable attitude associated with social pressure to undertake environmentally conscious behaviors, perceived desirability, and feasibility related to the perception of his/her capabilities. However, research suggests that the discourse related to sustainability drivers should be done from an institutional perspective rather than an individual one (De Clercq & Voronov, 2011; Greco & De Jong, 2017). Therefore, to fill this gap, we identified in the literature the following drivers of SE.

3.1. Innovation

The social and environmental disruptions are rooted in business activities and industries at a larger scale. However, a business with a market-oriented approach understands that there is a direct link between innovation and sustainability and that sustainability-driven innovations and entrepreneurship lie at the core of achieving economic, ecological, and societal benefits. Businesses that are sustainability-oriented through innovation engage in producing environmentally superior products and services that are also economically viable in the marketplace (e.g., Tesla in the automobile industry). Both innovation and entrepreneurship are the most effective tools to diffuse sustainability values, simultaneously ensuring economic benefits (Haldar, 2019).

Although innovation has been widely acknowledged as the key driver of sustainability in the literature on SE, still there are limitations in defining the linkage between innovation and SE. To achieve sustainable growth, businesses must develop sustainable innovations that take into account economic, social, and environmental concerns (Cillo, Petruzzelli, Ardito, & Del Giudice, 2019). At the heart of SE is the ability to develop new products and solutions that will address environmental and social problems. Sustainability-oriented entrepreneurs bring organizational and technological innovations at the firm level, not necessarily by accident. Hence, sustainability-oriented entrepreneurs foster innovative products and services in organizational and technological ways that positively impact the environment and quality of life (Haldar, 2019; Schaltegger & Wagner, 2011).

The potentiality of digital technologies allows the development of new sustainable business models, which, though, still need to gain legitimation to be accepted (Biloslavo, 2020). Disruptive innovations are considered new opportunities that entrepreneurs can embrace, especially in developing economies that can grow by establishing new industries (Si, Zahra, Wu, & Jeng, 2020). Evans et al. (2017) have identified some challenges that businesses face when using innovation to build sustainable business models (Table 1).

3.2. Organizational Governance

Organizational governance plays an essential role in driving SE by demonstrating that sustainability is incorporated into the business strategy where sustainable goals are clearly defined and accountability for goal achievement in sustainable manner

Table 1. Challenges of Innovative Sustainable Business Models.

Challenges	Description
Triple bottom line	The co-creation of profits, social and environmental benefits, and the balance among them is challenging for moving toward sustainable business models
Mindset	The business rules, guidelines, behavioral norms, and performance metrics prevail in the mindset of firms and inhibit the introduction of new business models
Resources	Reluctance to allocate resources to business model innovation and reconfigure resources and processes for new business models
Technology innovation	Integrating technology innovation, for example, clean technology, with business model innovation is multidimensional and complex
External relations	Engaging in extensive interaction with external stakeholders and the business environment requires extra effort
Methods and tools	Existing business modeling methods and tools are few and rarely sustainability driven

Source: Evans et al. (2017).

is monitored and reported on a regular basis. Business ventures should take a long-term view of sustainability and consider the influence of their decisions on future generations. Additionally, organization governance can help businesses identify and manage risks (Hoogendoom, Zwan, & Thurik, 2019), related to sustainability such as climate change, social unrest, and resource scarcity by ensuring that organizations are resilient to these risks and are competent to operate sustainably.

3.3. Collaboration

At the company level, companies can engage in innovating their processes and products, and transform their systems of governance and transparency in serving the purpose of sustainability. However, their engagement can surpass the company level to expand the impact of their sustainable activities and actions. By collaborating on a cross-sectorial level, the different members of supply chains developed in various industries can share knowledge, learn from the best practices, and establish standards of excellence to be followed by everyone (Dyllick & Muff, 2016).

3.4. Education

Education is a powerful driver of SE, since it provides individuals with the necessary knowledge, skills, and resources to establish socially responsible businesses and to operate in the environment's best interest. Education supports SE by raising awareness about environmental and social issues, so entrepreneurs can develop sustainable practices that prioritize sustainability, stimulate innovation, and generate added value (Gast, Gundolf, & Cesinger, 2017). Education can help in promotion and enhancement of sustainable business practices (Kuckertz & Wagner, 2010) as it supports entrepreneurs to generate knowledge to create a venture that prioritizes sustainability, from reducing waste and carbon emissions to promoting fair labor practices. Furthermore, education can stimulate creativity and drive innovation toward development of new products and technologies that are sustainable yet profitable and environmentally friendly.

3.5. Consumer Preferences

There is an increasing trend toward sustainable products among consumers (Petro, 2022), as they are attracted to and are willing to pay more for sustainable products. Sustainable entrepreneurs can respond to their needs for sustainable products by developing ventures that offer sustainable alternatives rather than conventional products.

Considering the above, an SE framework is presented in Fig. 1.

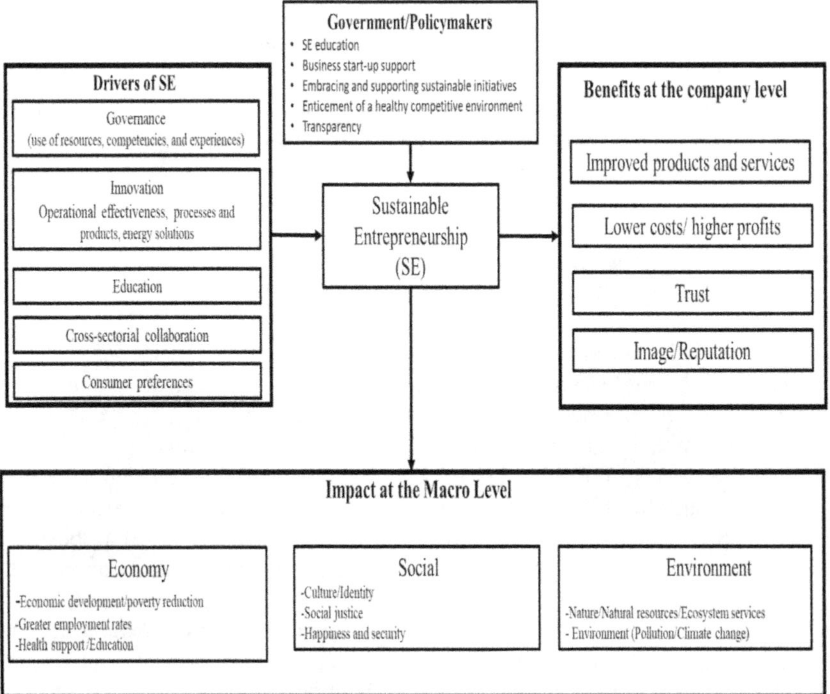

Fig. 1. SE Framework. *Source*: Authors, based on literature.

4. Sustainable Entrepreneurship in NM

A competitive market economy based on sustainable enterprises has been, and remains, one of the key priorities for NM. The sustainable growth of vibrant, innovative, and resilient companies is to a large extent influenced by the environment in which they operate. Thus, governments' efforts throughout recent years were focused on continually improving the conditions in which NM companies operated and on creating an enabling ecosystem for sustainable enterprises.

According to the Minister of Labor and Social Policy, the legislation is focused on adopting a broader sustainability approach, including support for social services as one of its domains (Chichevaliev, 2019).

4.1. Challenges of Adopting Sustainable Solutions in NM

The growth of the economy in NM is heavily dependent on entrepreneurship, therefore supporting entrepreneurs has become crucial to the country's future.

Toward strengthening inclusive economic growth and creating productive and sustainable jobs, the Republic of NM has developed and adopted a National Small and Medium Enterprise Strategy (2018–2023) and Action Plan (2018–2021). The goal was to establish a framework for cooperation between the public sector, the private sector, and civil society so that Micro. Small. and Medium Enterprises can develop and innovate, and thus enhance competitiveness, through:

- Creating a favorable business environment that encourages entrepreneurship and investment.
- Enhancing and expanding the development opportunities for SMEs to enhance their productivity, competitiveness, and internationalization to European and other international markets.
- Creating a dynamic ecosystem of entrepreneurship and innovation.

Despite the opportunities, there are many challenges that companies in NM are facing. A report of ILO (2019) has focused on five key areas as priorities to develop:

- *Enabling legal and regulatory environment.* As per the assessment of the World Bank, the Governance indicators show an improvement in the quality of regulatory policies and regulations related to businesses. However, challenges remain in terms of the burden of government regulation and labor market efficiency and flexibility. The decision of the government to increase taxes on personal income and minimum wage might affect the cost of doing business and worsen the business climate. While the draft of the new labor law should strive to provide workers with higher flexibility and security.
- *Rule of law and secure property rights.* It remains difficult to create a healthy business environment and beneficial to sustainable companies without a guarantee of the rule of law implementation. Significant policy reforms have been undertaken in anti-corruption legislation, public procurement, and inspection.

However, the main challenge of the NM government is to ensure that the legislation is executed properly.

- *Access to financial services.* According to International Monetary Fund, NM is a developing country. As such, financial instruments are not utilized to benefit from their potential due to low levels of financial education. Business services related to this area are still in their infancy and domestic firms need to improve their capacity in exploiting available financial instruments.
- *Fair competition.* In the last few years, local companies have become more competitive based on efficiency improvement rather than employing innovative processing in developing existing or innovative products. The key challenge for companies is unfair competition in an informal economy.
- *Entrepreneurial culture.* The entrepreneurial activity in NM has been in a stagnation phase due to a lack of entrepreneurial knowledge in identifying opportunities. Most new ventures start as a necessity rather than an endeavor to exploit the existing opportunities in the dynamic environment.

Although entrepreneurship strived to be promoted through education, in reality, the educational system in NM still does not provide the relevant knowledge and skills to the needs of the economy and business sector. In this context, young entrepreneurs should be supported with knowledge and facilitating policies that can lessen the cost of a start-up business.

Coherent collaboration across sectors is vital for the development of SE. There is evidence of an incoherent system of support in NM. The need for coherent moving forward across sectors and levels is highlighted as key to enabling effective and efficient social enterprises to deliver on their objectives (Chichevaliev, 2022).

5. The Case of Ecolog[1]

Ecolog International (Ecolog) is serving the community since 1998 under the leadership of Nazif Destani. Achieving environmental excellence is at the heart of Ecolog's mission as a leading global provider of integrated services, technology, environmental solutions, energy, logistics, engineering, and construction. The company continues to impact the quality of life in its communities while being responsible and sustainable in its business practices. Ecolog continues to support and participate in the United Nations Global Compact ("UNGC") initiative by

---

[1]This case is based on published information by the company T: Communication On Progress (2021), https://ungc-production.s3.us-west-2.amazonaws.com/attachments/cop_2021/498575/original/Ecolog_UNGC_COPReport_08062021.pdf?1623137746; Press Desk (2020). Ecolog International and Centre for Organic Electronics at the University of Newcastle-Australia Signed a Strategic Memorandum of Understanding to Commercialize Printed Solar – A Revolutionary Low-cost, Ultra-lightweight and Highly Portable Solar Energy Solution. https://solarquarter.com/2020/04/13/ecolog (Accessed 14.02.2023).

adopting sustainable, socially responsible human rights, labor, environment, and anti-corruption policies. By incorporating the UNGS's principles into strategies, policies, and procedures, and establishing a culture of integrity, the company aims not only to uphold its primary responsibilities to people and the planet but also to pave the way for long-term success. The company has undergone a due diligence process in 2018 and has been certified by Trace International, which underlines Ecolog's commitment to transparency in international commercial transactions.

Ecolog is committed to providing value to its employees and customers while also helping to develop local communities and reduce environmental impact. Ecolog is fulfilling its mission by hiring hardworking and dedicated employees, establishing strong business ethics, developing innovative products, and upholding consistent service standards. With the *Living Code of Business Ethics and Conduct (Code),* Ecolog strives to conduct its work with the utmost honor and integrity. The Code describes the company's ethics and compliance policies, explains where employees can get help if they have ethical questions or encounter ethical dilemmas, and provides guidelines for dealing with ethical and compliance issues.

Ecolog is steadfast on:

- *Developing a positive workplace* – by treating employees with dignity and respect. Each employee upon joining the company, receives mandatory training covering aspects of human and labor rights, and these types of training are retrained on yearly bases.
- *Preventing nepotism and favoritism* – applying fair selection and performance-based compensation to more than 12,000 employees from 57+ nationalities. According to the company, managing such a diverse workforce is not a challenge but an enriching experience.
- *Coming together as good corporate citizens* – getting involved in local community projects that promote higher economic welfare and standards of living. In 2021, Ecolog donated ten ambulances to hospitals in Tetova with one aim: To strengthen their capacity and provide better emergency services when needed most by citizens during the COVID-19 pandemic. Moreover, in recognition of Breast Cancer Awareness Month the company organized various imitative across different countries to raise awareness and stress the importance of early detection of the disease including free screening and checkups for their employees. Ecolog has demonstrated its CSR by launching COVID-19 testing and vaccination services to governments around the globe under the "Eco-Care" division as soon as the outbreak started.
- *Protecting the Environment* – Ecolog supports environmental sustainability through pollution mitigation and prevention, waste management, recycling, energy conservation, and energy-saving innovations. The company is implementing new technologies and smart solutions to reduce waste and energy consumption to achieve sustainability. In addition to its core business, Ecolog offers renewable energy solutions in the form of Water-as-a-Service and Energy-as-a-Service. Ecolog and the Centre for Organic Electronics at the University of Newcastle – Australia signed a Strategic Memorandum of Understanding to commercialize its revolutionary low-cost, lightweight, and

highly portable solar energy solution. Ecolog has an established Environmental Management System (EMS) that has been certified to ISO 14001:2015 by British Standard Institute (BSI) with UKAS accreditation.

The Sustainable Development Goals (SDGs) from United Nations are a clear call for global action. The 17 broad SDGs, and the 169 targets, aim to end poverty, protect the planet and ensure prosperity for everybody in every place by 2030. SDGs are a shared responsibility between businesses and governments to combat climate change, injustice, and inequality; Ecolog supports SDGs in the following areas:

- *SDG 4 – Ensuring quality education and lifelong learning for all.* To attain the Sustainable Development Goals, Ecolog works with local communities in underdeveloped economies where they have installed a state-of-the-art computer facility at the University of Bangui in the Central African Republic.
- *SDG 9 – Industry, innovation, and infrastructure.* This is a unique opportunity to develop a niche market with new and innovative technologies. Ecolog has developed innovative green technologies, such as Hybrid Power Project, which integrates solar panels with mobile generators to reduce fuel consumption by 30% and create critical infrastructure for remote business sites.
- *SDG 17 – Partnership for the goals.* Ecolog engages in collaborative partnerships with non-governmental organizations and international governments to harness the power of all stakeholders.

6. Managerial Implications

Once understanding the impact of sustainability entrepreneurship, businesses in NM should consider taking actions that contribute to society beyond their profitable goals. A business oriented toward sustainability should answer two significant questions to confirm that it is on the right track toward a sustainable approach:

First, the company should raise the question of how to address the sustainability problems that are concerning society while running the business. Second, it should ask how to combine its resources, skills, and knowledge in such a way as to utilize them for addressing the economic, social, and environmental issues that our society is dealing with, such as poverty, pollution, climate change, unemployment, or corruption.

As demonstrated by the case study of Ecolog, SE can be an effective transforming force for the achievement of sustainable development as well as leading to economic gains that are consistent with sustainable development principles. Furthermore, it demonstrates how SE helps to innovate new products and processes, generate employment, change lives, and preserve the natural environment through identifying opportunities and setting up new business partnerships with governments and international organizations, including the UN, NGOs, and leading commercial companies in diverse sectors.

Additionally, the findings of this study are relevant to the academic community because they provide a case study of sustainability and therefore boost ongoing scholarly discussions on sustainable development, innovation, and entrepreneurship.

Beyond improving their products and operational effectiveness, following the example of Ecolog, companies in NM should focus on providing answers to the questions below:

1. What are the resources, knowledge, talents, and experiences needed to address the main issues concerning the environment and society?
2. How can these resources be utilized to resolve environmental, societal, or economic issues?
3. How can the business's new products contribute to the community, society, and the environment?
4. How to transform operations to provide solutions that would benefit the community and the wide society?
5. How can the governance structure of the business be more flexible to respond more efficiently to the community's concerns?

Considering the challenges of SE development in NM as a developing country, it is worth highlighting the government and policymakers' role in identifying SE activities and strengthening the policies that push business organizations toward sustainability. These include activities related to reducing pollution and promoting the use of friendly-environmental products to diminish environmental issues in NM. Furthermore, the role of the NM government should be supportive in encouraging SE initiatives while having a close collaboration with businesses. This can be achieved by considering the following:

- SE education should be provided not only for young entrepreneurs.
- Government should provide business start-up support. New business ideas that bring innovative solutions to the market should be supported by the government.
- Embracing and supporting sustainable initiatives for businesses. The government can promote these initiatives as a great example to be followed by other businesses and support them financially.
- Enticement of a healthy competitive environment through increased transparency, equal treatment, and avoidance of corruptive procedures.

7. Future Research Agenda

In the context of developing countries, the need for more research has been identified in the following directions:

- Investigating the current acceptability of the SE approach from the side of businesses operating in NM and similar economies.
- The relationship between sustainability and performance needs to be elaborated to provide evidence on how the performance of a company can be improved due to sustainability progress.

- Identifying the predictors for SE success at the individual and organizational levels.
- More research is needed in the identification and elaboration of the barriers that impede the development of SE in developing countries.
- Using more quantitative research methods in SE studies to provide empirical evidence on the relationships between SE drivers and outcomes.
- Develop an assessment tool with non-financial indicators to measure the SE performance of various organizations.

References

Adams, B. (2019). *Green development: Environment and sustainability in a developing world.* London: Routledge.

Anderson, A. R. (1998). Cultivating the Garden of Eden: Environmental entrepreneurs. *Journal of Organizational Change Management*, *11*(2), 135–144.

Bansal, P., & Gao, J. (2006). Building the future by looking to the past: Examining research published on organizations and environment. *Organization & Environment*, *19*(4), 458–478.

Biloslavo, R., Bagnoli, C., Massaro, M., & Cosentino, A. (2020). Business model transformation toward sustainability: the impact of legitimation. *Management Decision*, *58*(8), 1643–1662.

Binder, J. K., & Belz, F. M. (2015). Sustainable entrepreneurship: What it is. In P. Kyrö (Ed.), *Handbook of entrepreneurship and sustainable development research* (pp. 30–72). Cheltenham: Edward Elgar Publishing.

Bowen, H. R. (1953). *Social responsibilities of the businessman.* New York, NY: Harper and Row.

Chichevaliev, S. (2019). *Feasibility study – Exploring the emergency button service and the need for other support services for the elderly in North Macedonia.* City Red Cross of Skopje. Retrieved from https://ckgs.org.mk/wp-content/uploads/2020/03/FF_Feasibility-Study_eng_final-2019_31_10_final-za-web.pdf. Accessed on February 16, 2023.

Chichevaliev, S. (2022). Social entrepreneurship and the use of sustainable business models in developing countries and the need for coherent intersectoral collaboration: The case of North Macedonia. In L. Michelini, A. Minà, & P. Alaimo Di Loro (Eds.), *Proceedings of the 7th international conference on new business models: Sustainable business model challenges: Economic recovery and digital transformation.* Rome: LUMSA University.

Cillo, V., Petruzzelli, A. M., Ardito, L., & Del Giudice, M. (2019). Understanding sustainable innovation: A systematic literature review. *Corporate Social Responsibility, and Environmental Management*, *26*(5), 1012–1025.

Cohen, B., & Winn, M. I. (2007). Market imperfections, opportunity, and sustainable entrepreneurship. *Journal of Business Venturing*, *22*(1), 29–49.

De Clercq, D., & Voronov, M. (2011). Sustainability in entrepreneurship: A tale of two logics. *International Small Business Journal*, *29*(4), 322–344.

Dean, T. J., & McMullen, J. S. (2007). Toward a theory of sustainable entrepreneurship: Reducing environmental degradation through entrepreneurial action. *Journal of Business Venturing*, *22*(1), 50–76.

Doing Business. (2019). *Training for reform.* Washington, DC: The World Bank Group.

Dyllick, T., & Muff, K. (2016). Clarifying the meaning of sustainable business: Introducing a typology from business-as-usual to true business sustainability. *Organization & Environment*, *29*(2), 156–174.

Evans, S., Vladimirova, D., Holgado, M., Van Fossen, K., Yang, M., Silva, E. A., & Barlow, C. Y. (2017). Business model innovation for sustainability: Towards a unified perspective for creation of sustainable business models. *Business Strategy and the Environment*, *26*(5), 597–608.

Gast, J., Gundolf, K., & Cesinger, B. (2017). Doing business in a green way: A systematic review of the ecological sustainability entrepreneurship literature and future research directions. *Journal of Cleaner Production*, *147*(1), 44–56.

Greco, A., & De Jong, G. (2017). *Sustainable entrepreneurship: Definitions, themes and research gaps*. Groningen: University of Groningen, Campus Fryslân.

Haldar, S. (2019). Towards a conceptual understanding of sustainability-driven entrepreneurship. *Corporate Social Responsibility and Environmental Management*, *26*(6), 1157–1170.

Hockerts, K., & Wüstenhagen, R. (2010). Greening Goliaths versus emerging Davids – Theorizing about the role of incumbents and new entrants in sustainable entrepreneurship. *Journal of Business Venturing*, *25*(5), 481–492.

Hoogendoom, B., Zwan, P., & Thurik, R. (2019). Sustainable entrepreneurship: The role of perceived barriers and risks. *Journal of Business Ethics*, *157*(4), 1133–1154.

Hummels, H., & Argyrou, A. (2021). Planetary demands: Redefining sustainable development and sustainable entrepreneurship. *Journal of Cleaner Production*, *278*, 123804.

ILO. (2019). *The enabling environment for sustainable enterprises in North Macedonia*. Retrieved from https://www.ilo.org/budapest/what-we-do/publications/WCMS_723390/lang-en/index.htm. Accessed on February 16, 2023.

Jayaratne, M., Mort, G. S., & D'Souza, C. (2019). Sustainability entrepreneurship: From consumer concern towards entrepreneurial commitment. *Sustainability*, *11*(24), 7076.

Koe, W. L., Omar, R., & Majid, I. A. (2014). Factors associated with propensity for sustainable entrepreneurship. *Procedia-Social and Behavioral Sciences*, *130*, 65–74.

Kuckertz, A., & Wagner, M. (2010). The influence of sustainability orientation on entrepreneurial intentions – Investigating the role of business experience. *Journal of Business Venturing*, *25*(5), 524–539.

Muñoz, P., & Cohen, B. (2018). Sustainable entrepreneurship research: Taking stock and looking ahead. *Business Strategy and the Environment*, *27*(3), 300–322.

Petro, G. (2022, March 11). Consumers demand sustainable products and shopping formats. Forbes. Retrieved from https://www.forbes.com/sites/gregpetro/2022/03/11/consumers-demand-sustainable-products-and-shopping-formats/?sh=5a8b116c6a06. Accessed on February 13, 2023.

Ramadani, V., Agarwal, S., Caputo, A., Agrawal, V., & Dixit J. K. (2022). Sustainable competencies of social entrepreneurship for sustainable development: Exploratory analysis from a developing economy. *Business Strategy and the Environment*, *31*(7), 3437–3453.

Ramadani, V., & Schneider, R. (2013). *Entrepreneurship in the Balkans: Diversity, support and prospects*. Heidelberg: Springer.

Rosário, A. T., Raimundo, R. J., & Cruz, S. P. (2022). Sustainable entrepreneurship: A literature review. *Sustainability*, *14*(9), 5556.

Schaltegger, S., & Wagner, M. (2011). Sustainable entrepreneurship and sustainability innovation: categories and interactions. *Business Strategy and the Environment*, *20*(4), 222–237.

Sharma, E. (2019). A review of corporate social responsibility in developed and developing nations. *Corporate Social Responsibility and Environmental Management*, *26*(4), 712–720.

Shepherd, D. A., & Patzelt, H. (2011). The new field of sustainable entrepreneurship: Studying entrepreneurial action linking "what is to be sustained" with "what is to be developed". *Entrepreneurship Theory and Practice*, *35*(1), 137–163.

Shepherd, D. A., Patzelt, H., Shepherd, D. A., & Patzelt, H. (2017). *Trailblazing in entrepreneurship: Creating new paths for understanding the field*. Cham: Springer.

Si, S., Zahra, S. A., Wu, X., & Jeng, D. J. F. (2020). Disruptive innovation and entrepreneurship in emerging economics. *Journal of Engineering and Technology Management*, *58*(1), 101601.

Terán-Yépez, E., Marín-Carrillo, G. M., Casado-Belmonte, M. del P., & Capobianco-Uriarte, M. (2020). Sustainable entrepreneurship: Review of its evolution and new trends. *Journal of Cleaner Production*, *252*(April), 119742.

Tregidga, H., Kearins, K., & Milne, M. (2013). The politics of knowing "organizational sustainable development". *Organization & Environment*, *26*(1), 102–129.

Vasilescu, M. D., Dimian, G. C., & Gradinaru, G. I. (2023). Green entrepreneurship in challenging times: A quantitative approach for European countries. *Economic Research – Ekonomska Istraživanja*, *36*(1), 1828–1847.

Whiteman, G., Walker, B., & Perego, P. (2013). Planetary boundaries: Ecological foundations for corporate sustainability. *Journal of Management Studies*, *50*(2), 307–336.

Chapter 12

Gender Differences in Early-stage Entrepreneurship: The Case of Romanian Entrepreneurs

Ana Iolanda Voda and Andrei Stefan Nestian

Abstract

The present study explores gender inequalities in the entrepreneurial landscape in Romania, based on Global Entrepreneurship Monitor (GEM) data, highlighting similarities and differences between women and men entrepreneurs. Even if the GEM reports include data on entrepreneurship since 1999, Romania has been among the participating countries only since 2007 for the Adult Population Survey (GEM, APS). Thus, to include Romania in the analysis, the data from this study were selected for nine years, namely from 2007 to 2015. Our results indicate that among Romanian men and women, similar drivers influence the odds of engagement in entrepreneurial activities relative to not being involved in businesses. For both men and women, having confidence in their knowledge and skills had the highest odds ratio values. Also, identifying opportunities proved to be positive and significant for both genders, while fear of failure had the opposite effect. Knowing other entrepreneurs can lead to great benefits generated through social exchange. Findings reveal that the external knowledge that an entrepreneur's environment gives rise to can prove to be supportive in the discovery of opportunities and their exploitation.

Keywords: Entrepreneurship; gender gap; opportunity perception; self-confidence; fear of failure; knowing other entrepreneurs; Global Entrepreneurship Monitor

1. Introduction

This chapter is focused on differences in the characteristics and attitudes (e.g., opportunity perception, confidence in own knowledge and skills, networking,

Entrepreneurship Development in the Balkans: Perspective from Diverse Contexts, 213–235

Published under exclusive licence by Emerald Publishing Limited
doi:10.1108/978-1-83753-454-820231012

and fear of failure) adopted by women and men entrepreneurs. In achieving this goal, we based our analysis on Global Entrepreneurship (GEM Global Report) data. GEM consortium monitors annually the entrepreneurial attributes and activities using as main instruments – APS and National Expert Survey (NES). In this chapter, the data were collected using APS – individual measurements obtained through the gathering of standardized and national representative survey responses. The questionnaires were administered to the Romanian population from 2007 to 2015. The sample included only the adult population aged 18–64 years old, and a minimum of 2,000 individuals/year which allowed us to monitor different patterns and trends in entrepreneurship characteristics and attitudes. The survey was implemented according to GEM methodology that implied a randomly selected adult population in a nationally representative sample, stratified by age, household income, geographical region, and status of the locality the respondents' residence in (GEM Global Report, 2015).

Romania is one of the largest Balkan nations, and since its acceptance as a European Union member state in 2007, considerable progress has been made especially concerning the increasing number of SMEs and entrepreneurial activity. The SME sector plays a key role in the Romanian economy, generating more than half of the total added value and two-thirds of total employment. The main SME sectors are wholesale trade, and manufacturing (OECD, 2020). However, although a growing number of enterprises have emerged, less emphasis has been put on their impact on the ecosystem and added value for society (European Commission, 2016). This quantitative assessment of entrepreneurial performance (i.e., the total number of new enterprises created) determined an entrepreneurial orientation mostly toward necessity-driven entrepreneurship (as a result of the lack of alternatives on the labor market) which had the opposite than expected results, determining a widening effect in the innovation production gap and a damaging effect in the country's overall growth and development (OECD, 2018; UEFISCDI, 2021).

While there is an interest in intensifying entrepreneurial activity, Romania is still struggling with gender disparities. Women's self-employed rate is significantly below that of their counterparts (GEM Global Report, 2015). In other words, women are less likely than men to be active in entrepreneurship, and even if this situation occurs "they are more likely to do so out of necessity" (Kelley et al., 2017, p. 25). However, as studies showed in many countries the number of female entrepreneurs has arisen, as entrepreneurship can be seen as an important alternative for their incorporation into the productive system (Carter, Anderson, & Shaw, 2001; Greene, Hart, Gatewood, Brush, & Carter, 2003; Sánchez-Escobedo, Fernández-Portillo, Díaz-Casero, & Hernández-Mogollón, 2016). Still, developing effective policies to improve gender equality in entrepreneurship requires a general overview of comprehensive and comparable data for the two genders. Starting from this premise the study focused on both gender-specific natures of the drivers of involvement in entrepreneurial activities.

This chapter is organized as follows. In Section 2, a review of the existing literature on entrepreneurial activities and attitudes and gender differences is presented in brief. Section 3 presents the methodological approaches, data, and sample. Section 4 presents the estimated results and their interpretation. Discussion and concluding remarks follow in Sections 5 and 6.

2. Literature Review

2.1. Entrepreneurial Activity and Gender Differences

At least two aspects are interesting when we consider gender differences in entrepreneurial activity. *The first one* is the fact that the general perception of the entrepreneur has traditionally been masculinized and rooted in masculine discourse (Ahl, 2006). This is a cultural starting point influencing all gender studies. *The second* aspect is the fact that narrowing the gender gap in terms of entrepreneurial activity remains a priority focus for policymakers in all economies (GEM Global Report, 2017), making useful studies about gender differences in entrepreneurial activity. Over the past years, the percentage of female entrepreneurs has increased, yet it is still far below that of males (Zampetakis, Bakatsaki, Litos, Kafetsios, & Moustakis, 2017). GEM studies' findings have consistently reported greater involvement in entrepreneurship among men than women in most economies (GEM Global Report, 2012). A consistent finding in GEM studies is that men are more likely to be involved in entrepreneurial activity, regardless of the level of economic development (GEM Global Report, 2017). Yet, the results of the special topic published in 2013 suggest that female entrepreneurs are generally more satisfied: on average they exhibit higher scores on subjective well-being and work–life balance (GEM Global Report 2013, p. 14).

In this chapter, entrepreneurship activities were measured using Total early-stage Entrepreneurial Activities (TEA), an indicator that estimates the percentage of the adult population (18–64 years old) involved in starting a business or new business owners (individuals who are managing a business that is less than 42 months old). Fig. 1 shows that TEA has increased in Romania from 4.02% in 2007 to 10.83% in 2015, a value that positions the country above the EU28 average (see OECD, 2020; Vodă, Butnaru, & Butnaru, 2020; Vodă, Haller, Anichiti, & Butnaru, 2020). During the analyzed period, Romania's early-stage entrepreneurial activity was more orientated toward manufacturing, construction, farming, forestry, fishing, and mining (European Commission, 2016). Even though in Romania special programs have been designed to stimulate disadvantaged groups in entrepreneurship (such as women), their effects are far away from achieving the set goals (Ioana & Dodescu, 2018). Fig. 1 also shows the female/male TEA indicator, which estimates the percentage of the females 18–64 population who are either nascent entrepreneurs or owned managers of a new business divided by the equivalent percentage of their male counterparts. Results indicate that women are less likely than men to engage in entrepreneurial activities, and their entrepreneurial rate is still much lower in comparison to men.

As studies show there is a constant difference found between men and women in developing their entrepreneurial activity due to gender characterization (Carter et al., 2001; Greene et al., 2003; Marlow, 2002). Yet, behind the visible gender

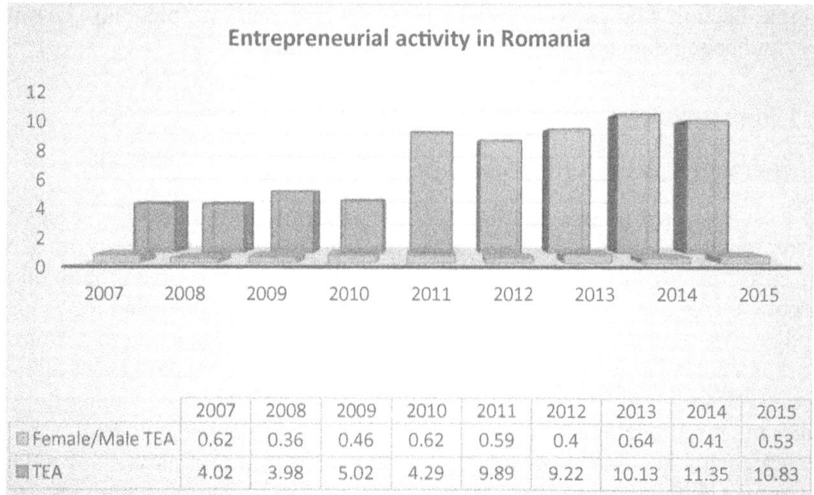

	2007	2008	2009	2010	2011	2012	2013	2014	2015
Female/Male TEA	0.62	0.36	0.46	0.62	0.59	0.4	0.64	0.41	0.53
TEA	4.02	3.98	5.02	4.29	9.89	9.22	10.13	11.35	10.83

Fig. 1. Entrepreneurial Activity in Romania. *Source:* Author's representation based on GEM 2007–2015 data.

difference, there are other factors explaining it. In a study from 2020, entrepreneurial idea generation by students was considered as comprising elements about academic support, access to an incubator, opportunities to brainstorm, education & training, and family encouragement & support (Smith, Hamilton, & Fabian, 2020).

In the GEM studies, we found a set of psychological deterministic factors considered as contributing together to the entrepreneurial intention or activities: opportunity perception, perceived capabilities, and fear of failure (GEM Global Report, 2012, p. 23). The entrepreneurship process is triggered by perceiving some favorable business opportunities in their area of interest or expertise. Yet, the opportunity itself might not be enough. Individuals are also reflecting on whether they believe they have the necessary capabilities to successfully start a venture. Another subjective assessment, an evaluation of the environment, can prevent the individual from starting a business if the perceived fear of failure is too intense. The GEM study published in 2016

> assesses individual self-perceptions regarding whether people see opportunities around them, whether those seeing opportunities would feel constrained by fear of failure, whether they believe they are capable of starting a business, and whether they intend to do so within the next three years. (GEM Global Report, 2016, p. 18)

We found a similar selection of variables in the study of Camelo-Ordaz, Diánez-González, and Ruiz-Navarro (2016), which focuses on entrepreneurial self-efficacy, the ability to recognize opportunities, and the fear of failure, aiming to examine the mediating role of perceptual factors on the relationship between gender and entrepreneurial intention. In the study of Maes, Leroy, and Sels (2014), gender was again included as a mere control variable, but the results show that women correlate negatively to personal attitude, perceived behavioral control, and social norms compared to men.

Starting from the elements mentioned above, for this chapter, we took into consideration four psychological deterministic factors considered as contributing together to entrepreneurship: opportunity perception, self-confidence, knowing other entrepreneurs, and fear of failure.

2.2. Opportunity Perception

The first step in the entrepreneurship process may occur when people perceive favorable business opportunities in their area (GEM Global Report, 2012, p. 23). But, the GEM studies also recognize that entrepreneurs may be pushed or pulled into entrepreneurship. By this, we understand that some will start a business because they find an appealing opportunity, despite the fact that they were not considering becoming entrepreneurs before that, and that some others will start a business because they have no other work options and need a source of income (GEM Global Report, 2012, p. 29). Based on this distinction, in the GEM studies, we find two categories of entrepreneurs.

> Individuals who start businesses in response to a lack of other options for earning an income are deemed to be necessity entrepreneurs, while those who start businesses with the intention to exploit an opportunity are identified as opportunity entrepreneurs. (GEM Global Report, 2012, p. 14)

Opportunity entrepreneurs are separated into other two categories, based on their different motivations. Some individuals aim to maintain or improve their income, while others aim to enhance their independence (GEM Global Report, 2012, p. 14).

Other studies also identify and provide findings about the relationship between entrepreneurship and opportunity perception. In prior GEM research, it recognized the relationship between the proportion of adults engaged in entrepreneurship and the level of economic development (Wennekers, Van Wennekers, Thurik, & Reynolds, 2005). This idea is considered proof of the differences in the entrepreneurial intention/activities created by the existence of more or fewer opportunities.

2.3. Self-confidence

For entrepreneurs, the belief that they have the necessary capabilities to successfully start a new business is related to perceived opportunities. It is in fact the belief that they can manage to economically exploit the opportunities. Favorable perceptions with respect to opportunities may not necessarily lead to intentions to start a business (GEM Global Report, 2012, p. 8) because a certain level of self-confidence is also needed. The concept of self-confidence is a subjective personal perception of capabilities, skills, knowledge, and experience. Individuals are likely to avoid challenging tasks and situations exceeding their perceived level of skills and take up challenges where they are comfortable with their own skills and capabilities (Thornton & Klyver, 2019). In the GEM studies, the "perceived capabilities" were considered as reflecting the percentages of individuals who believe they have the required skills, knowledge, and experience to start a new business" (GEM Global Report, 2013, p. 28). But, "capabilities perceptions may reveal not only people's skills but also confidence in their ability to start a business – as such, they are likely to play a significant role in the transition from potential to intentional entrepreneur" (GEM Global Report, 2017, p. 20). Self-belief, and confidence in one's ability to succeed, "are indicators of one's readiness for entrepreneurship" (GEM Global Report, 2020, p. 16).

The indicator "perceived capabilities" and the question related to it in the GEM instruments are nowadays interpreted with meanings related to the idea of self-capacity and self-confidence to act upon the opportunities, all set within the distinct conditions of their local environment with its own specific mix of social values, ecosystem supports, and economic resources (GEM Global Report, 2021). High entrepreneurial intentions to start a new business are positively associated with high self-efficacy and with the extent to which entrepreneurs believe in their own capabilities (Krueger, Reilly, & Carsrud, 2000).

Self-confidence has been found as the foundation of gender differences The Australian female students cited a lack of confidence, lack of leadership skills, not having found the right idea, fear of failure, and concern about having limited relevant experience, scoring significantly higher at these, compared with the male sample (Smith et al., 2020). As Camelo-Ordaz et al. (2016) stated,

> young women who presented reasonable levels of entrepreneurial self-efficacy showed less inclination to choose an entrepreneurial career compared with men and believed they would have more opportunities in other professional fields.

2.4. Knowing Other Entrepreneurs

The entrepreneurial intention or activities have been proven to be related to the knowledge about entrepreneurship of the potential entrepreneur. According to GEM, "knowing other entrepreneurs means exposure to role models and mentors, hardwires the motivating factors or drivers for being successful, and provides connections to relevant stakeholders and advice" (GEM Global Report, 2020). Knowing other entrepreneurs' influence on entrepreneurial activities involvement has been confirmed by several empirical research (Van Auken, Stephens, Fry, & Silva, 2006). Knowing someone else who has started their own business can increase awareness of entrepreneurship, as well as heighten appreciation of the associated costs and benefits, and can provide the potential entrepreneur with a benchmark (GEM Global Report, 2020). From a sociological perspective, social networks which include entrepreneurs play an important role in enhancing entrepreneurs' growth aspirations both directly, and more importantly, through compensating for the macro-level institutional weakness (GEM Global Report, 2013). In this context, parental or social environment-specific type entrepreneurial role models can indirectly influence the entrepreneurial intentions of individuals (Feder & Nițu-Antonie, 2017).

2.5. Fear of Failure

To clarify the concept of "fear of failure," we will start with the GEM's conceptualization of entrepreneurship. Since the state of the entrepreneur changes with the circumstances and the status of him and his business, entrepreneurship is seen as a multiphase process, with conditions marking the pass to the next status. The potential entrepreneurs, having passed the conditions of identifying opportunities and believing they have the capabilities to manage the opportunities are not yet free of doubts. They still can be dissuaded from creating a new venture by fear of failing. The perceived fear of failure is an important component of the risk attached to starting a new business (Camelo-Ordaz et al., 2016). This emotional state is not based so much on the inner belief of the personal ability but on the external uncontrollable factors, such as unpredictable or unknown threats, and relational or status-related social representations of the entrepreneur (GEM Global Report, 2012, p. 14). In these cases, even if they perceive opportunities and believe they have the skills necessary for entrepreneurship, fear of failure may prevent them from actually starting a business (GEM Global Report, 2012, p. 23).

The fear of failure

> can counteract the drive to start a business, even when the expected returns from entrepreneurship have better prospects than the next best alternative. People may have differing levels of fear of failure related to conditions in the institutional environment, such as bankruptcy legislation, which could deter would-be entrepreneurs. (GEM Global Report, 2012, p. 24)

Among the barriers to entrepreneurial activity, Shinnar uses the fear of failure and the perceived competence as variables (Shinnar, Rachel, Giacomin, & Janssen, 2012). Fear of failure generally increases as one moves from early-stage to advanced development levels (GEM Global Report, 2012). Also, fear of failure tends to be more common in developed economies, where the greater prevalence of alternative career options can create the impression that people have more to lose by forgoing these other opportunities (GEM Global Report, 2017).

3. Methodological Approach

3.1. Data and Variables

The analysis was based on GEM data, a research consortium that tracks entrepreneurship rates across multiple phases and rates the characteristics, motivations, and ambitions of entrepreneurs, and the attitudes societies have toward this activity. The consortium gathers data from more than 60 countries using APS and the NES. In this chapter, we collected data from the APS, from 2007 to 2015, the period when Romania participated in the survey. The APS survey is being administered to a minim of 2000 adults yearly, by country, and is nationally representative. The survey implemented as such, captures the business characteristics, individuals' motivation, attitudes, and actions considered to become an entrepreneur.

In Table 1, we present the dependent and independent variables included in the study. Total early-stage entrepreneurial activity (TEA), male entrepreneurial activity (MEA), and female entrepreneurial activity (FEA) are taken as dependent variables.

Table 1. Description of the Variables.

Name	Codes	Type	Description
Total early-stage entrepreneurial activity	TEA	Dependent/binary	Individuals aged 18–64 years who are actively involved in early-stage entrepreneurial activities Yes=1; no=0
Male entrepreneurial activity	MEA	Dependent/binary	Males in the age group of 18–64 years, who are actively involved in early-stage entrepreneurial activities Yes=1; no=0
Female entrepreneurial activity	FEA	Dependent/binary	Females in the age group of 18–64 years, who are actively involved in early-stage entrepreneurial activities Yes=1; no=0
Opportunity perception	opport	Independent/binary	Individuals' self-perceptions regarding whether they see opportunities around them Yes=1; no=0
Self-confidence	suskill	Independent/binary	Individuals' self-perception regarding their confidence in their own knowledge, skills, and experience Yes=1; no=0

(*Continued*)

Table 1. (*Continued*)

Name	Codes	Type	Description
Knowing other entrepreneurs	knowent	Independent/binary	Individuals who indicated whether they personally know someone who has started a business in the past two years Yes=1; no=0
Fear of failure	fearfail	Independent/binary	Share of total/females/males who indicated whether fear of failure would be an obstacle to launching a business Yes=1; no=0
Age	age	Control/categorial	The respondents were asked to indicate their age in years 1=18–24; 2=25–34; 3=35–44; 4=45–54; 5=55–64 years old
Household income	Income	Control/Categorial	Total annual household income 1=lowest 33%; 2= middle 33%; 3= upper 33%
Year	Year	Control/categorial	The year the survey was administered 2007–2010=1; 2011–2015=2

Source: Author's representation based on GEM data, 2007–2015.

TEA includes individuals aged between 18 and 64 years, who are currently involved in setting up a business or owning-managing new firms. MEA takes into consideration the share of males, aged between 18 and 64 years, involved in opening a business or managing a new one (less than 3.5 years). FEA includes females involved in early-stage entrepreneurial activities or who are actively involved in setting up a business.

The independent and control variables include the following: opportunity perception (opport) – individuals self-perception regarding whether there sees opportunities around them (females/males) (binary variable – yes=1; no=0); self-confidence (suskills) – indicates whether individuals have confidence in their own knowledge, skills, and experience (binary variable; yes=1; no=0); knowing other entrepreneurs (knowent) – assessing whether the respondents personally know someone who has started a business in the past two years (binary variable; yes=1; no=0); fear of failure (fearfail) – respondents were asked whether they consider that fear of failure would prevent them in starting a business (binary variables; yes=1; no=0); respondents age (age) – respondents were asked to indicate their age in years (five categories; 1=18–24; 2=25–34; 3=35–44; 4=45–54; 5=55–64 years old); household income (income) – total annual household income (3 categories; 1=lowest 33%; 2= middle 33%; 3= upper 33%); year – the year the survey was administered (2 categories; 2007–2010=1; 2011–2015=2).

3.2. Regression Analysis

Given the type of collected data, we performed a binomial logistic regression analysis, which indicates the probability that early-stage entrepreneurial activity can be predicted based on entrepreneurs' opportunity perception, self-confidence, network and fear of failure, age, and household income. We performed three regression models with three dependent variables: TEA, FEA, and MEA. The analysis was performed on data collected from 2007 until 2015, using SPSS statistical package and binary logistic models. The validation of the models was tested using Omnibus Test, Cox and Snell Pseudo R^2, Nagelkerke R^2, indicating the usefulness of the explanatory variables in predicting the response variable, and −2 Log Likelihood. We also apply Hosmer and Lemeshow test for checking the goodness of fit of the logistic regression models.

4. Results and Interpretation

The results indicate that only a small percentage of the respondents were engaged in entrepreneurial activities or taking the necessary steps to set up a business. As data in Table 2 show, in 2007 only 2.54% of the Romanian respondents were involved in such activities (52 in total; 31 males and 21 females), however, this percentage increased during the following years, reaching its peak points in 2014 (10.99% of the total sample; out of which were 152 males and 67 females) and 2015 (10.94% of the total sample; 219 in total out of which 138 males and 81 females). Although the number of female entrepreneurs has increased over the years, its average level is still 55.24%, lower than that of their counterparts during the 2007–2015 time period.

On average, around 27% of working-age, Romanian adults see good opportunities around them, while around 46% would be constrained from starting a business due to fear of failure. However, from the total sample on average around 35% consider that they have the necessary knowledge, and skills to start a business, and more than 31% know someone who has started a business in the past two years. From the total sample, 12.8% of the respondents were aged between 18 and 24 years old, 20.3% between 25 and 34 years; 23.7% were aged between 35 and 44 years old; 20.8% range between 45 and 54 years old and 22.3% were between 55 and 64 years old. On average 34.4% of respondents have registered in revenues the lowest 33% annual household income; 33.8% were situated in the middle 33% and 31.8% registered an income situated in the upper 33%.

In Table 3, we presented the values for the logistic regression coefficient (*B*) and their associated significance probability (Sig.) (in brackets), SE, rating scale (Wals), and odds ratio (Exp(β)) for each independent and control variable included in the study. The SE, measures of uncertainty of the logistic regression coefficient, the Wald test indicates the significance of the model coefficients, while

Table 2. Descriptive Statistics of Variables Distribution Based on the Year of the Survey.

		The Year the Survey Was Administered (Country: Romania)									Total
		2007	2008	2009	2010	2011	2012	2013	2014	2015	
Involved in TEA	No	1,994	2,141	2,027	2,174	1,857	1,840	1,824	1,781	1,783	17,421
	Yes	52	65	66	61	171	164	197	220	219	1,215
Total		2,046	2,206	2,093	2,235	2,028	2,004	2,021	2,001	2,002	18,636
Involved in TEA, male	No	925	980	956	980	853	860	878	810	825	8,067
	Yes	31	45	44	36	106	110	120	152	138	782
Total		956	1,025	1,000	1,016	959	970	998	962	963	8,849
Involved in TEA, female	No	1,069	1,161	1,071	1,194	1,004	980	946	973	959	9,357
	Yes	21	20	22	25	65	54	77	67	81	432
Total		1,090	1,181	1,093	1,219	1,069	1,034	1,023	1,040	1,040	9,789
opport	No	1,120	1,266	991	1,531	1,163	1,070	1,278	1,177	1,191	10,787
	Yes	401	428	161	264	591	620	508	558	591	4,122
Total		1,521	1,694	1,152	1,795	1,754	1,690	1,786	1,735	1,782	14,909
suskill	No	1,283	1,554	985	1,431	1,241	1,195	1,056	1,008	1,033	10,786
	Yes	484	434	365	566	710	722	895	940	920	6,036
Total		1,767	1,988	1,350	1,997	1,951	1,917	1,951	1,948	1,953	16,822

(Continued)

Table 2. (*Continued*)

		The Year the Survey Was Administered (Country: Romania)									Total
		2007	**2008**	**2009**	**2010**	**2011**	**2012**	**2013**	**2014**	**2015**	
knowent	No	1,178	1,381	1,000	1,464	1,438	1,350	1,420	1,407	1,348	11,986
	Yes	763	711	453	653	533	594	562	562	634	5,465
Total		1,941	2,092	1,453	2,117	1,971	1,944	1,982	1,969	1,982	17,451
fearfail	No	1,253	1,212	655	845	1,000	927	963	943	935	8,733
	Yes	526	737	577	997	876	917	934	964	975	7,503
Total		1,779	1,949	1,232	1,842	1,876	1,844	1,897	1,907	1,910	16,236
Age	18–24	189	229	194	212	258	252	262	253	213	2,062
	25–34	332	352	312	318	367	328	449	421	401	3,280
	35–44	391	378	340	346	421	431	516	501	500	3,824
	45–54	427	356	349	350	326	329	397	389	431	3,354
	55–64	400	352	424	422	360	358	394	432	456	3,598
Total		1,739	1,667	1,619	1,648	1,732	1,698	2,018	1,996	2,001	16,118
Income	1.00	587	607	518	600	539	582	536	667	681	5,317
	2.00	590	640	523	593	613	575	634	529	537	5,234
	3.00	408	521	419	632	573	515	672	555	625	4,920
Total		1,585	1,768	1,460	1,825	1,725	1,672	1,842	1,751	1,843	15,471

Source: Authors' contributions based on GEM data from 2007 to 2015.

Table 3. TEA Drivers (Logistic Regression Results).

	B	SE	Wald	Exp(*B*)
Intercept	−5.633**** (0.000)	0.189	887.844	0.004
opport	0.390**** (0.000)	0.079	24.473	1.477
knowent	0.912**** (0.000)	0.082	124.461	2.488
suskill	1.600**** (0.000)	0.098	266.613	4.955
fearfail	−0.330**** (0.000)	0.080	17.038	0.719
Age category 18–24 years	0.900**** (0.000)	0.152	35.081	2.459
Age category 25–34 years	0.810**** (0.000)	0.137	35.056	2.248
Age category 35–44 years	0.811**** (0.000)	0.135	35.895	2.250
Age category 45–54 years	0.469**** (0.001)	0.147	10.205	1.598
Income: middle 33rd percentile	0.363**** (0.002)	0.117	9.662	1.437
Income: upper 33rd percentile	0.631**** (0.000)	0.109	33.305	1.879
Year (2011–2015)	1.061**** (0.000)	0.105	101.952	2.891
Nagelkerke R^2		0.245		
Cox and Snell Pseudo R^2		0.110		
Omnibus test (sig. level)		0.000		
−2 Log Likelihood		4,736.511		
Hosmer and Lemeshow Test		0.561		

Source: Authors' contributions based on GEM data from 2007 to 2015.
Note: Standard errors (SE) in parentheses.
****$p<0.01$; ***$p<0.05$; **$p<0.10$; and *$p<0.15$.

the odds ratio (Exp(β)) – indicates the constant effects of the predictor, in the likelihood that the event will occur (the engagement in early-stage entrepreneurial activity). We used data from the GEM APS, from 2007 until 2015, for the Romania population. The average response rate was around 2070 individuals per year, with a total of 18636 respondents for the entire period of analysis (see Table 2).

The coefficients described in Table 3 show the effects of the independent and control variables on the odds of engagement in TEA relative to not being involved in such a business at all. A positive value of the coefficient indicates that an increase in the independent variable raises the likelihood of involvement in early-stage entrepreneurial activity (imposed condition: all the other variables remain equal). In the logistic regression model, besides the psychological determinants (opportunity perception, knowing other entrepreneurs, confidence in own skills, and fear of failure), two socio-demographic factors (age and household income) have been included, alongside the year of the survey.

The data show that the probability of starting a business is positively influenced by the perception of good business opportunities, confidence in own knowledge and skills, and personally knowing someone who has recently started a business. The highest odds ratios for the independent variables have been registered for self-confidence (odds ratio 4.955) and knowing other entrepreneurs (odds ratio 2.488). The odds ratio was 4.955 for an additional unit score of self-confidence in their skills when the scores for opportunity perception, knowing other entrepreneurs, and fear of failure remain constant, which indicates that individuals who have confidence in their skills are 4.955 times more likely to engage in TEA than those who do not. Similarly, knowing other entrepreneurs increase the odds of engaging in TEA (Sig.<0.01; odds ratio 2.488). On the other hand, fear of failure has a significant (Sig.<0.01) but the opposite effect, showing an inverse relationship between this psychological determinant and TEA. Our results also suggest that belonging to all 4 age categories significantly increases the odds of involvement in early-stage entrepreneurial activities, in comparison to the base category 55–64 years old. Both household incomes (belonging to the middle and upper 33rd percentile) increase the odds of involvement in TEA. As regards the year category (2011–2015), it showed a positive and significant effect.

The result of the logistic regression shows that all psychological determinants of men's involvement in entrepreneurship are significant (Table 4). The results of the logistic regression analyses indicate that for the male category (MEA), the highest odds ratio for the independent variables are registered for confidence in own skills and knowing other entrepreneurs have the highest odds ratio (4,947 and 2,251, respectively), followed by opportunity perception (odds ratio = 1.392). Our findings suggest that there is a positive and significant (Sig.<0.01) relationship between opportunity perception, confidence in own skills and personally knowing someone who started a business, and the odds of involvement in early-stage entrepreneurial activities among the male population. The odds ratio was 4.947 for an additional unit score of self-confidence when the scores for opportunity perception, knowing other entrepreneurs, and fear of failure remain constant, which indicates that individuals who have confidence in their skills are 4.947 times more likely to engage in TEA than those who do not.

Similarly, knowing other entrepreneurs increase the odds of engaging in TEA (Sig.<0.01; odds ratio 2.251), while fear of failure however is significantly and negatively related to the odds of starting or being involved in an early-stage business that is less than 42 months old. Findings also suggest that belonging to all 4

Table 4. MEA Drivers (Logistic Regression Results).

	B	SE	Wald	Exp(*B*)
Intercept	−5.299**** (0.000)	0.247	461.928	0.005
opport	0.331**** (0.001)	0.100	11.036	1.392
knowent	0.811**** (0.000)	0.103	61.782	2.251
suskill	1.599**** (0.000)	0.133	144.578	4.947
fearfail	−0.368**** (0.000)	0.104	12.654	0.692
Age category 18–24 years	1.020**** (0.000)	0.193	27.945	2.774
Age category 25–34 years	0.747**** (0.000)	0.177	17.837	2.110
Age category 35–44 years	0.796**** (0.000)	0.175	20.584	2.216
Age category 45–54 years	0.472*** (0.012)	0.187	6.349	1.603
Income: middle 33rd percentile	0.326*** (0.032)	0.152	4.601	1.385
Income: upper 33rd percentile	0.545**** (0.000)	0.141	14.844	1.724
Year (2011–2015)	0.989**** (0.000)	0.133	54.837	2.687
Nagelkerke R^2		0.233		
Cox and Snell Pseudo R^2		0.119		
Omnibus test (sig. Level)		0.000		
−2 Log Likelihood		2,859.816		
Hosmer and Lemeshow Test		0.189		

Source: Authors' contributions based on GEM data from 2007 to 2015.
Note: SE in parentheses.
****p<0.01; ***p<0.05; **p<0.10; and *p<0.15.

age categories significantly increases the odds of involvement in early-stage entrepreneurial activities in comparison to the base category 55–64 years old. Both household incomes (the middle and upper 33rd percentile) increase the odds of involvement in TEA. Similar to the previous model, the year category coefficient value shows a positive and significant effect.

The coefficients in Table 5 describe the effects of psychological factors and control variables on FEA.

The results indicate that the odds of starting an entrepreneurial activity among females are positively influenced by identifying opportunities, having the necessary skills in managing a business, and knowing other individuals who recently

Table 5. FEA Drivers (logistic Regression Results)

	B	SE	Wald	Exp(*B*)
Intercept	−6.036**** (0.000)	0.301	402.504	0.002
opport	0.495**** (0.000)	0.130	14.442	1.640
knowent	1.081**** (0.000)	0.134	62.399	2.889
suskill	1.511**** (0.000)	0.147	105.324	4.531
fearfail	−0.191* (0.138)	0.129	2.200	0.826
Age category 18−24 years	0.656**** (0.009)	0.251	6.834	1.926
Age category 25−34 years	0.901**** (0.000)	0.217	17.283	2.463
Age category 35−44 years	0.809**** (0.000)	0.214	14.299	2.245
Age category 45–54 years	0.425 ** (0.075)	0.239	3.169	1.530
Income: middle 33rd percentile	0.396*** (0.031)	0.184	4.638	1.486
Income: upper 33rd percentile	0.713**** (0.000)	0.174	16.813	2.039
Year (2011−2015)	1.149**** (0.000)	0.172	44.824	3.156
Nagelkerke R^2		0.236		
Cox and Snell Pseudo R^2		0.087		
Omnibus test (sig. Level)		0.000		
−2 Log Likelihood		1,851.630		
Hosmer and Lemeshow Test		0.497		

Source: Authors' contributions based on GEM data from 2007 to 2015.
Note: SE in parentheses.
****p<0.01; ***p<0.05; **p<0,10; and *p<0.15.

engaged in a business. Although the registered odds ratio is lower than in the case of males, for female entrepreneurs' activity the higher odds are registered for confidence in their skills (odds ratio = 4.531).

Knowing other entrepreneurs register higher odds for female entrepreneurs (odds ratio=2.889) than for men (odds ratio=2.251). The odds ratio was 2.889 for an additional unit score of knowing other entrepreneurs when the scores for self-confidence, opportunity perception, and fear of failure remain constant, which indicates that females who have confidence in their skills are 2,889 times more likely to engage in TEA than those who do not.

Our findings suggest that there is a positive and significant (Sig.<0.01) relationship between opportunity perception, and the odds of involvement in early-stage entrepreneurial activities among the female population (odds ratio=1.640; Sig.<0.01). Like men, fear of failure represents for women as well an important determinant in engaging in entrepreneurial activities.

As results indicate the relation between entrepreneurial activities in women and fear of failure shows a negative and significant coefficient. Results also indicate that belonging to age categories 18–24 years, 24–34 years, 35–44, and 45–54 years in comparison to base category 55–64 years old, significantly increases the odds of involvement in entrepreneurship.

Nevertheless, a positive relationship between household income from the middle and upper 33rd percentile, in comparison to the base category lower 33rd percentile, was observed, which significantly increases the odds of engagement in entrepreneurial activities.

The obtained data indicate the results for Omnibus Test, Cox and Snell R^2, Nagelkerke R^2, −2 Log Likelihood, and Hosmer and Lemeshow test. The results for all the models, indicated that the Omnibus tests of model coefficients are significant ($p < 0.05$), confirming the causal relationship of the proposed logit models.

The likelihood ratio test indicates that the included variables significantly contribute to early-stage entrepreneurial activity for all cases. The values for Cox and Snell R^2, and Nagelkerke R^2 are less than 1 and indicate how useful are the explanatory variables in predicting the response variable (the effect size).

For the logistic models, the obtained values are between 0.236 and 0.245 for Nagelkerke R^2 and 0.087 and 0.119 for Cox and Snell R^2. Hosmer and Lemeshow test values in all logistics models are above Sig.>0.05 which indicates a good fit (Tables 3–5).

5. Discussion of Our Findings

Entrepreneurial activity is considered an important source of innovation and job creation (Lukeš, Longo, & Zouhar, 2019; Munyo & Veiga, 2022). Although many studies have contributed to the literature by indicating the influence of different drivers on early-stage entrepreneurial activity, few have focused on the role played by both women and men in the business environment, especially in the Romanian framework. Our chapter contributes to the existing literature in two directions: first, it focused on both women and men drivers of early-stage entrepreneurial activities as not only men but also women play a crucial role in this activity; second, the analysis was built by taking into consideration the whole period that Romania participated in the GEM survey collection of data.

Our results indicate that in total and among Romanian men and women similar drivers influence the odds of engagement in entrepreneurial activities, relative to not being involved in businesses. Both men and women, having confidence in their knowledge and skills had the highest odds ratio values (odd ratio men = 4.947; odd ratio women=4.531). These skills may refer to the business and financial planning, risk management assessment, and problem-solving capacity, among others (OECD, 2019). Our results are in line with other findings that have demonstrated that high levels of self-confidence are positively related to engagement in entrepreneurship (Holienka, Jančovičová, & Kovačičová, 2016; Wong & Lee, 2005).

Also, identifying opportunities proved to be positive and significant in both cases, while fear of failure had the opposite effect. Perception of good entrepreneurial opportunities is related to one's capacity to be aware of the unexploited business chances, being a necessary precondition for entrepreneurial action. Although the registered odds ratio is higher for women (odd ratio=1.640) than for men (odd ratio=1.392), for both categories it represents an important determinant in engaging in entrepreneurial activities. Comparable results that prove the importance of opportunity perception toward engagement in entrepreneurship have been found in other empirical studies (Holienka et al., 2016; Vodă, Butnaru et al., 2020). Fear of failure, on the other hand, can act as an inhibitor of entrepreneurial actions. This variable has the highest odd ratio for women than for their counterparts (odds ratio women = 0.826; odd ratio men = 0.692. The odds ratio was 0,826 for an additional unit to the score of fear of failure when the scores for the opportunity, self-confidence, and networking remain constant, suggesting that women who indicate high levels of value for this variable are 0.826 times less likely to engage in TEA than those who do not. In comparison to men, the results indicate that those who registered important levels value for this variable are 0.692 times less likely to engage in TEA than those who do not. Other studies have reported that women are more likely to register important levels for this variable, as it can prevent them to engage in a part- or full-time productive activity (OECD, 2019).

Knowing other entrepreneurs can lead to great benefits generated through social exchange. The literature reports that this variable can affect entrepreneurial potential by providing role models and access to networks and knowledge (Sendra-Pons, Belarbi-Munoz, Garzón, & Mas-Tur, 2021). The external knowledge that an entrepreneur's environment gives rise to, can prove to be supportive in the discovery of opportunities and their exploitation, as well as in an efficient resource allocation towards high ended values activities (Markussen & Røed, 2017; Ramos-Rodriguez, Medina-Garrido, Lorenzo-Gómez, & Ruiz-Navarro, 2010). In our sample, knowing an entrepreneur also proved to positively influence engagement in entrepreneurship for both genders (odds ratio men =2.251; odds ratio women = 2.889). The odds ratio was 2.251 for an additional unit to the score of knowing other entrepreneurs when the scores for the opportunity, self-confidence, and fear of failure remain constant, suggesting that men who indicate high levels of value for this variable are 2.251 times more likely to engage in TEA than those who do not. Higher odds ratio values were obtained by women, indicating that women who score high levels at this indicator are 2.889 times more likely to engage in TEA than others who do not.

In the entrepreneurship literature, we commonly find the use of control variables such as age and income. Age is important because starting a new venture can come early, in the first years of someone's career, or later, after many years of experience. In a study about entrepreneurship among students, we found that the sample was made up of 80% of the respondents between 21 and 25 years of age (Karimi et al., 2013). In another study on graduate students, we found out that the respondents had an average age of 22 years with a small standard deviation of 1.74 (Maes et al., 2014). The decision to pursue a career as an entrepreneur is shaped by a range of individual realities such as educational, socio-cultural, and gendered factors, and labor market conditions. Among them, personal income and the average income in the region are important determinants. In many high-income countries, men are almost twice as likely to be early-stage or established business owners (Maes et al., 2014). Choosing income and age as control variables, and not as main variables, is sustained also by the study of Koellinger, Minniti, and Schade (2013) who concluded, using a sample from 17 countries, that "a significant portion of the gender gap in entrepreneurial propensity is explained by subjective perceptions whereas socio-economic variables appear to play a smaller role." For the age category variable, we took into consideration the working population between 55 and 64 years old as the base category, as in our sample we register the lowest involvement rate in entrepreneurship. Based on this, we could establish that all other categories significantly increased the likelihood of involvement in early-stage entrepreneurial activity for men and women. For the year, we establish as base category the period between 2007 and 2010, as the lowest number of involvements in entrepreneurship was registered for men and women. From the data, we could observe a constant increase of both men and women in entrepreneurial activities starting from 2011.

6. Conclusion

The study focused on the major importance of psychological factors in the field of entrepreneurship. By focusing on the total and both genders-specific nature of the drivers of involvement in early-stage entrepreneurship, this chapter documents an empirical case study on the Romanian situation, from 2007 until 2015.

The chapter presents the descriptive statistics of the psychological factors, and control variables and also uses three logistic regression models to estimate the odds ratio as total (TEA) or belonging to a specific group (MEA and FEA) on engaging in entrepreneurial activity relative to not being involved in such business at all. The logistic regression models were used as methods of analysis as the vast majority of the indicators were binary variables (yes=1; no=1).

The descriptive statistics indicated that in Romania, the women's rate is more than 50% lower than men, in terms of entrepreneurship (see the Female/Male

TEA ratio for 2007–2015). More than a quarter of the total sample consider identifying opportunities as a good determinant, while more than half of respondents attribute to fear of failure their incapacity of engaging in entrepreneurship. Similarly, more than 30% of the sample consider that both knowledge and skills to start a business and networking are among factor-driven determinants. Most individuals aged between 18 and 54 years old are involved in entrepreneurship, while those aged between 55 and 64 years old registered the lowest score. In terms of household income those belonging to the lower thirty-three percentile record the lowest involvement rate in entrepreneurship.

The results from the logistics regression indicate that the odds of starting an entrepreneurial activity among females and males are positively influenced by identifying opportunities, having the necessary skills in managing a business, and knowing other individuals who recently engaged in a business. Fear of failure has a significant and negative effect for both gender categories, with a higher odds ratio among the female population.

In terms of study limitation, we mention the following aspects: first, the data collected from GEM APS consists mostly of binary variables, which limits the use of other empirical models. Second, the analyzed period includes only data from 2007 until 2015, being the period when Romania participated in the survey (although Romania participated in the 2021 survey data collection, the full datasets are not yet available on GEM). Third, additional justification of the entrepreneurial activity rate could also include variables related to the institutional environment where entrepreneurs operate, which might offer a more accurate image of the county's drivers understanding.

References

Ahl, H. (2006). Why research on women entrepreneurs needs new directions. *Entrepreneurial Theory and Practice. 30*, 595–621. doi:10.1111/j.1540-6520.2006.00138.x

Camelo-Ordaz, C., Diánez-González, J. P., & Ruiz-Navarro, J. (2016). The influence of gender on entrepreneurial intention: The mediating role of perceptual factors: La influencia del género sobre la intención emprendedora: El papel mediador de los factores de percepción. *BRQ Business Research Quarterly*, *19*(4), 261–277. https://doi.org/10.1016/j.brq.2016.03.001

Carter, S., Anderson, S., & Shaw, E. (2001). *Women's business ownership: A review of the academic, popular and internet literature*. Report to the Small Business Service, RR002/01. Glasgow: Department of Marketing University of Strathclyde.

European Commission. (2016, November). In A. Radauer & L. Roman (Eds.), *The Romanian entrepreneurial ecosystem background report horizon 2020 policy support facility*. Brussels: Technopolis Group. Retrieved from https://ec.europa.eu/research-and-innovation/sites/default/files/rio/report/KI%2520AX%252017%2520002%2520EN%2520N%2520Romania_Background.pdf

Feder, E.-S., & Niţu-Antonie, R.-D. (2017). Connecting gender identity, entrepreneurial training, role models and intentions. *International Journal of Gender and Entrepreneurship*, *9*(1), 87–108.

Global Entrepreneurship Monitor (GEM). (2012). Global Entrepreneurship Monitor 2012 global report. Retrieved from https://gemconsortium.org/file/open?fileId=48545

Global Entrepreneurship Monitor (GEM). (2013). Global Entrepreneurship Monitor 2013 global report. Retrieved from https://gemconsortium.org/file/open?fileId=48772

Global Entrepreneurship Monitor (GEM). (2014). Global Entrepreneurship Monitor 2014 global report. Retrieved from https://gemconsortium.org/file/open?fileId=49079

Global Entrepreneurship Monitor (GEM). (2015). Global Entrepreneurship Monitor 2015/2016 report. Retrieved from https://www.gemconsortium.org/file/open?fileId=49480

Global Entrepreneurship Monitor (GEM). (2016). Global Entrepreneurship Monitor 2015/2016 global report. Retrieved from https://www.gemconsortium.org/file/open?fileId=49480

Global Entrepreneurship Monitor (GEM). (2017). Global Entrepreneurship Monitor 2016/2017 global report. Retrieved from https://gemconsortium.org/file/open?fileId=49812

Global Entrepreneurship Monitor (GEM). (2018). Global Entrepreneurship Monitor 2017/2018 global report. Retrieved from https://gemconsortium.org/file/open?fileId=50012

Global Entrepreneurship Monitor (GEM). (2019). Global Entrepreneurship Monitor 2018/2019 global report. Retrieved from https://gemconsortium.org/file/open?fileId=50213

Global Entrepreneurship Monitor (GEM). (2020). Global Entrepreneurship Monitor 2019/2020 global report. Retrieved from https://gemconsortium.org/file/open?fileId=50443

Global Entrepreneurship Monitor (GEM). (2021). Global Entrepreneurship Monitor 2020/2021 global report. Retrieved from https://gemconsortium.org/file/open?fileId=50691

Greene, P. G., Hart, M., Gatewood, E., Brush, C. G., & Carter, N. (2003). *Women entrepreneurs: Moving front and center. An overview of research and theory*. White Papers, United States Association for Small Business and Entrepreneurship (USASBE).

Holienka, M., Jančovičová, Z., & Kovačičová, Z. (2016). Drivers of women entrepreneurship in Visegrad countries: GEM evidence. *Procedia-Social and Behavioral Sciences*, *220*, 124–133. doi:10.1016/j.sbspro.2016.05.476

Ioana, P. C., & Dodescu, A. (2018). Inclusive entrepreneurship programmes in Romania in 2014–2020. There is an improvement compared to 2007–2013? *Annals of Faculty of Economics, University of Oradea, Faculty of Economics*, *1*(1), 80–93.

Karimi, S., Biemans, H. J., Lans, T., Chizari, M., Mulder, M., & Mahdei, K. N. (2013). Understanding role models and gender influences on entrepreneurial intentions among college students. *Procedia-Social and Behavioral Sciences*, *93*, 204–214. doi:10.1016/j.sbspro.2013.09.179

Kelley, D. J., Baumer, B. S., Brush, C., Greene, P. G., Mahdavi, M., Majbouri, M., … Heavlow, R. (2017). *Global Entrepreneurship Monitor: Women's entrepreneurship 2016/2017 report*. London: Global Entrepreneurship Research Association.

Koellinger, P., Minniti, M., & Schade, C. (2013). Gender differences in entrepreneurial propensity. *Oxford Bulletin of Economics and Statistics*, *75*(2), 213–234. https://doi.org/10.1111/j.1468-0084.2011.00689.x

Krueger, N., Reilly, M. D., & Carsrud, A. L. (2000). Competing models of entrepreneurial intentions. *Journal of Business Venturing*, *15*(5–6), 411–432. doi:10.1016/S0883-9026(98)00033-0

Lukeš, M., Longo, M. C., & Zouhar, J. (2019). Do business incubators really enhance entrepreneurial growth? Evidence from a large sample of innovative Italian start-ups. *Technovation*, *82*, 25–34. https://doi.org/10.1016/j.technovation.2018.07.008

Maes, J., Leroy, H., & Sels, L. (2014). Gender differences in entrepreneurial intentions: A TPB multi-group analysis at factor and indicator level. *European Management Journal*, *32*(5), 784–794. https://doi.org/10.1016/j.emj.2014.01.0

Markussen, S., & Røed, K. (2017). The gender gap in entrepreneurship – The role of peer effects. *Journal of Economic Behavior & Organization*, *134*, 356–373. https://doi.org/10.1016/j.jebo.2016.12.013

Marlow, S. (2002). Women and self-employment: A part of or apart from theoretical construct? *International Journal of Entrepreneurship and Innovation*, *3*(2), 83–91. https://doi.org/10.5367/000000002101299088

Munyo, I., & Veiga, L. (2022). Entrepreneurship and economic growth. *Journal of the Knowledge Economy*, 1–18. doi:10.1007/s13132-022-01032-8

Organisation for Economic Co-operation and Development (OECD). (2018). Inclusive entrepreneurship policies: Country assessment notes Romania. Retrieved from https://www.oecd.org/cfe/smes/ROMANIA-IE-Country-Note-2018.pdf

Organisation for Economic Co-operation and Development (OECD). (2019). Women's self-employment and entrepreneurship activities. Retrieved from https://www.oecd-ilibrary.org/sites/07d6d841-en/index.html?itemId=/content/component/07d6d841-en

Organisation for Economic Co-operation and Development (OECD). (2020). *Inclusive entrepreneurship policies*. Country Assessment Notes Romania. Retrieved from https://www.oecd.org/cfe/smes/Romania-IE-2020.pdf

Ramos-Rodriguez, A. R., Medina-Garrido, J. A., Lorenzo-Gómez, J. D., & Ruiz-Navarro, J. (2010). What you know or who you know? The role of intellectual and social capital in opportunity recognition. *International Small Business Journal*, *28*(6), 566–582. doi:10.1177/0266242610369753

Sánchez-Escobedo, M. C., Fernández-Portillo, A., Díaz-Casero, J. C., & Hernández-Mogollón, R. (2016). Research in entrepreneurship using GEM data. Approach to the state of affairs in gender studies. *European Journal of Management and Business Economics*, *25*(3), 150–160. https://doi.org/10.1016/j.redeen.2016.09.002

Sendra-Pons, P., Belarbi-Munoz, S., Garzón, D., & Mas-Tur, A. (2021). Cross-country differences in drivers of female necessity entrepreneurship. *Service Business*, *16*(4), 1–19. doi:10.1007/s11628-021-00470-9

Shinnar, R., Giacomin, O., & Janssen, F. (2012). Entrepreneurial perceptions and intentions: The role of gender and culture. *Entrepreneurship: Theory and Practice*, *36*(3), 465–493. https://doi.org/10.1111/j.1540-6520.2012.00509.x

Smith, S., Hamilton, M., & Fabian, K. (2020). Entrepreneurial drivers, barriers and enablers of computing students: gendered perspectives from an Australian and UK university. *Studies in Higher Education*, *45*(9), 1892–1905. https://doi.org/10.1080/03075079.2019.1637840

Thornton, P. H., & Klyver, K. (2019). Who is more likely to walk the talk? The symbolic management of entrepreneurial intentions by gender and work status. *Innovation*, *21*(1), 102–127. doi:10.1080/14479338.2018.1497448

UEFISCDI. (2021). Sustainability and innovation in the Romanian entrepreneurial ecosystem an exploratory study. Retrieved from https://accelerate.gov.ro/storage/sustainability-and-innovation-in-the-romanian-entrepreneurial-ecosystem.pdf

Van Auken, H., Stephens, P., Fry, F. L., & Silva, J. (2006). Role model influences on entrepreneurial intentions: A comparison between USA and Mexico. *The International Entrepreneurship and Management Journal*, *2*, 325–336. https://doi.org/10.1142/S1084946706000349

Vodă, A. I., Butnaru, G. I., & Butnaru, R. C. (2020). Enablers of entrepreneurial activity across the European Union—An analysis using GEM individual data. *Sustainability*, *12*(3), 1022. https://doi.org/10.3390/su12031022

Vodă, A. I., Haller, A. P., Anichiti, A., & Butnaru, G. I. (2020). Testing entrepreneurial intention determinants in post-transition economies. *Sustainability*, *12*(24), 10370. https://doi.org/10.3390/su122410370

Wennekers, S., Van Wennekers, A., Thurik, R., & Reynolds, P. (2005). Nascent entrepreneurship and the level of economic development. *Small Business Economics*, *24*(3), 293–309.

Wong, P. K., & Lee, L. (2005). *Antecedents for entrepreneurial propensity in Singapore*. Working Paper No. WP2005-12, NUS Entrepreneurship Centre, Singapore.

Zampetakis, L. A., Bakatsaki, M., Litos, C., Kafetsios, K. G., & Moustakis, V. (2017). Gender-based differential item functioning in the application of the theory of planned behavior for the study of entrepreneurial intentions. *Frontiers in Psychology*, *8*, 451. https://doi.org/10.3389/fpsyg.2017.00451

Chapter 13

Development of Entrepreneurship in Serbia: Main External Factors and Influences

Ondrej Jaško, Mladen Čudanov, Jovan Krivokapić and Ivan Todorović

Abstract

The main aim of this chapter is to systematize observations regarding changes in entrepreneurship in Serbia during the previous decade, having in mind some key factors such as high-impact low-probability (HILP) events, dynamic development in the sphere of information technologies (IT), and foreign direct investments (FDI). The choice of these factors was made in accordance with the fact that there were no significant changes in other external factors in the sphere of entrepreneurship (regulatory framework, financial conditions, and socio-political instability). This chapter discusses the assumptions that HILP events and FDI can have both positive and negative impacts on individual sectors or agglomerations of entrepreneurship, while only positive impacts are attributed to IT development. Using official databases and annual financial and business reports given by entrepreneurial agencies and micro and small enterprises we created a set of reports that indicate the strength and direction of the influence of the mentioned factors and their consequences in the sphere of entrepreneurship at the level of Serbia and selected cities, based on the fact that the entrepreneurial ecosystem in those cities faced greater than average challenges. The selected ratios indicate changes in the growth rate of the entrepreneurship sector (number of entrepreneurs and employees) as well as in the improvement of its competitiveness (productivity, assets, and profit per employee).

Keywords: Entrepreneurship; HILP events; FDI; performance measurement; information technologies; Serbia

Entrepreneurship Development in the Balkans: Perspective from Diverse Contexts, 237–260

Published under exclusive licence by Emerald Publishing Limited
doi:10.1108/978-1-83753-454-820231013

1. Introduction

The importance of entrepreneurship in Serbia is reflected in the realization of the roles attributed to them, such as innovation, taking risks, creating new jobs and employment, utilization of insufficiently engaged resources (Smith, 2010), increasing productivity, all of which contribute to economic growth and development in their full significance. According to many evaluations, the main role of entrepreneurship is the transformation of knowledge into products, services, new markets, which is significant not only from economic but also from social functioning point of view (Zahra & Wright, 2016). The significance and roles of entrepreneurship develop and change over time, adapting to general economic trends (Burke & van Stel, 2009), global, national, and regional business conditions.

Serbian entrepreneurship derives its potential from the position of Serbia. It is among the largest countries and economies in the Balkans, with a population of 6.690.887, according to the 2022nd census. According to the National Bank of Serbia, real gross domestic product (GDP) growth averaged 2.3% between 2012 and 2021, and was 4.2%, 3.8%, 1.0%, and 0.4% during the four quarters of 2022, averaging 2.4%. According to the same source, unemployment dropped from 25.9% in 2012 to 11% in 2021 and was measured at 8.9% in the Q3 of 2022, greatly influencing necessity entrepreneurship. Average wage for 2022 was 632.25 EUR (National Bank of Serbia, 2023). Additionally, start-up skills in Serbia are above the regional and especially global average, although some other factors in the entrepreneurial environment should be improved (Krivokapić & Jaško, 2015).

2. Dataset

Data for our research are coming from the trifold sources. The first hard dataset was provided by the Serbian Business Register Agency, as the aggregate dataset with sums and averages for entrepreneurs (sole proprietors) as well as for the incorporated business entities which are under the condition by the Serbian law to be classified as micro, small, or medium enterprises, having less than 50 employees. For this chapter, we classified enterprises with less than 50 employees in the entrepreneurship sector. Due to the change in methodology, some data were used as a timeseries up to 2019 and to the lack of data, aggregate numbers for the year 2020 and 2021 were estimated according to the data for all the companies.

The second hard dataset was provided by the Chamber of Commerce, Republic of Serbia. It contains basic financial data for all the incorporated business entities (LLC and Public companies), as well as for the entrepreneurs. Dataset was not the sample, but a large set of population. It included all the companies which prepared and submitted annual financial report. Due to the change in state regulation and subsidies policy, that number radically changed in the year 2019, making our dataset aiming at different population of entrepreneurs before and after the year 2019. While we can define both parts as the "resilient" entrepreneurs, part prior to 2019 has proven their resilience by submitting the financial report for each year since the year 2013 (and therefore surviving in the business sense), while the second part was the entrepreneurs which were lured by the subsidies to start submitting financial reports after the year 2019, paid flat-rate tax and did not keep the books prior to that. All in all, 439,539 annual business records were analyzed for the incorporated business entities, and 80,308 for entrepreneurs, in the time period of 9 years between 2013 and 2021. Data were all based on annual reports due at the end of each year, 31st December 2021. Chamber of Commerce was not able to provide the number of employees for the year 2021, since reliable data were not available at the time of this research.

The third source of data was relevant institutions, like the National Bank of Serbia, entrepreneurship hubs, and clusters. Those were the sources of aggregate quantitative data, as well as qualitative data and assessments.

All the obtained were used in order to analyze the changes in the sphere of entrepreneurship under the impact of three strong factors that emerged in the previous decade, regarding the creation of the economic environment and growth of the country. These factors are:

- HILP events (floods 2014, COVID-19 pandemic 2020),
- development of the IT industry, and
- FDI.

3. Strategic Framework and Financial Support for the Development of Entrepreneurship

Different authors suggest that the relationship between entrepreneurship and economic growth is mostly determined by the volume of newly created and sustainability of entrepreneurial ventures. The analysis of these two performances of the dynamics of entrepreneurship in Serbia determines much more than a quantitative assessment of the development of this economic activity. According to some findings (Aghion & Howitt, 1998), the dynamics in the entrepreneurship sector will influence the conversion in the market structure, the volume of capital in the economy and the innovative process, which are the necessary conditions for growth in the entrepreneurship sector, creating free capital for investment in the research and development process, which should generate new products, markets, and technologies, in accordance with the description of the positive growth spiral.

Significant funds and efforts are allocated to encourage entrepreneurs to start and develop their own businesses in accordance with the determination to develop the knowledge and private initiative-based economy (Todorović, Komazec, Jevtić, Obradović, & Marič, 2016). State support for entrepreneurship in Serbia was formalized in several documents and strategies provided by the Government of the Republic of Serbia:

- Strategy for the Development of Small and Medium Enterprises and Entrepreneurs, 2023–2027 (in development).
- Concept of the Policy for Development Financing of the Field of Entrepreneurship in the Republic of Serbia, 2022.
- Information Society and Information Security Development Strategy of the Republic of Serbia for the period 2021–2026.

- The Strategy for the Development of Artificial Intelligence in the Republic of Serbia for the period 2020–2025.
- Strategy on Scientific and Technological Development of the Republic of Serbia for the period 2016–2020.
- Intellectual Property Development Strategy for the period 2018–2022.
- Strategy for the Support of Development of Small and Medium Enterprises, Entrepreneurship and Competitiveness (with the action plan), 2015–2020.
- National Youth Strategy 2015–2020.

Direct financial support for the development of entrepreneurship is being performed through programs coordinated by the Ministry of Economy. Distribution is achieved through public tenders announced by the Ministry, then the Development Agency of Serbia – RAS, regional development agencies, Serbia Innovation Fund, and all in cooperation with the banks and leasing companies that provide support in the operationalization of distributing grants and loans. The funds allocated from the state budget (without local self-governments) for direct financial support in 2019 amounted to around EUR 200 million. The amount and method of distribution of support to entrepreneurship were changed during the COVID-19 pandemic, but during 2022 they reached the pre-pandemic level (Local Economic Development Office of Niš, 2023), and the consequences of those changes in the sphere of entrepreneurship are described in the part of the text dedicated to it.

4. Dynamics in the Entrepreneurship Sector

By virtue of support measures, stable economic growth (Table 1) and significant improvements have been achieved in the entrepreneurship sector in recent years. The growth dynamics of the number of entrepreneurs increased from 0.3% in 2013 to 5.3% in 2019, when it decreased, under the strong influence of the consequences of the COVID-19 pandemic. The change in dynamics in 2019, which can be seen in the official data of the Serbian Business Registers Agency, was influenced by the change in the number of entrepreneurs who are obliged to submit business reports, which came into force in 2019, when the number of natural persons–entrepreneurs increased 9 times, which significantly changed the official performance of the entrepreneurship sector. The fact that the reduction in 2019 is only approximate, and not realistic, clearly indicates the growth in this sector that was achieved even in the following year, despite the fact that it was marked by the consequences of the "closure" of the economy due to the mentioned pandemic. The change in the way and scope of collecting financial reports changed the dynamics of the ratios we have analyzed, so we draw some conclusions on the trends until 2019, and the impact of the COVID-19 pandemic is discussed in a separate part of the text.

The creators of public policies in Serbia should reconsider the policies of very significant incentives for the creation of new economic entities in the light of the limits of Perrett's model, in which there is an optimum at the top of the inverted U, between the number of firms and stable growth (Peretto, 1998). The number

Table 1. Dynamics of Entrepreneurship Sector Performance.

Performance indicator	**2013**	**2014**	**2015**	**2016**	**2017**	**2018**	**2019**	**2020**
Total number of entrepreneurs and small businesses	332,610	340,861	347,879	365,825	385,273	405,520	400,933	405,787
Growth rate of the number of entrepreneurs (%)	0.32	2.48	2.06	5.16	5.32	5.26	−1.13	1.21
Average number of employees	3.41	3.45	3.54	3.54	3.57	3.64	2.81	2.94
Productivity per employee (in 000)	8,834	8,823	8,878	9,206	9,418	9,579	8,607	8,298
Assets per employee (in 000)	13,899	12,155	12,440	12,944	12,846	13,207	10,722	10,816
Net profit per employee (in 000)	−65.09	−145.35	51.41	30.16	170.80	210.22	211.38	191.09

Source: Authors' calculations based on data from Serbian Business Registers Agency (2023).

of entrepreneurs and employees in that sector is an important factor of economic growth, but their excessive fragmentation and retention in the initial stages of the life cycle (birth), without dynamic productivity growth, based on the development and application of R&D results, will make a weak contribution.

The necessity to change something in the sphere of entrepreneurship is evidenced by the data on the trend of productivity in the sector of entrepreneurship, which, despite the described growth, remained almost unchanged. It is perceived that the number of new entrepreneurs affects the reduction of the average number of employees, which indicates a reduction in the competitive power of entrepreneurs, because too many of them remain in the initial development phase for too long. Hamilton (2007) talks about the effects of the increase in the number of firms on specialization, bearing in mind that as a result the market share of each firm decreases through the effect of fragmentation.

In Table 1, we see that the number of employees of entrepreneurs – natural persons is increasing, starting from 2013, from 1.93 to 2.71 employees, while in companies with up to 50 employees, that number is growing very slowly, from 3.9 to 4.18 employees.

In order to analyze the dynamics of the entrepreneurship sector in Serbia, it is useful to refer to the categorization that recognizes entrepreneurial ventures created on the basis of the compulsion-need to generate one's own business in the absence of employment opportunity (Amidžić, Leković, & Ivanović-Đukić, 2022), which we characterize as necessity-driven entrepreneurs (NDE) and entrepreneurial ventures based on opportunities to develop a new product, service, to create a new market, which are the key motives of opportunity-driven entrepreneurs (ODE) (Albulescu & Tămăşilă, 2014; Bosma & Kelley, 2018). In such cases, the need for greater achievement and independence are identified as motivators (Bjekić, Strugar Jelača, Berber, & Aleksić, 2021). Given the mentioned decline in the unemployment rate in Serbia in the observed period and the increase in average wages, the assumption is that the motivation of NDEs to start or stay in business will weaken, while in the future, according to the dynamics in more developed countries, ODE will provide an increasing contribution to growth and development (Amidžić, Leković, & Ivanović-Đukić, 2022; Stephan, Hart, & Drews, 2015). One of the illustrations of the turnaround in the entrepreneurship sector in Serbia is the overview of the development in the ICT sector, which can be found below.

5. Major HILP Events in Serbia During the Last Decade

The most significant HILP events that took place in Serbia in the previous decade were the large floods in May 2014 and the appearance of the COVID-19 virus, which officially began in this region in March 2020, but whose effects and consequences are still present worldwide.

The year 2014 evidenced the highest amount of precipitation in the last few decades in Serbia (Republic Hydrometeorological Service of Serbia, 2014; Vulević, Čudanov, & Kešetović, 2022). During May, it has been raining continuously for several days, which led to an increase in the water level of the rivers and their overflowing, as well as to great material damage and the evacuation of the population, because the floods endangered a huge number of residential and commercial buildings, and significantly threatened the economic infrastructure. This blow was twofold, because on the one hand, it required investments in rehabilitation and reparation of roads and land, reconstruction of buildings and destroyed equipment, and on the other hand, it led to a halt in economic activities, not only at that moment, but also permanently, while the conditions for continuing business were not met again.

It is estimated that the total value of damage and losses caused by floods was 1.53 billion euros, where the mining and energy industry suffered the most (487.7 million euros), followed by agriculture (228 million euros) (World Bank, 2014). Bearing in mind the nature of the mining and energy industry and thus the fact that it is predominantly handled by large companies, the impact of floods on their results will not be analyzed here. On the other hand, when it comes to entrepreneurship, the data collected for the purposes of this research confirm the negative effects of floods on agriculture, especially in certain areas that were directly affected by this natural disaster (Serbian Business Registers Agency, 2023).

A significant drop in the business results of entrepreneurs engaged in agriculture was felt in the Pomoravlje District, where 20,000 hectares of agricultural land were damaged by floods (Pomoravlje District, 2014). In this district, the number of entrepreneurships engaged in this activity did not change significantly compared to the year 2013, but the total income decreased by more than one third, which could not be stabilized even in the following years (Serbian Business Registers Agency, 2023). Similar trends, although not so extreme, were noted in certain parts of Vojvodina, as well as in the Zaječar District.

It is interesting that in the group of entrepreneurs that were particularly affected by floods, there are also those whose main activity is related to tourism. Experts believe that the image of Serbia as a safe destination was damaged, not only in those parts that were directly hit with the floods, and that fact affected the decrease in the interest of foreign tourists in visiting otherwise favorite destinations. Given that the floods occurred after the end of the winter tourist season, the negative effects were particularly felt in regions that are generally popular in the summer months, so Belgrade and Zlatibor suffered great losses because of reduced tourist interest. In Belgrade, there was a slight increase in the number of entrepreneurs engaged in tourism in 2014 compared to 2013, but the income from this activity had significant decline of 27%, while in the Zlatibor District, the number of entrepreneurs remained almost unchanged, but the income has declined by 12% (Serbian Business Registers Agency, 2023). However, from 2015 incomes from tourism in both districts are starting to show a growing trend again.

Less than 6 years later Serbia faced a new HILP challenge. The first cases of coronavirus infection appeared at the end of 2019 in China. Considering the high transferability of the virus and the general unpreparedness to fight it on a global level it spread very quickly to other countries and continents. This virus appeared in Serbia at the beginning of March 2020, and a state of emergency in the country was declared in the middle of the same month. It formally lasted about a month and a half with numerous restrictive measures that included, among other things, a ban on the gathering, reduced working hours, and the curfew in the afternoon and evening hours. Such provisions have redefined the way work was done in most industries, which, combined with the panic over the health situation, has left its mark on economic frameworks and business results.

In view of the ban on movement and gatherings, the hospitality and tourism sectors experienced a special blow. The hospitality industry was particularly affected by the fact that even after the cancelation of the state of emergency many restrictive measures affecting these activities remained on, but there was also the psychological barrier of a significant part of the population which avoided spending time in closed space because of fear of infection. This branch is the only one with a significant decrease in the number of employees, since the objects were closed for a long time or were working in significantly changed circumstances, which became unsustainable for many of them (Institute for Development and Innovation, 2021). The situation was improved to some extent by the fact that the weather conditions were favorable, so many restaurants and cafes used the opportunity to provide their services in open spaces, but the fact is that despite this, the financial blow was huge.

The best indicator of the decline in the performance of the hospitality sector in the group of entrepreneurs is the situation in Belgrade, which, apart from being the capital of the country, is also known for its rich gastronomic offer and evening entertainment. In 2020, however, this sector in Belgrade experienced a drastic drop in business income of 26%, which additionally continued in 2021 with the new wave of the coronavirus, though to a significantly smaller extent of 5% (Serbian Business Registers Agency, 2023).

On the other hand, the coronavirus has influenced many hospitality organizations to start thinking about redefining their business model, so a large number of them have started to offer a delivery service for their products. In those conditions, companies for the delivery of food (and other basic products soon after that) took advantage of the opportunity and gained significant benefits due to the fact that people were prevented from moving and making purchases in person.

Tourism has also suffered a serious blow in the first year of the coronavirus, but, unlike the hospitality industry, it has stabilized very quickly, so that already in 2021 the value of business income returned to the period before the pandemic or even exceeded it, and this is largely a consequence of the fact that many citizens of Serbia decided to spend their vacations in their own country, while the conditions of travel were consolidated at the global level, so Belgrade became a popular tourist destination for foreigners again. In 2020, in Belgrade, there was a slight increase in the number of entrepreneurs engaged in tourism. However, their income declined by as much as 36%, but in 2021 they managed to return to the values achieved in 2019. In the Zlatibor District, the income in 2020 had declined by 8%, but in 2021 it has increased by as much as 32% (Serbian Business Registers Agency, 2023).

When it comes to industries that have experienced expansion with the emergence of the coronavirus, it is necessary to highlight the IT sector, where a significant increase in activity and improvement in business results are noted, both at the level of the capital city and in other regions of Serbia, which will be discussed in the following part of this chapter. This is certainly a consequence of the trends in this sphere, which is constantly developing at the global level, but it took on a different shape in the conditions of the coronavirus pandemic.

Finally, when summarizing the impact of the coronavirus on the business results of companies in Serbia, it can be concluded that it was rather negative, and it has significantly slowed down the country's economic development. On the other hand, a series of measures adopted by the Republic's Government very soon after the start of the pandemic had a significant effect on mitigating these consequences. The government introduced 3 packages of measures with a total value of almost 6 billion euros, where the first two included a combination of tax policy measures, direct payments, and measures to maintain the liquidity of economic entities, and the third was aimed at tourism (Institute for Development and Innovation, 2021). Particularly, significant measure was the provision of three minimum net wages for all employees in micro-, small-, and medium-sized enterprises and entrepreneurs, and for many of them, it was the only way to maintain continuity in the payment of wages to their employees, reduce costs and create conditions for more permanent stabilization. Consequently, although the number of newly opened entrepreneurs and companies decreased in 2020 compared to 2019, the data indicate that the number of closed entrepreneurs and companies also decreased (Serbian Business Registers Agency, 2023), which implies that these measures were successful and justified, and that made it possible to maintain economic stability even in difficult conditions not only for business, but also for everyday life, thus creating conditions for further economic development. These measures were particularly significant when we take into consideration the entire economic situation in the country, so Serbia in 2020 was among the least affected countries in Europe with a GDP drop of 1.1% (OECD, 2021), while the GDP would increase by 7.4% during the following year (World Bank, 2023). Also, when observing the financial results, both in the group of entrepreneurs and in the group of SMEs, there can be noted an increasing trend in the value of business income and net profit in the previous three years (Serbian Business Registers Agency, 2023), which indicates the justification of the measures that were taken and their role in achieving stability and economic growth of the state.

6. Overview of the IT Entrepreneurship in Serbia

IT has constantly been among fastest growing industries in the Serbian economy for years, as shown in Fig. 1, thanks to the combination of numerous factors. Education for IT jobs is at a prominent level and is developing, with great support and investments from the state, which provide staff for the realization of these jobs. The general level of knowledge of the English language is high, therefore also among the people who perform this activity, which enables them to work for foreign companies or with foreign clients, and this is very significant for any type of concrete work that belongs to IT. On the other hand, the general level of wages compared to the countries of the European Union, and especially North America (USA and Canada) or Australia, still makes Serbia a very suitable market for outsourcing jobs that can be carried out remotely, which creates a huge space for

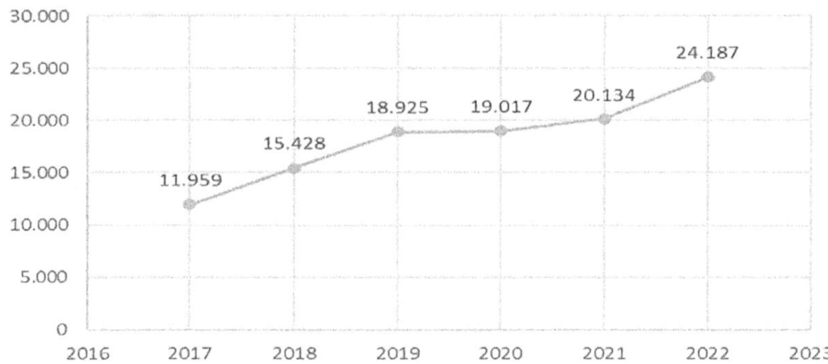

Fig. 1. Total Number of IT Legal Entities in Serbia. *Source*: Authors' illustration based on data from Serbian Business Registers Agency (2023).

opening IT companies that will offer these services in foreign markets and for the opening of representative offices of foreign IT companies in Serbia.

IT entrepreneurship is recognized as an important pillar for the development of the entire Serbian economy, which is why the Council for Innovative Entrepreneurship and Information Technologies was formed in 2017. The very fact that the prime minister at the time was appointed president of the council speaks volumes about Serbia's strategic determination regarding the development of the IT sector. Thanks to the strategic recognition of the importance of this topic, numerous initiatives have been implemented at the state level in the past few years, which can be classified into several categories (CIEIT, 2020).

The first concerns the support for education. Concrete activities included the introduction of subjects that increase digital literacy in the first cycle of primary education, as well as specialized IT subjects in the second cycle of primary education and high schools. The schools have also introduced special IT departments. The IT offices in schools are equipped with computers with the help of state funds. Also, the development of numerous undergraduate and master's degree programs in the areas of creative industries, programming, IT, data analysis, and similar fields is supported. It is also planned to increase the capacity of technical faculties through an increased number of students.

Additionally, investments in the construction of innovation infrastructure are provided. This includes buildings of technical faculties, institutes where innovative activities are studied, then data centers, as well as science and technology parks, and regional start-up centers. Schools have received new computers and secure internet connections. Entrepreneurship Portal has also been created, where relevant and updated information about all current support programs available to small- and medium-sized enterprises and entrepreneurs can be found. The plan is also to build a national telecommunications network.

The next one is about tax incentives. The founders of new companies that conduct innovative activities have the option of being exempt from paying taxes and contributions based on the founder's salary for a period of 36 months. Also, companies that invest capital in a newly founded company that performs innovative activities are enabled to reduce their tax liability in the amount of 30% of the investment.

Furthermore, the Government has adopted the amendments to the Law on Business Companies that introduced the right to acquire shares, which was not possible until then. This significantly expanded the possibilities of cooperation of registered companies with other stakeholders, investors, and consultants above all, but also opened up space for rewarding employees through the acquisition of rights to a share in the company's ownership. At the same time, through the Law on Citizens' Income Tax, it is defined that income in the form of ownership is exempt from taxes and contributions until the moment of alienation.

The combination of described market factors and government measures led to the continuous growth of IT entrepreneurial ventures in Serbia in recent years. By the term IT entrepreneurial venture, we mean IT legal entity up to 50 employees. The regulation in Serbia allows several institutional forms of organizing legal entities. In addition to the standard forms that exist in most states, the limited liability company (LLC) and the joint stock company (JSC), entrepreneurial agencies are very common. So entrepreneurial venture can either have a legal form of entrepreneurial agency or micro or small company registered as LLC or JSC.

The agencies are popular because the range and volume of administrative work that must be performed when running a legal entity is often reduced, but primarily because flat-rate taxation is possible for certain activities. This type of business drastically reduces allocations for taxes and contributions if the monthly income exceeds the corresponding amounts. The practice that has existed for many years consisted in the fact that natural persons do not conclude an employment contract with an employer, but rather register as entrepreneurial agency, and then conclude contracts for the provision of services with the principal, who is essentially the employer. This way contractor manages to secure significant savings on gross salaries, while the employer receives higher net income at the same time. Such practice was particularly widespread in the IT sector, as presented in Fig. 2.

The possibility of creating such contractual relationships was one of the pillars of the development of the IT industry in Serbia, as well as significantly higher average wages in the IT sector compared to other industries. The motive for such a business and legal arrangement was legal tax optimization, since the tax and contributions on earnings are significantly higher, compared to the tax and contributions on flat income. However, in addition to tax optimization, there are other reasons for this behavior, which often consist of the desire of persons engaged in sought-after occupations on the market to be independent in choosing the persons with whom they will cooperate, that is, not to be tied to the employer through employment.

Amendments to the Personal Income Tax Act from January 1, 2020, introduced a test of independence of entrepreneurs with flat-rate taxation, with the aim of preventing evasion of establishing an employment relationship by applying the described practice. The law defines nine criteria that indicate the lack of independence of the entrepreneur in relation to the client, and if it is determined that in a specific case at least five of those nine criteria are fulfilled, the income

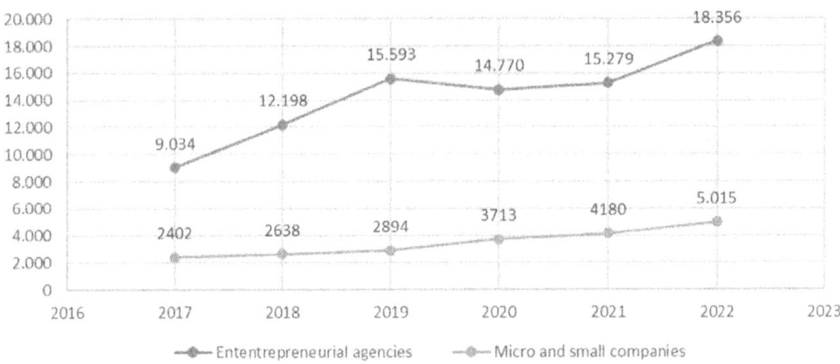

Fig. 2. IT Entrepreneurial Agencies Versus Small IT Companies in Serbia. *Source*: Authors' illustration based on data from Serbian Business Registers Agency (2023).

that the entrepreneur receives from that client will be taxed as regular income, and not as income from self-employment activities (Paragraf, 2020).

In Fig. 2, it is notable that the number of IT entrepreneurial agencies declined in 2020 due to new legislation. Although the introduction of such a test appears negative for IT entrepreneurship at first glance, it did not slow down the growth of the IT industry as it was accompanied by additional measures to encourage employment. Namely, at the same time, tax benefits for the employment of persons who were not previously employed began to apply. These reliefs included exemption from the calculation and payment of part of the obligations for the calculated wages, namely:

- during 2020: 70% of taxes and 100% of contributions;
- during 2021: 65% of taxes and 95% of contributions;
- during 2022: 60% of taxes and 90% of contributions.

The reliefs also began to be valid from January 1, 2020, and although they were supposed to last until the end of 2022, they were extended until 2025. What is significant is that all persons who, until the time of employment, had entrepreneurial agencies considered newly employed. Therefore, all employees in the IT sector who used the benefits of the cooperation model described earlier could transfer to their employers for the same net earnings as they had, while the costs of their engagement for the employer did not change.

Thanks to these facilities, IT entrepreneurship in Serbia continued to grow, and the observed decrease in the number of agencies actually spilled over into IT companies. Namely, the previous graph shows only trends related to the total number of entities, but not the number of newly opened entities, which can be seen in Fig. 3. It is obvious that in 2020 due to the test of independence certain number of agencies whose owners wanted to stay independent entrepreneurs or were working for principals outside Serbia was simply converted to companies, mostly LLCs.

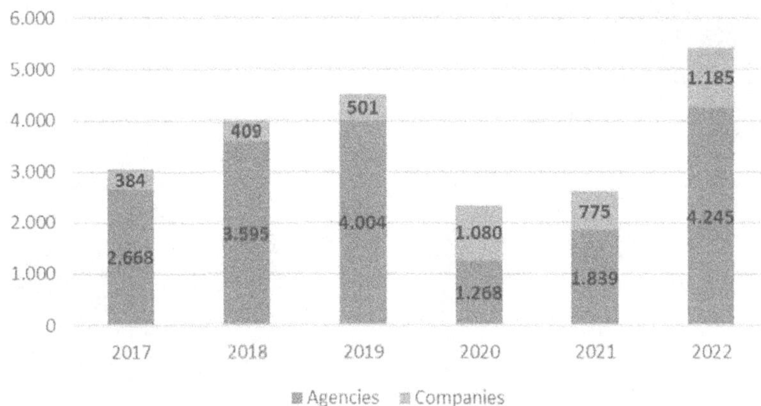

Fig. 3. Number of Newly Registered IT Legal Entities Per Year.
Source: Authors' illustration based on data from Serbian Business Registers Agency (2023).

On the other hand, some ex-entrepreneurs started working for their old contractors, which resulted in the increased number of employees in micro and small IT companies as presented in Fig. 4. The entrepreneurial agencies are also allowed to hire employees, but data about the number of employees in agencies are not available. However, in IT sector in Serbia, the most widespread practice is that only the owner works in the IT agency. Having that in mind, it can be concluded that entrepreneurial ventures within IT sector in Serbia employ more than 50,000 people, while total number of employees in IT sector is estimated to around 120,000 in 2022.

In general, Serbian IT industry has been constantly rising in previous years. Fig. 5 shows the revenues generated by IT companies, excluding entrepreneurial

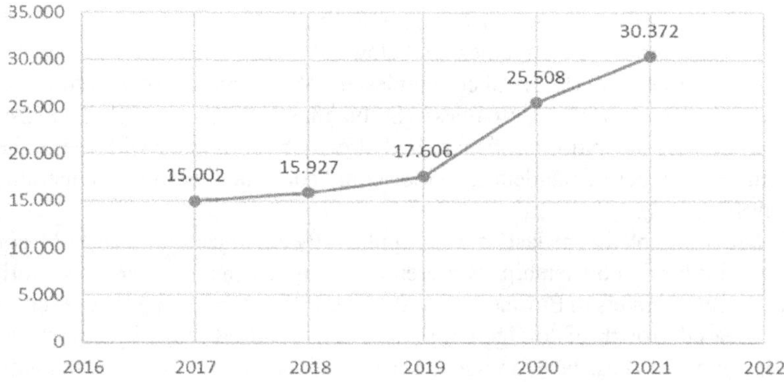

Fig. 4. Total Number of Employees in Micro and Small IT Companies Per Year. *Source*: Authors' illustration based on data from Serbian Business Registers Agency (2023).

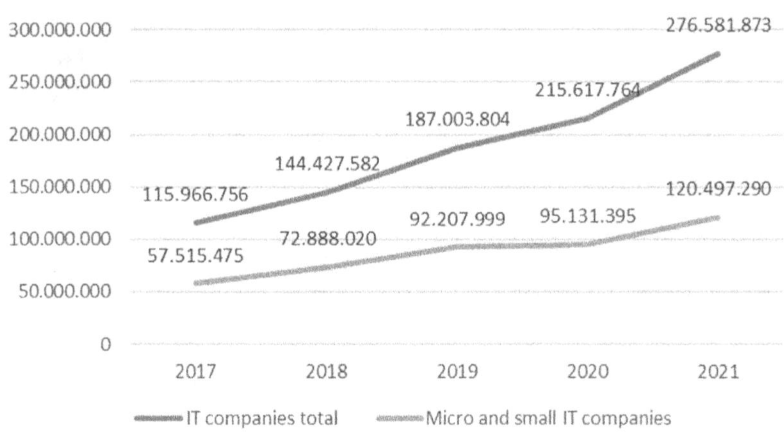

Fig. 5. Total Revenues of All IT Companies and Micro and Small IT Companies in Serbia. *Source*: Authors' illustration based on data from Serbian Business Registers Agency (2023).

agencies as the data for them are not available. However, the revenues of most agencies are below €50,000 per year, since in other case, they would lose the option of flat-rate taxation, which is the main benefit of having a form of agency instead of LLC.

The data show that described HILP events had no negative influence, as many companies were forced to quickly develop new methods of communication and work, and to adapt to the new situation, which turned out to be a good practice, so many of them retained it even in the period when the coronavirus began to weaken. Computer equipment and related systems have become not only crucial, but in many cases also the only tool for the regular work, so the growth and the development of this sector can be observed in the years of the pandemic at the level of whole country. Furthermore, Serbian IT mostly refers to software and services, hardware companies are below 5% in the total number of IT entities, and if just micro and small companies are observers, this share additionally drops. This means that IT companies in Serbia mostly did not face global logistics issues, and that the majority of them had already been familiar with the concept of remote work before pandemic, so they could continue their normal operations relatively quickly.

What is notable in the last year is significantly enhanced number of IT companies with foreign ownership, as presented in Fig. 6. The main cause is another HILP event, conflicts in Europe, which triggered migrations of people. Of course, the increased growth of foreign companies is not caused solely by migration in Europe, most of these new foreign companies appeared as a logical continuation of previous trends when it comes to the number of IT legal entities in Serbia of foreign ownership, but they definitely had an impact.

As for the activities for which foreign companies are registered, these are most often computer programming, consulting activities in the field of IT, specialized

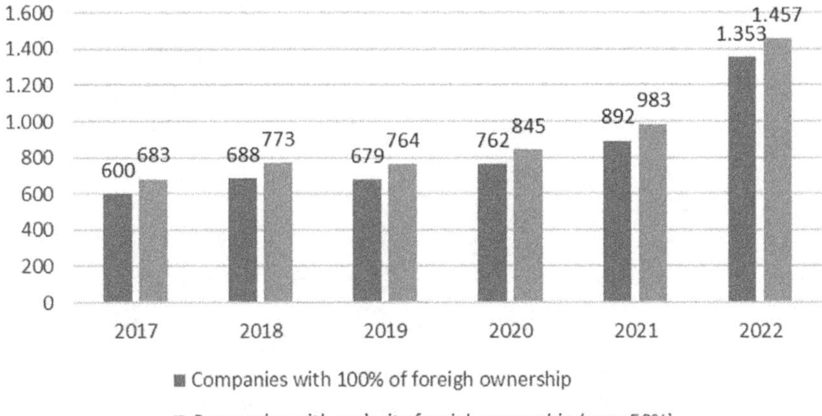

Fig. 6. Number of IT Companies with Foreign Ownership.
Source: Authors' illustration based on data from Serbian Business Registers Agency (2023).

design activities, activities of advertising agencies, etc. Recent migrations obviously reflected positively on the IT sector in Serbia, but it is yet to be seen how this new HILP is going to affect Serbian economy in total.

7. Impact of FDI on Entrepreneurship in Serbia

According to data from the World Investment Report (WIR) for 2022, Serbia is the absolute leader in attracting FDI among the countries of the Western Balkans (WIR includes Albania, Bosnia and Herzegovina, Montenegro, North Macedonia, and Serbia in the group of countries of the Western Balkans). The development of Serbia's economy demonstrates a significant connection with FDI, bearing in mind that in recent years the participation of FDI in GDP has expanded to the level of almost 7%. During the period from 2007 to 2023, Serbia attracted more than EUR 41 billion of FDI, with a particularly growing trend in the last 5 years (Fig. 7).

The state created and used a wide range of subsidies and incentives in order to maintain such a trend in the FDI growth (Development Agency of Serbia, 2023), implicitly taking the view that FDI contributes to economic growth and the development of entrepreneurship, while in public policies, FDI incentives are linked to increased employment, with increased incentives for investment in high technologies (Vasa & Angeloska, 2020), as well as other economic performances of the country. Our determination regarding the impact of FDI is also based on observations regarding the impact of FDI in the area of the countries belonging to the Visegrad group (V4) (Bobenič, Bruothová, Kubíková, & Ručinský, 2018) and the entire Southeast Europe.

On a global scale, it is reported that the two most common forms of incentives are tax holidays (50%) and direct subsidies (40%) (Delević, 2020), which is

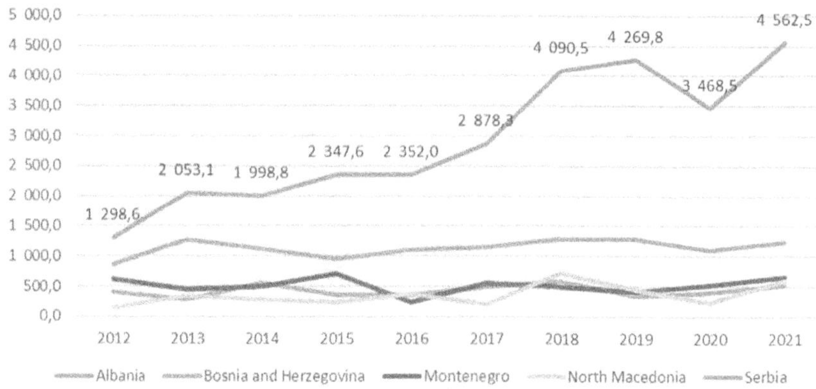

Fig. 7. FDI Inflow in the Countries of the Western Balkans by Year in Millions of dollars. *Source*: Authors' illustration based on data from United Nations UNCTAD (2022).

very similar to the policy of attracting FDI in the Republic of Serbia, but there remains a need to investigate whether and to what extent FDI contributes to the growth of average productivity, the evolution of employees and the technological level of the domestic economy (Burger, Jaklič, & Rojec, 2012) as well as to the entrepreneurship.

Our understanding of the contribution of FDI to economic development and entrepreneurship is based on research evidence that FDI contributes to the initiation of new businesses (Ayyagari & Kosová, 2010), the motivation of domestic entrepreneurs in the phase of total early-stage entrepreneurial activity (TEA), and established business ownership rate (EBOR) (Albulescu & Tămăşilă, 2014), on the one hand, and increasing the competitiveness of existing companies on the domestic and international markets (Desbordes & Franssen, 2019), on the other hand. The positive effect of FDI on the performance of domestic companies is seen through connections with domestic suppliers (vertical backward linkage), subcontracting of domestic suppliers on the domestic or international market, as well as the possibility to increase the export of complementary products of domestic producers, but also to improve the productivity and competitiveness of domestic companies based on "diffusion of new technologies and management practices" (Apostolov, 2017; De Mello, 1997; He & Tien-Liu, 2019).

On the other hand, in the conclusions of all research on the impact of FDI on entrepreneurship in the host countries, the risks and often real damages from FDI are also pointed out. They could crowd out domestic entrepreneurs through their selections in product and labor markets, they can make it difficult to access or increase the prices of local resources and wages to employees (De Backer & Sleuwaegen, 2003), can make it difficult to access state incentives for the development of entrepreneurship and employment, increase technological barriers (Albulescu & Tămăşilă, 2014) and more, which contributes to the effect of crowding out local entrepreneurship. In addition, some FDI use the country as a platform for their export-oriented activities, revealing weak linkages with the domestic market (Barbosa & Eiriz, 2009) while trying to take advantage of low labor costs and local resources. The effect of crowding out local entrepreneurs due to FDI is short term and refers to NDE entrepreneurs (Ha, Chu, Nguyen, Nguyen, & Nguyen, 2021).

The general conclusion is that the impact of FDI on the entrepreneurship of the domestic economy is ambivalent, and especially depends on the ability of local firms and entrepreneurs to absorb benefits from advanced technologies and managerial practices (Meyer & Sinani, 2009; Moran, 1999), which deserves further and deeper analysis, especially of the influences of FDI that have the character of Greenfield investments compared to mergers and acquisitions (M&A).

There are prevailing views that Greenfield investments have a predominantly positive effect on the domestic economy, increasing employment and capital flows, while the effect of FDI in the form of M&A is not significant, or even has a negative effect on local entrepreneurship (He & Tien-Liu, 2019) since they do not always bring new technologies, new export markets or changes in managerial practices, they are exclusively financially motivated (Kim, 2009), thereby increasing the risks of corruption and mismatch of cultural characteristics (Estrin, Hülya Danakol, Reynolds, & Weitzel, 2014).

The most harmful type of M&A was identified as FDI that was accompanied by the conclusion of contracts with elements of protection against competition on the domestic market and burdened with high domestic content, mandatory joint venture, and technology-sharing requirements (Moran, 1999). M&A can be associated with the activation of potential that is hidden within the low-productivity local companies with a large number of employees and a long tradition in business.

Evidence of FDI in the form of M&A can be seen in the examples of the takeover of the iron factory in Smederevo by HBIS GROUP (Smederevo-2017) and the mining and smelting basin of copper RTB Bor (Bor-2018) by the Zijin company, both of which are Chinese-owned. Each of the companies has more than five thousand employees, and these are the two largest exporters from the Republic of Serbia, which until the takeover by the new owners were among the biggest unprofitable companies. It is also useful for comparison that these are companies working in the metallurgy branch, which are large exporters and located in municipalities of similar size, about 100,000 inhabitants.

From the data in Table 1, it can be seen that the above-mentioned M&A did not trigger the "crowding out" effect, that growth continued in the entrepreneurial sphere, measured by the number of registered entrepreneurs, companies, total and average turnover, but not in the average number of employees, which corresponds with the trends of entrepreneurship in all of Serbia. The fact that both companies increased the number of employees, especially Zijin (more than 1,000 employees), as well as the fact that the average wages in Bor, after Belgrade, are the highest in Serbia (about €1,000 net), still did not have noticeable negative effects on the regional entrepreneurship sector, predominantly on NDE. Part of the effects was achieved by connecting the local economy to the global production network of foreign investors. Tens of thousands of FDI in the world testify to similar impacts on the regional development of entrepreneurship (Park, 2018).

Table 2. Entrepreneurship Dynamics on the Territory of Selected Cities.

Performance indicator	City	2013	2014	2015	2016	2017	2018	2019	2020
Growth rate of the number of entrepreneurs	Serbia	0.32%	2.48%	2.06%	5.16%	5.32%	5.26%	−1.13%	1.21%
	Bor		9.65%	4.40%	8.81%	14.79%	5.83%	6.67%	7.61%
	Smederevo		2.94%	7.79%	7.05%	7.25%	6.76%	8.06%	5.33%
	Pančevo		5.34%	8.04%	6.83%	6.49%	5.65%	7.97%	9.35%
	Kragujevac		2.87%	8.13%	9.45%	9.42%	8.52%	10.41%	7.86%
	Belgrade		5.73%	8.61%	8.19%	8.98%	8.99%	8.51%	9.49%
Average number of employees	Serbia	3.41	3.45	3.54	3.54	3.57	3.64	2.81	2.94
	Bor	4.71	4.57	4.56	4.18	3.86	3.80	3.84	3.59
	Smederevo	4.90	4.86	4.78	4.94	5.09	4.99	4.87	4.69
	Pančevo	5.07	4.83	4.85	4.82	4.81	4.89	4.72	4.59
	Kragujevac	5.94	5.85	5.79	5.72	5.79	5.72	5.66	5.41
	Belgrade	14.50	13.84	14.24	14.19	13.63	13.37	12.85	12.49

Source: Authors' calculations based on data from Serbian Business Registers Agency (2023).

Greenfield FDI has the potential to increase the productivity of domestic entrepreneurs and firms, especially if it is knowledge-based FDI, which can benefit local competitors, research centers, universities, and entrepreneurs with high development competencies (Castellani & Pieri, 2016), while it can reduce the competitiveness of the region from which foreign investments come from, if it is about the relocation of R&D activities outside the home country. Pančevo was included in the list of towns for comparison of the investments made by high-tech companies in the automotive industry, ZF Friedrihshafen, and Brosse-Germany in 2020 since the structure and dynamics of entrepreneurship before FDI is very important for assessing the potential of investment goals achievement.

Deepening the analysis of the impact of FDI on entrepreneurship in a country or in some region must also include the localization of production and service capacities in a geographical sense. While some scientific papers analyze the impact of FDI on several economic performances of the region's development (Getzner & Moroz, 2020), others specifically examine the impact on employment (Delević, 2020) and linking of the region into global value chains (Crescenzi & Iammarino, 2017).

The creation of FDI accumulation points within the country increases differences in the development of regions (Mallick & Zdražil, 2018), which are more pronounced in less developed countries. By conducting an FDI incentive policy that is sensitive to differences in terms of development in the regions in the long term, it is possible to achieve equalization effects and avoid demographic drains, as the most difficult to remove consequences of unequal development. On the other hand, the cities themselves are trying to improve the ways of attracting FDI, taking into account the evidence that regions with a higher rate of starting new businesses (entrepreneurs) show higher growth rates in the later period (Audretsch & Fritsch, 2002), even after the withdrawal of the foreign investor or his poor performance (FCA Serbia-Kragujevac). The data on the economic growth of Kragujevac's economy after several years of decline in business results are very clear evidence.

On an international scale, choosing a location for FDI is not just a matter of choosing between several countries. Models of location selection between different regions and cities themselves are increasingly being developed, which include analysis of absorptive capacity, availability of competent executors, networking opportunities with local firms and entrepreneurs, and more, and this is especially evidenced for the knowledge-based FDI (Belderbos, Du, & Slangen, 2020). In this sense, the application of an endogenous strategy of entrepreneurship development (Romer, 1986) is a prerequisite for attracting high-tech FDI, which has a far greater impact on economic growth than FDI which primarily provides employment. In order to attract them, the strategies of FDI incentives like education, innovation, research, etc. are needed, which do not provide a short-term effect, but cumulatively and in the long term ensure accelerated and sustainable economic growth and development. Research shows that company success is in correlation with, for example, entrepreneur's creative abilities (Peljko, Jordan, Jeraj, Todorović, & Marič, 2017), openness, and entrepreneurial curiosity (Jeraj, Marič, Todorović, Čudanov, & Komazec, 2015), and such factors that need to

Table 3. Improved Competitiveness of Entrepreneurship Sector in Selected Cities.

Performance indicator	City	2013	2014	2015	2016	2017	2018	2019	2020
Productivity per employee (in 000)	Serbia	8,834	8,823	8,878	9,206	9,418	9,579	8,607	8,298
	Bor	8,995	8,182	10,416	9,878	9,930	8,680	8,841	10,719
	Smederevo	7,574	8,480	8,450	9,053	9,702	10,229	9,732	8,574
	Pančevo	9,057	8,854	8,082	7,670	8,660	7,639	8,256	8,562
	Kragujevac	8,676	8,217	7,788	7,885	7,542	7,249	7,181	7,172
	Belgrade	9,262	9,582	9,479	9,845	10,424	10,741	11,230	10,772
Assets per employee (in 000)	Serbia	13,899	12,155	12,440	12,944	12,846	13,207	10,722	10,816
	Bor	8,207	7,712	7,715	7,747	7,994	7,607	8,528	8,573
	Smederevo	9,556	8,904	8,514	9,504	10,231	10,912	11,199	10,675
	Pančevo	10,979	9,100	10,047	10,572	9,353	9,809	13,139	13,404
	Kragujevac	18,849	9,225	9,044	9,316	10,216	9,944	9,685	10,823
	Belgrade	15,902	15,533	16,293	16,626	16,595	16,790	17,508	17,718
Net profit per employee (in 000)	Serbia	−65.09	−145.35	51.41	30.16	170.80	210.22	211.38	191.09
	Bor	−913.39	−811.25	49.11	241.64	361.01	380.74	434.86	355.72
	Smederevo	48.05	213.01	325.32	390.42	−120.79	32.45	−4,214.94	252.58
	Pančevo	11.32	71.11	0.01	104.53	−197.88	27.97	183.74	122.00
	Kragujevac	171.81	−535.76	−197.62	209.07	375.43	366.89	397.23	339.96
	Belgrade	57.99	−58.82	278.21	275.38	413.53	414.02	370.68	354.24

Source: Authors' calculations based on data from Serbian Business Registers Agency (2023).

be addressed through educational system and innovation inducement, which is a long-term process.

8. Conclusions

Global economic trends indicate that the development of entrepreneurship and small enterprises is in a special focus, which is not surprising considering their important role in the economy of the largest number of countries, which especially applies to the developing countries. Bearing in mind the advantages of entrepreneurship, which are reflected in flexibility and easier adaptation to changes on the one hand, but also innovation and the possibility of creating new or different business solutions on the other hand, it is obvious that their importance in the development of the economic stability of a country is exceptional. This is also recognized in Serbia, where the preconditions for the development of entrepreneurship are constantly being improved. This is supported by the adoption of numerous strategies and other documents at the state level that are important for this part of the economy, as well as the establishment of many organizations whose main objective is to create networks between entrepreneurs and provide support for their growth. Serbia also encourages entrepreneurship through numerous tax and other financial measures that facilitate the establishment of startups. In addition, cooperation between innovative enterprises and science is encouraged through technology centers, which also positively affects the entrepreneurial ideas in the country. Consequently, in the last decade, there can be noted significant increase in the number of entrepreneurs and small enterprises, as well as in the total number of their employees. It is also possible to observe a generally stable trend of income growth in this segment of the Serbian economy.

In this chapter, we emphasized that the growth in the number of entrepreneurs was higher than the growth in the number of employees in that sector. Also, there was a very small increase in productivity and value of assets per employee, which indicates that the growth of the entrepreneurship sector is not followed by the improvement of competitiveness in comparison to the rest of the economy.

Growth in the entrepreneurship sector was partially threatened under the influence of two major HILP events (floods in 2014 and the coronavirus pandemic in 2020), but it can be concluded that Serbia has successfully coped with these challenges. The measures adopted by the Government of Serbia in order to reduce the negative impact of these HILP events helped a large number of entrepreneurs and small businesses to "survive" the shocks caused by them. At the time of the coronavirus pandemic, it was particularly noticeable that there is growth in the number of services, employees, and turnover in the sphere of IT entrepreneurship.

Finally, it should be said that the economic growth of Serbia is significantly related to the growth of FDI, which affects the development of entrepreneurship, the start of new businesses in the investment allocation regions, the engagement of domestic companies in global production and supply chains, either in the role of suppliers or subcontractors of some specific services. FDI, however, to a certain extent also bring risks for the development of entrepreneurship considering that they influence the increase in the prices of local resources, services, average wages, competitiveness in the employment of new executors, the unavailability of incentives aimed at attracting foreign investments, etc. Potentially bigger losers due to the impact of FDI are NDEs, while the number of ODEs and their competitiveness is boosted through the regional or global networks initiated with foreign investments.

References

Aghion, P., & Howitt, P. (1998). A Schumpeterian perspective on growth and competition. In F. M. Coricelli (Ed.), *New theories in growth and development* (pp. 9–49). London: Palgrave Macmillan.

Albulescu, C., & Tămăşilă, M. (2014). The impact of FDI on entrepreneurship in the European countries. *Procedia-Social and Behavioral Sciences*, *124*, 219–228.

Amidžić, R., Leković, B., & Ivanović-Đukić, M. (2022). Factors affecting opportunity and necessity-driven intentions of entrepreneurs: The case of south east Europe. *Teme*, *46*(1), 129–144.

Apostolov, M. (2017). The impact of FDI on the performance and entrepreneurship of domestic firms. *Journal of International Entrepreneurship*, *15*(4), 390–415.

Audretsch, D. B., & Fritsch, M. (2002). Growth regimes over time and space. *Regional Studies*, *36*(2), 113–124.

Ayyagari, M., & Kosová, R. (2010). Does FDI facilitate domestic entry? Evidence from the Czech Republic. *Review of International Economics*, *18*(1), 14–29.

Barbosa, N., & Eiriz, V. (2009). The role of inward foreign direct investment on entrepreneurship. *International Entrepreneurship and Management Journal*, *5*, 319–339.

Belderbos, R., Du, H. S., & Slangen, A. (2020). When do firms choose global cities as foreign investment locations within countries? The roles of contextual distance, knowledge intensity, and target-country experience. *Journal of World Business*, *55*(1), 1–40.

Bjekić, R., Strugar Jelača, M., Berber, N., & Aleksić, M. (2021). Factors affecting entrepreneurial intentions of faculty students. *Management: Journal of Sustainable Business and Management Solutions in Emerging Economies*, *26*(2), 1–14.

Bobenič, H. A., Bruothová, M., Kubíková, Z., & Ru⊠inský, R. (2018). Determinants of foreign direct investment inflows: A case of the Visegrad countries. *Journal of International Studies*, *11*(2), 222–235.

Bosma, N., & Kelley, D. (2018). *Global Entrepreneurship Monitor – 2018/2019 global report*. Retrieved from https://www.gemconsortium.org/file/open?fileId=50213

Burger, A., Jakli⊠, A., & Rojec, M. (2012). The effectiveness of investment incentives: The Slovenian FDI co-financing grant scheme. *Post-Communist Economies*, *24*(3), 383–401.

Burke, A., & van Stel, A. (2009). *The entrepreneurial adjustment process in is equilibrium*. Amsterdam: Tinbergen Institute.

Castellani, D., & Pieri, F. (2016). Outward investments and productivity: Evidence from European regions. *Regional Studies*, *50*(12), 1945–1964.

CIEIT. (2020). The plan for the year 2020 with the annual report on the priorities and activities for 2019, the goals of state administration bodies and government services for the improvement of the IT sector in Serbia. Retrieved from https://www.srbija.gov.rs/extfile/sr/448737/plan-za-2020-sa-izvestajem-za-2019.pdf

Crescenzi, R., & Iammarino, S. (2017). Global investments and regional development trajectories: The missing links. *Regional Studies*, *51*(1), 97–115.

De Backer, K., & Sleuwaegen, L. (2003). Does foreign direct investment crowd out domestic entrepreneurship? *Review of Industrial Organization*, *22*, 67–84.

De Mello, L. R., Jr. (1997). Foreign direct investment in developing countries and growth: A selective survey. *Journal of Development Studies*, *34*(1), 1–34.

Delević, U. (2020). Employment and state incentives in transition economies: are subsidies for FDI ineffective? The case of Serbia. *Transnational Corporations*, *27*(2), 31–63.

Desbordes, R., & Franssen, L. (2019). Foreign direct investment and productivity: A cross-country, multisector analysis. *Asian Development Review*, *36*(1), 54–79.

Development Agency of Serbia. (2023). Retrieved from https://ras.gov.rs/invest-in-serbia/why-serbia/financial-benefits-and-incentives

Estrin, S., Hülya Danakol, S., Reynolds, P., & Weitzel, U. (2014). *Foreign direct investment and domestic entrepreneurship: Blessing or curse?* CEP Discussion Papers dp1268, Centre for Economic Performance, LSE, London.

Getzner, M., & Moroz, S. (2020). Regional development and foreign direct investment in transition countries: a case-study for regions in Ukraine. *Post-Communist Economies*, *32*(6), 813–832.

Ha, T. S., Chu, V. T., Nguyen, M. T. T., Nguyen, D. H. T., & Nguyen, A. N. T. (2021). The impact of Greenfield investment on domestic entrepreneurship. *Journal of Innovation and Entrepreneurship*, *10*, 1–16.

Hamilton, B. (2007). Book review: Economic development through entrepreneurship. *International Small Business Journal*, *25*(5), 568–570.

He, Q., & Tien-Liu, T.-K. (2019). The impact of FDI on entrepreneurship in European countries: Mechanism and strength. *Journal of Advanced Computational Intelligence and Intelligent Informatics*, *23*(4), 649–657.

Institute for Development and Innovation. (2021). *Efekti ekonomskih mera za ublažavanje negativnih posledica COVID-19 na privredu*. Beograd: NALED.

Jeraj, M., Marič, M., Todorović, I., Čudanov, M., & Komazec, S. (2015). The role of openness and entrepreneurial curiosity in Company's growth. *Amfiteatru Economic Journal*, *17*(38), 371–389.

Kim, Y.-H. (2009). Cross-border M&A vs. Greenfield FDI: Economic integration and its welfare impact. *Journal of Policy Modeling*, *31*(1), 87–101.

Krivokapić, J., & Jaško, O. (2015). Global indicators analysis and consultancy experience insights into correlation between entrepreneurial activities and business environment. *Amfiteatru Economic Journal*, *17*(38), 291–307.

Local Economic Development Office of Niš. (2023). Retrieved from https://investnis.rs/srlat/poslovno-okruzenje/podsticaji-privrednicima/

Mallick, J., & Zdražil, P. (2018). FDI and regional income disparity in the Czech Republic. *Scientific Papers of the University of Pardubice*, *25*(43), 159–171.

Meyer, K. E., & Sinani, E. (2009). When and where does foreign direct investment generate positive spillovers? A meta-analysis. *Journal of International Business Studies*, *40*, 1075–1094.

Moran, T. H. (1999, September 20–21). Foreign direct investment and development: A reassessment of the evidence and policy implications. *OECD conference on the role of international investment in development, corporate responsibilities and the OECD*. Paris: OECD Publications Service.

National Bank of Serbia. (2023). *Key macroeconomic indicators*. Belgrade: National Bank of Serbia.

OECD. (2021). The Covid-19 crisis in Serbia. Retrieved from https://www.oecd.org/south-east-europe/COVID-19-Crisis-in-Serbia.pdf. Accessed on February 25, 2023.

Paragraf. (2020). Test samostalnosti preduzetnika u skladu sa Zakonom o porezu na dohodak građana. Retrieved from https://www.paragraf.rs/100pitanja/posao/test-samostalnosti-za-preduzetnike-kriterijumi-objasnjenja-u-skladu-sa-zakonom.html#1. Accessed on February 25, 2023.

Park, J. (2018). *The effects of foreign direct investment on regional growth and productivity*. Asian Growth Research Institute. Retrieved from https://ideas.repec.org/p/agi/wpaper/00000149.html. Accessed on February 26, 2023.

Peljko, Ž., Jordan, G., Jeraj, M., Todorović, I., & Marič, M. (2017). Do entrepreneur's creative abilities influence company's growth? *Management: Journal of Sustainable Business and Management Solutions in Emerging Economies*, *22*(1), 25–35.

Peretto, P. F. (1998). Technological change, market rivalry, and the evolution of the capitalist engine of growth. *Journal of Economic Growth*, *3*(1), 53–80.

Pomoravlje District. (2014). Retrieved from http://puo.rs/poplave-2/?sr=lat. Accessed on February 01, 2023.

Republic Hydrometeorological Service of Serbia. (2014). Godišnji bilten za Srbiju. Retrieved from https://www.hidmet.gov.rs/data/klimatologija/latin/2014.pdf. Accessed on February 1, 2023.

Romer, P. M. (1986). Increasing returns and long run growth. *Journal of Political Economy*, *94*(5), 1002–1037.

Serbian Business Registers Agency. (2023). Retrieved from https://pretraga2.apr.gov.rs/APRMapePodsticaja/. Accessed on February 1, 2023.

Smith, D. (2010). The role of entrepreneurship in economic growth. *Undergraduate Economic Review*, *6*(1), 1–17.

Stephan, U., Hart, M., & Drews, C.-C. (2015). *Understanding motivations for entrepreneurship: A review of recent research evidence*. Birmingham: Enterprise Research Centre.

Todorović, I., Komazec, S., Jevtić, M., Obradović, V., & Marič, M. (2016). Strategic management in development of youth and women entrepreneurship – Case of Serbia. *Organizacija*, *49*(4), 197–207.

United Nations UNCTAD. (2022). Statistical annex tables of the world investment report – FDI inward stock, by region and economy, 1990–2021. Retrieved from https://unctad.org/system/files/non-official-document/WIR2022_tab03.xlsx

Vasa, L., & Angeloska, A. (2020). Foreign direct investment in the Republic of Serbia: Correlation between foreign direct investments and the selected economic variables. *Journal of International Studies*, *13*(1), 170–183.

Vulević, B., Čudanov, M., & Kešetović, Ž. (2022). Organisational design-learning from engagement during high-impact low-frequency events. *Lex Localis*, *20*(2), 393–410.

World Bank. (2014). *Poplave u Srbiji 2014*. Washington: WBP.

World Bank. (2023). Serbia-data. Retrieved from https://www.worldbank.org/. Accessed on February 26, 2023.

Zahra, S. A., & Wright, M. (2016). Understanding the social role of entrepreneurship. *Journal of Management Studies*, *53*(4), 610–629.

Chapter 14

Intrapreneurship, Ecopreneurship, and Digitalization in Slovenia

Jasna Auer Antončič and Boštjan Antončič

Abstract

This chapter covers intrapreneurship, ecopreneurship, and digitalization, and presents qualitative research findings on eco-innovations and digitalization in Slovenia. Eco-innovations and digitalization are important aspects of intrapreneurship and the performance of existing companies. Practices of the participating company in circular economy and eco-innovations and digitalization are presented and discussed.

Keywords: Intrapreneurship; ecopreneurship; digitalization; Slovenia; eco-innovations; performance

1. Introduction

Slovenia is a developed country with 2.1 million population, 29,291 US Dollars in gross domestic product (GDP) per capita in 2021, and 6.5 metric tons of CO_2 emissions per capita in 2019 (World Bank, 2023). Slovenia quickly became a member of the Organisation for Economic Co-operation and Development (OECD) and the European Union (EU) and was the most developed in terms of industry and other production in the former Yugoslavia, despite the fact that it had only 8% of the total area of the former Yugoslavia (Auer Antončič, Antončič, & Hisrich, 2020; Panthi, Antoncic, & Hisrich, 2018). Kraus et al. (2022) reviewed business and management research on digital transformation and concluded that digital transformation has gained interest recently (in particular, from 2019 onwards), but this research field remains fragmented, including certain shortcomings, which expose several areas for future research. This study contributes to research on

Entrepreneurship Development in the Balkans: Perspective from Diverse Contexts, 261–274

doi:10.1108/978-1-83753-454-820231014

intrapreneurship, ecopreneurship, digitalization, and digital transformation by exploring the characteristics of ecopreneurship and digitalization in existing companies. In this chapter, we cover aspects of intrapreneurship, ecopreneurship, and digitalization, and present the results of a qualitative study of ecopreneurship and digitalization in Slovenia.

2. Literature Review

2.1. Intrapreneurship

Intrapreneurship or corporate entrepreneurship is defined as entrepreneurship within an existing organization (e.g., Antončič & Hisrich, 2001, 2003, 2004; Antončič, 2007, 2008). Due to its positive effects on the business results of companies (growth, profits, and new value), it is of extreme importance both for the development of an individual company or organization as well as for the development of a region or the national economy. Intrapreneurship can significantly increase the annual growth of company revenues, for example, from around 4% to 7% (Antončič, 2004). Intrapreneurship means how companies behave and emphasizes introducing innovations in various areas (products/services, technologies, strategies, organization, etc.). Intrapreneurial behavior is important for companies of various sizes, not only for large companies or corporations, which allows them greater flexibility and thus a better position on the market (Antončič & Antončič, 2022).

Intrapreneurship works on the border of the existing in the company, as it represents the creation of innovations. Seven main dimensions of intrapreneurship are listed as follows (Antončič, 2002):

- new business: pursuing and entering into new business related to the company's current products or markets;
- new units and companies: establishment of new organizational units;
- innovation of products and services: the creation of new products and services;
- technological innovation: innovating existing and introducing new technology and processes;
- self-renewal: reorganization, redefinition of mission, vision, and strategies;
- risk-taking: pursuing new opportunities and mobilizing resources to exploit these opportunities;
- proactiveness: the tendency of the top management to improve the competitive position, orientation toward the future, and a leading position in the introduction of changes in the market.

The dimensions of intrapreneurship differ from each other, but at the same time, they are also related to each other and complement each other. The dimensions are the joint introduction of innovations in various fields, and the development and search for innovations and new solutions, which are the foundations of the concept of intrapreneurship. Market conditions offer companies new challenges and constantly open new windows of opportunity. Companies respond to this by finding innovative solutions in the areas of products, services, markets, technology, strategies, administration, etc., while proactive companies create the future by responding to expected future market conditions or by co-creating the future of the market with innovations that will be accepted by the market in the future (Auer Antončič & Antončič, 2022).

Organizations, in which the atmosphere encourages intrapreneurship, have the following characteristics (Antončič, Hisrich, Petrin, & Vahčič, 2002): the organization works at the frontier of technology, new ideas, trials, and errors are encouraged (while failures are allowed), there are no barriers to opportunities, support from the top management and reachability and availability of sponsors, leaders and resources, long-term vision, team approach characterized by multidisciplinarity and volunteerism, while at the same time, an appropriate reward system is provided. By giving intrapreneurs the right to rewards (Pinchot, 1985) in proportion to the new value created, the organization approaches independent entrepreneurship in terms of material incentives.

The findings of the research on a sample of 477 Slovenian companies were as follows (Antončič, 2002): (1) environmental factors have a positive effect on intrapreneurship, (2) internal organizational factors have a positive effect on intrapreneurship, (3) factors related to strategic connections have a positive effect on intrapreneurship, (4) the most important are the factors of the internal organization over which management has the greatest influence, (5) internal organizational support and the number of strategic connections are the factors that have the strongest influence on the development of intrapreneurship (the number of strategic connections has a favorable effect on intrapreneurship, but only up to a certain limit, as too many connections can have an inhibitory effect), and (6) intrapreneurship has a positive effect on company growth and profits. It follows from the model and empirical research that those companies that establish a stimulating environment for intrapreneurs and create an organizational structure that will have a favorable impact on entrepreneurial activities will be more successful. Open communication, control over projects, thorough analysis of the environment, management and organizational support, organizational values, and cooperation in strategic connections contribute to a higher level of intrapreneurship. Management can greatly contribute to the development of intrapreneurship by supporting employees, encouraging their independence, and providing resources. The support of management and organization is the most important factor for the development of intrapreneurship.

Research findings (Auer, 2009; Auer Antončič & Antončič, 2009, 2011) based on data from Slovenia show a connection between employee satisfaction, intrapreneurship, and growth. Based on the results of the research, recommendations were made to companies.

In the research, it was found that rewards, benefits, and organizational culture have the strongest influence on intrapreneurship and growth among the factors of employee satisfaction. Companies should ensure that employees are satisfied with their salary, learning should be treated as a value, and education as an investment. It is also important that superiors share important information with subordinates and provide sufficient information about the performance of work tasks. Companies should adapt to changes and strive for improvements. They should ensure that there are opportunities for personal growth and development in the company and that employees are satisfied with their working hours.

Overall employee satisfaction is important for intrapreneurship and growth. It is crucial that employees are satisfied with various elements of their work, such as with the work itself, type of work, interestingness of the work, challenge at work, personal satisfaction at work, pleasure of performing work, independence of decision-making in performance of work and tasks, and its importance in the workplace within the company. The general satisfaction of employees is also related to financial rewards for work and some elements of employee affiliation with the organization.

Relationships with colleagues are important especially for company growth, and for intrapreneurship in service industries. For the company, it is important that employees understand each other well, that they are satisfied with their mutual relations, that they are surrounded by the kind of colleagues they would like, and that they have a stimulating effect on them.

Employee belonging is important mainly in terms of overall satisfaction while belonging itself is not important for intrapreneurship or company growth in service industries. Affiliation is important for growth in manufacturing industries. Companies should try to ensure that employees belong to the organization with elements of overall satisfaction.

Intrapreneurship is also crucial for company growth in terms of new business, product innovation, technology innovation, and self-renewal. The following factors are important: stimulating new demand, dealing with new business in new markets, finding new market niches, offering and developing new products, developing own technology, introducing technological novelties and innovations, defining the mission of the company, checking the business concept, redefining industries, in which the company will compete, reorganizing parts of the company, increasing unit autonomy, coordinating activities between units, and establishing a flexible organizational structure to improve the company's innovation. Companies will achieve all this by increasing employee satisfaction.

From the point of view of economic growth, different dimensions of intrapreneurship have different importance and influence depending on the level of economic development of the country. For example, researchers (Antončič, Antončič, Douglas, Hisrich, & McLaughlin, 2022) proposed an intrapreneurship model of economic development and growth after comparing the intrapreneurship model in the United States, Australia, and Slovenia. They considered four dimensions (new business and new units, innovation, self-renewal, and proactiveness) and suggested that in order to promote growth at the level of the national economy in countries with low GDP, companies should increase the levels of all dimensions until they reach medium to high GDP levels. Then the emphasis should be on innovation and self-renewal, when they reach a high level of GDP, they should focus on new businesses and new units, and proactivity, to finally become the best (the highest level of GDP) innovation is decisive. Innovativeness is a factor of continuous progress, which can also be seen in the economic guidelines of the EU, which emphasize innovation, competitiveness, and entrepreneurship (Auer

Antončič & Antončič, 2022). In the following sections, two special aspects of intrapreneurship are discussed: ecopreneurship and digitalization.

2.2. Ecopreneurship

Green entrepreneurship or eco-entrepreneurship or ecopreneurship is defined as the activity of consciously addressing environmental and social problems or needs through the implementation of entrepreneurial ideas with a high level of risk, which has net positive effects on the natural environment and is at the same time financially sustainable (GREENT, 2019, in Hojnik, 2022, p. 109). A green entrepreneur or an eco-entrepreneur or ecopreneur is defined as someone who starts and runs an entrepreneurial business that is designed to be "green" or environmentally friendly in its products and processes from the moment it is founded (GREENT, 2019, in Hojnik, 2022, p. 109). Eco-entrepreneurs become so-called agents of change, destroying existing conventional methods of production, existing conventional products, market structures, and models of consumption and replacing them with new, superior ecological products and services (GREENT, 2019, in Hojnik, 2022, p. 109). Ecopreneurship can be reflected in the following ways (GREENT, 2019, in Hojnik, 2022, p. 110): (1) with softer forms of ecological modernization that preserve existing economic structures and mechanisms by achieving higher levels of ecological efficiency through the use of better technologies; and (2) with more radical forms that arise from the reconsideration of economic paradigms and the achievement of disruptive innovations. An example of such an innovation is community farming, which allows farmers to be financed by the community in solidarity at the beginning of the crop-growing season, so that community members have access to fresh and clean food later.

Just like innovation is central to intrapreneurship, eco-innovation is central to ecopreneurship. The defining properties of eco-innovations are (Hojnik, 2022, p. 111):

- They represent a subset of all innovations in the economy (Wagner, 2008).
- Eco-innovation is defined as the production, use, or exploitation of a good, service, production process, organizational structure or method, the management or business method that is new for a company or user and is expressed throughout its entire life cycle in reducing environmental risk, pollution and negative impacts of resource use (including energy use) compared to relevant alternatives (according to the Measuring Eco-innovation project, Kemp & Pearson, 2007, p. 7).
- Eco-innovation is any innovation that reduces the use of natural resources and the release of harmful substances throughout its life cycle, reflecting its environmental component. Enterprises ought to know more about the feasible values that can be gained from the introduction of eco-innovations, and therefore they should be encouraged to implement eco-innovations on a larger scale, which is a critical point for gaining competitive advantage and expanding into foreign markets, and in the long term, they improve the company's performance (Eco-innovation Observatory, 2013).

The path to achieving sustainability is the introduction of eco-innovations that bring benefits to the environment and companies and thus represent a win–win situation (win for both sides) (Hojnik, 2022, p. 111). One of the most exposed peculiarities of eco-innovations, which also had a decisive influence on the study of the driving forces of eco-innovations, is the "double externality problem," in which eco-innovations create double positive external effects (Rennings, 2000, Rennings et al., 2004, in Hojnik, 2016, in Hojnik, 2022, p. 112):

- The first positive effect refers to knowledge spillovers (innovation and R&D activities and talks about the fact that companies investing in eco-innovation cannot fully appropriate the creation of value, as other companies and the economy take advantage of the spillover of knowledge, and for this reason, various incentives are needed, such as public funding and subsidies).
- The second positive effect refers to environmental effects (society and the environment gain benefits from the point of view of the positive effects of eco-innovation – a lower negative/harmful effect of the company on the environment, while the company itself bears the costs of eco-innovation).
- Because of these positive effects, eco-innovations differ from conventional innovations and above all demonstrate the need for environmental policy instruments, such as taxes, regulations, and various incentives to introduce eco-innovations, which solve this problem at least partially, so that companies that introduce eco-innovations can competitive on the market, but not harmed, because they pay attention to the environment.

Eco-innovation types are (Hojnik, 2017): (1) product eco-innovation; (2) process eco-innovation; (3) technological eco-innovation; (4) organizational eco-innovation; (5) marketing eco-innovation; (6) social eco-innovation; and (7) system eco-innovation. The benefits that companies can have from the successful introduction of eco-innovations are mainly the following (Shrivastava, 1995, in Hojnik, 2022, p. 120): (1) cost savings; (2) improved image of the company; (3) improved connection and relationship with local communities; (4) access to new green markets; and (5) greater competitive advantage.

Hojnik, Ruzzier, Antončič, and Rus (2015) studied drivers of eco-innovation and found based on a quantitative study of Slovenian companies that competitive pressure operates as a driver of all three eco-innovation types (product, process, and organizational eco-innovation) and different factors stimulate different eco-innovation types (product eco-innovation is driven by customer demand and competitive pressure; process eco-innovation is propelled by managerial environmental concern, competitive intensity, and competitive pressure; organizational eco-innovation is driven by competitive pressure).

2.3. Digitalization

Digitalization in business refers to the improvement and transformation of business activities, processes, and models through the use and adoption of digital technologies and the wider use and context of digitized data transformed into intelligence and effective knowledge (Bradač Hojnik, Huđek, & Močnik 2022). The key technologies of digital transformation are (OECD, 2019, in Bradač Hojnik et al., 2022, p. 88): (1) Internet of Things, (2) next-generation wireless networks (5G and beyond), (3) cloud computing, (4) Big data analytics, (5) artificial intelligence, (6) blockchain, and (7) computing power.

Digitalization led to the datafication of society (Redden, 2018) and allows for building wealth, data access, better integration, and wider accessibility (Palszkiewicz & Skarzynska, 2022). The main consequence of digitalization is the optimization of processes and their better management, while digital transformation refers to strategies or processes that go beyond the use of digital technologies and mean a profound change in the entire business model and the arrangement of the way of work (Bradač Hojnik et al., 2022). The process of digital transformation takes place sequentially in three phases (Digital Business Innovation, 2022; in Bradač Hojnik et al., 2022, pp. 89–90; Savić, 2019):

1. *Digitization:* Conversion of analog information into digital; the product becomes digital. Focus: data conversion. Objective: change from analog to digital format. Activity: Digital conversion of paper documents, photographs, microfilms, records, films, and VHS tapes. Tools: Computing and conversion equipment for encoding. Challenge: scope (material challenge). Example: scanning paper registration forms.
2. *Digitalization:* Analysis of digital information and digitalization of the business model; the business model becomes digital. Focus: Information Processing. Goal: automation of existing business operations and processes. Activity: the creation of fully digital business processes. Tools: IT systems and computer applications. Challenge: Price (financial challenge). Example: fully electronic registration process.
3. *Digital transformation:* Transforming the entire economy into a digital one; the entire systematic restructuring of companies, society, economy, and institutions. Focus: achieving leverage in knowledge. Goal: changing the company's culture, its way of working, and its thinking. Activity: Creating a new digital business or transforming it into a digital business. Tools: matrix of new digital technologies. Challenge: resistance to change (the challenge is human resources). Example: the entire process is electronic, from registration to content delivery.

Digital entrepreneurship can be defined as (Bradač Hojnik et al., 2022, p. 93) a form or type of entrepreneurship in which something or everything that is traditionally physical is now digital (Hull, Hung, Hair, Perotti, & DeMartino, 2007). In international settings, companies can benefit by developing three key themes (Falcioglu, 2022): digital storytelling, cultural intelligence, and digital literacy. The Slovenian economy faces serious challenges brought about by the strongly expressed need for digitalization and renewal of business models, as not all companies have the necessary capabilities to carry out this transformation, which can be an obstacle to digitalization, especially for small companies that lag behind in digital transformation in comparison with large companies (Bradač Hojnik et al., 2022). The key findings of a study about digitization in Slovenia are (Bradač Hojnik et al., 2022, pp. 83–84):

1. Digitalization represents a trend that will experience tremendous momentum in the coming decades. That is why the EU and Slovenia are renewing the strategic framework that will enable such development. In 2022, a new Strategy for the digital transformation of the economy was adopted in Slovenia, which represents the basic strategic document for the digital development of Slovenia in the next decade.
2. The DESI digital economy and society index ranks Slovenia 13th among EU member states and shows a total score of 52.8 (the EU average is 50.7). Improving its ranking on the DESI index is the key goal of Slovenia in the next decade.
3. Micro-, small-, and medium-sized companies are the ones that have more problems in the transition to digitalization compared to large companies. The problems they face are multifaceted, from a lack of financial resources and relevant knowledge to difficulties in implementing and maintaining technological and digital solutions. SMEs cannot overcome these obstacles alone, so they need adequate support from the business ecosystem and policies.
4. General information and knowledge of the strategic framework for digitization in Slovenia is relatively poor, as 40% of surveyed companies do not know about it, and among those who do, 16% think that it is very effective, and 43% that it is only partially effective or not at all.
5. For the comprehensive implementation of digitalization, it is necessary to define a digital strategy in the company. The research showed that 39% of micro, 43% of small, 43% of medium, and 54% of large companies have this defined. It is an encouraging fact that most of them have all key areas included in their strategy, which shows the comprehensiveness of digital strategies in companies. The supportive environment certainly contributed to this with its measures, including a voucher for the development of a digital strategy.
6. Companies mainly use simpler digital technology solutions and tools, and more demanding, complex, or newer ones significantly less. Thus, the implementation and use of websites, tools to support teamwork, and software solutions for paperless businesses dominate. Only then do the digitalization of business processes, the Internet of Things, and comprehensive software solutions for customer support follow. At the very least, companies use the latest technologies, such as 3D printing and blockchain.
7. Companies mainly highlighted financial problems with digitalization and the lack of employees with relevant skills. SMEs will not be able to overcome these kinds of problems by themselves, so there is an urgent need to support the business ecosystem with appropriate measures in these areas. On one hand, these are financial measures, and on the other hand, enabling access to relevant skills for existing employees as well as for young people who are yet to join the labor market.

8. In the field of digitalization, the task of the support environment, especially for SMEs, will be multifaceted. These companies do not even have enough information about digitalization as a basis for its successful implementation in the company. They lack financial resources, perceive a skills deficit, and express problems with implementation. After the introduction of various solutions, their maintenance and upgrading follow, which represents an additional obstacle that SMEs may not even be aware of at the beginning.

Characteristics of digitalization in companies with at least 10 employees in Slovenia in 2021 are (SURS, 2021; Bradač Hojnik et al., 2022, p. 112):

- 83% of companies have a website;
- 59% of companies use social media;
- 58% of employees and self-employed with access to the Internet for work purposes;
- 58% of companies sent e-invoices in 2020;
- 53% of companies use tools to support teamwork and collaboration;
- 49% of companies use smart devices or systems;
- 43% of companies rent cloud computing services;
- 36% of companies use an ERP software solution;
- 36% of employed and self-employed with an assigned portable device with internet access;
- 22% of companies use a CRM software solution;
- 17% of companies have a digital transformation strategy;
- 16% of companies use a software solution for paperless business;
- 12% of companies use artificial intelligence technology; and
- 9% of companies use human resource management software solutions.

Digitalization is a necessary condition for competitiveness, so companies in Slovenia need an appropriate digitalization strategy that will cover digital strategic goals, models, products and services, key processes and digital solutions, personnel development, data strategy, and cyber security, and in the case of manufacturing companies also an appropriate strategy for the transition to Industry 4.0 (Bradač Hojnik et al., 2022). In January 2022, a new strategy for the digital transformation of the Slovenian economy from 2021 to 2030 was adopted, in which an ambitious vision was set to become the leading junction of advanced digital technologies in Europe and how Slovenia will ensure the transition to a modern digital economy in the next decade, on three key areas (MGRT, 2022; Bradač Hojnik et al., 2022, p. 103): (1) advanced digital technology; (2) an efficient ecosystem for a competitive economy; and (3) an open and sustainable society as a basis for the growth of the digital economy.

Hojnik, Ruzzier, Ruzzier, Sučić, and Soltwisch (2023) studied the role of demographic changes and digitalization in eco-innovations and the circular economy using results derived from semi-structured interviews with Slovenian companies. They found (1) all 10 analyzed companies implement practices of the circular economy (e.g., the digitalization of production, development of green, sustainable materials and green technologies, closed resource loops (e.g., materials and water), rental and remote monitoring of their products, recycling, and reuse of materials, using excess heat during the technological process, and open-circle recycling); (2) the companies stressed the role of digitalization for the future and the circular economy and emphasized automation, robotization and the use of advanced digital tools in business processes in the digital transformation; and (3) digitalization is eliminating low-productivity jobs and brings higher productivity and energy efficiency, and in some companies resource efficiency; effects of digitalization on eco-innovation and circular economy bring better transparency, control, and manageability of technological processes, and reducing energy consumption and environmental impact.

3. Methods

Qualitative methods were used in this study in order to answer a research question: How does a company perform ecopreneurial activities and how does it look at circular economy, eco-innovations, and digitalization? The participant was one company from the electric and electronics sector in Slovenia. The company was purposely selected on the basis of the knowledge of researchers that the company exhibits circular economy or eco-innovation activities, and has environmentally friendly products and sustainable solutions included in both the company's vision and mission. The company started introducing circular economy/eco-innovations in the early 1990s and received awards for corporate responsibility and innovations in the reduction of emissions in the environment and longer product life. Data collection was performed via a semi-structured interview questionnaire. Findings are presented in an anonymized form in the following section.

4. Findings

The main factors that encouraged the company to practice the circular economy and introduce eco-innovations are internal (the management's decision on the brand's sustainable orientation) and external (customer satisfaction), in this case, the company developed, for example, an online application for intuitive ordering of spare parts for their products. The main obstacles and challenges that prevented the company from implementing and developing ecopreneurial activities represented the search for suitable providers for the production of personalized clickable parts lists for their products. This also had organizational effects, as by transferring the sale of products to the online store, the company recognized the need for new skills (e-commerce and digital marketing) and for this purpose formed the marketing department as an independent unit, which, in addition to the aforementioned skills, is distinguished by advanced knowledge of graphic design and system integration.

Circular economy practices or eco-innovations are visible in the company's circular model, which ensures a long-term product life extension, in the direction of reducing the carbon footprint and lower total costs. The company has a sustainable approach, follows trends, and offers a better user experience to customers by simplifying the purchase process. When changing the business model, the company emphasized new sales channels, an online store, and digital marketing. The circular business model of extending product life has been positively received by customers and other stakeholders (e.g., banks and media). The company achieved impacts on a cleaner environment and lower costs with a circular business model of product life extension. Especially during the crisis in the electronics supply chain, which is implemented in the company's products, the business model proved to be one of the elements for easier operation in such economic conditions.

Many departments of the company participated in the implementation of the circular economy, eco-innovations, and their acceptance by consumers: management, development, technology, marketing, and sales. All departments contributed to the brand's new operational approach. To inform actual and potential consumers about the practices it uses in the field of circular economy or eco-innovations, the company uses communications via independent mailings, social networks, a website, or an online store, regularly shares its circular practices with stakeholders in the municipal newsletter, interviews in regional newspapers, and participation in various organizations and round tables.

The company emphasized: Both digitalization and the circular business model have contributed to the overhaul of the communication strategy. The production of video and other interesting web content has increased thanks to new communication channels. By addressing the younger and more environmentally aware generation, the tone of communication is also being adjusted on the fly.

The company is aware that digital technologies in the new digital age have a strong impact on products, services, and business processes in companies. The company recognizes the opportunities that digital concepts offer (digitalization of processes, automation, simplified communication channels with customers, suppliers, and within the company), and at the same time, their customers are also aware of these opportunities and rapid progress.

The company focuses on concrete opportunities, which will strengthen in the future:

- establishment of a B2B platform for attaining new suppliers;
- systematic data processing and analysis;
- updated website with the possibility of an offer configurator;
- raising digital culture and competencies, training employees in the field of digital literacy and the use of ERP;
- at the expense of the time gained due to digitization, the opportunity to acquire new customers;
- use of circular business models also with their other brands; and
- digital technologies enabled them to bring the circular business model to life faster, as well as cheaper and faster communication about new practices with their existing and potential customers.

5. Discussion and Conclusion

The participating company provided good insights into its view and activities related to the circular economy, eco-innovations, ecopreneurship, and digitalization. This study contributes to ecopreneurship research and complements the findings of Hojnik et al. (2023) on the role of digitalization in eco-innovations and the circular economy.

The participating company's circular business model of extending product life contributed to the reduction of the carbon footprint and costs and has been positively received by customers and other stakeholders. The ecopreneurial activity of changing the business model can be achieved using new sales channels, online stores, and digital marketing. Digitalization improves communication with actual and potential customers and can be an enabler of ecopreneurship and faster creation of new circular business models.

Implications of this study are for: (1) theory (e.g., eco-innovations and digitalization can be viewed as two special aspects of intrapreneurship, digitalization can be viewed as a part of circular economy activities); (2) practice (e.g., by following the practices of circular economy and eco-innovation of the participating company, companies can improve their performance); and (3) economic policies (e.g., governmental and development institutions should emphasize digitalization as an important driver in the practices of eco-innovation and the circular economy).

This study has limitations, for example, the method (qualitative), the selection, and the number of participating companies (only one Slovenian company). In future research, for example, the aspects from this study can be assessed more in detail in focused qualitative studies or examined on a large number of respondents in a quantitative study.

In this chapter, we covered intrapreneurship, ecopreneurship, and digitalization, and presented research findings on eco-innovations and digitalization in Slovenia. Eco-innovations and digitalization warrant further study because they are important aspects of intrapreneurship and the performance of existing companies.

Funding

This work was supported by the Public Agency for Research of the Republic of Slovenia [grant numbers J5-3106 and P5-0117].

References

Antončič, B. (2002). *Notranje podjetništvo. Prenova konstrukta in razvoj integrativnega modela* [*Intrapreneurship: Construct refinement and an integrative model development*]. Koper: Društvo za aplikativne in akademske raziskave.

Antončič, B. (2004). Nujni ukrepi za gospodarsko rast in spodbujanje podjetništva. *Finance*, 247, 26.

Antončič, B. (2007). Intrapreneurship: A comparative structural equation modeling study. *Industrial Management & Data Systems*, *107*(3), 309–325.

Antončič, B. (2008). Notranje podjetništvo. In M. Ruzzier, B. Antončič, T. Bratkovič, & R. D. Hisrich (Eds.), *Podjetništvo* (pp. 93–101). Koper: Društvo za akademske in aplikativne raziskave.

Antončič, B., & Hisrich, R. D. (2001). Intrapreneurship: Construct refinement and cross-cultural validation. *Journal of Business Venturing*, *16*(5), 495–527.

Antončič, B., & Hisrich, R. D. (2003). Clarifying the intrapreneurship concept. *Journal of Small Business and Enterprise Development*, *10*(1), 7–24.

Antončič, B., & Hisrich, R. D. (2004). Corporate entrepreneurship contingencies and organizational wealth creation. *Journal of Management Development*, *23*(6), 518–550.

Antončič, B., Hisrich, R. D., Petrin, T., & Vahčič, A. (2002). *Podjetništvo*. Ljubljana: GV Založba.

Auer, J. (2009). *Zadovoljstvo zaposlenih in notranje podjetništvo. Magistrska naloga*. Koper: Univerza na Primorskem, Fakulteta za management.

Auer Antončič, J., & Antončič, B. (2009). *Zadovoljstvo zaposlenih, notranje podjetništvo in rast podjetja*. Koper: Društvo za akademske in aplikativne raziskave.

Auer Antončič, J., & Antončič, B. (2011). Employee satisfaction, intrapreneurship and firm growth: A model. *Industrial Management & Data Systems*, *111*(4), 589–607.

Auer Antončič, J., & Antončič, B. (2022). Notranje podjetništvo in skrb za zaposlene. In B. Antončič (Ed.), *Podjetništvo: glavni dejavnik razvoja* (pp. 145–174). Ljubljana: School of Economics and Business, University of Ljubljana.

Auer Antončič, J., Antončič, B., Douglas, E. J., Hisrich, R. D., & McLaughlin, T. (2022). The impact of intrapreneurship on growth and profitability. *FAIMA Business & Management Journal*, *10*(2), 16–30.

Auer Antončič, J., Antončič, B., & Hisrich, R. D. (2020). Women's entrepreneurship in Slovenia. In R. Palalić, E. Knezović, & L.-P. Dana (Eds.), *Women's entrepreneurship in former Yugoslavia: Historical framework, ecosystem and future perspectives for the region* (pp. 161–176). Cham: Springer.

Bradač Hojnik, B., Hudek, I., & Močnik, D. (2022). Podjetniška demografija in značilnosti digitalizacije malih in srednje velikih podjetij. In M. Rebernik & B. Bradač Hojnik (Eds.), *Slovenski podjetniški observatorij 2021* (pp. 1–140). Maribor: Univerzitetna založba. doi:10.18690/um.epf.2.2022

Eco-Innovation Observatory (EIO) & CfSD. (2013). Eco-innovate! A guide to eco-innovation for SMEs and business coaches. Retrieved from http://cfsd.org.uk/site-pdfs/eco-innovate-sme-guide.pdf

Falcioglu, P. (2022). Future of digital work practices in multicultural business settings: A systematic literature review. *FAIMA Business & Management Journal*, *10*, 109–118.

GREENT. (2019). Definition of green entrepreneurship. Retrieved from http://greentproject.eu

Hojnik, J. (2016). *Model eko inovacij: določljivke, glavne dimenzije in posledice = Eco-innovation model: antecedents, main dimensions and consequences. Doctoral dissertation*. Koper: Univerza na Primorskem, Fakulteta za management.

Hojnik, J. (2017). *In pursuit of eco-innovation: Drivers and consequences of eco-innovation at firm level*. Koper: Založba Univerze na Primorskem.

Hojnik, J. (2022). Zeleno podjetništvo: eko inovacije. In B. Antončič (Ed.), *Podjetništvo: glavni dejavnik razvoja* (pp. 109–125). Ljubljana: School of Economics and Business, University of Ljubljana.

Hojnik, J., Ruzzier, M., Antončič, B., & Rus, M. (2015). What drives eco-innovations in Slovenia. In *Management international conference*, Portorož, Slovenia, May 28–30, 2015. Koper: University of Primorska, Faculty of Management.

Hojnik, J., Ruzzier, M., Ruzzier, M. K., Sučić, B., & Soltwisch, B. (2023). Challenges of demographic changes and digitalization on eco-innovation and the circular economy: Qualitative insights from companies. *Journal of Cleaner Production, 396* (136439): 1–9.

Hull, C. E. K., Hung, Y. T. C., Hair, N., Perotti, V., & DeMartino, R. (2007). Taking advantage of digital opportunities: A typology of digital entrepreneurship. *International Journal of Networking and Virtual Organisations*, *4*(3), 290–303.

Kemp, R., & Pearson, P. (2007). Final report MEI project about measuring eco innovation. Retrieved from http://scholar.google.com/scholar?hl=en&btnG=Search&q=intitle:Final+report+MEI+project+about+measuring+eco-+innovation#3

Kraus, S., Durst, S., Ferreira, J. J., Veiga, P., Kailer, N., & Weinmann, A. (2022). Digital transformation in business and management research: An overview of the current status quo. *International Journal of Information Management*, *63*(102466), 1–18.

MGRT. (2022). Strategija digitalne transformacije gospodarstva. Retrieved from https://www.gov.si/assets/ministrstva/MGRT/Dokumenti/DIPT/StrategijaDTG.pdf

OECD. (2019). *The missing entrepreneurs 2019: Policies for inclusive entrepreneurship*. Berlin: OECD Publications Centre.

Palszkiewicz, J., & Skarzynska, E. (2022). Trust and digitalization. *FAIMA Business & Management Journal*, *10*, 119–128.

Panthi, L., Antoncic, B., & Hisrich, R. D. (2018). Entrepreneurship in Slovenia. In R. Palalic, L.-P. Dana, & V. Ramadani (Eds.), *Entrepreneurship in former Yugoslavia: Diversity, institutional constraints and prospects* (pp. 131–143). Cham: Springer. https://doi.org/10.1007/978-3-319-77634-7

Pinchot, G., III. (1985). *Intrapreneuring*. New York, NY: Harper & Row.

Redden, J. (2018). Democratic governance in an age of datafication: Lessons from mapping government discourses and practices. *Big Data & Society*, *5*(2), https://doi.org/10.1177/2053951718809145

Rennings, K. (2000). Redefining innovation – Eco-innovation research and the contribution from ecological economics. *Ecological Economics*, *32*(2), 319–332.

Rennings, K., Bartolomeo, M., Kemp, R., Miles, I., & Arundel, A. (2004). The impact of clean production on employment in Europe – An analysis using surveys and case studies (IMPRESS). Retrieved from http://ec.europa.eu/research/social-sciences/pdf/impress_en.pdf

Savić, D. (2019). From digitization, through digitalization, to digital transformation. Retrieved from https://www.researchgate.net/publication/332111919

Shrivastava, P. (1995). Environmental technologies and competitive advantage. *Strategic Management Journal*, *16*, 183–200.

SURS. (2021). *Težave pri digitalni preobrazbi poslovanja in uporaba tehnologij umetne inteligence v podjetjih*. Ljubljana: Statistični urad Republike Slovenije. Retrieved from https://www.stat.si/StatWeb/news/Index/9100

Wagner, M. (2008). Empirical influence of environmental management on innovation: Evidence from Europe. *Ecological Economics*, *66(2–3)*, 392–402.

World Bank. (2023). *GDP per capita, PPP (current international $) – Slovenia*. New York, NY: The World Bank Group. Retrieved from https://data.worldbank.org/country/slovenia

Chapter 15

Entrepreneurship Studies in Türkiye: Where are We? Where Should We Go? Analysis of International Publications

Mehmet Bağış, Mehmet Nurullah Kurutkan and Liridon Kryeziu

Abstract

This research aims to determine the contribution of publications in the context of Türkiye to the international entrepreneurship literature between 2005 and 2022. We examined 471 articles published in international journals in the Web of Science (WoS) Core Collection database using bibliometric analysis techniques. We analyzed the data with the software Biblioshiny+Bibliometrix, SciMAT, and VOSViewer. We used performance, theme and evolution, co-authorship, and document analysis in data analysis. Performance analysis findings show that the most publications were made in 2021, the journal with the most publications was sustainability, and the author with the most publications was Bakır, C. Theme and evolution analysis revealed that the motor themes were corporate entrepreneurship, gender and entrepreneurial intentions in the first period (2005–2014), while institutional entrepreneurship stood out as the niche theme. In the second period (2015–2022), "corporate entrepreneurship" and "performance" emerged as the motor themes, while the niche themes in this period were "Syrian refugees" and "entrepreneurial intentions." Document analysis findings show that the most studied entrepreneurship types are gender, family, corporate, social, and small business, respectively. In addition, immigrant/refugee entrepreneurship is emerging as a new topic, while indigenous entrepreneurship, informal entrepreneurship, sustainable entrepreneurship, and religion entrepreneurship are the most minor studied topics in entrepreneurship. Evidence-based decision-making inputs were obtained for those holding the resource allocation authority in Türkiye. Policymakers and funders, as well as individuals and institutions that want to design the future in terms of

Entrepreneurship Development in the Balkans: Perspective from Diverse Contexts, 275–302

Published under exclusive licence by Emerald Publishing Limited
doi:10.1108/978-1-83753-454-820231015

resources, can benefit from the findings and analysis of this chapter. Türkiye, which ranks 26th in the world regarding entrepreneurship, must develop a policy based on data.

Keywords: Entrepreneurship; Türkiye; publication performance; bibliometric analysis; document analysis; Web of Science

1. Introduction

Entrepreneurship scholars have expressed their concerns that current knowledge in the field is based on research produced in Western societies (Acs & Audretsch, 1993; Fayolle, Kyrö, & Ulijn 2005) and made calls for the need to examine the phenomena of entrepreneurship in different cultural contexts (Anggadwita, Luturlean, Ramadani, & Ratten, 2017a; Bird & West, 1998). Therefore, in recent years, there has been a significant increase in the number of studies focusing on understanding the factors affecting entrepreneurship in non-Western sociocultural and economic contexts (Anggadwita et al., 2017a; Grimm, Gubert, Koriko, Lay, & Nordman, 2013; Verver, Passenier, & Roessingh, 2019). These studies have reinforced research trends on entrepreneurship outside Western societies and have contributed to the global knowledge base with contributions from national and regional studies.

In this research, we examine the development of entrepreneurship research conducted in Türkiye and published in international journals. Türkiye's entrepreneurship culture has not reached the expected levels compared to other developed and developing countries (Gürol & Atsan, 2006; Tekin, Ramadani, & Dana, 2021). Still, the country aims to move from an efficiency-oriented economy to an innovation-oriented economy (Ozaralli & Rivenburgh, 2016). Studies show that financial support (Cetindamar, Gupta, Karadeniz, & Egrican, 2012), the presence of an entrepreneur in a family (Celik, Yıldız, Aykanat, & Kazemzadeh, 2021), and education affect entrepreneurship in Türkiye (Altınay & Wang, 2011; Gürol & Atsan, 2006). In addition, socio-psychological and cognitive factors (Naktiyok, Nur Karabey, & Caglar Gulluce, 2010), individual characteristics such as locus of control, entrepreneurial self-efficacy, and external factors such as social networks and capital have also been found to affect entrepreneurship (Cetindamar et al., 2012; Sesen, 2013). Despite this increase in the literature, there have been a few previous studies on the development pattern of entrepreneurship research in Türkiye (Caylan, 2014; Cem et al., 2019; Deveciyan, Korkarer, & Çetin, 2021). However, none of these studies examined the entire knowledge base of articles published in Turkish and international journals. Among these studies focusing on the international arena, strategic entrepreneurship (Caylan, 2014) and ethical entrepreneurship (Deveciyan et al., 2021) were partially analyzed. Also, a mix of different bibliometric tools used in the production of mapping and visualization in previous research has not been used. Taking these gaps into account, in this research, we reveal the intellectual foundations of entrepreneurship researches of

Turkish origin indexed in the WoS and published in international journals. In this way, we aim to offer suggestions to researchers and policymakers. In this context, we seek answers to the following research questions.

1. Which are the most influential journals and authors in Turkish-based entrepreneurship research in WoS?
2. What are the prominent and declining themes in Turkish-based entrepreneurship studies in WoS between 2005–2014 and 2015–2022? How have these themes evolved?
3. Which authors stand out in co-authorship patterns in Turkish-based entrepreneurship studies in WoS?
4. Which types of entrepreneurship research are prominent and under-studied in Turkish-based entrepreneurship studies in WoS?

We structured the remainder of the research into four sections. In Section 2, we gave the method of the study. In Section 3, we presented the findings. In Section 4, we introduced the theoretical implications of the research, recommendations for policymakers, limitations, and future research directions.

2. Methods

We obtained the research data from the WoS database. We preferred this database because it is widely used by management and business scientists (Bağış, 2020, 2021a, 2021b; Bağış et al., 2022; Zupic & Čater, 2015). We searched on 02/11/2022 with the term "entrepreneurship" in the "Topic" tab of WoS. At the end of this initial search strategy, we reached N=58,843 publications. Second, "Turkey" and "Türkiye" were chosen from the "country" criteria. As a result of this selection, the number of publications became $N = 690$. We reached $N = 522$ publications in the third stage by choosing "Article" and "Review." In the fourth stage, we filtered the duplication publications created by recording some "Articles" twice as a book chapter and proceeding paper in WoS. As a result, we reached N=471 publications. We have given the search strategy in Fig. 1. Finally, we exported the filtered publications in the database in "plain text" format and uploaded them to bibliometric softwares.

We analyzed the data with four analysis techniques and software. (i) Performance analysis (Biblioshiny+Bibliometrix), (ii) Theme and evolution analysis (SciMAT) (Cobo, 2011), (iii) Co-authoring (Bibliometrix+VOSViewer) (Donthu, Kumar, Mukherjee, Pandey, & Lim, 2021), and (iv) Document Analysis (Excel). The first three techniques are bibliometric analysis techniques. Bibliometric analysis is a quantitative analysis technique that determines trends in the field by digitizing and visualizing some specific research features in a particular field (Kasemodel, Makishi, Souza, & Silva, 2016). In this context, we *first* made a performance analysis. This is an analysis technique that aims to evaluate the impact of the activities of scientific actors or actor groups, such as the most efficient researchers, journals, departments, universities, and countries, based on the number of publications and the data in the bibliography (Donthu et al., 2021;

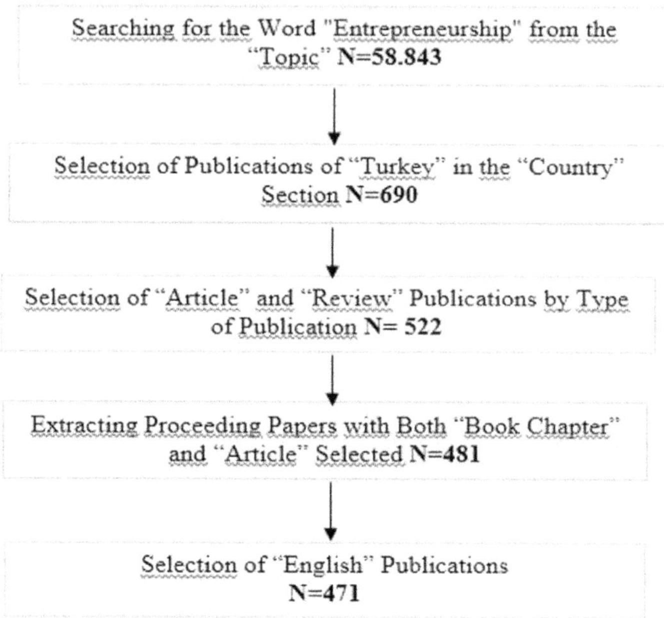

Fig. 1. Search Strategy.

Gutiérrez-Salcedo, Martínez, Moral-Munoz, Herrera-Viedma, & Cobo, 2018). In this analysis, we used the publications as the unit of analysis. *Second*, we performed a co-occurrence word analysis using keywords. We classified the analysis as the first period and second period to determine the evolution pattern and the thematic development course of entrepreneurship publications based in Türkiye. This analysis is done with "author keywords." However, in the absence of these words, analyzes are performed by removing notable words from "article titles," "summaries," and "full texts" for analysis (Baker, Pandey, Kumar, & Haldar, 2020; Donthu, Kumar, & Pattnaik, 2020). In this analysis, we used the author keywords as the analysis unit. *Third*, we conducted a co-authorship analysis. This analysis is the production of a study by two or more authors and examines the social networks that the authors have created by collaborating for publications (Acedo, Barroso, Casanueva, & Galán, 2006; Huang & Chang, 2011). In this analysis, we used the authors as the unit of analysis. *Finally*, we conducted a document analysis to determine which types of entrepreneurship exist in the research. This systematic analysis technique allows for reviewing and evaluating printed and electronic publications. Like other analytical methods in qualitative research, document analysis requires examining, interpreting, and classifying data to reveal meaning and develop empirical knowledge (Bowen, 2009). In this context, we used publications as a unit of analysis. In the theme and evolution analysis, we designed the processing process of the study made with the SciMAT program similar to both the SciMAT guide and the method of Kurutkan and Terzi (2022). We have given this process in Fig. 2.

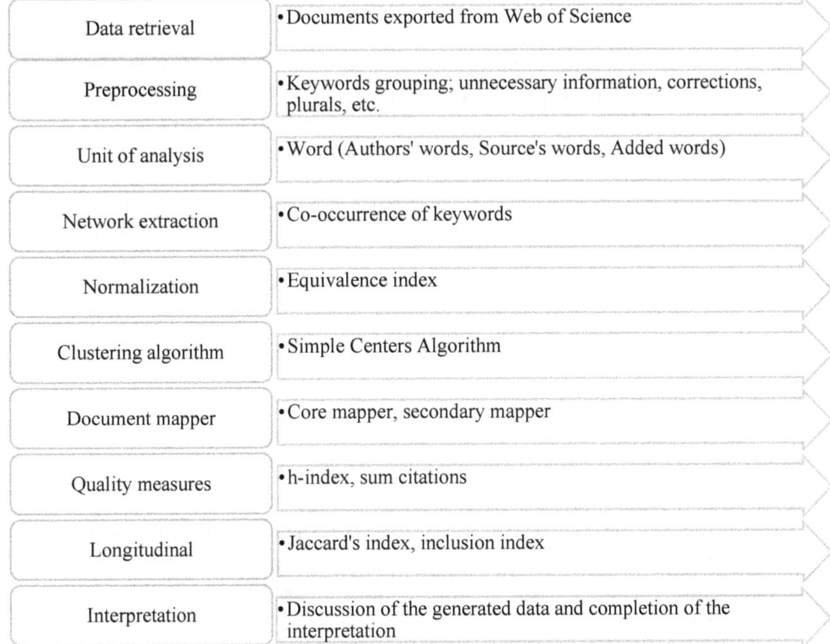

Fig. 2. SciMAT Analysis Process. *Source*: Based on Cobo (2011) and Kurutkan and Terzi (2022).

In the SciMAT analysis process, we analyzed the co-occurrence of keywords to identify nodes and relationships between clusters. To do this, we used the co-occurrence matrix in the SciMAT software. We calculated the similarity between the themes according to the equivalence index. We chose the Simple Centers Algorithm for clustering, which creates connection networks between themes. To define the mesh of clusters, we set the mesh size as a maximum of 12 and a minimum of 2. Then, in cluster analysis, we drew a strategic diagram in which density (vertical axis) measures the internal bonding strength and centrality (horizontal axis) measures the density of binding one cluster with other clusters. The themes in strategic diagrams are placed according to centrality and density (Cobo, López-Herrera, Herrera-Viedma, & Herrera, 2012). The centrality feature is related to the external relations of the theme, and the themes with a high level of relationship with the other themes in the diagram approach the right side of the diagram. The density feature, which shows the development of the theme, is related to the internal relations of the theme, and the themes with a high level of relationship in themselves approach upwards in the diagram. The themes are placed in four quadrants in the strategic diagram according to their centrality and density values (Kurutkan & Terzi, 2022). We have given which themes these areas represent in Fig. 3.

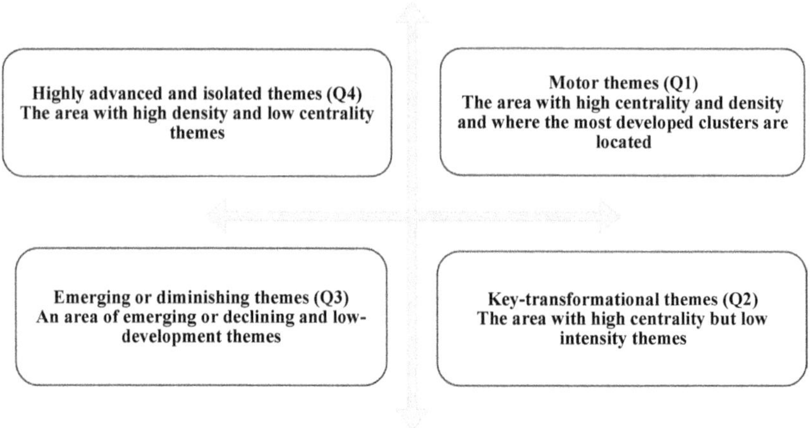

Highly advanced and isolated themes (Q4)
The area with high density and low centrality themes

Motor themes (Q1)
The area with high centrality and density and where the most developed clusters are located

Emerging or diminishing themes (Q3)
An area of emerging or declining and low-development themes

Key-transformational themes (Q2)
The area with high centrality but low intensity themes

Fig. 3. Quadrants of the Strategic Diagram.

Accordingly, motor themes (Q1) are the related field's most studied and developed themes. On the other hand, the core and transformational themes (Q2) show the themes that have the highest relations with different external themes but have not developed much (Furstenau et al., 2021). Emerging or declining themes (Q3) are weak or marginally advanced in the relevant field. On the other hand, highly developed or isolated themes (Q4) are highly developed themes in themselves, although they do not have many relations with different external themes in the relevant field. These themes are considered well-developed in the relevant field but are of marginal importance for the field (Karayel & Kurutkan, 2022).

The size of the clusters in which the themes are included in the thematic development map indicates that there are more publications in the relevant theme, the thickness of the lines indicates the level of relations between the themes, and the use of the same keywords as the theme names. The dashed lines on the same map reveal that different common words are used apart from the theme names. The overlap map shows the inter-period development of the keywords in the publications and what percentage of the keywords used in the previous period were transferred to the next period (Cobo, López-Herrera, Herrera-Viedma, & Herrera 2011). The overlap map also presents the number of keywords that are not used in the next period and are obsolete and the number of keywords that were not used in the previous periods but that have started to be used in the new period (Murgado-Armenteros, Gutiérrez-Salcedo, Torres-Ruiz, & Cobo, 2015).

3. Findings

3.1. Performance Analysis

The publications cover the period between 2005 and 2022. Nine hundred thirty-nine authors wrote 471 articles in 288 different journals. The number of articles with a single author is 106. The average number of authors per document is 2.5. This means that the number of pieces with multiple authors in the field is low. We have given basic information about 471 articles in Fig. 4.

When the number of publications is analyzed by years, the number before 2016 is relatively low. In particular, the number of publications before 2009 indicates that the number of publications sent from Türkiye to journals accepted as international sales points is relatively low. However, since 2016, it has been seen that the publications have increased steadily. This indicates the increasing interest in entrepreneurship research among scientists in Türkiye. Furthermore, since 2022 is not over, it is estimated that the number of publications will increase by the end of the year. In Table 1, we have given the distribution of publications by years, journals, and authors.

According to Table 1, Sustainability is among the journals with 12 publications, Eskişehir Osmangazi University Journal of Economics and Administrative Sciences with 10 publications, and Journal of Mehmet Akif Ersoy University. Considering the index of the journals, only the Sustainability (2021 impact factor: 3.889) journal is in SSCI, while other journals are indexed within the scope of ESCI. The authors with the most publications are Bakır C (nine publications), Baycan T, Nijkamp P, and Temel S (seven publications each), and Sesen H has six publications. When Bakır's publications are examined collectively, it is seen that the effect of public regulatory institutions and financial incentive mechanisms on entrepreneurship types is emphasized (Bakır, 2009, 2022; Bakır, Akgunay, & Coban, 2021; Bakır & Gunduz, 2020). In addition, Alrawadieh Z., Aydin E., Dabic M., Deveci I., Durst S., Koçak A., and Kryeziu L. each contributed to the field with five publications.

3.2. Theme and Evolution Analysis

3.2.1. Motor Themes. In first period, the motor themes were corporate entrepreneurship, gender, knowledge, social structure, and entrepreneurial orientations. The niche themes of the field are job satisfaction, survival, market orientation, and institutional entrepreneurship. In the second period, corporate entrepreneurship and performance are motor themes. Niche themes in this period

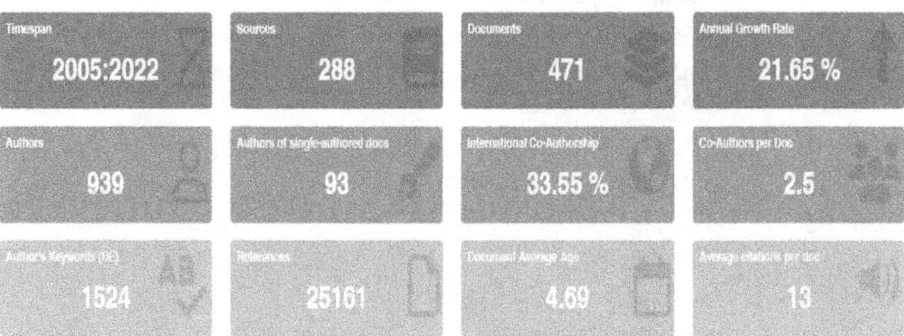

Fig. 4. Main Information About the Data.

Table 1. Performance Analysis.

Year	Articles	Sources	Articles	Authors	Articles
2022	56	*Sustainability*	13	Bakır C	9
2021	60	*Eskişehir Osmangazi University Journal of Economics and Administrative Sciences*	10	Baycan T	7
2020	58	*Journal of Mehmet Akif Ersoy University Economics and Administrative Sciences Faculty*	8	Nijkamp P	7
2019	51	*Journal of Small Business Management*	8	Temel S	7
2018	37	*African Journal of Business Management*	6	Alrawadieh Z	6
2017	32	*Education and Training*	6	Sesen H	6
2016	24	*International Journal of Contemporary Economics and Administrative Sciences*	6	Aydın E	5
2015	10	*Istanbul Business Research*	6	Cetindamar D	5
2014	14	*Journal of Entrepreneurship in Emerging Economies*	6	Dabic M	5
2013	17	*Istanbul University Journal of the School of Business*	5	Deveci I	5
2012	19	*Journal of Agriculture and Nature*	5	Durst S	5
2011	13	*Small Business Economics*	5	Koçak A	5
2010	14	*Yükseköğretim Dergisi*	5	Kryeziu L	5
2009	16	*Çukurova University Faculty of Education Journal*	4	Altınay L	4
2008	3	*Entrepreneurship Research Journal*	4	Arun K	4
2007	4	*IEEE Transactions on Engineering Management*	4	Bağış M	4
2006	5	*Istanbul Journal of Sociological Studies*	4	Baycan-Levent T	4
2005	2	*Journal of Organizational Change Management*	4	Karadeniz EE	4

are Syrian refugees, ideas, and entrepreneurial intentions. Fig. 5 shows the evolutionary pattern in themes from the first period to the second period.

3.2.2. Scientific Evolution Structure of Entrepreneurship. When we look at the first period in terms of the scientific development map, the themes of corporate entrepreneurship, gender, knowledge, entrepreneurship, and entrepreneurialism were able to position themselves in the field. We determined that the themes that could not pass from the first to the second period were survival, job satisfaction, market orientation, and perceptions. In the second period, we determined prominent themes: performance, corporate entrepreneurship, Syrian refugees, education, and Business. In the second period, the themes unrelated to the past are "Syrian refugees, ideas" and institutions (see Fig. 6). In particular, the concept of Syrian Refugees indicates that refugee/immigrant entrepreneurship has come to the fore in research specific to Türkiye in this period.

3.3. Co-Author Analysis

A total of six clusters were identified in the co-authorship analysis (see Fig. 7). The size of the nodes of each color indicates a large number of cooperation. For example, in the cluster shown in red, there are predominantly entrepreneurial intentions working in the international entrepreneurship initiatives of family companies in transition economies (Coskun, Kryeziu, & Krasniqi, 2022; Kryeziu, Bağış, Kurutkan, Krasniqi, & Haziri, 2022; Kryeziu, Coskun, & Krasniqi, 2022). Liridon Kryzieu is the most collaborative. The field represented by the green cluster is the field of rural development-based enterprise and immigrant entrepreneurship (Baycan, Sahin, & Nijkamp, 2012; Nijkamp, Sahin, & Baycan-Levent, 2010). In the cluster represented by the dark yellow cluster, the most collaborating author is Alrawadieh, Z. It is emphasized in this cluster that refugee (refugee) entrepreneurship is mainly represented in the accommodation sector in Türkiye (Alrawadieh, Altinay, Cetin, & Şimşek, 2021; Alrawadieh, Karayilan, & Cetin, 2019; Shneikat & Alrawadieh, 2019).

3.4. Document Analysis

Considering the scope of this book, we have classified the entrepreneurship types according to the following ten entrepreneurship types: government policy on entrepreneurship, indigenous entrepreneurship, gender and entrepreneurship, religion and entrepreneurship, social entrepreneurship, corporate entrepreneurship, sustainable entrepreneurship, family entrepreneurship, informal entrepreneurship, immigrant entrepreneurship, and small businesses in ethnic enclaves. Within the scope of the document review, three authors examined 471 articles separately and in detail. In this review, we read the articles' titles, keywords, abstracts, and introductions. Then we compared the classifications we made on the types of entrepreneurship. Where there were contradictions, we decided by compromise. As a result, we determined that we could evaluate 233 articles within the scope of related entrepreneurship types. As a result of our analysis, the most studied entrepreneurship types are gender (65 publications), family business

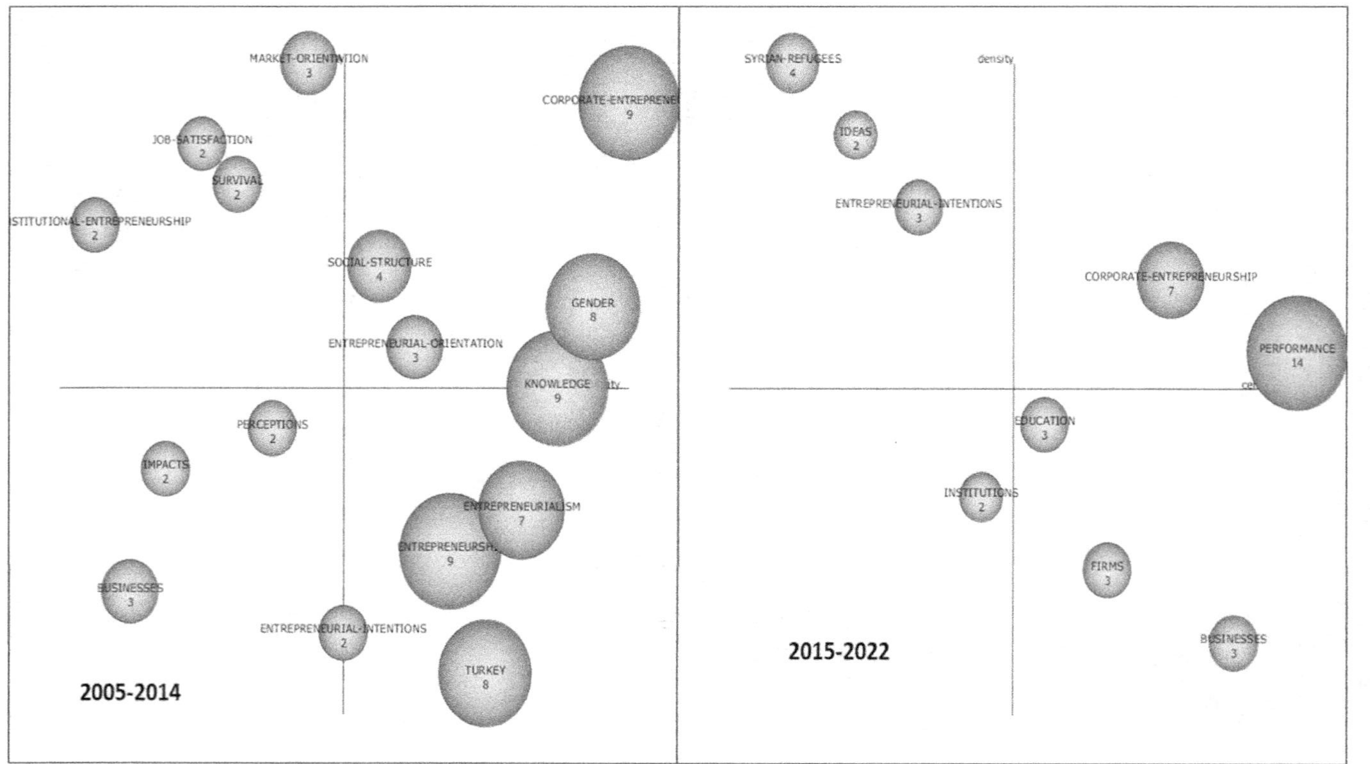

Fig. 5. Theme Analysis.

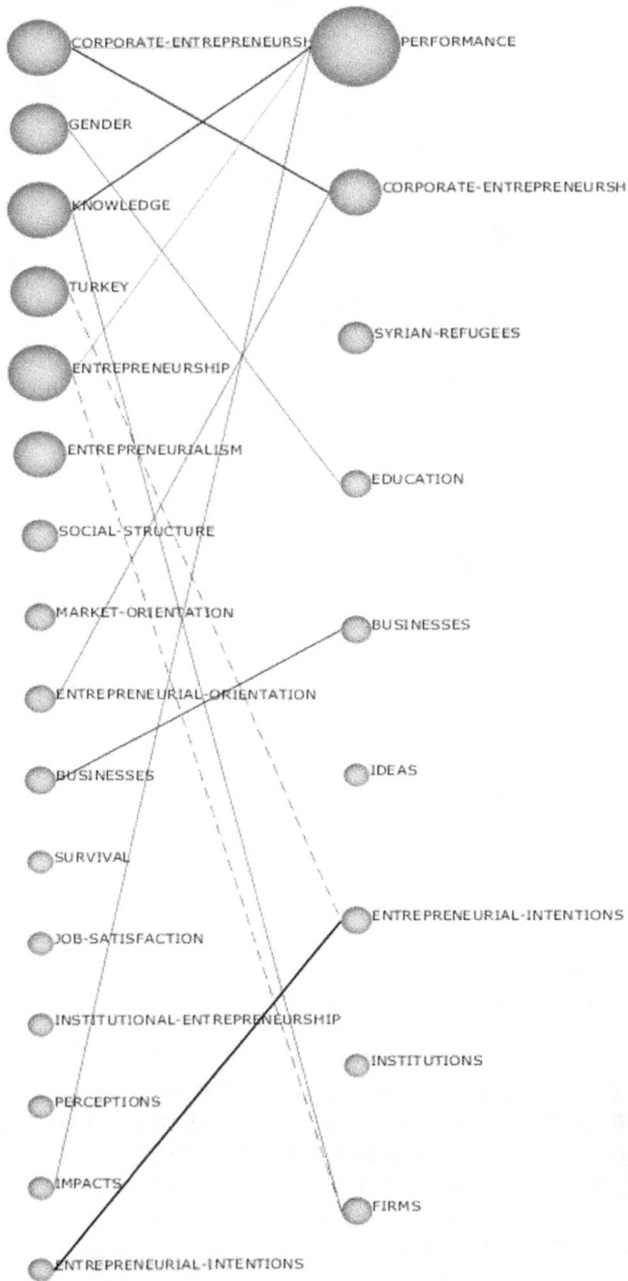

Fig. 6. Scientific Evolution Map.

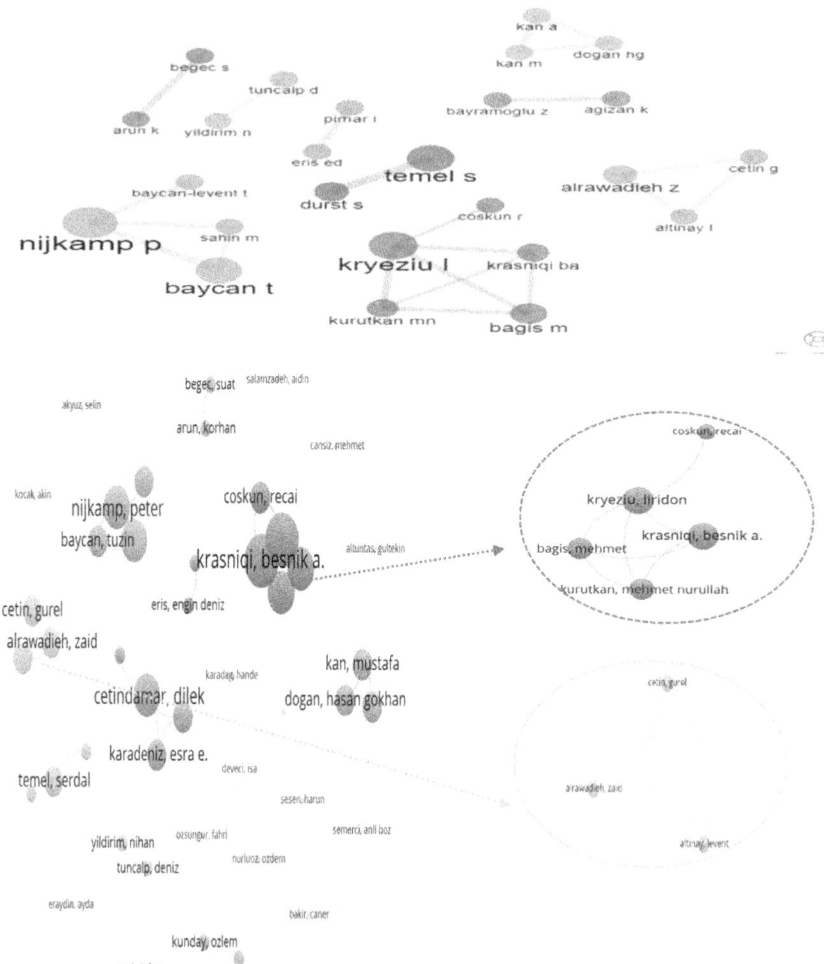

Fig. 7. Co-author Analysis Networks.

(52 publications), corporate entrepreneurship (37 publications), social entrepreneurship (28 publications), small business (23 publications), immigrant/refugee entrepreneurship (14 publication), and sustainable entrepreneurship (10 publications) are types of entrepreneurship. On the other hand, we found that the least studied subjects are indigenous (one publication), informal, and religion (three publications) entrepreneurship types.

3.4.1. Gender and Entrepreneurship. Research on gender entrepreneurship can be grouped as follows: *First*, a group focused on entrepreneurial intentions. In this group, Gupta, Goktan, and Gunay (2009) concluded no difference in entrepreneurial intentions between men and women. This study reported male and female perceptions based on masculine/feminine gender roles. Likewise, Gupta,

Turban, Wasti, and Sikdar (2014) show that, compared to women, men were more successful in opportunity evaluation when gender information was not presented. Whereas when gender–neutral attributes were equally presented, men and women evaluated entrepreneurial opportunities equally.

The differences in evaluating entrepreneurial orientation based on gender depend on feminine/masculine stereotypical information. In this context, Dabic, Daim, Bayraktaroglu, Novak, and Basic (2012) research found that the desire to be an entrepreneur is gender-dependent and that women are less entrepreneurial-oriented than men. The source of this difference is related to self-confidence and family support. The differences in gender-based entrepreneurial intentions depend on personality traits, where there is a difference between the two genders in terms of perceived feasibility and desirability. Examining gender differences within the framework of human capital, family capital, and financial capital, Cetindamar et al. (2012) discussed the importance of these capitals for being an entrepreneur. This study shows that human capital is essential for women, family capital is necessary depending on family size, and there are no differences between men and women regarding financial capital and the likelihood of becoming entrepreneurs.

The *second* group of studies focuses on cultural settings and personality traits within entrepreneurship and entrepreneurial intentions. Research show that there is a difference in terms of country culture, entrepreneurial intentions, and personality traits. Shneor, Metin Camgöz, and Bayhan Karapinar (2013) revealed that students in Türkiye have higher entrepreneurial intentions and self-efficacy than students in Norway, regardless of gender. Regarding gender, despite cultural context, males have entrepreneurial intentions, self-efficacy, and social norms in both countries. Aygun, Arslan, and Güney (2008) investigated entrepreneurship values in two different cultural environments (United States and Türkiye) and determined that entrepreneurship values differed between the two cultures. Men are more entrepreneurially oriented in Türkiye, where men value femininity and entrepreneurship more than in the United States. Studies on personality traits and entrepreneurial intentions have determined that successful women in Türkiye are persistent, determined, patient, mentally robust, visionary, and innovative (Maden, 2015; Zulfiu, Ramadani, & Dana, 2015). In addition, Altan-Olcay's (2014) study focuses on promoting women's entrepreneurship in Türkiye and on the role of civil society organizations in enhancing women's entrepreneurship. This study shows how civil society organization fs promote entrepreneurial attitudes discussing within a neoliberal ideological framework.

3.4.2. Entrepreneurship in Family Businesses. In the context of entrepreneurship in the family business, Erdogan, Rondi, and De Massis (2020) examined the innovative approach to improve long-established family firms' products and production processes. They demonstrated that tradition is a crucial driver of firm innovation and how the family's generations of experience shape firm strategy and reflect the strategic decisions of the current generation. This study argued that tradition and innovation are not contradictory, as they can be essential for the current generation of family businesses to focus on innovation. Kozan, Öksoy, and Özsoy (2006) researched the intensity and the business environment challenges as predictors of SME growth. This research reveals that the compelling factors do not fall into family business role conflict but the importance of other factors such as lack of knowledge and financial access. Maden's (2015) study shows that the source of finances and motivation for women entrepreneurs in Türkiye are family members, business partners, and other sources of finances. In another research, Altındag, Zehir, and Acar (2011) examined the strategic orientations of family businesses based on performance. This study shows that family companies use strategic aspects such as innovation and entrepreneurship to achieve sustainable competitive advantage and that the strategic orientation of family companies depends on the implementation, not the type of strategy. Sabah, Carsrud, and Koçak (2014) focus on family firms' entrepreneurial intensity by examining cultural openness, religion, and nationalism. They found that family businesses characterized as high nationalism have a low frequency and degree of entrepreneurship and, therefore, cannot compete in the global economy. Karataş-Özkan, Erdoğan, and Nicolopoulou (2011) focused on women in family firms by emphasizing the importance of cultural dynamism. The authors concluded that flexible working conditions and a sense of responsibility and belonging motivate women in family businesses in Türkiye. The rapid change in cultural values has positively reflected in women's involvement in family firms, which has driven them to contribute to their family business. This research also shows that women in family businesses contribute in several ways, such as entry into new industry markets, business growth, restructuring the company, establishing new ventures, and shifting the firm's direction.

3.4.3. Corporate Entrepreneurship. Regarding studies on corporate entrepreneurship, generally speaking, studies have focused on innovation and corporate performance. Gunday, Ulusoy, Kilic, and Alpkan (2011) examine the impact of types of innovation as a driving factor on firm performance. They show innovation positively affects firm performance mediated by the kinds of innovation. Ağca, Topal, and Kaya (2012) focus on the relationship between intrapreneurship activities and firm performance. The authors reveal that self-renewal is negatively associated with profitability and positively related to innovation and risk-taking. Another study by Alpkan, Bulut, Gunday, Ulusoy, and Kilic (2010) researches innovative firms and the impact of an internal supportive environment that led to intrapreneurial activities. This study confirms that organizational support, management support for idea development, and tolerance for risk-taking positively influence a firm's innovative performance at the individual level. While the reward system, free time, and work discretion have a distinct impact, the latter has a negative impact, whereas the former does not affect innovative performance. In addition, this study shows that human capital is the driving factor for innovative performance when organizational support is limited. Kantur's (2016) study focused on strategic entrepreneurship and attempted to distinguish between behavioral intentions and actual entrepreneurial events at the firm level. This study reports that the relationship fully mediates strategic entrepreneurship between entrepreneurial orientation and organizational performance, influenced by financial and non-financial performance.

Regarding performance, Kaya, Koc, and Topcu (2010) showed a positive relationship between human resources management activities in which all human resources management activities are correlated and positively influence organizational climate. Ozen and Berkman's (2007) study focuses on how the discourse that corporate executive elites produce to legitimate total quality management. This study shows ethos justifications have been exploited at the macro level, which has led to reconstructing comprehensive quality management as a source of solutions for different societal groups. Adopting total quality management instead of source discourse involves ethos justification, which is essential when actors promote these practices to produce social legitimacy. Furthermore, ethos justification is necessary when managerial procedures are attempted to implement in another context. Likewise, these actors are more likely to promote total quality management to the public, not their specialized field.

3.4.4. Social Entrepreneurship. Researches examining social enterprises are networks (Özeren, Saatcioglu, & Aydin, 2018; Sakarya, Bodur, Yildirim-Öktem, & Selekler-Göksen, 2012), institutions (Özdemir, 2013; Turker & Vural, 2017), cognitive factors (Konaklı, 2015; Özdemir, 2013), and life stories (Asarkaya & Keles Tayşir, 2019). On this subject, Sakarya et al. (2012) revealed the reasons and consequences of establishing alliances of commercial and social enterprises. The authors analyzed the goals, inputs, and effects of social alliances. They also explored the motives for forming social alliances at the alliance and partner levels and in terms of alliances of social influence created in micro, mezzo, and macro contexts and cultural, economic, and political domains. In a different study based on social networks, Özeren et al. (2018) examined the role of network processes in innovative activities carried out by social entrepreneurs and suggested that network processes are more critical for social innovation than network structure/design. Turker and Vural (2017) found the effect of institutional gaps and supports embedded in the logic of social welfare, commercial or public sectors on social innovation in their research, which they associate with social innovation. In a different study, Özdemir (2013) examined the effects of a corporate environment, cognitive factors, and social intention on the social value creation process for for-profit and non-profit organizations and presented a conceptual model. In another study focusing only on cognitive factors, Konaklı (2015) researched the effect of pre-service teachers' self-efficacy on social entrepreneurship characteristics. Finally, Asarkaya and Keles Tayşir (2019) analyzed the life stories of some Turkish social entrepreneurs and determined which factors in their backgrounds influenced their decision to create a social enterprise. Our review of 10 of the 23 publications shows that the literature on social networks, institutions, and cognitive factors dominates social entrepreneurship research.

3.4.5. SMEs (Small- and Medium-Sized Enterprises) and Entrepreneurship. Koçak and Abimbola (2009) listed the factors that lead to the successful internationalization of firms in developing economies as organizational structures, creating the entrepreneurial process of firms, and marketing and learning orientation. In further research regarding modes of open innovation and types of innovation outcomes, Hinteregger, Durst, Temel, and Yesilay (2019) showed the time different categories of SMEs use other modes of open innovation and their impact on different innovation outcomes. This study, by making a distinction between small- and medium-size enterprises and the tension between openness and firm size, shows that both use different modes of opening and types of innovation. Altınay et al. (2016) examined small business performance. They determined a positive relationship between entrepreneurial orientation and sales and market shares, compared to a negative relationship between entrepreneurial orientation and employment growth. This study also revealed that organizational learning capability and entrepreneurial orientation correlate positively. Another study by Karadag (2017) focuses on industry, SME age, and education and shows that the education level of SME owners and managers is positively related to financial management performance.

Demirel and Danisman (2019) focused on the circular economy and its impact on eco-innovations and external finances available. This research shows that a significant threshold investment into circular eco-innovations is required for SMEs to benefit from the circular economy. Compared to circular eco-innovations that do not successfully increase their growth rates of SMEs, eco-design investors successfully increase the growth rates of SMEs. In addition, equity finances positively influence SMEs' growth compared to traditional finances. Abimbola and Koçak (2007) examined SMEs' branding, reputation, and organizational identity. This study finds that branding and reputation are primary factors for SMEs to get resources that influence firms' success over a long period. Furthermore, this study shows that the interdisciplinary approach to exploiting identity, reputation, and entrepreneurship is the most suitable research design and method SMEs adopt. Finally, Asgary, Ozdemir, and Özyürek (2020) revealed that SMEs in the Turkish context listed global economic and geopolitical risks followed by environmental risks.

Regarding economic risks, fiscal crisis and unemployment rate are two primary sources SMEs list as the highest risks. Likewise, failure of regional, global, and national governance and its consequences, followed by risk of large-scale cyberattacks, social instability, failure of urban planning, manufactured environmental risks, disasters, and significant natural hazards, are the main risks the SMEs perceive. Some studies on this subject have focused on the contribution of SMEs to the economy in different ways and their impact on quality of life (Erdin & Ozkaya, 2020). This study found that quality of life and socioeconomic development are related to the initiatives of SMEs. As a result, SMEs significantly impact living standards in eastern and western Türkiye, including economic growth in these regions.

3.4.6. Immigrant/Refugee Entrepreneurship. Studies on immigrant/refugee entrepreneurship mainly focused on various forms of capital they employ to achieve sustainable competitive advantage and growth, their impact on host-country impact, and integration in the host country. Alrawadieh et al. (2019) focused on refugee entrepreneurs' challenges in Türkiye. This study revealed that refugee entrepreneurs face legislative and administrative challenges, access to finances, and obstacles related to the market. Eraydin, Tasan-Kok and Vranken (2010) examined the contribution of immigrant entrepreneurs on urban economic performance in two contexts: Belgium and Türkiye. This research finds that diversity is essential for urban financial performance, facilitated by the skills and social networks that lead to increased production and services. The main factor that helps immigrant entrepreneurs survive is social capital, as well as the talent these entrepreneurs have to fill the gap regarding the lack of a skilled labor force. According to Shneikat and Alrawadieh's (2019) study, refugee entrepreneurs' impact on economic performance is the motivation to survive, the willingness to become independent, and the resources available. This study also determines the hiring practices, social networks, and other factors essential in their entrepreneurial activities in the host country. As shown in the above studies, the importance of human and social capital is confirmed by Shinnar and Zamantılı Nayır (2019), which suggest that immigrant entrepreneurs have a unique human and social capital resource for opportunity identification, and knowledge. Likewise, these entrepreneurs are characterized by the ability to build relationships based on their ability of language, culture, and religious knowledge. The economic integration through entrepreneurial activities of immigrant entrepreneurs was examined by Alrawadieh et al. (2021) cross-country study. This study identified the importance of language skills, family and ethnic networking, and relationships with host communities as crucial factors for entrepreneurial success and integration.

In this vein, Atasü-Topcuoğlu (2019) focused on the ability of immigrant entrepreneurs to utilize various forms of cultural, social, economic, and symbolic capital to establish and build sustainable competitive strategies. This research shows that immigrant entrepreneurs maximize different forms of capital to seek entrepreneurial opportunities and become integrated. However, the informal economy as the primary form of entrepreneurial chance for these immigrants at the start-up stage is essential but limits growth and economic integration. Likewise, establishing start-ups for immigrants was the focus of Kachkar's (2019) study which maintains that approximately one-third of immigrants found their businesses in refugee camps. The primary financial source was savings or sponsorship from close-knit relatives. This study also shows that most immigrants have indicated their intentions to become entrepreneurs. Finally, various forms of capital were the main focus of Karadal, Shneikat, Abubakar, and Bhatti (2021) which focuses on Turkish immigrants in the United States and maintains that entrepreneurial, intellectual, social, family, and financial capital are the leading driving factors of entrepreneurial activities. In addition, Yetim's (2008) study focuses on female entrepreneurship. It distinguishes between immigrant and non-immigrant female entrepreneurs and shows that social capital is essential for social status.

3.4.7. Sustainable Entrepreneurship. Vatansever and Arun (2016), in their research on sustainable entrepreneurship, aim to analyze individual cases of green entrepreneurs to understand local authorities and dynamics from the perspectives of ecological modernization and network society theories. The authors discussed the relatively new and unique dynamics of green entrepreneurship in Türkiye and the opportunities and barriers to green entrepreneurs. Fidlerová, Stareček, Vraňaková, Bulut, and Keaney (2022) provided findings from six countries, including Türkiye, in a different study. The authors concluded that there are differences in approaches to sustainability issues, the scope of knowledge, interest, competencies in sustainable development and sustainable development goals, and practice content in organizations in different sectors, regions, and countries. Our document analysis findings found that only 2 out of 10 articles on sustainable entrepreneurship are directly related to the Turkish context. This situation has implications for the inadequacy of empirical studies in sustainable entrepreneurship research in Türkiye.

4. Implications and Conclusions

4.1. Theoretical Implications

In recent years, developments in entrepreneurship research produced in non-Western societies have encouraged researchers to look at the entrepreneurship literature in terms of national (Zheng, 2018) and emerging market (Indarti, Hapsari, Lukito-Budi, & Virgosita, 2020) dynamics. This chapter aimed to contribute to a more diverse knowledge base by examining the international performance and development of entrepreneurship literature in Türkiye. This section will discuss the theoretical and practical implications of the research, its limitations, and recommendations for future research.

Firstly, performance analyses show that the interest in entrepreneurship research has increased in Türkiye. However, when we look at the quality of the journals in which the articles are published, we see that the publications from Türkiye are insufficient in journals with high impact factor. This finding reveals that publications in journals with high impact factors, such as Entrepreneurship Theory and Practice, Entrepreneurship & Regional Development, and the International Journal of Entrepreneurial Behavior & Research, are insufficient. However, the performance analysis shows that there are authors from different countries. This situation reveals the importance of international cooperation in sending Turkish-origin publications to global sales points.

Secondly, the theme and evolution analysis findings show that the motor themes, such as corporate entrepreneurship, gender, and entrepreneurial orientation in the first period, gave way to the motor themes, such as institutional entrepreneurship and performance, in the second period. Corporate entrepreneurship describes entrepreneurial behavior within established, medium-sized and large organizations and refers to the organizational renewal process (Phan, Wright, Ucbasaran, & Tan, 2009). On the other hand, institutional entrepreneurship relates to the activities of actors interested in specific institutional arrangements and using resources to create new institutions or transform existing ones (Maguire, Hardy, & Lawrence, 2004, p. 657). When the two definitions and findings are evaluated together, it is seen that the research in Türkiye has evolved from the first period to the second period at the level of the organization firm to a point where the actor and the institutional environment interact together. However, this inference does not provide information about the interaction of managers and the corporate environment in firms and is a motivation for future research. In the niche, themes show that while institutional entrepreneurship issues were studied in the first period, the entrepreneurial intentions of Syrian refugee entrepreneurs came to the fore in the second period. This finding shows that the turmoil in Syria affected Türkiye (Alrawadieh et al., 2021). Especially the migration from Syria to Türkiye has revealed this result. We see many studies on this subject (Alrawadieh et al., 2019, 2021; Atasü-Topcuoğlu, 2019; Kachkar, 2019). In addition to this, we found that entrepreneurship studies were conducted with different international (Eraydin et al., 2010; Karadal et al., 2021; Shinnar & Zamantılı Nayır, 2019; Yetim, 2008) and migrant-nonmigrant comparisons (Yetim, 2008).

Thirdly, the results of the co-authorship analysis show that there are co-authorships within specific clusters in Türkiye. The authors in the first group are Kryeziu, L. Bağış, M., Kurutkan, M. N., and Krasniqi B. A. The collaborative work of these authors focused on entrepreneurial intentions (Bağış et al., 2022). The second group of authors is Alrawadieh, Z., Çetin, G., and Altınay, L. The research of this group of authors focused on Syrian refugee entrepreneurs in the tourism and hospitality industry (Alrawadieh et al., 2019, 2021). However, the findings show that the co-authorship relationship within the group is not reflected in the co-authorship relationships between the groups. This situation reveals that co-authorship relationships are limited to certain scientists.

Finally, the document analysis results show that the most studied types of entrepreneurship are gender, family, corporate, social, and small business, respectively. In addition, while immigrant/refugee entrepreneurship is emerging as a new topic, indigenous entrepreneurship, ethnic entrepreneurship, informal entrepreneurship, sustainable entrepreneurship, and religious entrepreneurship are the least studied topics. This finding showed that many issues in the international entrepreneurship literature were insufficiently researched in Türkiye.

4.2. Policy Implications

In this context, the research has some implications for policymakers. *Firstly*, scientists who direct entrepreneurship research can design new studies by addressing the missing points we have listed within the framework of research results, and policymaker can provide resources for incomplete research. *Secondly*, the findings show that refugee entrepreneurs have emerged as an important problem and research area in Türkiye. Therefore, policymakers can design policies for the issues of these entrepreneurs. In this topic, one of the most common problems refugee entrepreneurs face is the lack of language skills to facilitate their integration into the host society. In this regard, policymakers can open language courses that will enable the integration of refugee entrepreneurs into society. Such programs can serve as a platform for the coexistence of refugees and for improving their language skills (Alrawadieh et al., 2021). *Finally*, considering the concepts of entrepreneurship that emerged in the research, such as immigrant, refugee, and Syrian refugee, we suggest that policymakers make formal regulations to ensure that such entrepreneurs fit into the economy and society. In this regard, it is essential to provide entrepreneurship training and resource allocation, facilitate legal mechanisms, and provide infrastructure for relevant refugees. In addition, enacting laws that will distance entrepreneurs from the informal economy will benefit economic development and growth.

4.3. Limitations and Future Research

The research limitations and future research recommendations can be grouped under four headings. *Firstly*, while this research draws a static view, the structuring of the field of entrepreneurship is dynamic (Déry & Toulouse, 1996). Although our research is a longitudinal analysis, it gives a snapshot of research published in international journals from Türkiye (Teixeira & Ferreira, 2013). Considering the possibility of development and the dynamic structure of the literature while the research is going on, we may have overlooked new research. Therefore, future research can examine emerging research.

Secondly, we only examined the WoS database. For example, Scopus and EBSCO databases may have valuable research from Türkiye (Donthu et al., 2021; Li, Spry, & Woodall 2020; Zupic & Čater, 2015). Therefore, future research can do a more comprehensive review by combining research from these databases. *Thirdly*, we only examined studies in English. Consequently, we did not read the Turkish and English studies in Türkiye. On this basis, future research can compare and review the Turkish and English research in Türkiye with the Turkish and English research in the international arena.

Fourthly, we could not provide information on how Türkiye is doing compared to the entrepreneurship literature in other emerging economies. Therefore, future research can compare research in Türkiye and other emerging economies. In addition, making a comparison that will cover research originating from Türkiye and developed countries (Ding, Ge, Wu, & Zheng, 2013) deserves a new research. In this way, it will be possible to say something about the scope of entrepreneurship research between developing and developed countries.

Fifthly, we analyzed performance, co-author, and co-word from bibliometric analyses. However, we did not perform co-citation, and bibliographic coupling analyzes. Bibliography matching refers to the similarity of the bibliographies of two different studies (Donthu et al., 2021; Vogel & Güttel, 2013). This occurs due to citing the same study (or studies) in two studies (Rehn & Kronman, 2006). This analysis can identify new publications not yet mentioned, emerging fields, and smaller subdomains (Bağış, 2021b). For this reason, future research can analyze to determine the sub-fields that will appear in the future in international publications originating from Türkiye.

Finally, despite the critical literature on religion and entrepreneurship (Anggadwita, Mulyaningsih, Ramadani, & Arwiyah, 2015; Anggadwita, Ramadani, Alamanda, Ratten, & Hashan, 2017b; Block, Fisch, & Rehan, 2020; Ramadani, Dana, Gërguri-Rashiti, & Ratten, 2017; Ramadani, Dana, Ratten, & Tahiri, 2015), we concluded that this subject has never been researched in Türkiye. Therefore, future research can examine the entrepreneurship of Türkiye's Islamic, Christian, Jewish, and other religious communities as an institution. In addition, there is a well-developed literature on informal entrepreneurship (Santos & Ferreira, 2017). However, we concluded that the studies in Türkiye on this subject are quite limited (Atasü-Topcuoğlu, 2019; Kus, 2014). Considering the differences between the productivity of informal and formal firms in Türkiye (Taymaz, 2009), future research may focus on possible differences between formal and informal entrepreneurs. In addition, despite the literature on sustainable entrepreneurship (Tunçalp & Yıldırım, 2022) and ethnic entrepreneurship (Indarti et al., 2021), we see that research on both types of entrepreneurship is insufficient in international publications from Türkiye. This creates a potential research area for future research.

For example, how does Türkiye's full accession to the Paris Climate Agreement and Green Deal Action Plan on October 7, 2021, shape the new entrepreneurship strategies of medium and large-sized companies? In addition, considering the ethnic texture of Türkiye, the field of ethnic entrepreneurship emerges as an essential field of study. The points where ethnic identities enrich and complicate entrepreneurial behavior in Türkiye seem to be worth investigating and constitute a motivation for potential research in the future.

References

Abimbola, T., & Koçak, A. (2007). Brand, organization identity and reputation: SMEs as expressive organizations: A resources-based perspective, *Qualitative Market Research*, *10*(4), 416–430.https://doi.org/10.1108/13522750710819748

Acedo, F. J., Barroso, C., Casanueva, C., & Galán, J. L. (2006). Co-authorship in management and organizational studies: An empirical and network analysis. *Journal of Management Studies*, *43*(5), 957–983.https://doi.org/10.1111/j.1467-6486.2006.00625.x

Acs, Z. J., & Audretsch, D. B. (1993). *Small firms and entrepreneurship: An East–West perspective*. Cambridge: Cambridge University Press.

Ağca, V., Topal, Y., & Kaya, H. (2012). Linking intrapreneurship activities to multidimensional firm performance in Turkish manufacturing firms: An empirical study. *International Entrepreneurship and Management Journal*, *8*(1), 15–33.https://doi.org/10.1007/s11365-009-0132-5

Alpkan, L., Bulut, C., Gunday, G., Ulusoy, G., & Kilic, K. (2010). Organizational support for intrapreneurship and its interaction with human capital to enhance innovative performance. *Management Decision*, *48*(5), 732–755.https://doi.org/10.1108/00251741011043902

Alrawadieh, Z., Altinay, L., Cetin, G., & Şimşek, D. (2021). The interface between hospitality and tourism entrepreneurship, integration and well-being: A study of refugee entrepreneurs. *International Journal of Hospitality Management*, *97*(1–12), 103013. https://doi.org/10.1016/j.ijhm.2021.103013

Alrawadieh, Z., Karayilan, E., & Cetin, G. (2019). Understanding the challenges of refugee entrepreneurship in tourism and hospitality. *The Service Industries Journal*, *39*(9–10), 717–740.https://doi.org/10.1080/02642069.2018.1440550

Altan-Olcay, Ö. (2014). Entrepreneurial subjectivities and gendered complexities: Neoliberal citizenship in Turkey. *Feminist Economics*, *20*(4), 235–259. https://doi.org/10.1080/13545701.2014.950978

Altınay, L., Madanoglu, M., De Vita, G., Arasli, H., & Ekinci, Y. (2016). The interface between organizational learning capability, entrepreneurial orientation, and SME growth. *Journal of Small Business Management*, *54*(3), 871–891. doi:10.1111/jsbm.12219

Altınay, L., & Wang, C. L. (2011). The influence of an entrepreneur's socio-cultural characteristics on the entrepreneurial orientation of small firms. *Journal of Small Business and Enterprise Development*, *18*(4), 673–694. https://doi.org/10.1108/14626001111179749

Altındag, E., Zehir, C., & Acar, A. Z. (2011). Strategic orientations and their effects on firm performance in Turkish family owned firms. *Eurasian Business Review*, *1*(1), 18–36. https://doi.org/10.14208/BF03353796

Anggadwita, G., Luturlean, B. S., Ramadani, V., & Ratten, V. (2017a). Socio-cultural environments and emerging economy entrepreneurship: Women entrepreneurs in

Indonesia. *Journal of Entrepreneurship in Emerging Economies*, *9*(1), 85–96. https://doi.org/10.1108/JEEE-03-2016-0011

Anggadwita, G., Mulyaningsih, H. D., Ramadani, V., & Arwiyah, M. Y. (2015). Women entrepreneurship in Islamic perspective: A driver for social change. *International Journal of Business and Globalisation*, *15*(3), 389–404. https://doi.org/10.1504/IJBG.2015.071914

Anggadwita, G., Ramadani, V., Alamanda, D. T., Ratten, V., & Hashani, M. (2017b). Entrepreneurial intentions from an Islamic perspective: A study of Muslim entrepreneurs in Indonesia. *International Journal of Entrepreneurship and Small Business*, *31*(2), 165–179. doi:10.1504/IJESB.2017.10004845

Asarkaya, C., & Keles Taysir, N. (2019). Founder's background as a catalyst for social entrepreneurship. *Nonprofit Management and Leadership*, *30*(1), 155–166. https://doi.org/10.1002/nml.21353

Asgary, A., Ozdemir, A. I., & Özyürek, H. (2020). Small and medium enterprises and global risks: Evidence from manufacturing SMEs in Turkey. *International Journal of Disaster Risk Science*, *11*(1), 59–73. https://doi.org/10.1007/s13753-020-00247-0

Atasü-Topcuoğlu, R. (2019). Syrian refugee entrepreneurship in Turkey: Integration and the use of immigrant capital in the informal economy. *Social Inclusion*, *7*(4), 200–210. https://doi.org/10.17645/si.v7i4.2346

Aygun, Z. K., Arslan, M., & Güney, S. (2008). Work values of Turkish and American university students. *Journal of Business Ethics*, *80*, 205–223. doi:10.1007/s10551-007-9413-5

Bağış, M. (2020). A longitudinal analysis on the micro-foundations of strategic management: where are micro-foundations going?. *Business & Management Studies: An International Journal*, *8*(2), 1310–1333. https://doi.org/10.15295/bmij.v8i2.1454

Bağış, M. (2021a). A research on the cognitive and behavioral foundations of strategic management: 1995–2020. *Ege Academic Review*, *21*(3), 163–180. https://doi.org/10.21121/eab.959904

Bağış, M. (2021b). Bibliyometrik araştırmalarda kullanılan başlıca analiz teknikleri. *Editörler: Oğuzhan Öztürk ve Gökhan Gürler), Bir Literatür İncelemesi Aracı Olarak Bibliyometrik Analiz, 3.Baskı*, 97–109.

Bağış, M., Kryeziu, L., Kurutkan, M. N., Krasniqi, B. A., Hernik, J., Karagüzel, E. S., ... Ateş, Ç. (2022). Youth entrepreneurial intentions: A cross-cultural comparison. *Journal of Enterprising Communities: People and Places in the Global Economy*, ahead-of-print.

Bağış, M., Kryeziu, L., Kurutkan, M. N. & Ramadani, V. (2022). Women entrepreneurship in family business: Dominant topics and future research trends, *Journal of Family Business Management*, Vol. ahead-of-print No. ahead-of-print. https://doi.org/10.1108/JFBM-03-2022-0040

Baker, K. H., Pandey, N., Kumar, S., & Haldar, A. (2020). A bibliometric analysis of board diversity: Current status, development, and future research directions. *Journal of Business Research*, *108*, 232–246. https://doi.org/10.1016/j.jbusres.2019.11.025

Bakır, C. (2009). Policy entrepreneurship and institutional change: Multilevel governance of central banking reform. *Governance*, *22*(4), 571–598. https://doi.org/10.1111/j.1468-0491.2009.01454.x

Bakır, C. (2022). What does comparative policy analysis have to do with the structure, ınstitution, and agency debate? *Journal of Comparative Policy Analysis: Research and Practice*, *24*(5), 415–429. https://doi.org/10.1080/13876988.2022.2045867

Bakır, C., Akgunay, S., & Coban, K. (2021). Why does the combination of policy entrepreneur and institutional entrepreneur roles matter for the institutionalization of policy ideas? *Policy Sciences*, *54*(2), 397–422. https://doi.org/10.1007/s11077-021-09417-3

Bakır, C., & Gunduz, K. A. (2020). The importance of policy entrepreneurs in developing countries: A systematic review and future research agenda. *Public Administration and Development*, *40*(1), 11–34. https://doi.org/10.1002/pad.1864

Baycan, T., Sahin, M., & Nijkamp, P. (2012). The urban growth potential of second-generation migrant entrepreneurs: A sectoral study on Amsterdam. *International Business Review*, *21*(6), 971–986. https://doi.org/10.1016/j.ibusrev.2011.11.005

Bird, B. J., & West, G. P. (1998). Time and entrepreneurship. *Entrepreneurship Theory and Practice*, *22*(2), 5–9. https://doi.org/10.1177/104225879802200201

Block, J., Fisch, C., & Rehan, F. (2020). Religion and entrepreneurship: A map of the field and a bibliometric analysis. *Management Review Quarterly*, *70*(4), 591–627. https://doi.org/10.1007/s11301-019-00177-2

Bowen, G. A. (2009). Document analysis as a qualitative research method, *Qualitative Research Journal*, *9*(2), 27–40. https://doi.org/10.3316/QRJ0902027

Celik, A. K., Yıldız, T., Aykanat, Z., & Kazemzadeh, S. (2021). The impact of narrow personality traits on entrepreneurial intention in developing countries: A comparison of Turkish and Iranian undergraduate students using ordered discrete choice models. *European Research on Management and Business Economics*, *27*(1), 100 138. https://doi.org/10.1016/j.iedeen.2020.100138

Cem, I., Küçükaltan, E. G., Çelebi, S. K., Çalkın, Ö., Enser, İ., & Çelik, A. (2019). Turizm ve girişimcilik alanında yapılmış çalışmaların bibliyometrik analizi. *Güncel Turizm Araştırmaları Dergisi*, *3*(1), 119–149. https://doi.org/10.32572/guntad.519018

Cetindamar, D., Gupta, V. K., Karadeniz, E. E., & Egrican, N. (2012). What the numbers tell: The impact of human, family and financial capital on women and men's entry into entrepreneurship in Turkey. *Entrepreneurship & Regional Development*, *24*(1–2), 29–51. https://doi.org/10.1080/08985626.2012.637348

Chen, C. (2006). CiteSpace II: Detecting and visualizing emerging trends and transient patterns in scientific literature. *Journal of the American Society for information Science and Technology*, *57*(3), 359–377. https://doi.org/10.1002/asi.20317

Chen, C. (2014). The citespace manual. *College of Computing and Informatics*, *1*(1), 1–84.

Chen, C., Ibekwe-SanJuan, F., & Hou, J. (2010). The structure and dynamics of cocitation clusters: A multiple-perspective cocitation analysis. *Journal of the American Society for information Science and Technology*, *61*(7), 1386–1409. https://doi.org/10.1002/asi.21309

Cobo, M. (2011). *SciMAT: Software tool for the analysis of the evolution of scientific knowledge. proposal for an evaluation methodology*. Doctoral dissertation, University of Granada.

Cobo, M., López-Herrera, A., Herrera-Viedma, E., & Herrera, F. (2011). An approach for detecting, quantifying, and visualizing the evolution of a research field: A practical application to the fuzzy sets theory field. *Journal of Informetrics*, *5*(1), 146–166. https://doi.org/10.1016/j.joi.2010.10.002

Cobo, M. J., López-Herrera, A. G., Herrera-Viedma, E., & Herrera, F. (2012). SciMAT: A new science mapping analysis software tool. *Journal of the American Society for Information Science and Technology*, *63*(8), 1609–1630. https://doi.org/10.1002/asi.22688

Coskun, R., Kryeziu, L., & Krasniqi, B. A. (2022). Institutions and competition: Does internationalisation provide advantages for the family firms in a transition economy?. *Journal of Entrepreneurship and Public Policy*, *11*(2/3), 253–272. https://doi.org/10.1108/JEPP-01-2022-0010

Caylan, D. Ö. (2014). Stratejik girişimcilik alanına ilişkin bibliyometrik bir değerlendirme. *Journal of Entrepreneurship and Innovation Management*, *3*(2), 61–80.

Dabic, M., Daim, T., Bayraktaroglu, E., Novak, I., & Basic, M. (2012). Exploring gender differences in attitudes of university students towards entrepreneurship: An international survey. *International Journal of Gender and Entrepreneurship*, *4*(3), 316–336. https://doi.org/10.1108/17566261211264172

Déry, R., & Toulouse, J. M. (1996). Social structuration of the field of entrepreneurship: A case study. *Canadian Journal of Administrative Sciences/Revue canadienne des sciences de l'administration, 13*(4), 285–305. https://doi.org/10.1111/j.1936-4490.1996.tb00739.x

Demirel, P., & Danisman, G. O. (2019). Eco-innovation and firm growth in the circular economy: Evidence from European small- and medium-sized enterprises. *Business Strategy and the Environment, 28*(8), 1608–1618. https://doi.org/10.1002/bse.2336

Deveciyan, M. T., Korkarer, S., & Çetin, C. (2021). Etik girişimcilik alanında yapılmış ulusal ve uluslararası çalışmaların bibliyometrik analizi. *İşletme Araştırmaları Dergisi, 13*(3), 2455–2472. https://doi.org/10.20491/isarder.2021.1271

Ding, Z. Q., Ge, J. P., Wu, X. M., & Zheng, X. N. (2013). Bibliometrics evaluation of research performance in pharmacology/pharmacy: China relative to ten representative countries. *Scientometrics, 96*(3), 829–844. https://doi.org/10.1007/s11192-013-0968-x

Donthu, N., Kumar, S., Mukherjee, D., Pandey, N., & Lim, W. M. (2021). How to conduct a bibliometric analysis: An overview and guidelines. *Journal of Business Research, 133*, 285–296. https://doi.org/10.1016/j.jbusres.2021.04.070

Donthu, N., Kumar, S., & Pattnaik, D. (2020). Forty-five years of Journal of Business Research: A bibliometric analysis. *Journal of Business Research, 109*(1), 1–14. https://doi.org/10.1016/j.jbusres.2019.10.039

Eraydin, A., Tasan-Kok, T., & Vranken, J. (2010). Diversity matters: Immigrant entrepreneurship and contribution of different forms of social integration in economic performance of cities. *European Planning Studies, 18*(4), 521–543. https://doi.org/10.1080/09654311003593556

Erdin, C., & Ozkaya, G. (2020). Contribution of small and medium enterprises to economic development and quality of life in Turkey. *Heliyon, 6*(2), e03215. https://doi.org/10.1016/j.heliyon.2020.e03215

Erdogan, I., Rondi, E., & De Massis, A. (2020). Managing the tradition and innovation paradox in family firms: A family imprinting perspective. *Entrepreneurship Theory and Practice, 44*(1), 20–54. https://doi.org/10.1177/104225871983971

Fayolle, A., Kyrö, P., & Ulijn, J. M. (2005). *Entrepreneurship research in Europe: Outcomes and perspectives*. Cheltenham: Edward Elgar Publishing.

Fidlerová, H., Stareček, A., Vraňaková, N., Bulut, C., & Keaney, M. (2022). Sustainable entrepreneurship for business opportunity recognition: Analysis of an awareness questionnaire among organisations. *Energies, 15*(3), 849. https://doi.org/10.3390/en15030849

Furstenau, L. B., Sott, M. K., Homrich, A. J. O., Kipper, L. M., Dohan, M. S., López-Robles, J. R., … & Tortorella, G. L. (2021). An overview of 42 years of lean production: Applying bibliometric analysis to investigate strategic themes and scientific evolution structure. *Technology Analysis & Strategic Management, 33*(9), 1068–1087. https://doi.org/10.1080/09537325.2020.1865530

Grimm, M., Gubert, F., Koriko, O., Lay, J., & Nordman, C. J. (2013). Kinship ties and entrepreneurship in Western Africa. *Journal of Small Business & Entrepreneurship, 26*(2), 125–150. https://doi.org/10.1080/08276331.2013.771854

Gunday, G., Ulusoy, G., Kilic, K., & Alpkan, L. (2011). Effects of innovation types on firm performance. *International Journal of Production Economics, 133*(2), 662–676. https://doi.org/10.1016/j.ijpe.2011.05.014

Gupta, V. K., Goktan, A. B., & Gunay, G. (2014). Gender differences in evaluation of new business opportunity: A stereotype threat perspective. *Journal of Business Venturing, 29*(2), 273–288. https://doi.org/10.1016/j.jbusvent.2013.02.002

Gupta, V. K., Turban, D. B., Wasti, S. A., & Sikdar, A. (2009). The role of gender stereotypes in perceptions of entrepreneurs and intentions to become an entrepreneur. *Entrepreneurship Theory and Practice, 33*(2), 397–417. https://doi.org/10.1111/j.1540-6520.2009.00296.x

Gutiérrez-Salcedo, M., Martínez, M. Á., Moral-Munoz, J. A., Herrera-Viedma, E., & Cobo, M. J. (2018). Some bibliometric procedures for analyzing and evaluating research fields. *Applied İntelligence*, *48*(5), 1275–1287. https://doi.org/10.1007/s10489-017-1105-y

Gürol, Y., & Atsan, N. (2006). Entrepreneurial characteristics amongst university students: Some insights for entrepreneurship education and training in Turkey. *Education + Training*, *48*(1), 25–38. https://doi.org/10.1108/00400910610645716

Hinteregger, C., Durst, S., Temel, S., & Yesilay, R. B. (2019). The impact of openness on innovation in SMEs. *International Journal of Innovation Management*, *23*(01), 1950003. https://doi.org/10.1142/S1363919619500038

Huang, M. H., & Chang, Y. W. (2011). A study of interdisciplinarity in information science: Using direct citation and co-authorship analysis. *Journal of Information Science*, *37*(4), 369–378. https://doi.org/10.1177/0165551511407141

Indarti, N., Hapsari, N., Lukito-Budi, A. S., & Virgosita, R. (2021). Quo vadis, ethnic entrepreneurship? A bibliometric analysis of ethnic entrepreneurship in growing markets, *Journal of Entrepreneurship in Emerging Economies*, *13*(3) 427–458. https://doi.org/10.1108/JEEE-04-2020-0080

Kachkar, O. A. (2019). Refugee entrepreneurship: Empirical quantitative evidence on microenterprises in refugee camps in Turkey. *Journal of Immigrant & Refugee Studies*, *17*(3), 333–352. https://doi.org/10.1080/15562948.2018.1479913

Kantur, D. (2016). Strategic entrepreneurship: Mediating the entrepreneurial orientation-performance link. *Management Decision*, *54*(1), 24–43. https://doi.org/10.1108/MD-11-2014-0660

Karadag, H. (2017). The impact of industry, firm age and education level on financial management performance in small and medium-sized enterprises (SMEs): Evidence from Turkey, *Journal of Entrepreneurship in Emerging Economies*, *9*(3), 300–314. https://doi.org/10.1108/JEEE-09-2016-0037

Karadal, H., Shneikat, B. H. T., Abubakar, A. M., & Bhatti, O. K. (2021). Immigrant entrepreneurship: The case of Turkish entrepreneurs in the United States. *Journal of the Knowledge Economy*, *12*(4), 1574–1593. https://doi.org/10.1007/s13132-020-00684-8

Karataş-Özkan, M., Erdoğan, A., & Nicolopoulou, K. (2011). Women in Turkish family businesses: Drivers, contributions and challenges. *International Journal of Cross Cultural Management*, *11*(2), 203–219. https://doi.org/10.1177/1470595811399189

Karayel, T., & Kurutkan, M. N. (2022). Covid 19 Sürecinde Yapay Zekâ ve Bileşenleri ile İlgili Yayınların Bibliyometrik Analizi. *Sağlık Akademisyenleri Dergisi*, *9*(3), 220–233. https://doi.org/10.52880/sagakaderg.1070774

Kasemodel, M. G. C., Makishi, F., Souza, R. C., & Silva, V. L. (2016). Following the trail of crumbs: A bibliometric study on consumer behavior in the food science and technology field. *International Journal of Food Studies*, *5*(1), 73–83. https://doi.org/10.7455/ijfs/5.1.2016.a7

Kaya, N., Koc, E., & Topcu, D. (2010). An exploratory analysis of the influence of human resource management activities and organizational climate on job satisfaction in Turkish banks. *The International Journal of Human Resource Management*, *21*(11), 2031–2051. https://doi.org/10.1080/09585192.2010.505104

Koçak, A., & Abimbola, T. (2009). The effects of entrepreneurial marketing on born global performance, *International Marketing Review*, *26*(4/5), 439–452. https://doi.org/10.1108/02651330910971977

Konaklı, T. (2015). Effects of self-efficacy on social entrepreneurship in education: A correlational research. *Research in Education*, *94*(1), 30–43. https://doi.org/10.7227/RIE.0019

Kozan, M. K., Öksoy, D., & Özsoy, O. (2006). Growth plans of small businesses in Turkey: Individual and environmental influences. *Journal of Small Business Management*, *44*(1), 114–129. https://doi.org/10.1111/j.1540-627X.2006.00157.x

Kryeziu, L., Bağış, M., Kurutkan, M. N., Krasniqi, B. A., & Haziri, A. (2022). COVID-19 impact and firm reactions towards crisis: Evidence from a transition economy.

Journal of Entrepreneurship, Management and Innovation, *18*(1), 169–196. https://doi.org/10.7341/20221816

Kryeziu, L., Coskun, R., & Krasniqi, B. (2022). Social networks and family firm internationalisation: Cases from a transition economy. *Review of International Business and Strategy*, *32*(2), 284–304. https://doi.org/10.1108/RIBS-03-2021-0052

Kurutkan, M. N., & Terzi, M. (2022). Sağlık Hizmetlerinde Dış Kaynak Kullanımının Bibliyometrik Analizi. *Sağlık Bilimlerinde Değer*, *12*(3), 417–431. https://doi.org/10.33631/sabd.1072053

Kus, B. (2014). The informal road to markets: Neoliberal reforms, private entrepreneurship and the informal economy in Turkey. *International Journal of Social Economics*, *41*(4), 278–293. https://doi.org/10.1108/IJSE-11-2012-0209

Li, S., Spry, L., & Woodall, T. (2020). Corporate social responsibility and corporate reputation: A bibliometric analysis. *International Journal of Industrial and Systems Engineering*, 14(11), 1041–1045. doı:10.36756/JCM.v2.3.2

Maden, C. (2015). A gendered lens on entrepreneurship: Women entrepreneurship in Turkey. *Gender in Management*, *30*(4), 312–331. https://doi.org/10.1108/GM-11-2013-0131

Maguire, S., Hardy, C., & Lawrence, T. B. (2004). Institutional entrepreneurship in emerging fields: HIV/AIDS treatment advocacy in Canada. *Academy of Management Journal*, *47*(5), 657–679. https://doi.org/10.5465/20159610

Murgado-Armenteros, E. M., Gutiérrez-Salcedo, M., Torres-Ruiz, F. J., & Cobo, M. J. (2015). Analysing the conceptual evolution of qualitative marketing research through science mapping analysis. *Scientometrics*, *102*(1), 519–557. https://doi.org/10.1007/s11192-014-1443-z

Naktiyok, A., Nur Karabey, C., & Caglar Gulluce, A. (2010). Entrepreneurial self-efficacy and entrepreneurial intention: The Turkish case. *International Entrepreneurship and Management Journal*, *6*(4), 419–435. https://doi.org/10.1007/s11365-009-0123-6

Nijkamp, P., Sahin, M., & Baycan-Levent, T. (2010). Migrant entrepreneurship and new urban economic opportunities: İdentification of critical success factors by means of qualitative pattern recognition analysis. *Tijdschrift Voor Economische En Sociale Geografie*, *101*(4), 371–391. https://doi.org/10.1111/j.1467-9663.2009.00546.x

Ozaralli, N., & Rivenburgh, N. K. (2016). Entrepreneurial intention: Antecedents to entrepreneurial behavior in the USA and Turkey. *Journal of Global Entrepreneurship Research*, *6*(1), 1–32. https://doi.org/10.1186/s40497-016-0047-x

Ozen, Ş., & Berkman, Ü. (2007). Cross-national reconstruction of managerial practices: TQM in Turkey. *Organization Studies*, *28*(6), 825–851. https://doi.org/10.1177/0170840607079863

Özdemir, Ö. G. (2013). Entrepreneurial marketing and social value creation in Turkish art industry: An ambidextrous perspective. *Journal of Research in Marketing and Entrepreneurship*, *15*(1), 39–60. https://doi.org/10.1108/JRME-03-2013-0012

Özeren, E., Saatcioglu, O. Y., & Aydin, E. (2018). Creating social value through orchestration processes in innovation networks: The case of "Garbage Ladies" as a social entrepreneurial venture. *Journal of Organizational Change Management*, *31*(5), 1206–1224. https://doi.org/10.1108/JOCM-06-2017-0213

Phan, P. H., Wright, M., Ucbasaran, D., & Tan, W. L. (2009). Corporate entrepreneurship: Current research and future directions. *Journal of Business Venturing*, *24*(3), 197–205. https://doi.org/10.1016/j.jbusvent.2009.01.007

Ramadani, V., Dana, L. P., Gërguri-Rashiti, S., & Ratten, V. (2017). An introduction to entrepreneurship and management in an Islamic context. In V. Ranmadani (Ed.), *Entrepreneurship and management in an Islamic context* (pp. 1–5). Cham: Springer. doi:10.1007/978-3-319-39679-8_1

Ramadani, V., Dana, L. P., Ratten, V., & Tahiri, S. (2015). The context of Islamic entrepreneurship and business: Concept, principles and perspectives. *International Journal of Business and Globalisation*, *15*(3), 244–261. https://doi.org/10.1504/IJBG.2015.071906

Rehn, R., & Kronman, U. (2006). *Bibliometric handbook for Karolinska Institutet*. Stockholm: Karolinska Institutet: University Library Publications.

Sabah, S., Carsrud, A. L., & Koçak, A. (2014). The impact of cultural openness, religion, and nationalism on entrepreneurial intensity: Six prototypical cases of Turkish family firms. *Journal of Small Business Management*, *52*(2), 306–324. doi:10.1111/jsbm.12101

Sakarya, S., Bodur, M., Yildirim-Öktem, Ö., & Selekler-Göksen, N. (2012). Social alliances: Business and social enterprise collaboration for social transformation. *Journal of Business Research*, *65*(12), 1710–1720. https://doi.org/10.1016/j.jbusres.2012.02.012

Santos, E. M. M. D., & Ferreira, J. J. (2017). Analyzing informal entrepreneurship: A bibliometric survey. *Journal of Developmental Entrepreneurship*, *22*(04), 1750022. https://doi.org/10.1142/S1084946717500224

Sesen, H. (2013). Personality or environment? A comprehensive study on the entrepreneurial intentions of university students. *Education & Training*, *55*(7), 624–640. https://doi.org/10.1108/ET-05-2012-0059

Shinnar, R. S., & Zamantılı Nayır, D. (2019). Immigrant entrepreneurship in an emerging economy: The case of Turkey. *Journal of Small Business Management*, *57*(2), 559–575. https://doi.org/10.1111/jsbm.12408

Shneikat, B., & Alrawadieh, Z. (2019). Unraveling refugee entrepreneurship and its role in integration: Empirical evidence from the hospitality industry. *The Service Industries Journal*, *39*(9–10), 741–761. https://doi.org/10.1080/02642069.2019.1571046

Shneor, R., Metin Camgöz, S., & Bayhan Karapinar, P. (2013). The interaction between culture and sex in the formation of entrepreneurial intentions. *Entrepreneurship & Regional Development*, *25*(9–10), 781–803. https://doi.org/10.1080/08985626.2013.862973

Taymaz, E. (2009). *Informality and productivity: Productivity differentials between formal and informal firms in Turkey*. Country Economic Memorandum (CEM) – Informality: Causes, Consequences, Policies.

Teixeira, A. A., & Ferreira, E. (2013). Intellectual structure of the entrepreneurship field: A tale based on three core journals. *Journal of Innovation Management*, *1*(2), 21–66. https://doi.org/10.24840/2183-0606_001.002_0005

Tekin, E., Ramadani, V., & Dana, L.-P. (2021). Entrepreneurship in Turkey and other Balkan countries: Are there opportunities for mutual co-operation through internationalisation?. *Review of International Business and Strategy*, *31* (2), 297–314. https://doi.org/10.1108/RIBS-10-2020-0133

Tunçalp, D., & Yıldırım, N. (2022). Sustainable entrepreneurship: Mapping the business landscape for the last 20 years. *Sustainability*, *14*(7), 38–64. https://doi.org/10.3390/su14073864

Turker, D., & Vural, C. A. (2017). Embedding social innovation process into the institutional context: Voids or supports. *Technological Forecasting and Social Change*, *119*(1), 98–113. https://doi.org/10.1016/j.techfore.2017.03.019

Vatansever, Ç., & Arun, K. (2016). What color is the green entrepreneurship in Turkey?. *Journal of Entrepreneurship in Emerging Economies*, *8*(1), 25–44. https://doi.org/10.1108/JEEE-07-2015-0042

Verver, M., Passenier, D., & Roessingh, C. (2019). Contextualising ethnic minority entrepreneurship beyond the west: Insights from Belize and Cambodia. *International Journal of Entrepreneurial Behavior & Research*, *25*(5), 955–973. https://doi.org/10.1108/IJEBR-03-2019-0190

Vogel, R., & Güttel, W. H. (2013). The dynamic capability view in strategic management: A bibliometric review. *International Journal of Management Reviews*, *15*(4), 426–446. https://doi.org/10.1111/ijmr.12000

Yetim, N. (2008). Social capital in female entrepreneurship. *International Sociology*, *23*(6), 864–885. https://doi.org/10.1177/0268580908095913

Zheng, Y. (2018). The past, present and future of research on Chinese entrepreneurship education: A bibliometric analysis based on CSSCI journal articles. *Educational Sciences: Theory & Practice*, *18*(5), 1255–1276. https://doi.org/10.12738/estp.2018.5.025

Zulfiu, V., Ramadani, V., & Dana, L. P. (2015). Muslim entrepreneurs in secular Turkey: Distributors as a source of innovation in a supply chain. *International Journal of Entrepreneurship and Small Business*, *26*(1), 78–95.

Zupic, I., & Čater, T. (2015). Bibliometric methods in management and organization. *Organizational Research Methods*, *18*(3), 429–472. https://doi.org/10.1177/1094428114562629

Index

Printed in the USA
CPSIA information can be obtained
at www.ICGtesting.com
JSHW061632270923
49265JS00004B/53

9 781837 534555